Gender and Timebound Commandments in Judaism

The rule that exempts women from rituals that need to be performed at specific times (so-called timebound, positive commandments) has served for centuries to stabilize Jewish gender. It has provided a rationale for women's centrality at home and their absence from the synagogue. Departing from dominant popular and scholarly views, Elizabeth Shanks Alexander argues that the rule was not conceived to structure women's religious lives, but rather became a tool for social engineering only after it underwent shifts in meaning during its transmission. Alexander narrates the rule's complicated history, establishing the purposes for which it was initially formulated and the shifts in interpretation that led to its being perceived as a key marker of Jewish gender. At the end of her study, Alexander points to women's exemption from particular rituals (Shema, tefillin, and Torah study), which, she argues, are better places to look for insight into rabbinic gender.

Elizabeth Shanks Alexander is an associate professor of religious studies, teaching ancient Judaism, at the University of Virginia. She received her PhD from Yale University in 1998. She formerly taught at Smith and Haverford Colleges. Alexander received a Brandeis-Hadassah Research Grant for her work on this book and is also the author of *Transmitting Mishnah: The Shaping Influence of Oral Tradition* (Cambridge, 2006).

Gender and Timebound Commandments in Judaism

ELIZABETH SHANKS ALEXANDER
University of Virginia

CAMBRIDGE
UNIVERSITY PRESS

CAMBRIDGE UNIVERSITY PRESS
Cambridge, New York, Melbourne, Madrid, Cape Town,
Singapore, São Paulo, Delhi, Mexico City

Cambridge University Press
32 Avenue of the Americas, New York, NY 10013-2473, USA

www.cambridge.org
Information on this title: www.cambridge.org/9781107035560

First published 2013

Printed in the United States of America

A catalog record for this publication is available from the British Library.

Library of Congress Cataloging in Publication Data

Alexander, Elizabeth Shanks, 1967–
Gender and timebound commandments in Judaism / Elizabeth Shanks Alexander.
    pages   cm
Includes bibliographical references and index.
ISBN 978-1-107-03556-0 (hardback)
1. Women in Judaism.   2. Sex role – Religious aspects – Judaism   3. Feminism – Religious
aspects – Judaism.   4. Jewish women – Religious life.   I. Title.
BM729.W6A44
2013   2012035661

ISBN 978-1-107-03556-0 Hardback

For my parents,
who came before

For my children,
who come after

For my husband,
who shared the journey
from here to there

Contents

Preface

Sometimes I call this book my "Smith book." My first teaching job out of graduate school was at Smith College, an elite liberal arts institution for women in New England. The largest major there was Women and Gender Studies, and the first class I was asked to teach was "Women in Rabbinic Literature." The class enrolled twenty-five students. A more prosaic "Introduction to Rabbinic Literature" registered only two. Clearly, Smith students had a passion for women's issues. I was glad to tailor my material to fit their interests. My training was in the hermeneutics of rabbinic literature, rabbinic theories of textuality, and text criticism. I saw my class on women as a backhand way to teach students the complex skills of decoding rabbinic texts. If students needed to hook into the material by connecting it to questions that were pressing to them in the contemporary world, so be it. My pedagogical goals could be achieved by doing a close reading of rabbinic texts on any topic. What I learned from teaching the course on women is the power of our contemporary questions. When people look at ancient texts through the lens of issues that matter today, their motivation to understand the foreign, the unfamiliar, and the esoteric increases exponentially. The truth of the matter is that very little distinguished the teaching objectives for my general introductory course from those of my course on women. The only significant difference between the two classes was the number of students I reached.

This book grows out of my experiences teaching women and rabbinic literature during my three years at Smith College. I was deeply moved by my students' enthusiasm for the material. This book exploits all that is positive in our contemporary interest in the social standing of women and the construction of gender. When teaching the course, however, I felt it vitally important to make sure the lens of student interest did not overdetermine our reading of rabbinic texts. We needed to balance our interest in gender with an understanding of the goals and purposes of the various genres of rabbinic writing. When students read rabbinic texts too selectively for gender, they risked misinterpreting ancient gender. Precisely because I wanted my students to understand rabbinic gender in sophisticated ways, I wanted them to be patient and attend to the broader cultural and literary contexts within which rabbinic gender is constructed. Like my course at Smith, this book draws its energy from contemporary cultural debates about the role of women in society today, and in Judaism in particular. But also like my course, it steps back from questions of gender where appropriate to make sure we read the ancient sources in light of the most recent research on the goals and purposes of rabbinic writing.

This book grows out of my Smith course in another, very specific way. When I sat down to construct my syllabus, I was no expert on women or gender in rabbinic literature. I figured I should start the course by exposing students to the most well-known texts regarding rabbinic views of women. Experiences in traditional Jewish communities had exposed me to the rule that women are exempt from the so-called timebound, positive commandments (m. Kid. 1:7). Jewish women, like Jewish men, are generally obligated to follow the laws laid out in the Torah. There is, however, a small subset of commandments from which women are exempt. According to the rule, women are not required to do certain "positive" ritual actions (the "thou shalts" as opposed to the "thou shalt nots") that need to be performed at a specified time of the day, week, or year (the "timebound commandments"). Contemporary interpreters of the rule universally assume that the rule exempts women because of its understanding of the way that women differ from men. Whatever it is that makes women unique also makes it inappropriate to require women to perform these commandments. The most common contemporary explanation is that women are exempt from these commandments because they are not in complete control of their time. Women are generally burdened with the care of young children, a demanding duty that respects no external clocks. Since women must be available to their children when they need attention, it is not fair to require women to perform timebound religious obligations. On this interpretation, the rule is grounded in the rabbinic understanding of women as the primary caretakers of children. In my experience, Jewish women react to this interpretation of the rule in various ways. Some are grateful that Judaism acknowledges and makes allowances for the intense efforts they exert in the care of children. Others feel constrained by a tradition that limits their ritual participation on the basis of its perception that their primary role is as mothers and caregivers. Either way, contemporary Jews are using the rule to help them figure out what it means to be a Jewish woman today.

When I was putting together my syllabus, I recalled the passion with which different people had spoken about the rule: both those who were edified by its vision and those who felt constrained by it. I figured that looking at the rule was a good place to start my study of rabbinic views of women. My plan was to find the definitive article on the rule, include it on the syllabus, and move on. As it turned out, I could not find a scholarly article that explained the rule to my satisfaction. So I did what any scholar in my shoes would do: I set about reading the primary sources on my own. At the time, I still assumed that the rule was motivated by a rabbinic understanding of how women differ from men. When the semester began, I still had not identified the "rabbinic view of women" implicit in the rule, but I figured I could work it out with my students. I developed a worksheet of primary sources that we would study together. During the first three weeks of the course, we read various articles that affirmed the importance of the rule and worked through relevant primary sources.

By the time I taught the course the fourth time, I no longer opened the course with the rule as a programmatic statement on gender by the rabbis. Something was not right, though I did not fully understand what. The more I worked with the sources, the less convinced I became that the rule could tell us anything about "the rabbinic view of Jewish womanhood." There was a major disconnect between the articles that read the rule as a programmatic statement of rabbinic gender and my own emergent understanding of the sources. Under these conditions, it no longer made sense to begin the course with a study of timebound, positive commandments. I was presenting students with a perspective – that the rule is a programmatic statement of rabbinic gender – that I immediately had to un-teach. This book represents my attempt to make sense of the dissonance I experienced when trying to reconcile the popular view with the results of my textual investigations. I am still not sure how to teach the course. Should I include a section on the rule if I am only going to show why the common perception is not true? Or should I excise discussion of the rule altogether since my discussion of the rule will not take the popular view as its starting point? I have learned a lot of interesting things about the rule and gender, although not the things I thought I would find when I first began my investigations. But the fact of the matter is that people want to understand the rule on the basis of its *perceived*, even if inaccurate, meaning. As I learned from my Smith students in my first year of teaching, contemporary questions play a useful role when they motivate and energize our study. At the same time, we need to make sure that we do not let our contemporary interests overdetermine the methods of our study. In this book, I try to balance these two *desiderata*.

In the body of the book, I argue that the rule was not formulated in dialogue with "rabbinic views of women." The rule eventually came to be seen as a "programmatic statement" of rabbinic gender, but this view of the rule is a function of *how the rule was transmitted, not how it was written*. I find myself in an awkward position. As in my course, I must both teach and un-teach the rule's prominence. On one hand, the energy for this book comes from the fact that in modern times the rule is taken to be the rabbis' premiere statement on the nature of Jewish womanhood. On the other hand, the central thesis of the book is that this view of the rule was constructed incrementally at particular moments in rabbinic history as the result of particular intellectual habits; it does not inhere in the rule.

In an ideal world, my book would be written for an audience that knows, like I did when I first began my investigations, that the rule exempting women from timebound commandments has been universally understood in the modern world to be a programmatic statement about the nature of Jewish womanhood. But I live in the real world where, even when talking with Jewish audiences, I must explain why I have chosen to focus my research on the rule in the first place. The problem is exacerbated by the fact that the phrase "timebound, positive commandments" sounds technical and esoteric if you are not already familiar with the concept. Most people wonder why I have chosen to focus on such an obscure topic. Ironically, in order to un-teach a widely held view, I need to teach it first.

This book, then, is the "article" I was seeking those many years ago. At the time I was looking, such an article did not, and could not, exist. As noted, the popular view of the rule – that it captures and defines the essence of Jewish womanhood – cannot be found in the rabbinic texts where the rule originates. So the article could not exist from the standpoint of ideas. But as I was to find out after eight years of textual labor, it could not exist as a mere article either. The book you have in your hands is the product of those efforts. To all those who facilitated the transition from inchoate intuition to coherent arguments and prose, acknowledgments are due.

First, I would like to thank Lois Dubin of Smith College, the study partner with whom I prepared the primary sources in anticipation of my first year of teaching. The questions that emerged from our study fueled my research for many years to come. I want also to thank the many Smith students who studied with me while I taught there and who shared their passion for women's issues with me.

Parts I and II of the book were initially researched and drafted during a sabbatical year in Jerusalem (2004–5). I would like to thank the institutions and individuals that supported my learning and work during that year. Thank you to Shaye Gafni and the Yad HaNadiv-Berachah Foundation for their financial support and mentoring. Thank you to the Hartman Institute for providing a collegial place to work and write during my year in Jerusalem and for welcoming me into its intellectual community. A highlight of my year was presenting my work in progress as a series of four lectures to the weekly seminar in "Advanced Jewish Studies." The feedback I received on technical issues was invaluable, and the seminar's general interest in my approach was heartening and encouraging. Two individuals from the Hartman Institute deserve special mention for their level of involvement with me. Shlomo Naeh was assigned to me as a "mentor" by the Yad HaNadiv-Berachah Foundation. Words cannot express the depth of my gratitude for his engagement with me and this project. The textual interpretations presented in this book emerged in an ad hoc manner as I pored over primary texts with a framing set of questions. Each time I settled on a new interpretation, I would hurry from the library where I was working to Shlomo's office. I would narrate my insight to him, and he would interrogate it on the spot on the basis of his intimate familiarity with the entire rabbinic corpus and manuscript variants. Shlomo was my harshest and best critic, and my work is infinitely better for his pointed questions and the resources to which he directed me. I do not think I was ever able to convince him that the Mekilta's midrashic presentation of the rule conceptually precedes the mishnaic formulation of the rule, although I hope that my latest version of Chapter 1 offers new evidence for my intuition. My great victory came at the end of the year, when Shlomo smiled wryly at me and said, "When you showed up at the beginning of the year I thought it would be impossible to say anything new about this topic, which has already been written about so extensively. You have wrung water from a stone." Ishay Rosen-Zvi also provided invaluable collegiality and intellectual support during my year at the Hartman Institute. He generously served as a sounding board while I tried out different versions of my argument. He was receptive to my emerging thesis and asked intelligent questions that pushed my thinking deeper. Thanks also go to the following scholars, who discussed my work with me during the year in Israel: Rahel Berkovits, Menahem Fisch, Yoni Garb, Moshe Halbertal, Avital Hochstein, Tal Ilan, David Levin-Kruss, Hindy Najman, Vered Noam, Chana Safrai obm, Aharon Shemesh, Hila Weinstein, and Noam Zohar.

Part III of the book was conceived, researched, and written back in Virginia over the next seven years. A special thanks to Jonathan Schofer, who served as cheerleader extraordinaire. He read multiple drafts at various stages, offered useful feedback, and suggested generative readings, but most of all believed in the project and helped me see it from a distance when I was too mired in the details. Our conversations were a source of sustaining and mobilizing energy. I am grateful to the following people, who exerted considerable effort reading drafts – often several times – provided valuable feedback, saved me from many errors, and alerted me to perspectives and resources I had not considered: Blaire French, Greg Goering, Christine Hayes, Richard Kalmin, and Rebecca Rine. I am also grateful to the following individuals, who read parts of the book, discussed my hypotheses with me, studied primary texts with me, and generally shared their expertise: Rachel Anisfeld, Cynthia Baker, Elisheva Baumgarten, Beth Berkowitz, Asher Biemann, Yehudah Cohn, Valerie Cooper, Jennifer-Rachel Cousineau, Natalie Dohrman, Kelly Figuera-Ray, Charlotte Fonrobert, Steven Fraade, Gregg Gardner, Chaya Halberstam, Martien Halvorson-Taylor, Judith Hauptman, Tal Ilan, Martin Jaffee, Mark James, Paul Jones, Gil Klein, Judith Kovacs, David Kraemer, Ben Laugelli, Marjorie Lehman, Rebecca Levi, M. David Litwa, Timothy Lytton, Barbara Mann, Chuck Mathewes, Rena May, Margaret Mohrman, Rachel Neis, Tzvi Novick, Peter Ochs, Vanessa Ochs, Tamar Ross, Suzanne Singer, Benjamin Sommer, and Barry Wimpfheimer. I presented all of the chapters at one point or another in public forums (at UVa, University of Tennesee, Yale, Jewish Theological Seminary, William and Mary College, Haifa University, Harvard Law School, Institut für Judaistik at the Freie Universität, Graduate Theological

Union, and Hartman Institute), and my work benefited from the comments and questions of all those in attendance. Thanks go also to the anonymous readers for Cambridge University Press, who gave generously of their time, making the effort to understand my arguments and offer thoughtful feedback and suggestions. The book is infinitely better for the input of all of these people. I, of course, am solely responsible for all shortcomings and errors that remain.

The following institutions have my heartfelt gratitude for the financial support they provided while I was researching and writing this book: the Yad HaNadiv-Beracha Foundation for a fellowship during the academic year of 2004–5; the University of Virginia for faculty research grants during the summers of 2006, 2007, 2009, and 2011 and for Sesquicentennial Fellowships during the academic years of 2004–5 and 2010–11; and the Hadassah-Brandeis Institute for a research grant in 2010.

I also extend my gratitude to Lewis Bateman, Shaun Vigil, Mark Fox, Brian MacDonald, Becca Cain, and others at Cambridge University Press, whose enthusiasm for the project, as well as hard work on its behalf, turned the manuscript into a book. I thank Mark James for his excellent work indexing the book.

Several of the chapters were originally published as discrete articles.

Chapter 1 originally appeared as "From Whence the Phrase 'Timebound, Positive Commandments'?" *Jewish Quarterly Review* 97/3 (2007): 317–46.

Chapter 3 originally appeared as "How *Tefillin* Became a *Non*-timebound, Positive Commandment: The *Yerushalmi* and *Bavli* on *mEruvin* 10:1," in *A Feminist Commentary to the Babylonian Talmud: Introduction and Studies*, ed. Tal Ilan et al. (Tübingen: Mohr Siebeck, 2007), 61–89.

Chapter 6 originally appeared as "Women's Exemption from Shema and Tefillin and How these Rituals Came to be Viewed as Torah Study," *Journal for the Study of Judaism* 42 (2011): 531–79.

I thank these journals and their publishers for permission to reprint them here.

The final and most important thanks go to my family: my parents, Hershel and Judith Shanks; my sister, Julia Shanks; my children, Nancy and Charlie; and my husband, Drew Alexander. I simply could not have reached this point without their enthusiastic support. They believed in me and my vision and encouraged me to keep going when my energy flagged. My mother and sister cheered me from afar and expressed their admiration. My immediate family supplied me with Starbucks coffee and chocolate bars, and kept me laughing. Nightly Mishnah study with my son in preparation for his Bar Mitzvah reminded me why study of rabbinic texts is important. On the day I completed the manuscript, my daughter bought me a card that read, "We are so proud of you for doing something so hard." I cannot thank you all enough for seeing into my heart and cheering me on.

An unexpected treat during the last three years of the writing process was sharing each chapter fresh off the press with my father. A writer and editor of works about ancient Judaism, he has extensive experience with scholarly research and writing in fields adjacent to mine. Despite the similarity of our interests, we often joke that we might as well be in different professions, so great is the disparity in our approaches. His focus is biblical archaeology and the historical reality that lies behind the biblical text. Mine is rabbinic texts and the religious life that lies in front of them. I thank my father for thoughtfully reading each chapter and for living in the ideas, even as they diverge from his primary interests. Our subsequent conversations were deeply moving; he engaged the arguments as if they mattered, not only in academia, but also for "real people" in the "real world." When I finished the final version of the Epilogue, I emailed him a copy, saying, "I won't feel it's done until it has seen the red ink of Hershel's pen." I am forever grateful to have had the opportunity to interact with him in a way that was both deeply personal and professionally sophisticated.

And last, because he is dearest of all, I thank my husband. He is the air I breathe, my source of sustenance. He believes in me, in my ideas and their importance, and in my ability to bring them to life in writing. He reminds me to keep the important things important and let the lesser things drop. He lets me work hard when I need to and makes me stop when I lose perspective. He keeps me in mind of the higher purposes for which we have been placed on this earth. For helping me be the best person I can, I thank him from the bottom of my heart.

For all of these blessings and the many others that go unspoken, I thank the Holy One.

Elizabeth Shanks Alexander
Richmond, Virginia
June 13, 2012

Abbreviations

b.	Bavli
b.	ben/bar
BB	Baba Batra
BCE	before the Common Era
Bekh.	Bekhorot
Ber.	Berakhot
Bik.	Bikkurim
BM	Baba Metzia
CE	Common Era
Deut	Deuteronomy
Eruv.	Eruvin
Exod	Exodus
Hag.	Hagigah
HUCA	*Hebrew Union College Annual*
Josh	Joshua
Kel. BM	Kelim Baba Metzia
Ker.	Keritot
Ket.	Ketubot
Kid.	Kiddushin
Lev	Leviticus
LXX	Septuagint
m.	Mishnah
Meg.	Megillah
Mek.	Mekhilta of Rabbi Ishmael
Men.	Menachot
MRSY	Mekhilta of Rabbi Shimon bar Yohai
Naz.	Nazir
Ned.	Nedarim

NJPS	New Jewish Publication Society edition of *Tanakh*
Num	Numbers
Pes.	Pesachim
Ps	Psalm
Pss	Psalms
QE	Qorban Edah
R.	Rabbi
RH	Rosh Hashanah
San.	Sanhedrin
Sem.	Semachot
Shab.	Shabbat
Sif. Dt.	Sifre Deuteronomy
Sif. Num.	Sifre Numbers
Sot.	Sotah
Suk.	Sukkah
t.	Tosephta
y.	Yerushalmi
Yev.	Yevamot

Introduction

The Mishnah (c. 200 CE) stipulates that men and women have different levels of ritual obligation.[1] Men are obligated to perform all of the commandments outlined in the Torah. Women, by way of contrast, are obligated to perform all the commandments except those which are "timebound" and "positive." "Timebound" commandments are those which must be performed at, by, or within a specified time frame. "Positive" commandments are those which must be actively performed rather than passively refrained from (the "thou shalts," as opposed to the "thou shalt nots").[2] In classical Judaism, one observes the commandments as an ennobling act of devotion to the God of Israel who redeemed Israel from Egypt. Through observance of the commandments, the religious actor realizes himself or herself a covenantal partner with God.[3] Insofar as the mishnaic rule indicates that men and women engage the commandments differently and insofar as observance of commandments is a central form of religious devotion in Judaism, the rule constructs men and women as different kinds of religious actors. This book seeks to understand what is at stake in that rule's stipulations. How did the rabbis who conceived this rule think about the differences between men and women such that this way of gendering religious obligation made sense?

The topic of this book (the rule that exempts women from timebound, positive commandments) and its driving question (how can analysis of the rule

---

[1] m. Kid. 1:7.

[2] For a discussion of two different ways in which the terms "positive" and "negative" were used to describe categories of commandments during the tannaitic period, see Aharon Shemesh, "Toward a History of the Terms Positive and Negative Commandment'" (Hebrew), *Tarbiz* 72/1 (1993): 133–50.

[3] Jon D. Levenson, *Sinai and Zion: An Entry into the Jewish Bible* (San Francisco: Harper and Row, 1987), 15–86.

shed light on rabbinic gender?) are conceived in the shadow of a contemporary cultural debate about the role of women in Judaism. In the late 1960s and 1970s, when the tide of social change was sweeping across America and Europe, feminism blew into the Jewish world. Jewish women began to ask many of the questions that feminism had raised for society-at-large. Jewish feminists observed the mechanisms by which gender is constructed in Judaism, and they proposed strategies for women to achieve greater levels of religious self-realization.[4] The rule that exempts women from timebound, positive commandments received significant attention in these conversations because at that time (and still today in certain circles) the rule was often cited as a cornerstone of traditional Jewish gender roles.

Two explanations of the rule – both of which affirm traditional gender roles – were circulating in the sixties and seventies, though they have their roots in medieval sources. The first explanation begins by acknowledging that women's involvement in the care of babies and children places heavy and unpredictable demands on their time. Since it is not fair to put women in the untenable position of being ritually obligated without a reasonable means of fulfilling the obligation, the rabbis gave women a ritual "out" by declaring them exempt.[5] For feminists, this vision of Jewish womanhood was less than inspiring. It tethered women to domestic responsibilities and kept them out of the "main business" of public and communal ritual where – they assumed – spiritual richness lay. The second explanation of women's exemption from timebound, positive commandments did little to placate feminists. It claims that women have an innately spiritual nature and do not need the mundane trivialities of timebound, positive commandments to achieve a rich relationship with God. For women, spirituality is intuitive. By way of contrast, men need the concrete engagements of timebound, positive commandments to lift them out of

---

[4] See Adler, who uses the language of "self-actualization" in her 1973 essay. Rachel Adler, "The Jew Who Wasn't There: Halakha and the Jewish Woman," in *Contemporary Jewish Ethics*, ed. Menachem Marc Kellner (New York: Sanhedrin Press, 1978), 352. See the early collection of feminist reflections in Elizabeth Koltun, ed., *The Jewish Woman: New Perspectives* (New York: Schocken Books, 1976). Later important works (in chronological order of appearance) include Judith Plaskow, *Standing Again at Sinai: Judaism from a Feminist Perspective* (San Francisco: Harper and Row, 1990); Rachel Adler, *Engendering Judaism: An Inclusive Theology and Ethics* (Philadelphia: Jewish Publication Society, 1998); and Tamar Ross, *Expanding the Palace of Torah: Orthodoxy and Feminism* (Hanover: Brandeis University Press, published by University Press of New England, 2004).

[5] Moshe Meiselman attributes this position to the medieval commentator Abudraham (d. 1345). See Moshe Meiselman, "The Jewish Woman in Jewish Law," in *The Jewish Woman in Jewish Law* (New York: Ktav Publishing House, 1978), 43. Moshe Benovitz points out, however, that Abudraham's rationale for the rule has more to do with a woman's obligation to her *husband* than to her children. Benovitz suggests that the modern rationale that links the exemption to women's duties to her children is a "modern, apologetic" version of the medieval explanation that suggests that women are at the beck and call of their husbands. Presumably contemporary traditionalists find it more palatable to suggest that women have a more unnegotiable obligation to their children than to their husbands. See Moshe Benovitz, "Time-Triggered Positive Commandments as Conversation Pieces," *HUCA* 78 (2007): 47.

spiritual lethargy.[6] To the feminists, this explanation smacked of apologetics.[7] It prodded women to see their meager ritual lot as a sign of election that was belied by social realities. They felt that anyone with eyes to see could discern that the multifaceted ritual life of men was more spiritually fulfilling than the glorified childcare that fell to women.[8] Mainstream feminism had created opportunities for women to achieve new levels of professional self-realization and economic remuneration. Jewish feminists also wanted to expand, rather than limit, their spiritual and ritual horizons. Contesting the gender roles implicit in women's exemption from timebound, positive commandments provided one concrete means to do so.[9]

Not surprisingly, traditionalists sensed that their social vision was under attack and rose to its defense.[10] Rabbis and traditionally minded women alike found meaning in the model of Jewish womanhood implied by the rule. They celebrated the importance of women as the spiritual center of the home.[11] They suggested that women do not need timebound commandments because they naturally synchronize themselves with the divine temporal rhythms through internal biological clocks in their bodies.[12] Above all, they stressed that different levels of ritual responsibility do not imply a denigration of women as religious actors.

Though the debate between feminists and traditionalists ostensibly centers on the rule that exempts women from timebound commandments, the underlying tension concerns how Jewish women should construct their religious lives today. When feminists say that the rule limits women's religious development

---

[6] Meiselman attributes this position to the Maharal of Prague (d. 1609) and Samson Raphael Hirsch (d. 1888). See Meiselman, "The Jewish Woman in Jewish Law," 43–44; the Maharal's *Drush al haTorah* included in *Sifrei Maharal* (Jerusalem, 1971) in the volume with *Be'er haGolah*, 27a of Prague; and Samson Raphael Hirsch, trans. and explained, *The Pentateuch*, vol. 3: *(Leviticus Pt. II)*, rendered into English by Isaac Levy (Gateshead: Judaica Press, 1976), s.v. 23:43, 711–12.

[7] Orthodox feminist Tamar Ross characterizes these two explanations of the rule as "patriarchalist and apologetic" insofar as she discusses them in her section on "The Conservative Response: Patriarchalists and Apologists." This judgment is not necessarily an indictment, in her view. See Ross, *Expanding the Palace of Torah: Orthodoxy and Feminism*, 35–37.

[8] See, for example, the remarks of Rachel Adler: "It is not unusual for committed Jewish women to be uneasy about their position as Jews. It was to cry down our doubts that rabbis developed their pre-packaged orations on the nobility of motherhood; the glory of childbirth." Adler, "The Jew Who Wasn't There," 348.

[9] See the trenchant essay by Rachel Adler, originally published in 1973. Adler, "The Jew Who Wasn't There." The fact that the first chapter in Rachel Biale's 1984 book examines women's ritual exemptions suggests that she too finds women's ritual exemptions to play a major role in structuring women's religious lives in Judaism. See Rachel Biale, *Women and Jewish Law: An Exploration of Women's Issues in Halakhic Sources* (New York: Schocken Books, 1984), 10–43.

[10] See especially Moshe Meiselman's rebuttal to Adler's 1973 article: Meiselman, "The Jewish Woman in Jewish Law," 43–62, esp. 52–57.

[11] See Saul Berman, "The Status of Women in Halakhic Judaism," in *The Jewish Woman: New Perspectives*, ed. Elizabeth Koltun (New York: Schocken Books, 1976), 114–28.

[12] Lisa Aiken, *To Be a Jewish Woman* (Northvale: J. Aronson, 1992), 34–36.

by tying them to domesticity and when traditionalists counter that the rule affirms uniquely feminine modes of religious expression by respecting the temporal rhythms in women's bodies, they are debating not just the meaning of the rule (although they are doing that too). The deeper disagreement involves whether the gendering of religious obligation proposed by the rule structures women's lives for better or worse. They are asking whether Jews today should accept or reject the picture of women's religious lives painted by the rule. This book does not attempt to adjudicate the question of what kind of religious identities Jewish women should adopt for themselves today. It neither contributes to a feminist critique of the roles suggested by the rule (though I would suffer in a society where these roles limited my own development) nor advocates traditional allegiance to the rule (though I am attracted to the idea of fealty to an ancient text). The book does, however, draw energy from these heated debates because at the center of them is the question of what the rule actually means. Whenever someone rejects or affirms the rule's social utility, he or she theorizes about how the rule structures gender. As a scholar of rabbinic literature and culture, I have tried in this book to shed light on this issue.

There is, of course, an important difference between my interest in the rule and that of parties to the debate just described. When feminists and traditionalists debate the meaning of the rule, they do so with a consciousness that it is a normative Jewish source with a voice in how Jews construct their identity today. I, on the other hand, approach the rule as an artifact of history: conceived, formulated, and transmitted by sages who lived in a world very different from ours. Both ways of reading are legitimate, of course, but it is important to be cognizant of the differences between them. As a historian, my interest is in reconstructing the cultural concerns of the world that produced the rule. I want to understand those aspects of the ancient world that explain why this way of configuring gender and religious obligation made sense. The question that this book raises is *how* best to elicit this information from the sources. This is a serious question because scholars who have all the best intentions of locating the rule in its historical context use paradigms derived from the contemporary cultural debate to reconstruct ancient gender in the rule.

Parties to the contemporary cultural debate (irrespective of whether they are "for" or "against" the rule) see the rule as a programmatic statement on rabbinic gender. They reach this conclusion on the basis of their understanding of the rule's literary structure. The rule juxtaposes the religious obligations of men and women, stipulating one important difference between the two. This structure leaves readers with both a *question* and a *strategy* for answering the following question: Why does the rule treat women differently from men? The strategy for answering the question involves discerning the distinctive features of timebound, positive commandments and linking them to a postulated characteristic of women. Consider the following example of this interpretive strategy: Timebound commandments allow little flexibility in the time of their performance. Women are exempt because they are otherwise engaged in time-consuming domestic responsibilities, especially childcare. From this we learn that the rabbis envisioned women as domestic creatures whose primary responsibilities revolve around childcare. Or: Timebound, positive commandments are necessary for the religious actor who forgets to be conscious of God at regular intervals. Women are not required to perform them because they are naturally in sync with divine rhythms. From this we learn that the rabbis envisioned women as spiritually intuitive and adept. Or: From this we learn that the rabbis envisioned womanhood in terms of the physical body with its distinct temporal rhythms. When one foregrounds the question implicit in the rule's literary structure and answers it using this procedure, the rule does indeed appear to be a programmatic statement by the rabbis about women's nature.

When academic scholars accept the common perception that the rule is a key piece of evidence regarding rabbinic views of women, they reflexively adopt this procedure as the best means of getting the rule to yield insight into rabbinic gender. Like the parties to the contemporary cultural debates, scholarly researchers direct their energy toward understanding why the rule treats women differently from men. They focus on the distinctive features of timebound, positive commandments and link them to postulated characteristics of women in tannaitic culture.

The following is a partial list of the conclusions historians of rabbinic culture have reached regarding the ancient rabbinic views of women on the basis of the rule:

- Timebound commandments *take* time. Women do not have much expendable time because of the all-consuming responsibilities of home and children. Conclusion: The rabbis constructed womanhood around domestic tasks and childcare.[13]
- Timebound commandments *mark* Jewish ritual time (holy occasions). The responsibility for marking such occasions falls to those in social order who resemble the priestly caste (not women). Conclusion: The rabbis constructed women as second-class citizens in their social order.[14]
- Timebound commandments need to be performed "*on time*," but women lack the self-control to respond appropriately. Conclusion: The rabbis constructed women as wild, untamed creatures.[15]

---

[13] Shmuel Safrai, "The *Mitzva* Obligation of Women in Tannaitic Thought" (Hebrew), *Bar Ilan Annual* 26–27 (1995): 233.

[14] Judith Hauptman, *Rereading the Rabbis: A Woman's Voice* (Boulder: Westview Press, 1998), 226–27. See also Natan Margalit, "Priestly Men and Invisible Women: Male Appropriation of the Feminine and the Exemption of Women from Positive, Time-Bound Commandments," *AJS Review* 28/2 (November 2004): 305–6.

[15] Lawrence Hoffman, *Covenant of Blood: Circumcision and Gender in Rabbinic Judaism* (Chicago: University of Chicago Press, 1996), 164–67.

- Timebound, positive commandments are *performed in the public domain*, but women should not be in the public domain. Conclusion: The rabbis constructed women as creatures of the private, domestic sphere.[16]

In much of their work on the rule, academic scholars make a point of explicitly rejecting popular explanations of the rule.[17] They strive to reach historically grounded conclusions regarding the rabbinic motivations for excluding women from this class of commandments. What they do not realize, however, is that by employing this procedure for getting the rule to yield insight into rabbinic gender, they have largely determined in advance the kind of information they will elicit from the rule. From the moment scholars accept the analysis that frames the rule as a key rabbinic statement on women, they cut off the most productive avenues for getting the rule to yield insight into rabbinic gender.

I argue that in order to unburden ourselves from the patterns of reading employed in the contemporary cultural debates, we must *explicitly* acknowledge our debt to the contemporary cultural context. This book chooses to focus on the rule and what it can tell us about rabbinic gender not because of an innate feature of the rule, but because of a *widespread perception* that the rule conveys important information about how the rabbis constructed gender in antiquity. Having attributed the book's line of inquiry to popular perceptions of the rule rather than a feature of the rule itself, I am free to conduct the research in the way that makes most sense for me as a historian of antiquity. Eliciting information about the role the rule played in the construction of rabbinic gender requires that we locate the rule in the cultural context in which it was produced. We must be careful *not to read the rule through the lens of later interpretation*, and we must be sure *to read the rule in the context of contemporary parallels*. Unfortunately, these standards for scholarly research have often been disregarded when scholars turn to examine the rule's role in the construction of rabbinic gender. The next section explores the roots of this unwitting neglect of standard scholarly procedure.

The Normative View of the Rule and the Reading Habits That Follow from It

Parties to the contemporary cultural debate make several assumptions about the rule that foster particular ways of reading it. Though scholars of ancient

---

[16] Judith Wegner, *Chattel or Person: The Status of Women in the Mishnah* (New York: Oxford University Press, 1988), 150–53. See also Shmuel Safrai, "The *Mitzva* Obligation of Women in Tannaitic Thought," 233.

[17] See, for example, Hauptman, *Rereading the Rabbis*, 221; Margalit, "Priestly Men and Invisible Women: Male Appropriation of the Feminine and the Exemption of Women from Positive, Time-Bound Commandments," 302; and Benovitz, "Time Triggered Positive Commandments," 59–64.

rabbinic culture do not share these assumptions, they have adopted many of the reading habits that follow from them.

Most significantly, contemporary Jews recognize the rule as a normative statement by the ancient rabbis. For them, the rule dictates how the social world *ought* to be constructed. Though the rule was composed in antiquity, it is assumed to have a normative force that extends through today. Whether "for" or "against" the rule, parties to the contemporary debate envision the process that produced the rule as one in which the rabbis tried to influence the shape of Jewish society. Traditionalists are inclined to accept the authority of the rule as determinative even today. Feminists may reject the authority of the rule in our time, but their interest in doing so is rooted in a recognition of the fact that originally the rule was formulated to function normatively. According to the normative view of the rule, the rabbis exerted social influence by deciding which commandments women should perform. To the extent that the parties to the contemporary cultural debates engage in historical reconstruction of the origins of the rule, they assume that the rabbis formulated the rule as a *prescriptive principle* to determine which of the many existing commandments women should be required to perform. Three reading habits follow from this normative view of the rule.

The first habit of reading involves focusing on the distinctive feature of timebound commandments and linking them with a posited characteristic of women. This habit of reading follows from the assumption that the rule *determines* women's ritual involvement. If the rule determines women's ritual involvement, then the best way to reveal rabbinic ideas about women is to reveal the rationale for the rabbinic prescription. This habit of reading, however, is not warranted by the prevailing scholarly opinions regarding the purpose of the Mishnah (the document in which the rule is preserved). In popular circles the Mishnah is viewed as the document by which the ancient rabbis promulgated (and continue to promote) their legal standards among the Jewish population. Scholars, however, are increasingly skeptical about the idea that the Mishnah functioned as an authoritative code of rabbinic law for the Jewish populace during the tannaitic period.[18] If the Mishnah did not serve as a law

---

[18] Skepticism regarding the popular view of the Mishnah arises from two different quarters. Those who examine the role of the rabbis in Jewish society-at-large have concluded that the rabbis did not have the sufficient social influence among the non-rabbinic population to enforce rabbinic legal norms as represented by the Mishnah. See Seth Schwartz, *Imperialism and Jewish Society, 200 B.C.E.–640 C.E.* (Princeton: Princeton University Press, 2001); Lee I. Levine, *The Rabbinic Class of Roman Palestine in Late Antiquity* (New York: Jewish Theological Seminary of America; Jerusalem: Yad Izhak Ben-Zvi Press, 1989); and Miriam Peskowitz, *Spinning Fantasies: Rabbis, Gender and History* (Berkeley: University of California Press, 1997). Scholars increasingly see the laws in the Mishnah as a kind of wishful thinking on the part of the rabbis that helped bring about the authority they envisioned for themselves. See Beth A. Berkowitz, *Execution and Invention: Death Penalty Discourse in Early Rabbinic and Christian Cultures* (New York: Oxford University Press, 2006); and Ishay Rosen-Zvi, *The Mishnaic Sotah Ritual: Temple, Gender and Midrash*, trans. Orr Scharf (Leiden: Brill, 2012). Skepticism also arises

code, then the rule may not have been included therein to determine women's ritual involvement. Nonetheless, scholars often focus on the distinctive characteristic of timebound, positive commandments as a means of articulating the view of women implied by the rule.

Even leaving aside the issue of the purpose of the Mishnah generally, many scholars explicitly reject the idea that the rule determined women's ritual involvement.[19] There are many rituals where women's obligations do not conform to the stipulations of the rule.[20] "Be fruitful and multiply," for example, is *not* a timebound commandment, and according to the rule women should be obligated, but according to tannaitic law they are exempt.[21] Likewise, saying the Amidah at appointed times *is* a timebound commandment, and according

from assessments of literary data within the Mishnah. New theories about the Mishnah propose that the laws therein were compiled to serve as a pedagogical tool in the training of sages or as expressions of philosophical positions. For the proposal that the Mishnah served a pedagogical purpose, see Abraham Goldberg, "The Mishna – a Study Book of Halakha," in *The Literature of the Sages*, part 1, ed. Shmuel Safrai (Philadelphia: Fortress Press, 1987), 211–51; and Elizabeth Shanks Alexander, *Transmitting Mishnah: The Shaping Influence of Oral Tradition* (Cambridge: Cambridge University Press, 2006). For the theory that the Mishnah functions like a philosophical essay, see Jacob Neusner, *Judaism: The Evidence of the Mishnah* (Atlanta: Scholars Press, 1988), 230–83. Dov Zlotnick documents the rules that amoraic scholars (particularly from the school of R. Yohanan) put in place in order to facilitate the Mishnah's functioning like a law code after the Mishnah was already a document. The fact that such rules were needed suggests to Zlotnick that there was a disparity between R. Yohanan's vision of the Mishnah as law code and Rabbi Judah the Patriarch's when he compiled it. See Dov Zlotnick, *The Iron Pillar – Mishnah: Redaction, Form, and Intent* (Jerusalem: Ktav, 1988), 206–17.

[19] The suggestion is made that the rule reflects a descriptive summary of some aspects of current popular practice. See Shmuel Safrai, "The *Mitzva* Obligation of Women in Tannaitic Thought"; Tal Ilan, *Jewish Women in Greco-Roman Palestine* (Peabody: Hendrickson Publishers, 1996), 117; and Biale, *Women and Jewish Law: An Exploration of Women's Issues in Halakhic Sources*, 17.

[20] Though the rule exempts women from timebound, positive commandments, other sources obligate them to the following timebound, positive commandments: *hakhel* (Deut 31:12), *simchah* offering (Deut 15:14 and t. Hag. 1:4), eating matzah on Passover (t. Pisha 1:34), *kiddush hayom* (b. Ber. 20b), lighting of Hanukah candles (b. Shab. 23a), drinking the four cups of wine on Passover (b. Pes. 108a–b), and reading the *megillah* on Purim (b. Meg. 4a). In addition, though the rule obligates women to perform non-timebound, positive commandments, women are exempt from a number of them: Torah study (Sif. Dt., Ekev, Piska 46, and t. Kid. 1:11), redemption of the firstborn son (t. Kid. 1:11), circumcising one's son (t. Kid. 1:11), and to "be fruitful and multiply" (m. Yev. 6:6) on the view of all except Yohanan b. Baroka. Modern scholars have hardly been the first to note the inconsistency of the rule with these exceptional cases. Already in the Talmud, R. Yohanan rejects the prescriptive utility of the rule (see b. Kid. 34a). Maimonides agrees with R. Yohanan that the rule should not be regarded as a prescriptive principle. Rather the term "all" in the phrase "all timebound, positive commandments" should be understood as describing *most* timebound, positive commandments. See Maimonides' commentary to m. Kid. 1:7. Shlomo Goren offers a useful overview of Maimonides' approach to this question: "Women as Regards Timebound, Positive Commandments" (Hebrew), *Mahanayim* 98 (1965): 10–16.

[21] See m. Yev. 6:6.

to the rule women should be exempt, but according to tannaitic law they are obligated.[22] Since the rule clearly did not determine women's involvement in the exceptional cases, scholars suggest that the rule did not determine women's ritual involvement even in the cases that do conform to the rule.[23] In their view, the rule summarizes and reflects the state of women's actual ritual practice when the rule was formulated. But even these scholars who recognize that the rule was not formulated to function normatively focus on the distinctive features of timebound commandments when they push the rule to yield insight into rabbinic gender.[24]

A second habit of reading the rule also follows from popular assumptions about the rule. Parties to the contemporary cultural debates generally focus on the mishnaic version of the rule while ignoring evidence of the rule in other compilations of tannaitic literature (tannaitic midrash and tosephtan baraitas). A focus on the mishnaic version of the rule makes sense if one holds the normative view of the rule because the Mishnah, and not other tannaitic documents, has a privileged status as part of the Jewish legal canon. Scholars, however, do not generally privilege mishnaic evidence as a *source of information about tannaitic culture* over extra-mishnaic evidence. From a historical perspective, evidence from other tannaitic sources has as much to tell us about tannaitic culture as mishnaic evidence does. Indeed, if one's goal is to reconstruct the world that lies behind the sources, the more diverse the sources that one brings to bear, the more fully one is able to reconstruct that world.[25] Nonetheless, scholarly studies of the rule tend to focus exclusively on the mishnaic version of the rule when analyzing the rule for insight into rabbinic gender.[26]

---

[22] See m. Ber. 3:3.

[23] See Shmuel Safrai, "The *Mitzva* Obligation of Women in Tannaitic Thought"; Ilan, *Jewish Women in Greco-Roman Palestine*, 178; and Biale, *Women and Jewish Law: An Exploration of Women's Issues in Halakhic Sources*, 17.

[24] See Shmuel Safrai, "The *Mitzva* Obligation of Women in Tannaitic Thought," 233–36.

[25] Several noteworthy examples of this type of scholarship are Steven D. Fraade, *From Tradition to Commentary: Torah and Its Interpretation in the Midrash Sifre to Deuteronomy* (Albany: State University of New York Press, 1991), esp. 28–49; Chaya T. Halberstam, *Law and Truth in Biblical and Rabbinic Literature* (Bloomington: Indiana University Press, 2009), esp. 91–105; and Rosen-Zvi, *The Mishnaic Sotah Ritual: Temple, Gender and Midrash*.

[26] There are some limited precedents to my approach, which takes the full range of tannaitic parallels to the rule into account when trying to reconstruct the meaning of the rule. Safrai, for example, examines the midrashic parallels to the rule, though in the end these do not impact how he uses the rule to reconstruct rabbinic gender. See Shmuel Safrai, "The *Mitzva* Obligation of Women in Tannaitic Thought." Margalit and Noam Zohar focus on the mishnaic rule, but they take the important step of examining the rule in the context of the chapter in which it appears. See Margalit, "Priestly Men and Invisible Women: Male Appropriation of the Feminine and the Exemption of Women from Positive, Time-Bound Commandments"; and Noam Zohar, "Women, Men and Religious Status: Deciphering a Chapter of Mishnah," in *Approaches to Ancient Judaism: New Series*, vol. 5, ed. Hebert Basser and Simcha Fishbane (Atlanta: Scholars

Finally, a third habit of reading characterizes discussion of the rule in the contemporary cultural debates and has penetrated scholarly study of the rule. The discussion assumes that the rule determined women's ritual involvement. But this understanding of the rule is attested only in the commentary to the Mishnah provided by the Babylonian Talmud (the Bavli, c. 600 CE), not in the Mishnah itself. While the Mishnah is commonly read through the lens of the Bavli in popular circles, scholars of rabbinic culture have worked hard to distinguish the cultural world of the tannaim (whose work is preserved in the Mishnah and other tannaitic documents) from that of the post-amoraic sages (whose work is preserved in the latest stratum of the Bavli).[27] When scholars read the rule as a prescriptive principle that determines women's ritual involvement, they inadvertently blur the distinction between the rule as it functioned during the tannaitic period and the rule as it was understood by its later talmudic interpreters.

Historians of rabbinic culture generally eschew these habits of reading because they prevent us from reconstructing the cultural and intellectual world

---

Press, 1993), 33–54. As far as I am aware, no scholarship on the rule examines the parallels to the rule in the Tosephta, which are the focus of Chapter 2 of this book.

[27] David Weiss Halivni laid the groundwork for distinguishing tannaitic and post-amoraic culture by identifying a stratum in the Bavli that was attributable to a group of sages who lived after the Amoraim. Halivni calls this generation of sages the "stammaim" ("anonymous ones") because their identity remains anonymous. Other scholars have suggested that the stratum that Halivni attributes to the stammaim is more properly attributed to the Saboraim. Since my discussions of this generation of sages do not turn on attributing the materials to either the stammaim or saboraim, I use the agnostic term "post-amoraic" sages to describe the sages that Halivni identified. See David Weiss Halivni, *Midrash, Mishnah, and Gemara: The Jewish Predilection for Justified Law* (Cambridge, Mass.: Harvard University Press, 1986); and Richard Kalmin, *The Redaction of the Babylonian Talmud: Amoraic or Saboraic?* (Cincinnati: Hebrew Union College Press, 1989).

Halivni's students have built on Halivni's findings and collectively worked on articulating the distinctive culture and intellectual interests of the post-amoraic sages. See David Kraemer, *The Mind of the Talmud: An Intellectual History of the Bavli* (New York: Oxford University Press, 1990); Jeffrey L. Rubenstein, *The Culture of the Babylonian Talmud* (Baltimore: Johns Hopkins University Press, 2003); and Barry Scott Wimpfheimer, *Narrating the Law: A Poetics of Talmudic Legal Stories* (Philadelphia: University of Pennsylvania Press, 2011).

Jacob Neusner first articulated the scholarly agenda of studying the Mishnah without the overlay of its talmudic framing. See Jacob Neusner, ed., *The Modern Study of the Mishnah* (Leiden: Brill, 1973). Since he first articulated this vision, a number of studies have explored distinctive features of tannaitic culture. See Fraade, *From Tradition to Commentary: Torah and Its Interpretation in the Midrash Sifre to Deuteronomy*; Halberstam, *Law and Truth in Biblical and Rabbinic Literature*; Berkowitz, *Execution and Invention: Death Penalty Discourse in Early Rabbinic and Christian Cultures*; and Rosen-Zvi, *The Mishnaic Sotah Ritual: Temple, Gender and Midrash*. In my own work, I have tried to attend to the differences among tannaitic, amoraic, and post-amoraic intellectual culture. I have been especially concerned with recognizing the Bavli as an interpretation of the Mishnah and not a statement of the Mishnah's "innate" meaning. See Alexander, *Transmitting Mishnah*.

of the tannaitic rabbis in all its diversity and distinctiveness. Nonetheless, over and over again scholars fall into these habits when reading the rule for insight into rabbinic gender. When scholars turn to the rule as a primary source of insight into rabbinic gender, the procedure for eliciting this information seems self-evident. I, on the other hand, stress that before we can shed light on how the rule contributes to the construction of rabbinic gender, we must follow standard scholarly procedure for setting the rule in the context of the tannaitic culture that produced it. When analyzing the rule, we must (1) allow for the possibility that the rule was not formulated to determine women's ritual involvement, (2) read the mishnaic version of the rule alongside the diverse tannaitic evidence regarding the rule, and (3) recognize the differences between the rule as it circulated in the tannaitic period and the rule as it was interpreted by the post-amoraic sages in the Bavli. Employing these methods, we will discover that there are ways to think about how the rule supported the construction of rabbinic gender other than by focusing on the distinctive qualities of timebound, positive commandments.

The Present Study

This book aims to understand how the rule supported the construction of gender during the rabbinic period (c. 80–600 CE). During this period the rule was conceived, formulated, and transmitted. Within the rabbinic period, I distinguish among the tannaitic period (c. 80–200 CE), the amoraic period (c. 200–450), and the post-amoraic period (c. 450–600), as is conventional in current rabbinic historiography.[28]

The book's interest in the tannaitic period, when the rule was conceived and formulated, appears self-evident at first. After all, during the tannaitic period sages produced the rule's stipulations. I suggest, however, that the rule was not necessarily formulated to determine women's ritual involvement. I therefore try to discern not only how the rule supported the construction of gender when it was formulated, but also how the rule became a tool in the construction of gender *when it was transmitted.* Transmission of the rule began in the tannaitic period shortly after it was formulated and continued into the amoraic and post-amoraic periods. Foundational to this study is a recognition of the fact that the rule was manipulated *in different ways* during each of these three

---

[28] See, for example, the time line of rabbinic history provided in Charlotte Elisheva Fonrobert and Martin S. Jaffee, eds., *The Cambridge Companion to the Talmud and Rabbinic Literature* (Cambridge: Cambridge University Press, 2007), xiv–xvi. This periodization builds on medieval historiography, which distinguishes between the tannaitic and amoraic periods. Modern talmudic scholarship posits the existence of an additional generation of scholars following the end of the amoraic period, but before the final editing of the Bavli.

rabbinic periods.[29] It is important to recognize that the rule supports the construction of rabbinic gender in different ways during each of the three rabbinic
periods.[30]

Although this book does not examine the post-rabbinic transmission and
interpretation of the rule in any detail, it does take into account the fact that
the rule supports the construction of gender in the medieval and modern periods in *yet a different manner* than it does during the three rabbinic periods. The
contemporary strategy of deducing the rabbis' view of women from the rule
has its roots in the medieval period. In the thirteenth and fourteenth centuries,
traditional scholars first articulated the *reasons* for women's exemption from
timebound, positive commandments. Jacob Anatoli (d. 1256), for example,
writes that "[the fact that a woman is a helpmeet to her husband] is ... the
reason (*hasibah*) she is exempt from timebound, positive commandments. For
if she was busy doing commandments at a specified time, her husband would
be without a helpmeet at those times and quarreling would break out between
them, and his authority, which benefits both him and her, would degenerate."[31]
Like the contemporary writers discussed above, Anatoli focuses on the distinctive features of timebound, positive commandments and links them with
a postulated characteristic of women. For Anatoli, the distinctive feature of
timebound commandments is that they must be performed at a specified time.
Women, however, have a primary obligation to serve as helpmeet to their husband at all times (see Gen 3:16). If our focus were on the medieval period,
we would explore the ways that Anatoli constructs womanhood as the fulfillment of wifely duties. Though this book does not focus on the medieval
period per se, the existence of Anatoli and others like him is important to the
shape of the present study. From Anatoli and others we learn that the rule was

---

[29] This emphasis builds on a tradition of scholarship that attends to the distinctive cultural
and intellectual trends of each of the three rabbinic periods. See Christine Elizabeth Hayes,
*Between the Babylonian and Palestinian Talmuds: Accounting for Halakhic Difference in
Selected Sugyot from Tractate Avodah Zarah* (New York: Oxford University Press, 1997);
Jeffrey L. Rubenstein, *Talmudic Stories: Narrative Art, Composition, and Culture* (Baltimore:
Johns Hopkins University Press, 1999); and David Kraemer, *The Mind of the Talmud: An
Intellectual History of the Bavli.*

[30] Scott emphasizes that since gender is a social construct, historians of gender need to be attuned
to the ways by which gender is constructed changes throughout history. See Joan Wallach
Scott, *Gender and the Politics of History* (New York: Columbia University Press, 1988), esp.
6, 41–50.

[31] Jacob Anatoli, *Sefer Malmad Hatalmidim* (Lyck, 1866; repr. Israel, 1968), s.v *lekh lekha*, 15b–
16a. Within a century's time, Abudraham (d. 1345) offers a similar rationale for the rule. He
writes that "the reason (*hata'am*) women are exempt from timebound, positive commandments
is because a woman is subservient to her husband and must fulfill his needs." Abraham Abudraham, *Sefer Abudraham* (Jerusalem, 1963), *sha'ar* 3, p. 25. In a forthcoming book, Elisheva
Baumgarten examines the cultural and historical contexts in which timebound, positive commandments assumed a new prominence in the gendering of religious life toward the end of the
thirteenth century.

eventually seen to be a foundational brick in the edifice of rabbinic gender.[32] *My goal when reading materials from the rabbinic period is to understand how rabbinic manipulations, transmission, and interpretation of the rule made possible later readings like this one of Anatoli.*

A concrete example will illustrate this facet of the book. In the body of the book, I argue that during the tannaitic period the rule was conceived as a descriptive summary of three exegetical conclusions. Initially the rule was legally inert; insofar as it summarized exegetical conclusions, it did not promulgate law de novo. Not only that, when the rule was originally formulated, it concerned both women *and slaves.* The questions that I ask are the following: What happened subsequent to the rule's formulation (but still during the rabbinic period) that led post-talmudic Jews to inherit the rule as a telling marker of the differences between men and women, while ignoring the rule's ability to yield insight into the differences between slaves and free men? Likewise, what happened subsequent to the rule's formulation (but still during the rabbinic period) that led post-talmudic Jews to inherit the rule as a prescriptive principle that determines women's ritual involvement? In examining the rabbinic sources, I clarify how rabbinic discussions of the rule laid the groundwork for post-talmudic readings of the rule that see it as a major statement on the role of women in Judaism.

My focus on the rabbinic period flows from the fact that this book was conceived in dialogue with the contemporary cultural debate about the rule. What scholars feel they have to contribute to the contemporary conversation is an understanding of the ancient world that produced the rule. It turns out that illuminating the world that produced the rule requires examining not only the process by which the rule was formulated, but also the process by which the rule came to be perceived as a programmatic statement about rabbinic gender.

Book Structure

This book is divided into three parts, each of which explores how the rule manifests and supports the construction of gender in a different way. The first two parts examine the rule's development along a historical trajectory, following rabbinic manipulations of the rule from the tannaitic period to the post-amoraic period. The first part explores how the rule was manipulated in the tannaitic period, and the second part focuses on the amoraic and post-amoraic periods. The third part returns to the tannaitic period and explores the rationale for several ritual exemptions implied by the rule.

---

[32] The following pre-contemporary traditional authors use the rule as a means of constructing gender: Jacob Anatoli (d. 1256), Abraham Abudraham (d. 1345), the Maharal (d. 1609), and Samson Raphael Hirsch (d. 1888). See also discussion of *Sefer Hakanah* (late fourteenth, early fifteenth century) in Talya Fishman, "A Kabbalistic Perspective on Gender-Specific Commandments: On the Interplay of Symbols and Society," *AJS Review* 17/2 (1992): 199–245.

Part I ("Gender and the Tannaitic Rule") examines the formulation and transmission of the rule during the tannaitic period. Central to the project is reading the mishnaic version of the rule alongside evidence of the rule from other tannaitic collections. Chapter 1 tries to reconstruct the process by which the category of timebound, positive commandments was originally formulated. It is generally assumed that the category of "timebound, positive commandments" was conceived by reflecting on how gender operates (or should operate) in the social world. Judith Hauptman, for example, notes that the category of "timebound, positive commandments" is used in no context other than those that discuss women's ritual obligations. She suggests that the category was "created solely for the purpose of distinguishing between women's ritual obligations and her exemptions."[33] The rabbis reflected, so it is thought, on the appropriate roles for women in social and religious life and created the category to structure women's place appropriately. In contrast to this dominant scholarly approach, I find that the category was formed as a descriptive summary of three exegetical conclusions about the so-called tefillin verses (Exod 13:9–10). Exegesis of these verses reveals important differences between tefillin and mezuzah, even though both rituals are "positive commandments." When the three distinctive features of tefillin are summarized, the category of timebound, positive commandments emerges. Among the exegetical conclusions referenced in the rule that exempts women from timebound, positive commandments is the stipulation that women are exempt from tefillin. Though the tannaitic creation of the category of timebound, positive commandments itself did not support the construction of gender, the exemption of women from tefillin did. Chapters 6 and 7 in Part III follow up on this conclusion by exploring the social and religious bases for women's exemption from tefillin. Part I, however, remains squarely focused on how tannaitic manipulations of the *rule as a rule* (not the underlying ritual exemptions) support the construction of gender.

Chapter 2 (also in Part I) takes its starting point from the fact that the rule appears in several lists of ways in which Jewish law treats women differently from men. One of the lists of male–female difference begins with a question: "What are the differences between man and woman?" It answers by saying things like whereas a man is stoned naked, a woman is not; whereas a man can be sold as a Hebrew slave, a woman cannot.[34] Most items of male–female difference in the lists are documented elsewhere in the tannaitic corpus. Like the exegesis discussed in the previous chapter, the lists do not represent an attempt to legislate de novo. Rather they represent efforts to organize existing legal traditions into meaningful categories. The stipulation that men, but not women, are obligated to perform timebound, positive commandments is

---

[33] Hauptman, *Rereading the Rabbis*, 226.
[34] See m. Sot. 3:8. Other lists of male–female difference can be found in t. Sot. 2:7–9; t. Bik. 2:3–7; m. Kid. 1:7–8; Sem. 6:1–5; and m. Shab. 6:1–5.

found in several of these lists. Chapter 2 investigates how the rule functioned in the context of the lists. First, I note that in the context of the lists the rule is not an overarching principle that explains or accounts for all other instances of male–female difference. Rather, the rule takes its place as a single piece of information in the complex collage of "male–female difference." This conclusion flies in the face of conventional wisdom that assumes that the rule functions as a programmatic statement of male–female difference. What the lists do indicate, however, is that the tannaitic rabbis found the project of cataloguing instances of male–female difference to be important and meaningful. They did not, for example, compile comparable lists of the differences between slaves and freemen or adults and minors. I argue that the rule drew its significance as a salient marker of male–female difference from the fact that it was transmitted in these lists. At this stage in the rule's transmission, it does not promote a particular vision of gendered identities (as scholars have generally assumed). Rather, citing the rule in the context of the lists was a way to affirm that men and women are different. Difference between men and women was conceived as a composite of *all* the legal differences listed.

Part II ("Talmudic Interpretation and the Potential for Gender") examines amoraic and post-amoraic interpretation of the rule and documents incremental shifts in the perception of the rule. Though the rule was not formulated to function prescriptively, the fact remains that later sages assumed it had been formulated in such a manner. I do not mean to claim that later sages invoked the rule to determine women's actual ritual involvement. It does appear, however, that later sages *assumed* that the rule *had* functioned prescriptively during the tannaitic period, when decisions about women's ritual involvement were first being made. My goal in Part II is to determine when and why this shift in perception occurred. I conclude that the idea that the rule functioned prescriptively is first in evidence during the post-amoraic period. The prescriptive interpretation of the rule made it possible for post-talmudic thinkers to ascribe gendering motivations to the rule's authors. I find no evidence, however, to indicate that the post-amoraic impulse to read the rule as a prescriptive principle was itself motivated by a concern with gender.

Chapter 3 identifies one moment in the process by which the rule came to be viewed as a prescriptive principle rather than a descriptive summary of exegesis. It will be recalled that Chapter 1 argues that the category of timebound, positive commandments emerged from exegesis of the tefillin verses. For the rule to be perceived as having been formulated prescriptively, it needed to be freed from its descriptive function with regard to tefillin. During the post-amoraic period, the view emerged that some tannaitic sages had characterized tefillin as *non*-timebound. Once it was determined that some tannaitic sages characterized tefillin as *non*-timebound, the theoretical possibility existed to conceive of the rule's genesis apart from its relationship to tefillin.

It is noteworthy that the creation of a fictional position that tefillin are not timebound was *not motivated by concerns with gender*. The attribution of this view to some tannaitic sages arose in the context of scholastic exercises.[35] Post-amoraic sages inherited several tannaitic sources about the prohibition of carrying on the Sabbath. Among these traditions was a source about tefillin. As part of an effort to harmonize the differences among the sources, it was suggested that certain tannaitic sages had thought that tefillin are not timebound. This conclusion made room for post-amoraic sages to assume that the rule had a history independent of tefillin. Freed from its descriptive relationship with tefillin, the rule could now be viewed as prescriptive.

Chapters 4 and 5 provide additional evidence that a shift in the perception of the rule occurred during the post-amoraic period. Chapter 4 analyzes the differences in approach exhibited by the two Talmuds in their analysis of an exceptional woman who did wear tefillin in antiquity. The earlier Yerushalmi (c. 375–425) insists that women are exempt from wearing tefillin. The commentary explains that the sages made a special allowance for this exceptional woman. The post-amoraic stratum of the Bavli (c. 450–600), on the other hand, explains that the sages who did not censor the exceptional woman were of the opinion that tefillin are not timebound. These sages apparently used the rule to determine women's ritual involvement generally; in their view, however, women's involvement with tefillin was not adjudicated by the rule because *tefillin are not timebound*. Only in the post-amoraic stratum of the Bavli does the discussion of this exceptional woman rest on the assumption that the rule was in force as a prescriptive principle early in the rabbinic period.

Chapter 5 brings yet more evidence to locate a shift in the perception of the rule during the post-amoraic period. The post-amoraic stratum of the Bavli invests extensive amounts of energy defending the idea that the rule was formulated to determine women's involvement in ritual. Medieval and modern

---

[35] José Cabezón defines scholasticism in a manner that proves useful for scholars working outside of the context of medieval Christian scholasticism, where the category was initially introduced. See José Ignacio Cabezón, *Buddhism and Language: A Study of Indo-Tibetan Scholasticism* (Albany: State University of New York Press, 1994), 11–25; and José Ignacio Cabezón, ed., *Scholasticism: Cross-cultural and Comparative Perspectives* (Albany: State University of New York Press, 1998), 4–6. Michael Swartz notes that not all of the features that Cabezón identifies with scholasticism are manifest in rabbinic scholasticism. See Michael D. Swartz, "Scholasticism as a Comparative Category and the Study of Judaism," in *Scholasticism: Cross-cultural and Comparative Perspectives*, ed. José Cabezón (Albany: State University of New York Press, 1998), 91–114. The features of scholasticism that are manifest in the post-amoraic stratum of the Bavli are (1) a preoccupation with exegesis and commentary of an authoritative text of tradition (in this case the Mishnah; Cabezón 1994, 23); (2) a concern with disembodied knowledge and theoretical questions for their own sake (Cabezón 1994, 18; 1998), and (3) an interest in the systematic elucidation of a body of tradition with the goal of eliminating inconsistencies (Cabezón 1998, 6). See also the useful discussion of scholasticism in Raimundo Panikkar, "Common Patterns of Eastern and Western Scholasticism," *Diogenes* 21/83 (1973): 103–13.

scholars note that there are numerous exceptions to the rule.[36] (The exceptions, by the way, are one good indication that the rule was *not* formulated to determine women's ritual involvement broadly. The rule certainly did not determine women's ritual involvement in the exceptional cases referred to above!) Chapter 5 reviews the Bavli's attempts to reconcile the exceptions with a supposedly prescriptive rule. The Bavli additionally tries to make sense of the places where tannaitic law *agrees* with the rule. In the Bavli's view, the Mishnah never explicitly states a case that can otherwise be learned from a general principle like the rule. The Bavli must therefore explain why the cases that agree with the rule had to be stated explicitly, given that the rule was in force as a prescriptive principle. Ironically, by the Bavli's count no single case of women's ritual involvement was actually ever determined by the rule. Nonetheless, fundamental to the Bavli's discussion of both the rule's instantiations and exceptions is the assumption that the rule was formulated to function prescriptively.

Both chapters 4 and 5 identify an important shift in the perception of the rule in the post-amoraic period. In the post-amoraic period, sages began to assume that the rule had been formulated to function prescriptively. The new perception, however, does not arise with an awareness of the rule's new potential to support an edifice of gender. Nowhere does the Bavli address the question of why women are exempt from the entire class of timebound, positive commandments.[37] The Bavli reads the rule as it does because it is engaged in the scholastic project of organizing inherited legal sources (including the rule) into a coherent and systematic whole.[38] Within the context of this work, reading

---

[36] Though the rule exempts women from timebound, positive commandments, other sources obligate them to the following timebound, positive commandments: *hakhel* (Deut 31:12), *simchah* offering (Deut 15:14 and t. Hag. 1:4), eating matzah on Passover (t. Pisha 1:34), *kiddush hayom* (b. Ber. 20b), lighting of Hanukah candles (b. Shab. 23a), drinking the four cups of wine on Passover (b. Pes. 108a–b), and reading the *megillah* on Purim (b. Meg. 4a). In addition, though the rule obligates women to perform non-timebound, positive commandments, women are exempt from a number of them: Torah study (Sif. Dt., Ekev, Piska 46, and t. Kid. 1:11), redemption of the firstborn son (t. Kid. 1:11), circumcising one's son (t. Kid. 1:11), and to "be fruitful and multiply" (m. Yev. 6:6), on the view of all except Yohanan b. Baroka.

[37] The Bavli does discuss the reasons for women's exemption or obligation regarding several specific rituals. B. Kid. 34a reflects on plausible reasons to obligate women to and exempt them from sukkah. B. Ber. 20b suggests reasons why women should not be exempt from Shema and tefillin and offers a rationale for obligating women to recite the Amidah.

[38] Most recently Barry Wimpfheimer has argued that an important component of the post-amoraic project consisted of organizing diverse tannaitic sources into a systematic whole. See Wimpfheimer, *Narrating the Law: A Poetics of Talmudic Legal Stories*. Other important insights into how post-amoraic sages imposed systematization and abstract conceptualization onto tannaitic sources can be found in Yitzhak Gilat, *Studies in the Development of Halakha* (Hebrew) (Israel: Bar Ilan University Press, 1992); Leib Moscovitz, *Talmudic Reasoning: From Casuistics to Conceptualization* (Tübingen: Mohr Siebeck, 2002); Jeffrey Rubenstein, "The Sukkah as Temporary or Permanent Dwelling: A Study in the Development of Talmudic Thought," *Hebrew Union College Annual* 64 (1993): 137–66; and Jeffrey Rubenstein, "On Some Abstract Concepts in Rabbinic Literature," *Jewish Studies Quarterly* 4 (1997): 33–73.

the rule as a prescriptive principle makes sense. Though the shift in perception had an enormous impact on the rule's significance for discussions of gender thenceforth, the shift does not appear to be occasioned by an interest in gender per se. We might think of the rule as a vessel crafted by the post-amoraic sages. They did not fill the vessel, but it now had the capacity to hold something. Post-amoraic sages did not themselves reflect on the reasons for women's exemptions from timebound, positive commandments. But by understanding the rule as one that had been formulated as a prescriptive principle, they left room for those who came later to do so.

By the end of Part II, we find ourselves in a paradoxical situation. Though I set out to understand what is at stake in the rule's stipulations, Part II concludes that this question is nonsensical when oriented toward those who formulated the rule. The tannaitic rabbis simply did not formulate the rule to determine women's ritual involvement. One can legitimately ask how *post-*talmudic scholars ascribed motivations to the rule's authors. Post-talmudic scholars encountered the rule as framed by the Bavli and therefore understood it to be a prescriptive principle determining the broad range of women's ritual involvement. Like Anatoli discussed above, they assume that a "reason" for the rule exists. But if the tannaim who framed the rule did not understand it to be a prescriptive principle, how can we inquire into their motivations when determining women's ritual involvement?

In Part III ("Gender in Women's Ritual Exemptions"), I recognize the extent to which the question with which the study begins – how do the rule's stipulations support the construction of rabbinic gender? – reflects our current understanding of the rule as a programmatic statement of rabbinic gender. Answering the question according to sound historical method requires that we modify it to reflect the way the rule was understood in the tannaitic period. Accordingly, rather than focusing on the rationale for women's exemptions from timebound, positive commandments as a class, I explore the reasons for women's exemptions from tefillin and related rituals, since women's exemption from tefillin undergirds the rule as a whole.

Chapter 6 examines women's exemption from tefillin in light of the long history of the practice during the Second Temple period. I argue that women's exemption from tefillin is intimately connected with their exemption from recitation of Shema. Chapter 6 concludes that women's exemption from both tefillin and Shema is rooted in the rabbinic understanding of these rituals as forms of Torah study. Since the rabbis claim to know from elsewhere that women are exempt from Torah study, they also exempt women from tefillin and Shema.

Chapter 7 explores the next obvious question: Why do the rabbis exempt women from Torah study? My analysis highlights the fact that the rabbis exempted women only from the type of Torah study associated with the Shema, which I characterize as ritual Torah study. A careful reading of tannaitic texts reveals that the rabbis were not opposed to women's Torah when it was a means to an end. The sources leave open the possibility that women may study Torah to gain information, perspective, or skills. What is the basis for distinguishing between ritual and instrumental Torah study? Why do the rabbis represent women as involved in one form of Torah study, but not the other? I draw on work from the field of ritual studies that suggests that ritual action (like Torah study) enables the ritual actor to inhabit, even if only temporarily, an ideal world.[39] Close readings of the tannaitic sources reveal that ritual Torah study by fathers and sons facilitated the creation of a world in which fathers reproduced their social and covenantal identity in the next generation.[40] Since daughters could never reproduce their father's (male) social identity, ritual Torah study was simply not relevant for them. Taking these insights back to women's exemption from tefillin suggests that women are exempt from tefillin (and Shema) because as forms of Torah study these rituals likewise enable the father to reproduce his social and covenantal identity.

Chapter 8 examines the one tannaitic case where the rule appears to have been used to determine women's ritual involvement. Tannaitic sources preserve a debate regarding women's obligation to wear tzitzit on the corners of their garments. One of the parties to the debate cites the rule relieving women from timebound, positive commandments as the basis for exempting women from tzitzit. Chapter 8 explores what the rule might have meant to the one sage who historically invoked it to determine women's ritual involvement. It is reasonable to assume that when *he* cited the rule as the basis for exempting women, *he was motivated by a vision of the distinct roles men and women should play in religious life*. Here then is where we finally receive an answer to the question posed at the outset of the book, though by the time it is offered it provides a much less comprehensive view of rabbinic gender than we initially hoped to find. I conclude that characterizing tzitzit as a timebound, positive commandment was akin to likening it to tefillin. To do so was to claim that tzitzit, like tefillin, are a ritual means for fathers to reproduce their social and covenantal identities in the next generation. The logic behind women's exemption from tzitzit is the same as that behind their exemption from tefillin.

---

[39] See Adam B. Seligman et al., *Ritual and Its Consequences: An Essay on the Limits of Sincerity* (Oxford: Oxford University Press, 2008).

[40] See Nancy Jay, *Throughout Your Generations Forever: Sacrifice, Religion, and Paternity*, foreword by Karen E. Fields (Chicago: University of Chicago Press, 1992); and Elisheva Baumgarten, *Mothers and Children: Jewish Family Life in Medieval Europe* (Princeton: Princeton University Press, 2004), 55–89. Generally, discussions of cultural reproduction in rabbinic culture have stressed how the disciple reproduces the identity of the master. Biological and cultural reproduction are often pitted against each other in literary contexts that highlight how the master's cultural line is continued through his disciples. See Martin S. Jaffee, "Gender and Otherness in Rabbinic Oral Culture: On Gentiles, Undisciplined Jews, and Their Women," in *Performing the Gospel: Orality, Memory and Mark*, ed. Richard Horsley, Jonathan Draper, and John Miles Foley (Minneapolis: Fortress Press, 2006), 21–43, 201–9; Daniel Boyarin, *Carnal Israel: Reading Sex in Talmudic Culture* (Berkeley: University of California Press, 1993), 197–225; and Jeffrey L. Rubenstein, *Talmudic Stories: Narrative Art, Composition, and Culture*, 176–211.

Since women will never be the *pater familias* of the next generation, rituals that aim to reproduce the father's social and covenantal identity simply are not relevant to them. The issue of time turns out to be a red herring. Ironically, the rule that exempts women from timebound, positive commandments provides more information about rabbinic ideas concerning male identity than it does about rabbinic ideas concerning female identity.

Part III investigates the rationale behind women's exemptions from only a limited number of commandments: tefillin, Shema, Torah study, and tzitzit. The list of commandments that I treat does not correspond to the list of commandments named in rabbinic sources as exemplars of the rule. In fact, Torah study is not a timebound commandment at all. My approach in Part III is determined by my conclusions in earlier chapters. I focus on explaining the exemptions that my analysis indicates are formative for the rule. I discuss tefillin, for example, because it is identified as a prototype of the rule.[41] I discuss tzitzit because women's involvement with them is adjudicated by the rule.[42] Other rituals receive attention because they are closely associated with tefillin. I discuss women's exemption from Shema because historical analysis reveals that this exemption is closely tied to the exemption from tefillin.[43] I discuss women's exemption from Torah study because tannaitic sources report that women's exemption from Torah study accounts for their exemption from tefillin.[44]

My way of conceiving the cases covered by the rule is an admittedly scholarly construct. If one were to ask the parties to the contemporary debate to list the timebound, positive commandments from which women are exempt, they would surely mention exemptions that I do not treat in Part III (most notably sukkah, lulav, and shofar). Though the contemporary cultural debates give energy and relevance to this scholarly inquiry, in the final analysis my procedure for illuminating how the rabbis used ritual exemption to construct gender is not dictated by the structures of thinking that dominate popular conceptions of the rule.

A Short Note about the Term "Timebound, Positive Commandments"

The Hebrew phrase *mizvot 'aseh shehazaman garama* is difficult to translate gracefully. My favorite way of rendering the phrase is "positive commandments occasioned by time." This translation has the merit of enabling the English reader to grasp conceptually how the category is constituted. "Timebound, positive commandments" are a subset of the broader category of positive commandments. The smaller category consists of those positive commandments

---

[41] See MRSY, ed. Epstein-Melamed, 41.
[42] Sif. Num. 115, ed. Horowitz, 124; t. Kid. 1:10.
[43] See discussion in Chapter 6.
[44] See Mek. Bo 17, ed. Horowitz-Rabin, 68.

that are "occasioned by time." Unfortunately, the English phrase "positive commandments occasioned by time" is bulky and does not fit gracefully into many English sentences. In a very few places I have used this translation. In most places, however, I use the awkward term "timebound," which was long ago coined as an English adjective to indicate the concept of being "occasioned by time." I place the adjective "positive" closest to the noun that it modifies because that placement in English indicates that "positive" is the primary descriptor:[45] thus "timebound, positive commandments" instead of the often used "positive, timebound commandments."

As noted above, the dominant scholarly approach investigates the rationale for women's exemption from this class of commandments. These studies focus on the distinctive features of this class of commandments and usually take the fact that they are "occasioned by time" to be their most noteworthy feature. Scholars who take this approach sometimes avoid the conventional translation ("timebound") because they want their readers to think about the concept of being "occasioned by time" in new ways. Moshe Benovitz, for example, creatively renders the Hebrew with the English phrase "time-triggered positive commandments." He explains that "while it is true that these commandments are conditioned upon time on both ends, the Hebrew phrase stresses the *terminus a quo* of the obligation; time... triggers the obligation... hence 'time-triggered.'"[46] My study, unlike the majority of scholarly work on the rule, does not find women's exemption from this class of commandments to flow from the fact that they are "occasioned by time." Employing one translation or another does not affect the substance of my argument. Consequently, I allow myself the liberty of using the slightly imprecise but conventional term "timebound" because it is familiar to readers and renders the prose slightly less awkward.

[45] I thank Shlomo Naeh for alerting me to this point of English grammar.

[46] Benovitz, "Time-Triggered Positive Commandments," 45n1. Safrai (in the English summary of his article) uses the term "time dependent." Shmuel Safrai, "The *Mitzva* Obligation of Women in Tannaitic Thought," English summary, X. Wegner uses the term "positive precepts whose obligation accrues at a specified time." Wegner, *Chattel or Person*, 150. Kraemer uses the term "affirmative precepts limited to time": Ross Shepard Kraemer, *Her Share of the Blessings: Women's Religions among Pagans, Jews, and Christians in the Greco-Roman World* (New York: Oxford University Press, 1992), 96. Stern explains that the term indicates a "commandment that becomes binding by the onset of its proper designated time." Sacha Stern, *Time and Process in Ancient Judaism* (Portland: Littman Library of Jewish Civilization, 2003), 28.

PART I

GENDER AND THE TANNAITIC RULE

I

The Rule and Social Reality

Conceiving the Category, Formulating the Rule

This chapter aims to reconstruct the process by which the category of time-bound, positive commandments was conceived and the rule exempting women from them formulated. The goal of this exercise is to gain insight into how this process contributed to the construction of social identities within Jewish society during the tannaitic period. The conventional understanding of this process envisions the rabbis as lawmakers seeking to influence or accommodate social reality. Judith Hauptman observes that "the Talmud mentions the phrase 'positive time-bound' or 'non-time-bound' mitzvot *only* in connection with women" (emphasis in the original). She concludes from this observation that the category "was created solely for the purpose of distinguishing between women's ritual obligations and her exemptions."[1] When formulating the rule, the rabbis would have reflected on the social standing of women, the nature of ritual obligation, and the way women already were using or ideally should use their time. They would have weighed a variety of issues and concluded on the basis of considered priorities that women need perform only a particular subset of ritual commandments. In this reconstruction of the process, the authors of the rule support the construction of women's social identities by encouraging women to use their time in some ways and not others, and to engage in some rituals and not others.[2] In contrast to the conventional understanding, I

---

[1] Hauptman, *Rereading the Rabbis*, 226.

[2] See, for example, Berman, "The Status of Women in Halakhic Judaism." He argues that though the rule refrains from *legislating* a particular role for women, it "was a tool used by the Rabbis to achieve a particular social goal, namely to assure that no legal obligation would interfere with the selection by Jewish women of a role which was centered almost exclusively in the home" (121–22). The language of many other scholars imputes a high level of conscious social engineering to the rule's authors. See esp. Wegner, *Chattel or Person*, 154–55; and Ross Shepard Kraemer, *Her Share of the Blessings: Women's Religions among Pagans, Jews, and Christians in the Greco-Roman World*, 96–97, who builds on Wegner.

argue that the category was conceived and the rule formulated in the process of rehearsing and consolidating knowledge of Jewish legal tradition. If any social identities were constructed in the process of conceiving the category and formulating the rule, it would have been the social identity of rabbinic masters and disciples as experts in legal tradition and Torah.

The textual evidence that is usually used to reconstruct this process is the rule as it appears in the Mishnah. In the Mishnah (which at least superficially resembles a law code), the rule appears to be a prescriptive principle. When the rule is encountered in this context, it is easy to imagine that the rule's authors functioned as lawmakers. By way of contrast, my approach emphasizes that the mishnaic evidence for this process should be read *in conjunction with* tosephtan and midrashic evidence. I do not let the fact that the rule is preserved in the codelike Mishnah overdetermine my understanding of what was accomplished when the category was conceived and the rule formulated. Instead I focus on how performance of the rule in the codelike genres of Mishnah and Tosephta was part of a larger endeavor that also included performance of tradition in the exegetical genre of midrash.[3] When the sages rehearsed legal tradition in the midrashic style, they emphasized its roots in biblical scripture. When they rehearsed it in the mishnaic/tosephtan style, they emphasized its place within an organized and coherent system of law. Both ways of rehearsing legal tradition helped mold it so that it could be mastered and refined. Both ways of rehearsing tradition were social acts insofar as they established the rabbis as an educated and pious elite within Jewish society.[4] I find no evidence to suggest that when the rabbis conceived the category of timebound, positive commandments and formulated the rule, they were reflecting on the relationship among women, ritual, and time in the "real world." Instead, they were reflecting on verses from the Torah, legal traditions associated with them, and the broader categories into which legal traditions could be organized. I conclude that the process of conceiving the category and formulating the rule did not *directly* contribute to the construction of women's social identities in the tannaitic period.[5] Rather, it

---

[3] In my attention to what is accomplished when legal tradition is rehearsed (in both mishnaic and midrashic modes), I build on my earlier work, which focuses on what was accomplished when mishnaic texts were performed in antiquity. See Alexander, *Transmitting Mishnah.* I also draw on the work of Steven Fraade, who discusses "the performative work" of the "discursive rhetoric" of midrash. See Fraade, *From Tradition to Commentary: Torah and Its Interpretation in the Midrash Sifre to Deuteronomy,* esp. 163–64.

[4] Here I draw on Fraade, *From Tradition to Commentary: Torah and Its Interpretation in the Midrash Sifre to Deuteronomy,* esp. 69–121.

[5] I am indebted to Chaya Halberstam for pointing me to literature in the subfield of law and society that helped me clarify my thinking on the relationship between the technical manipulations of legal materials in the mishnah and midrash and social reality. In an electronic communication (February 24, 2011), Halberstam summarizes the emerging regnant view in the subfield as follows: "Law is not hermetically sealed off from society, but it functions most overtly within its own internal disciplinary language, not answering *directly* to social pressures or constraints." My argument in this chapter explores how the rule emerged most immediately from formal concerns of the rabbis as legal technicians. On this view of the relationship between law and society, see

appears that this process, like many other academic exercises of a similar nature, supported the construction of rabbinic identities. By rehearsing the relationship between elements of legal tradition and verses of biblical scripture and by highlighting the categories into which tradition could be organized, rabbinic masters and disciples established themselves as the experts and guardians of this tradition.

This chapter documents how the category and rule emerged while the rabbis were rehearsing legal tradition in both midrashic modes, which emphasized the scriptural roots of legal tradition, and mishnaic modes, which emphasized the extent to which legal tradition can be organized into categories. The process appears to have begun in the context of midrashic style rehearsal of tradition and continued in the context of mishnaic style rehearsal of tradition, but the fact that the process cannot be fully reconstructed from either midrashic or mishnaic texts suggests that rehearsing tradition in both of these modalities was part of a single enterprise. Rehearsing legal tradition in both modalities helped establish the sages as an elite class of Torah experts. Though I argue that the category and rule have their roots in midrashic style rehearsal of legal tradition, it will be helpful to begin by examining the rule as it appears in the mishnaic and tosephtan contexts most familiar to readers.

Categories in the Mishnah and Tosephta

The Mishnah presents the rule exempting women from timebound, positive commandments alongside another rule that also circumscribes women's ritual obligations. The mishnah that records the two rules reads as follows:

כל מצות האב על הבן⁶ – אנשים חיבין, ונשים פטורות.
וכל מצות הבן על האב⁷ – אחד אנשים ואחד נשים חיבין.

וכל מצות עשה שהזמן גרמה – אנשים חיבין ונשים פטורות.
וכל מצות עשה שלא הזמן גרמה – אחד אנשים ואחד נשים חיבין.

Pierre Bordieau, "The Force of Law: Toward a Sociology of the Juridical Field," trans. Richard Terdiman, *Hasting Law Journal* 38/5 (1987): 805–50; Stanley Fish, "The Law Wishes to Have a Formal Existence," in *The Fate of Law*, ed. Austin Sarat and Thomas Kearns (Ann Arbor: University of Michigan Press, 1991), 159–208; and Gunther Teubner, ed., *Autopoietic Law: A New Approach to Law and Society* (Berlin: W. de Gruyter, 1988). For an application of these theories to rabbinic law, see Halberstam, *Law and Truth in Biblical and Rabbinic Literature*, 22–41.

6 Transcription follows the Palestinian tradition, as attested in MSS Cambridge, Lowe, and Parma and in the mishnah in the Palestinian Talmud. The mishnah in the Babylonian Talmud reverses the order of the subjects and reads "son-to-father commandments" (מצות הבן על האב,) but understands the meaning to be the same as in the Palestinian tradition. As the Bavli explains, "these are commandments *concerning* the son, which are *placed* upon the father" (b. Kid. 29b).

7 Transcription follows the Palestinian tradition, as attested in MSS Cambridge, Lowe, and Parma and in the mishnah in the Palestinian Talmud. The mishnah in the Babylonian Talmud reverses the order of the subjects and reads "father-to-son commandments" (מצות האב על הבן,) but understands the meaning to be the same as in the Palestinian tradition.

וכל מצות לא תעשה, בין שהזמן גרמה, בין שלא הזמן גרמה – אחד אנשים ואחד נשים
חיבין, חוץ מבל תשחית, ובל תקיף ובל תטמא למתים.

A. 1. All father-to-son commandments – men are obligated, women are exempt.

A. 2. All son-to-father commandments – men and women are equally obligated.

B. 1. All timebound, positive commandments – men are obligated, women are exempt.

B. 2. All non-timebound, positive commandments – men and women are equally obligated.

B. 3 and 4. All negative commandments, irrespective of whether they are timebound or non-timebound – men and women are equally obligated, except "do not mar [the corners of your beard," "do not round [the corners of your head]" and "do not become impurified through contact with the dead." (m. Kid. 1:7)

This mishnah consists of two parts, each of which considers women's obligation with regard to an interrelated set of categories of commandments. The first part of the mishnah (A) clarifies the extent of women's obligations regarding commandments pertaining to fathers and sons; the second part (B) clarifies their obligations regarding commandments that are negative and positive, timebound and non-timebound. In each part of the mishnah (A and B), the named categories display a rhetorical symmetry. In the first part (A), the symmetry is created by inverting the position of the two subjects, with the first line considering the father's obligations to his son and the second line considering the son's obligations to his father.[8] In the second part of the mishnah (B), the symmetry is a bit more complex, since more variables are subject to manipulation. Here each category is formed by pairing one adjective from the "positive"/"negative" binary set with one adjective from the "timebound"/"non-timebound" binary set, yielding a total of four possible combinations.[9] For each of the stated categories, the mishnah delivers a ruling concerning male and female obligation.

The Mishnah's presentation suggests that the two categories in the first part ("father-to-son" and "son-to-father" commandments) and the four categories in the second part ("timebound, positive"; "non-timebound, positive"; "timebound, negative"; and "non-timebound, negative" commandments) have the same ontological status. It is noteworthy, however, that in both parts of the mishnah only the ruling regarding the first category (A.1 and B.1) distinguishes between male and female obligation. The other categories of commandments (A.2 and B.2, B.3 and B.4) are legally unremarkable insofar as men and women are equally obligated to perform them. Only "father-to-son" and "timebound,

---

[8] Elizabeth Shanks Alexander ("The Fixing of the Oral Mishnah and the Displacement of Meaning," 1999) discusses the use of shifting variables to generate a series of rhetorically and structurally similar formulations.

[9] The duplication of a set of binary descriptors to produce a four-part structure is commonplace in the Mishnah. See the following examples: m. BB 8:1; m. Yev. 9:1; m. Men. 5:3; 5:5; m. Bekh. 8:1; m. Avot 5:10–14.

positive" commandments are legally significant, for in these cases women are exempt.[10] It is also noteworthy that only these "legally significant" categories ("father-to-son commandments" and "timebound, positive commandments") are independently attested in other tannaitic materials.[11] These facts suggest that the mishnaic presentation of all the categories as of equal conceptual status does not tell the whole story.

George Lakoff argues that the mind does not develop categories through disembodied abstract conceptual reason. Rather, the mind forms categories in organic ways that involve imaginative extensions of and oppositions to a generative prototype.[12] In other words, not all categories are created equally, though after they have been formed they can sometimes appear to be of the same conceptual status. By presenting the two categories in A and the four categories in B of equal conceptual status, the Mishnah obscures the organic cognitive process that led to the creation of these networks of related categories. The fact that only one category in each part of the mishnah (A.1 and B.1) is legally significant and the fact that only these categories are attested independently suggest that they are the prototypical categories from which the network of related categories was generated. To put the thesis in slightly different terms, I am proposing that in each set of interrelated categories (A and B), one of the categories (A.1 = "father-to-son commandments" and B.1 = "timebound, positive commandments") was conceived before the others were. Once the rule for this one category was formulated, it became possible to consider women's obligations for the variant categories, eventually producing the more complex rhetorical structure of the mishnah. One way to think about the formulation of the rule, then, is to focus on the conception of the category "timebound, positive commandments" that generates the more complex structure of interrelated categories in this mishnah.[13]

Lakoff argues that the formation of categories happens in a variety of ways. The preceding analysis of a network of interrelated categories emphasizes how

---

[10] Judith Hauptman makes a similar point. She notes that the characterization of commandments as "timebound" and "positive" is not used except in connection with women. She suggests that "this distinction was created solely for the purpose of distinguishing between women's ritual obligations and her exemptions." See Hauptman, *Rereading the Rabbis*, 226.

[11] I do not take the tosephtan parallel (t. Kid. 1:10–11) to this mishnah into account when I make this assessment. The tosephta is obviously familiar with the full mishnah and so comments on each of the named categories. Though the Sifra (Kedoshim, parshata 1:2) does refer to obligations children have with respect to their parents, it does not use the term "son-to-father commandments" to describe these obligations. The Sifra's failure to use this term is all the more significant in light of other parallels between the Sifra passage and t. Kid. 1:11.

[12] George Lakoff, *Women, Fire, and Dangerous Things: What Categories Reveal about the Mind* (Chicago: University of Chicago Press, 1987).

[13] Elsewhere I discuss the process that led to the conception of the generative category in the first part of the mishnah ("father-to-son commandments"). See Elizabeth Shanks Alexander, "From Whence the Phrase 'Timebound Positive Commandments'?" *Jewish Quarterly Review* 97/3 (2007): 325–34.

categories coexist alongside each other and map out the structure of a comprehensive field. In this way of thinking about categories, categories take a comprehensive field (like commandments) and divide it into appropriate groupings (positive and negative, timebound and non-timebound). The structure of categories, however, can also be examined "from the ground up." Such analysis focuses on what we can learn about a category by looking at the exemplars that make up the category.

The Tosephta offers insight into the category of timebound, positive commandments by providing a list of exemplary rituals.

איזו היא מצות עשה שהזמן גרמא?

כגון סוכה ולולב ותפילין.

What is a time-bound, positive commandment?

For example, sukkah, lulav, and tefillin.[14] (t. Kid. 1:10)

The Tosephta names three rituals as timebound, positive commandments: sukkah, lulav, and tefillin. The Yerushalmi's version of this baraita additionally includes shofar on the list of exemplary rituals. The term "for example" that introduces the list indicates that the named rituals are not the only members of this category, but illustrative examples. The Tosephta's presentation suggests that all three rituals exhibit the traits of timebound, positive commandments to the same extent. When we turn to the midrashic discussion of these three commandments, however, we find that the rule lies in the background

---

[14] The two Talmuds differ slightly from the Tosephta in their representation of this baraita. The Yerushalmi inserts shofar into the list in between sukkah and lulav. See y. Kid. 61c. The Bavli inserts shofar after lulav, but more significantly, adds tzitzit before the final item on the list, tefillin. See b. Kid. 33b–34a. The second of the Bavli's emmendations of the Tosephta's baraita has generated a fair amount of scholarly discussion, because it represents the amalgamation into the anonymous strata of tradition of, what in the Tosephta appears as, a minority view. In the Tosephta, the anonymous voice characterizes tzitzit as a *non*-timebound, positive commandment. R. Shimon disagrees, claiming that tzitzit is a timebound, positive commandment. The Bavli's version of the baraita represents R. Shimon's opinion as normative. For detailed discussion of the parallels to this baraita, see Saul Lieberman, *The Tosefta Ki-Fshutah: A Comprehensive Commentary on the Tosefta* (1955–73), vol. 8 (Hebrew) (Israel: Jewish Theological Seminary of America, 1995), 922–23; Louis Ginzberg, *A Commentary on the Palestinian Talmud: A Study of the Development of Halakhah and Haggadah in Palestine and Babylonia* (New York: Ktav, 1971), 159–63; Menachem Katz, "The First Chapter of Tractate Qiddushin of the Talmud Yerushalmi: Text, Commentary and Studies in the Editorial Process" (PhD diss., Bar Ilan University, 2003), 189–93. Following previous scholarly discussions, I view the inclusion of shofar in the list of timebound, positive commandments as less ideologically motivated than the inclusion of tzitzit. Consequently, I think it possible that shofar was on some of the lists that circulated during the tannaitic period, even though its presence there is not attested in explicitly tannaitic literature. I follow Martin S. Jaffee, *Torah in the Mouth: Writing and Oral Tradition in Palestinian Judaism, 200 BCE–400 CE* (New York: Oxford University Press, 2001), 135–40, in allowing that some amoraic variants to tannaitic teachings (like the Yerushalmi's version of this baraita) are part of the same discursive universe as the tannaitic teachings.

of the conversations concerning tefillin in a way that it does not lie in the background of conversations concerning sukkah and lulav.

Lakoff's discussion of how the mind forms categories again proves helpful as we try to make sense of these findings. Lakoff discusses a phenomenon called the "prototype effect" in which some members of a category are better representative of it than others.[15] To illustrate this point, he notes that a robin or a swallow is a better representative of the category "bird" than an owl or a penguin.[16] Many different cognitive processes can result in a "prototype effect," but the one most relevant to our discussion is where a category is defined by a "generator" that "has the status of a central, or 'prototypical,' category member."[17] In these cases, the qualities of the generative prototype are observed in things other than the prototype, and a category is formed that encompasses them all. The generative prototype will likely remain a "better" example of the categories than will other members. In our case study, midrashic sources suggest that tefillin is a "better" example of timebound, positive commandments than sukkah, lulav, or shofar. Midrashic sources link tefillin with the category in a way that they do not link sukkah, lulav, and shofar. In addition, two sources (of which, admittedly, only one is tannaitic) name women's exemption from tefillin as the *source* for the rule that women should be exempt from all timebound, positive commandments.[18] In the analysis that follows, I turn to the midrashic texts that lead me to conclude that tefillin is a prototype for this category.

Before I continue, however, it will be helpful to connect my conclusions regarding timebound, positive commandments as a category with my methodological approach that emphasizes the performative aspect of tannaitic literature. Both the Mishnah and the Tosephta present categories in a manner that makes them appear to be the product of abstract conceptual thinking. The four interrelated categories in the Mishnah appear to exist because they are a theoretically sound way to conceptualize groupings of commandments. Likewise, the Tosephta's exemplars of sukkah, lulav, and tefillin are assumed to exhibit a common set of traits that make them all equally valid members of the category on a theoretical level. But rather than thinking of the categories themselves as the product of abstract conceptual thought, I suggest that this impression *results from* the Mishnah and Tosephta's manner of rehearsing legal tradition.[19] Both the Mishnah and the Tosephta rehearse tradition in a way that highlights the integrity and coherence of the tradition. Performing tradition in these ways stresses that each datum has its place within an organized, rational,

---

[15] For a full definition of this term, see Lakoff, *Women, Fire, and Dangerous Things: What Categories Reveal about the Mind*, 40–45.

[16] Lakoff, *Women, Fire, and Dangerous Things: What Categories Reveal about the Mind*, 45.

[17] Lakoff, *Women, Fire, and Dangerous Things: What Categories Reveal about the Mind*, 12.

[18] See MRSY, ed. Epstein-Melamed, 41; b. Kid. 34a.

[19] Fraade's description of the Sifre informs conclusions here. He writes that these texts "might be seen not so much as *reports* of a transformation already completed as part of the very *work* of that transformation – as the discursive media of their *will*." Fraade, *From Tradition to Commentary: Torah and Its Interpretation in the Midrash Sifre to Deuteronomy*, 74.

and master-able system of tradition. The perception that the network of related categories maps out a comprehensive field of commandments, and the perception that the category of timebound, positive commandments includes all the commandments that share the traits of being "positive" and "timebound," do *not* reflect the way the categories actually function. Rather, this perception *results from* the mishnaic and tosephtan way of rehearsing legal tradition. Both the mishnaic and tosephtan presentations highlight the fact that tradition can be organized by categories and is therefore a coherent and master-able body of information.

Tefillin as a Prototype

When the sages rehearsed legal tradition as midrash, they stressed its roots in scripture.[20] In this section, I will argue that the category of timebound, positive commandments and the rule exempting women from them emerged in the context of rehearsing legal tradition as midrash. The Mekilta of Rabbi Yishmael (Mek.) links a number of instructions regarding tefillin practice to the so-called tefillin verses (Exod 13:9–10). By presenting the tefillin instructions in tandem with scriptural verses, the midrash suggests that the instructions have their roots in scripture. Reconstructing the process by which the category was conceived and the rule formulated, however, does not require that we interrogate the Mekilta's claims that the instructions originate in exegesis of scriptural verses.[21] Rather, I want to draw our attention to the fact that rehearsing these instructions in tandem with the scriptural verses *establishes* a connection among the instructions. The connection among the instructions is not innate, but a by-product of the midrashic rehearsal of the instructions alongside what is rhetorically represented as their scriptural roots.[22] I argue

[20] Azzan Yadin argues that the impulse to represent scripture as the *source* of legal tradition is a trait of midrashim from the school of R. Yishmael. The Mekhilta of R. Yishmael, on which the analysis in the next section builds, derives – as the name suggests – from the school of R. Yishmael. See Azzan Yadin, *Scripture as Logos: Rabbi Ishmael and the Origins of Midrash* (Philadelphia: University of Pennsylvania Press, 2004).

[21] Yadin argues that R. Yishmael midrashim present scripture as the generative force of halakhic norms. By way of contrast, R. Akiba midrashim present the connection between halakhic norms and scripture as an afterthought. Yadin argues that behind these two rhetorical strategies lie two different theories or ideologies about the origins of halakhic norms. Whereas the school of R. Yishmael sees halakhah as "scriptural instruction," produced by an exegetical process that is actively directed by scripture, the school of R. Akiba sees halakhah as independent teachings that derive their authority from the chain of teachers who have passed them on. In this way of thinking, the fact that halakhic norms are represented in midrash as scripturally derived is not a statement about their "real" origins, but a reflection of the ideology of those who compiled the midrashic collections. See Azzan Yadin, "Resistance to Midrash? Midrash and *Halakhah* in the Halakhic Midrashim," in *Current Trends in the Study of Midrash*, ed. Carol Bakhos (Leiden: Brill, 2006), 35–58.

[22] This way of conceiving the cultural significance of midrashic textual materials builds on earlier work that discusses the "performative effect" of rehearsing mishnaic materials. In my work

that the category of timebound, positive commandments and the rule exempting women from them was the by-product of rehearsing these instructions alongside scripture. In the Mekilta's discussion of the tefillin verses, one biblical phrase is linked to the instruction that exempts women and slaves from wearing tefillin. An adjacent biblical phrase is linked to the instruction to wear tefillin during daylight hours. A second analysis of the same phrase links the biblical verse to the instruction to refrain from wearing tefillin on the Sabbath and holidays. Throughout, the exegesis emphasizes that tefillin are a positive commandment. The rule, then, appears to be a summary of these three instructions about tefillin practice, one that also takes into account the fact that the midrash names tefillin as a positive commandment. The midrashic unit, when taken as a whole, characterizes tefillin as a "timebound, positive commandment from which women (and slaves) are exempt."

Undoubtedly, the instruction that exempts women (and slaves) from wearing tefillin contributes to the construction of the social identities of both men and women (and slaves and freemen). Chapters 6 and 7 explore at great length the social implications of this ritual exemption. As far as I can tell, however, the process of *conceiving the category* and *formulating the rule* did not require the sages to reflect on the social implications exempting women from tefillin. Rather, the category and the rule seem to have emerged when the sages reflected on the relationship between the tefillin verses and the tefillin instructions (of which women's exemption was one). To the extent that the process of conceiving the category and formulating the rule contributed to the construction of social identities, it solidified the rabbis' position as masters of legal tradition and Torah.

Both the earlier Mekhilta (Mek.). and the later Mekhilta of R. Shimon bar Yohai (MRSY)[23] discuss women's exemption from wearing tefillin in the context of Exod 13:9–10, from which the commandment to wear tefillin is rabbinically understood to derive.[24] Though Mek. never characterizes tefillin as a "timebound, positive commandment from which women are exempt," it

on Mishnah, I write that a focus on the performative effect "tries to imagine what would *result* from performing the materials. That is, it inquires into the 'effect' of oral performance." Alexander, *Transmitting Mishnah*, 169. See also Susan Handelman, "The 'Torah' of Criticism and the Criticism of Torah: Recuperating the Pedagogical Moment," in *Interpreting Judaism in a Post-modern Age*, ed. Steven Kepnes (New York: New York University Press, 1996), 236.

[23] Mehachem Kahana argues that at the very least the legal material in the Mek. is earlier than that in the MRSY. See Menahem I. Kahana, "The Halakhic Midrashim," in *Literature of the Sages*, part 2, ed. Shmuel (z"l) Safrai et al. (Amsterdam: Royal Van Gorcum and Fortress Press, 2006), 75–76. See also H. L. Strack and G. Stemberger, *Introduction to the Talmud and Midrash*, trans. Markus Bockmuehl (Minneapolis: Fortress Press, 1992), 277–78, 283.

[24] Yehudah Cohn argues that these verses were understood metaphorically in the early Second Temple period. Starting in the late Hellenistic period, these verses began to be understood as instructing one to place a literal sign on one's hand and a literal memorial between one's eyes. See Yehudah B. Cohn, *Tangled Up in Text: Tefillin and the Ancient World* (Providence: Brown Judaic Studies, 2008), esp. 45–48.

does provide the conceptual and linguistic building blocks for doing so. The potential that these building blocks embody is realized in the later MRSY, which characterizes tefillin as the prototypical timebound, positive commandment. I argue that the category and rule arose in the context of rehearsing the exegesis from the earlier Mek. in a manner like what we see in the later MRSY. Apparently, MRSY's explicit use of the category is possible only because Mek. rehearsal of tradition had already laid the groundwork. When understood in this manner, the process that leads to the formulation of the rule is not a *legislative* process at all. The rule's authors do not reflect on social reality in and of itself. To the extent that formulating the rule involves reflexively transmitting the instruction that women are exempt from tefillin, it has *indirect* social implications. These will be explored extensively in Chapters 6 and 7, where I explore the social motivations for women's exemption from tefillin. In the current chapter, however, I want to stress that the process that produced the rule was an academic process that *had the consolidation of legal tradition as its main objective*. The rule itself – with its stipulation that women are exempt from commandments exhibiting a particular set of traits – was, as far as I can tell, not formulated in order to encourage women toward particular forms of social and religious identity.

Exod 13:9–10 uses the following language to outline the obligation to wear tefillin: "And it shall be a sign for you on your hand and a memorial between your eyes, in order that the teaching (*torah*) of God shall be in your mouth, for with a strong hand did the Lord take you out of Egypt. You shall observe this law in its time, throughout your days." The rabbis assumed that the cryptic allusions to "a sign on your hand" and "a memorial between your eyes" specified the obligation to wear tefillin.[25] Other expressions used in the passage were taken to indicate specific aspects of the practice.

Mek. focuses on two key phrases in this passage: first, the fact that tefillin are to be worn "in order that the teaching (*torah*) of God be in your mouth," and second, the fact that this practice should be observed "throughout your days." The purpose of the midrashic exercise is to discern the unique import and legal significance of these phrases. The bolded words illustrate where features of the rule are anticipated by the midrash.

למען תהיה תורת ה' בפיך. למה נאמר, לפי שנאמר והיה לך לאות?
שומע אני אף נשים במשמע? והדין נותן הואיל ומזוזה מצות עשה ותפילין מצות עשה,
אם למדת על מזוזה שהיא נוהגת בנשים כאנשים, יכול אף תפילין ינהגו בנשים כאנשים?
ת"ל למען תהיה תורת ה' בפיך, לא אמרתי אלא במי שהוא חייב בתלמוד תורה.
מכאן אמרו: הכל חייבין בתפילין חוץ מנשים ועבדים.

                                                        . . .

---

[25] Cohn argues that these verses were not understood as requiring a physical ritual act until late in the Second Temple period. Yehudah B. Cohn, *Tangled Up in Text: Tefillin and the Ancient World*.

מימים ימימה. למה נאמר, לפי שהוא אומר והיה לך לאות?
שומע אני אף לילות במשמע? והדין נותן הואיל ומזוזה מצות עשה ותפילין מצות עשה,
אם למדת על מזוזה שנוהגת בלילות כבימים, יכול אף תפילין נוהגין בלילות כבימים?
ת"ל מימים ימימה, בימים אתה נותן ולא בלילות.
ד"א מימים ימימה. למה נאמר, לפי שהוא אומר והיה לך לאות?
שומע אני אף שבתות וימים טובים במשמע? והדין נותן הואיל ומזוזה מצות עשה
ותפילין מצות עשה, אם למדת על מזוזה שנוהגת בשבתות ובימים טובים, יכול אף תפילין ינהגו
בשבתות ובימים טובים?
ת"ל מימים ימימה, יצאו שבתות וימים טובים.

A.1. *In order that the teaching* (torah) *of God shall be in your mouth* (Exod 13:9). Why is this said, since it is also stated, *And it shall be for you a sign* (Exod 13:9)?

A.2. Could I learn that the meaning is to include women also? After all, logic suggests that since **mezuzah is a positive commandment** and **tefillin is a positive commandment,** if you learned with respect to mezuzah that it applies with respect to women as to men, could it be that tefillin also functions with respect to women as with men?

A.3. The Torah states, *"in order that the teaching* (torah) *of God shall be in your mouth."* It [the commandment of tefillin] has not been stated except with regards to he who is required to study Torah.

A.4. From here they said: Everyone is required [to perform the commandment of] tefillin, **except women** and slaves, [since they are exempt from studying Torah]....

B.1. *Throughout your days* (Exod 13:10). Why is this said, since it is also stated, *And it shall be for you a sign* (Exod 13:9)?

B.2. Could I learn that the meaning is to include nights? After all, logic suggests that since **mezuzah is a positive commandment** and **tefillin is a positive commandment,** if you learned with respect to mezuzah that it is performed in the nights as well as the days, could it be that tefillin is also performed in the nights as well as the days?

B.3. The Torah states, *throughout your days.* **During the day you put on [tefillin], but not at night.**

C.1. *Throughout your days* (Exod 13:10). Why is this said, since it is also stated, *And it shall be for you a sign* (Exod 13:9)?

C.2. Could I learn that the meaning is to include Sabbaths and holidays? After all, logic suggests that since **mezuzah is a positive commandment** and **tefillin is a positive commandment,** if you learned with respect to mezuzah that it is performed on the Sabbath and holidays, could it be that tefillin is also performed on the Sabbath and holidays?

C.3. The Torah states, *throughout your days.* **This excludes the Sabbath and holidays.** (Mek., Bo 17, ed. Horowitz-Rabin, 68–69)

The entire exercise consists of three paragraphs (A, B, and C), each of which uses the same rhetorical strategy to reach a different exegetical conclusion. Each paragraph begins by noting a redundancy between the phrase under examination and the verse's opening phrase, "it shall be a sign for you" (see lines A.1, B.1, and C.1). In each paragraph, the midrash rhetorically proposes that the verse's opening phrase ("it shall be a sign for you") renders the phrase under examination superfluous. In the first paragraph, the midrash inquires why it is necessary to state that tefillin are worn "in order that the teaching (*torah*) of God be in your mouth" when scripture has already said that they are to be a sign (A.1). In the second and third paragraphs, the midrash asks why scripture states that tefillin are to be worn "throughout your days," when scripture already states that tefillin are to be a sign (B.1 and C.1). After posing its questions, the midrash highlights the unique import of the phrases under examination by comparing tefillin with mezuzah (see lines A.2, B.2, and C.2). Though logic suggests that the laws concerning tefillin and mezuzah should be the same (since both are positive commandments), a pointed reading of scripture reveals otherwise.

The midrash reveals the legal import of each of the phrases under examination. The details of scripture are interpreted as specifying ways in which performance of tefillin differs from that of mezuzah, in spite of their common status of positive commandments. Whereas women are obligated to perform the positive commandment of mezuzah, the phrase "in order that the teaching (*torah*) of God be in your mouth" links the performance of tefillin with Torah study. Since women (and slaves) are exempt from the obligation to study Torah, they are also are exempt from performance of tefillin (lines A.3–4). In similar fashion, the import of the phrase "throughout your days" is deduced as limiting the wearing of tefillin to specifically designated times. Tefillin are not to be worn during the night (B.3) or on the Sabbath and holidays (C.3).

In each paragraph, the midrashist highlights how scripture indicates ways in which the rules for the observance of tefillin differ from those of mezuzah. Unlike mezuzah, this commandment is not an obligation for women and slaves (A), it is not observed at night (B), and it is not observed on the Sabbath and holidays (C). What emerges from the midrashic unit as a whole is the fact that tefillin and mezuzah are two positive commandments that scripture has nonetheless distinguished. The distinctive features of tefillin can be summarized by the exegetical conclusions of each of the three paragraphs: women and slaves are exempt from wearing them, and they are to be worn only at particular times, that is, not at night and not on the Sabbath and holidays. To phrase these conclusions in the familiar terms of the rule, tefillin is distinguished from mezuzah because it is a "timebound, positive commandment from which women and slaves are exempt." Except for the small variant – that in this formulation the category of timebound, positive commandments has legal significance for slaves, as well as women – this summary has strong resonances with the mishnaic formulation of the rule. Further strengthening the connection between Mek.'s exegesis and the rule concerning timebound, positive commandments is the fact that a more obscure version of the rule includes slaves, along with women, as its subjects.[26] It is highly likely, then, that the concept of "timebound, positive commandments from which women (and slaves) are exempt" emerged as a summary of the exegetical conclusions reached in this passage. The significance of the term "timebound" (lit. "occasioned or caused by time") would have been to distinguish tefillin from mezuzah, another positive commandment *whose observance was not occasioned by time.*

My conclusion is in part a negative conclusion: I am arguing that the term "timebound" is conceived *neither* to regulate *nor* to accommodate women's use of their time. Instead, I propose that the term is introduced to distinguish tefillin from mezuzah. Though both tefillin and mezuzah are positive commandments, scripture specifies that tefillin's distinction lies in its timebound nature and non-obligatory status for women and slaves. I further argue that the act of naming tefillin as a "timebound, positive commandment from which women (and slaves) are exempt" had implications beyond being a useful description of tefillin. Naming tefillin as a "timebound, positive commandment from which women are exempt" apparently suggested that a broader category of timebound, positive commandments existed, for which there might be other exemplars. Following Lakoff's theory regarding the cognitive processes that produce categories, I propose that the tosephtan list emerged as a secondary development. It would have been an attempt to see what other known phenomenon fit into the newly minted category. M. Kid. 1:7's structure of four interrelated categories would also have been a secondary development. The creation of an additional three categories would have filled out the conceptual map implied by the existence of the prototypical category (timebound, positive commandments).

When commenting on the same verses, the later MRSY presents women's exemption from tefillin as a prototype for the rule exempting them from *all* timebound, positive commandments.

ד"א: למען תהיה תורת ייי בפיך. להוציא את הנשים.

מה תפילין מיוחדת מצות עשה שהזמן גרמה נשים פטורות, כך כל מצות עשה שהזמן גרמה נשים פטורות.

---

[26] Sif. Num., Shellah, piska 115 (ed. Horowitz, 124), attributes the rule to R. Shimon and offers a slightly different presentation from the one we find in m. Kid. 1:7. There he states, "timebound, positive commandments apply to men and do not apply to women, to qualified people (*kasherim*) and not to unqualified people (*pasulim*)." The major interpretive question posed by this source is the following: Who are the qualified and unqualified people referred to by this source? This binary set of adjectives is most commonly applied to people in order to distinguish those who may offer testimony from those who may not. Those who are disqualified from offering testimony are dice players, usurers, pigeon flyers, traffickers in seventh-year produce, and slaves. See m. San. 3:3 and m. RH 1:8. Ginzberg states that the Sifre does not mean to exempt various male schemers (dice payers, pigeon flyers, etc.) from timebound, positive commandments. He suggests that R. Shimon certainly meant to exclude slaves (and only slaves) with his use of the term "unqualifed," though this is the only place in rabbinic literature where this term is used in this way. See Louis Ginzberg, *A Commentary on the Palestinian Talmud*, vol. 2 (New York: Ktav, 1971), 63n47.

1. Another interpretation: *In order that the teaching* (torah) *of God be in your mouth* (Exod 13:9). (This verse comes) to exclude women.

2. Just as tefillin are distinctive insofar as they are a timebound, positive commandment from which women are exempt, so too let women be exempt from all timebound, positive commandments. (MRSY, ed. Epstein-Melamed, 41)

This midrashic excerpt consists of two distinct units (1 and 2). The first unit summarizes the exegetical conclusions of the first paragraph of the earlier Mek. (A.1–A.4). As in the earlier passage, women's exemption from tefillin is derived from the section of the verse alluding to Torah study. Though the later MRSY does not make the inference explicit, we must assume that women are excluded from tefillin because elsewhere they are excluded from Torah study. The first line of this passage, then, appears to offer a summary of the more drawn-out exercise from the earlier Mek. in which women's exemption from tefillin is explicitly linked to their exemption from Torah study.

The second unit also builds on the exegetical conclusions of the earlier midrash. Here, however, the later MRSY goes beyond the conclusions explicitly stated in the earlier Mek. Though the Mek. provides the linguistic and conceptual basis to describe tefillin as a "timebound, positive commandment," it does not take that step; only MRSY does. Furthermore, the MRSY suggests that women's exemption extends to all commandments that share with tefillin the traits of being "timebound" and "positive." Even though MRSY is familiar with the stipulations of the rule (i.e., that women are exempt from all timebound, positive commandments), it does not frame women's exemption from tefillin as a function of its being "timebound" and "positive." Rather, women's exemption from timebound, positive commandments follows from the fact that tefillin is the prototypical exemplar of the category and women are exempt from tefillin (notably, for a reason other than tefillin's traits as "timebound" and positive"). Women's exemption from the acknowledged prototype of category (i.e., tefillin) is notably *not* determined by the rule. According to MRSY, women's exemption from tefillin is determined by force of scriptural language. Women are exempt from tefillin because scripture links tefillin practice to Torah study, from which women are assumed to be exempt. These observations suggest to me that even though MRSY is familiar with the stipulations of the rule (namely, that women are exempt from timebound, positive commandments), it does not think of the rule as prescriptive. In any event, the rule certainly is not seen as determining women's ritual obligations in the case of tefillin.

It appears that observing that tefillin possess certain traits (they are positive, they are occasioned by time, and women are exempt from them) is intimately linked to the creation of a broader category with other rituals that share these traits. I propose that when the rule was initially formulated, it was merely a descriptive summary of Mek.'s exegesis of the tefillin verses. Once the category and rule were articulated, however, they were assumed to function more broadly and to be independent of the exegetical sequence that they originally came to summarize.

Though the rule may have been initially formulated in the context of rehearsing scriptural exegesis, at least one sage seems to have thought that the rule – once formulated – could have full normative force. Unique among the tannaitic sages, R. Shimon uses the rule to *determine* women's ritual obligations regarding tzitzit.

ויאמר ה' אל משה לאמר דבר אל בני ישראל ואמרת אליהם ועשו להם ציצית. אף נשים במשמע.

רבי שמעון פוטר את הנשים מן הציצית מפני מצות עשה שהזמן גרמה נשים פטורות

שזה הכלל: אמר ר' שמעון כל מצות עשה שהזמן גרמה נוהגת באנשים ואינה נוהגת בנשים בכשרים ולא בפסולים.

1. *And God spoke to Moses saying: Speak to the children of Israel and tell them to make fringes* (tzitzit) *for themselves* (Num 15:37–38). Women are also included in the meaning.

2. R. Shimon exempts women from tzitzit because they are a timebound, positive commandment from which women are exempt.

3. For this is the rule: R. Shimon said all positive timebound commandments must be performed by men, but not by women, by those who are fit (to give testimony), but by not those who are unfit. (Sif. Num., Shelah 115, ed. Horowitz, 124)

This midrash examines the verse from which the ritual of wearing fringes (*tzitzit*) on the corner of one's garments is assumed to derive. The anonymous voice declares women, like men, obligated to perform this ritual. By way of contrast, R. Shimon declares them exempt. He uses the rule exempting women from timebound, positive commandments to reach this conclusion. Insofar as R. Shimon invokes the rule *to determine* women's ritual involvement, his use of the rule does have social implications. I will discuss these extensively in Chapter 8. For the moment, however, I wish merely to observe that even though the rule was not formulated or conceived to determine women's ritual participation, once formulated, the rule could function in that manner. R. Shimon's use of the rule to exempt women from tzitzit appears, however, to be the only clear-cut case of the rule being used to determine women's ritual exemptions.[27] In Chapter 8, I will discuss the social implications of R. Shimon's use of the rule.

On what basis do I conclude that R. Shimon's use of the rule to determine women's ritual involvement with tzitzit was unique? It will be recalled that the tosephtan list includes sukkah and lulav as exemplary items of the category, along with tefillin. The Yerushalmi additionally includes shofar.[28] How did these rituals come to be included as members of the category and subject to

[27] On this basis, Louis Ginzberg argued that the principle was formulated and endorsed by R. Shimon alone. See Ginzberg, *Commentary on the Palestinian Talmud*, 159–64. Shevah Yalon endorses and extends Ginzberg's position. Shevah Yalon, "'Women Are Exempted from All Positive Ordinances That Are Bound Up with a Stated Time': A Study in Tanaic and Amoraic Sources" (Ramat Gan: Bar Ilan University, 1989), 118–21.

[28] See y. Kid. 61c.

the rule? Are these rituals that R. Shimon submitted to his rule, in which case women's exemption from them was *determined* by the rule? Or are these examples of rituals whose female exemption *had already been determined by other means* and only ex post facto came to be associated with the rule because they had an appropriate profile (i.e., they were timebound, positive commandments from which women were *already* exempt)?

The existing evidence does not allow us to resolve this question with certainty, but in my view it favors the position that women's exemptions from these rituals were determined by other means before they came to be associated with the category and its attendant rule. Aside from the tosephtan list, no other tannaitic or amoraic source links women's exemption from sukkah, lulav, or shofar to the rule of their exemption from timebound, positive commandments. By way of contrast, the link between tefillin and the rule is attested in several tannaitic and amoraic contexts.[29] When the midrash does discuss women's exemption from sukkah, it derives the exemption from the particularities of scriptural language unrelated to the rule about timebound commandments.[30] Furthermore, as noted in the Introduction, women's obligations and exemptions regarding a number of rituals actually violate the terms of the rule,[31] suggesting that the rule did not determine women's involvement in those cases.

---

[29] See the Yerushalmi on m. Ber. 3:3 (y. Ber. 6b). Additionally, the link between tefillin and the rule is in the background of the Yerushalmi's discussion of m. Eruv. 10:1 (y. Eruv. 26a), though the connection is only made explicit in the Bavli's discussion of the same mishnah (b. Eruv. 96b).

[30] Sifra, Emor, Perek 17, derives women's exemption from sukkah in the following manner.

האזרח. להוציא נשים.

[In huts you shall dwell for seven days, each one,] the citizen. This comes to exclude women.

The midrashic exclusion of women is explained as a function of the extra letter *heh*, which is a direct article for the word "citizen." Though the appearance of an extra letter might not necessarily seem to warrant such extensive legal ramfications, it is important to remember that the midrashic collection of Sifra from which this passage derives is traditionally associated with the school of R. Akiba, which was known for attributing significance to extra letters. Elsewhere in the passage, minors are required to participate in the dwelling in huts on the basis of the apparently extraneous word "each." As the midrash states, "*Each one.* This comes to include minors." It seems arbitrary that one apparent redundancy leads to the exclusion of women and another to the inclusion of minors. It is likely that the exegesis is motivated by the external, rather than the textual. In other words, it is likely that the author of this midrash had a means of determining these outcomes other than pure exegetical concerns. Perhaps he had an inherited tradition? Perhaps he was reflecting custom as practiced? One thing is striking, however: He did not cite the principle of women's exclusion from positive, timebound commandments as the basis for his exemption of women. It is worth noting that the Sifra comes from the same block of midrashim as the MRSY, where the phrase first appears as a basis to derive other exemptions. The fact that the Sifra ignores the rule and makes no mention of it – though it could plausibly know of it – strikes me as significant. I would argue that the Sifra does not cite the principle because it was not the basis for its ruling.

[31] See notes 20–22 in the Introduction.

I am inclined to agree with those scholars who account for these exceptions to the rule by suggesting that the rule was formulated as a descriptive, and not prescriptive, statement.[32] Shevah Yalon argues that women's obligation with respect to each ritual was determined on an individual basis. Following Shmuel Safrai, he suggests that the rule as we know it was crafted as a descriptive summary only after the fact. The major difference between my argument and those of Yalon and Safrai is that these scholars believe that the rule was a descriptive summary of *prevailing social practice*. I, on the other hand, have argued that the process that produces the rule involves little to no reflection on social reality. Instead the rule's authors were reflecting on scriptural verses, their relationship to tefillin practice, and the categories into which legal tradition could be organized.

Conclusion

The rule designates some commandments as "timebound" and "positive." It is usually assumed that these characteristics (the "timeboundedness" and "positiveness" of these commandments) account for women's exemption from them. We have seen, however, that other factors give rise to women's exemptions. In the case of tefillin, women's exemption follows from the close link between tefillin and Torah study. Though we cannot determine with certainty the reason for women's exemption from sukkah, lulav, and shofar, it is highly likely that it was determined for reasons not connected with their being "timebound" and "positive." In the conventional way of thinking about the rule, it seeks to organize or accommodate women's use of their time. I have argued, however, that the rule's language is best explained as a summary of exegetical exercises that emerged in the context of rehearsing legal tradition. Social issues like the relationship between women and time do not appear to have been on the minds of the rule's authors. To the extent that the rule reflexively rehearses traditions that exempt women from various rituals (tefillin, sukkah, lulav, and shofar), it does have social implications. These implications are best understood, however, when we examine the discrete legal judgments that the sages made regarding women's ritual involvement. Part III of the book follows up on this conclusion by exploring the social motivations and implications for several of women's ritual exemptions. In this chapter, however, I have argued that the category of "timebound, positive commandments" and the rule stipulating women's exemption from them do not shed special light on the rabbis' social agenda. To the extent that the process of conceiving the category and formulating the rule supported the construction of social identities, it helped construct rabbis

---

[32] See Shmuel Safrai, "The *Mitzva* Obligation of Women in Tannaitic Thought"; Yalon, "'Women Are Exempted from All Positive Ordinances That Are Bound Up with a Stated Time'"; Ilan, *Jewish Women in Greco-Roman Palestine*, 117; and Biale, *Women and Jewish Law: An Exploration of Women's Issues in Halakhic Sources*, 17.

as the masters of Torah, legal tradition, and the relationship between them. By rehearsing legal tradition in the various ways documented in this chapter, the rabbis affirmed that their tradition had roots in scripture and that the tradition was a coherent and organized system.

To point out the rule's origins as a descriptive summary of exegesis is not, however, to deny that it had a long subsequent history in which it was *viewed* as a prescriptive principle. In its mishnaic formulation, the processes that produced the category and rule were obscured and lost. Part II of the book documents the process by which the view came to be universally seen as a prescriptive principle that determined women's ritual involvement. Even in the tannaitic period, R. Shimon used the rule to determine women's ritual involvement in the case of tzitzit. The point of this chapter is to point out that the dominant perception that the rule was formulated to determine women's use of time is achieved only gradually in the course of the rule's transmission; it is not an innate feature of the rule's language or structure. This observation is important because it helps us recognize that the numerous claims that have been made with respect to the rule's rationale – all of which attribute to the rule's authors social motivations – are not explanations of how the rule *came to be*. Rather, they reflect later understandings of the rule as prescriptive in its origins.

2

Between Man and Woman

Lists of Male–Female Difference

In the preceding chapter, I argued that when the sages rehearsed legal tradition in the manner that produced the rule, they were not actively or directly constructing gender. Their explicit goal was to review the relationship between scriptural verses and legal tradition (the rules about tefillin) and to clarify the categories into which legal tradition could be organized. In the course of rehearsing legal tradition, the sages did reflexively endorse women's exemption from tefillin (which certainly did have social implications). I found no evidence to indicate, however, that the sages' engagement with gender went beyond endorsing women's exemption from tefillin. When tannaitic sages formulated the rule, they appear to have been most interested in performing scholastic exercises that affirmed their status as masters of Torah.

In this chapter, I again reflect on how rehearsing legal tradition involving the rule contributed to the construction of social identities in the tannaitic period. Here I examine the social implications of rehearsing the rule as part of a grouping of related laws. The chapter takes as its starting point the observation that the rule appears in several tannaitic lists of the ways in which the law treats women differently from men. The list from which this chapter takes its name begins with this question: "What is the difference between man and women?"[1] When cultural critics encounter this question today, they assume it seeks to identify a biologically or culturally based difference between men and women. They may reject the idea that gender is natural and stable; they may argue that gender is socially constructed, rather than innate.[2] But however they respond

---

[1] See m. Sot. 3:8.
[2] The classic articulation of the view that gender is culturally conditioned and not biologically based is Simone de Beauvoir, *The Second Sex*, trans. Constance Borde and Sheila Malovany-Chevallier, with an introduction by Judith Thurman (New York: Alfred A. Knopf, 2010). See also Judith Lorber, *Paradoxes of Gender* (New Haven: Yale University Press, 1994); Judith Butler,

to this question, they assume it tries to elicit from the respondent insight into an (if not *the*) essential quality that gives men and women their distinctive characteristics. Judging by their response, the tannaitic sages of antiquity understood the question quite differently. They responded to the question by surveying their corpus of legal traditions and finding places where the law treats women differently from men. For example, in the collection of laws on the Nazirite oath, they found the stipulation that a man may submit his son to a Nazirite oath, but a woman may not.[3] In the exegesis on scriptural verses about slavery, they found the stipulation that a man may sell his daughter as a maidservant, but a woman may not sell her daughter as a maidservant.[4] In a collection of laws concerning capital punishment, they found the stipulation that a man is hanged naked, but a woman is not.[5] When the sages answered the question about the difference between man and woman, they were organizing known legal tradition into meaningful categories. Apparently, the best way to affirm that there are meaningful differences between men and women was to collate tradition that attests to this fact. I do not mean to deny that each legal stipulation that treats women differently from men constructed gender differences in its own legal domain. But the lists as a whole constructed gender at a different level. The lists lent a broader cultural significance to each stipulation, one that each stipulation did not have on its own. In the context of the lists, each stipulation helped construct the social entities of "man" and "woman" as distinct, abstract entities.

The rule that women are exempt from timebound, positive commandments is included in three of the four extant lists of male–female difference. Rehearsing the rule did apparently contribute to the construction of gender in antiquity, but not in the way that most scholars have assumed. The dominant scholarly view suggests that when the sages rehearsed the rule, they were engaged in a mild form of social engineering. They were encouraging women toward certain types of social and religious identity, and away from others more properly performed by men. By way of contrast, I argue that rehearsing the rule in the context of the lists helped construct gendered identities by affirming that there are meaningful differences between men and women. When the sages rehearsed the lists of instances where the law treats women differently from men, they asserted that men and women are legally distinct beings. They were, in the words of Joan Scott, constructing "knowledge about sexual difference."[6] Notably, the rule that exempts women from timebound, positive commandments did not

Gender Trouble: Feminism and the Subversion of Identity (New York: Routledge, 1990); and Scott, *Gender and the Politics of History*.
[3] See m. Naz. 4:6.
[4] Mek. on Exod 21:6, Mishpatim 3, ed. Horowitz-Rabin, 255.
[5] See m. San. 6:4.
[6] Scott, *Gender and the Politics of History*, 2.

contribute to the construction of gender as a *discrete* stipulation with direct social implications.[7] Rather, the rule contributed to the construction of gender insofar as it was rehearsed *alongside many other legal traditions* that attest to the fact that the law treats women differently from men. Gender, that is, *knowledge* about sexual difference, was constructed as a result of collating tradition. No single datum could accomplish this cultural work on its own. Only when different rules from diverse domains of law were gathered together into a structured collection did they perform the cultural work of affirming the existence of male–female difference on a broad scale.

The fact that the rule was rehearsed in the context of the lists of male–female difference has two major implications for understanding how the rule contributed to the construction of gender in the tannaitic period. First, when we observe the rule in the context of the lists, we are forced to recognize that the rule was not a comprehensive statement about how the law treats women differently from men. When rehearsed alongside many other traditions attesting to other ways in which the law treats women differently from men, the rule appears as a single discrete instance in which the law treats women differently. Taking the redactional context of the lists seriously, then, requires that we find a way to understand the rule as a *limited*, rather than comprehensive, statement of male–female difference. The first half of this chapter considers the question of whether the rule can legitimately be read as a limited statement of male–female difference.

Attending to the fact that the rule was rehearsed in the context of the lists has a second implication for the inquiry into how the rule contributes to the construction of gender in the tannaitic period. It gives us insight into the process by which the rule became a meaningful marker of male–female difference. Chapter 1 argues that the rule was formulated as a legally inert summary of exegesis that concerns both women *and slaves*. The second half of this chapter explores how the rule came to have cultural significance (though not necessary legislative significance) as a marker of male–female difference. Within the lists, the rule had new significance for the construction of gender, but its significance followed from the context of transmission rather than its legal content.

Finally, it is important to be clear about the extent and nature of the social implications of rehearsing the rule in the context of the lists of male–female difference. The evidence presented in this chapter enables us to reconstruct social processes only to a limited extent. The lists of male–female difference provide evidence of how gender operated as a meaningful category of knowledge *in the social context of the rabbinic disciple circles*. They reveal little, however, about how the sages employed this knowledge when interacting with "real"

---

[7] See discussion in Chapter 1.

women in the "real world."[8] In the previous chapter, I stressed the fact that rehearsing tradition in the form of the rule did not *directly* involve the sages in the construction of gender. By way of contrast, in this chapter, I highlight a moment when their academic activities *did* involve them directly in reflecting on the social meanings of sexual difference. Nonetheless, it remains unclear from the evidence presented in this chapter how rehearsing legal tradition in this manner played out in the wider social field where the rabbinic disciples and masters interacted with both men and women. The most we can conclude with confidence is that rehearsing tradition in this manner lent cultural significance to the rule for those within the academy. It was no longer a legally inert summary of exegesis; it was a marker of male–female difference, although for the time, it remained one among many such markers.

The Rule and Female Nature

Starting in the medieval period, scholars began to propose reasons for women's exemption from timebound, positive commandments. In seeking out the reasons for the rule, medieval and modern interpreters have assumed it was formulated to reinforce a natural or divinely ordained gender order.[9] Two major lines of interpretation emerge. One trend sees the rule as accommodating the social order in which women are subservient to men and occupied with domestic duties. God, so to speak, "bows out"[10] of the competition for women's time and leaves them free to attend to the duties that nature has ordained for them: care of husband, home, and children.[11] The second trend posits that the rule attends to the divinely ordained relationship between male and female. Drawing on kabbalistic descriptions of the upper realms, this line of interpretation suggests that men are wrapped up in the concrete workings of the world with all of its individuated features including time; women, on the other hand, are associated with the upper realms, where distinctions such as time do not

---

[8] It is almost certain that academic conversations within the social context of rabbinic disciple circles did affect people beyond their circles, but it is difficult to know from the evidence explored in this chapter precisely how. Pierre Bordieau, in his discussion of law and society in modern France, argues that the "juridical field" serves as the primary point of reference for legal conversations, even when they focus on issues of concern for society at large. The juridical field will take social issues into account when thinking through legal questions, but such questions are always filtered primarily through the categories and rubrics of the juridical field. Bordieau, "The Force of Law: Toward a Sociology of the Juridical Field."

[9] For a succinct summary of these tendencies, see Tamar Ross, *Expanding the Palace of Torah: Orthodoxy and Feminism*, 35–37.

[10] This phrase is borrowed from Biale, *Women and Jewish Law: An Exploration of Women's Issues in Halakhic Sources*, 14.

[11] Among the medievals see David Abudraham, *Sefer Abudraham*, section on "Blessings for Commandments and their Laws," 25; and Jacob Anatoli, *Malmad Hatalmidim*, Lekh Lekha, 16. Among contemporary scholars, most pointedly, see Berman, "The Status of Women in Halakhic Judaism."

exist.[12] Even while positing very different notions of the relationship between women, worldliness, and time, these two trends of interpretation share the fact that they see in the rule an allusion to women's essential nature. Women's nature may transcend the worldliness of time, or it may be completely bound up in the worldly constraints of time, but in either case the exemption from timebound commandments is assumed to be a legal response to women's "natural" relationship to time. Historically, one important function of the rule has been to authorize particular conceptions of female nature.[13]

Though the rule has worked to ground conceptions of female nature since medieval times, this function is by no means the necessary consequence of having such a rule on the books. In the tannaitic period, the rule contributed to the cultural project of distinguishing men from women, but (with one exception to be discussed at the end of this chapter) the rule did not support an essentialist notion of female nature. Instead, the rule found its place as a single item within the lists of male–female difference. Rather than seeing the rule as a leading principle through which all other gender differences were refracted, the tannaitic rabbis saw it as a single, albeit important, statement of male–female difference.

A Comprehensive Statement of Male–Female Difference?

When we examine the locus classicus of the rule, it is easy to see why later interpreters used it to reflect on essential differences between men and women. When read as a discrete source – independent of its surrounding literary context – the rule appears to offer a comprehensive statement of the way in which men and women differ in their relationship to the law.

וכל מצות עשה שהזמן גרמה – אנשים חיבין ונשים פטורות.
וכל מצות עשה שלא הזמן גרמה – אחד אנשים ואחד נשים חיבין.
וכל מצות לא תעשה, בין שהזמן גרמה, בין שלא הזמן גרמה – אחד אנשים ואחד נשים
חיבין, חוץ מבל תשחית, ובל תקיף ובל תטמא למתים.

---

[12] See the Maharal, "Drush al Hatorah," in *Sifrei Maharal* (Jerusalem, 1971) (volume with Be'er Hagolah), 27a. See also his *Tiferet Yisrael*, Perek 37, p. 110. For some of the earlier roots of the Maharal's view, see also *Sefer Hakanah*, p. 10. See also Ben Zion Rosenfeld, "The Maharal: A Chapter in the Theory of the Soul of Man and Woman." Meiselman ("The Jewish Woman in Jewish Law," 43–45) discusses this view and cites Samson Raphael Hirsch as its chief modern exponent. See Hirsch's *Commentary to Leviticus* (New York, 1971), s.v. 23:43, 711–12.

[13] The extent to which the issue of women's nature has become amalgamated with the issue of women's exemption from timebound, positive commandments can be seen also in the *Encylopedia Talmudit* (Hebrew). The entry entitled "Woman" (אשה) consists entirely of lists of commandments that women do and do not perform. Women are essentially defined by the commandments they perform. Modern feminists challenging and wrestling with the roles traditionally assigned to women have also assumed that the rule reflects a traditional understanding of female nature. See Biale, *Women and Jewish Law: An Exploration of Women's Issues in Halakhic Sources*, 13–17; Adler, "The Jew Who Wasn't There"; and Tamar Ross, *Expanding the Palace of Torah: Orthodoxy and Feminism*, 14–16.

1. All timebound, positive commandments – men are obligated, women are exempt.

2. All non-timebound, positive commandments – men and women are equally obligated.

3 and 4. All negative commandments, irrespective of whether they are timebound or non-timebound – men and women are equally obligated, except "do not mar [the corners of your beard," "do not round [the corners of your head]," and "do not become impurified through contact with the dead." (m. Kid. 1:7)

All commandments are divided into four basic categories: (1) timebound, positive; (2) non-timebound, positive; (3) timebound, negative; and (4) non-timebound, negative. Since the category divisions cover the entire range of all commandments, the statement that women are exempt from one of the four categories seems to be a comprehensive statement of how women differ from men. Only in the area of timebound, positive commandments is the legal implication of being female different from that of being male. In all other cases, men and women are regarded comparably. Read in this way, this source provides a *complete* summary of male–female difference under the law. The medieval interpreters who linked the rule to conceptions of female nature did so on the assumption that the rule does indeed provide a comprehensive statement of the ways in which the law regards women differently from men.

The idea that the rule offers a complete and comprehensive statement of the legal implications of being a woman is, however, undermined if we look just beyond the boundaries of the rule itself. In m. Kid. 1:7, the rule appears alongside another rule that appears to contradict the stipulations of the first rule. The complete text of m. Kid. 1:7, which we already examined in Chapter 1, reads as follows:

כל מצות האב על הבן – אנשים חיבין, ונשים פטורות.[14]
וכל מצות הבן על האב – אחד אנשים ואחד נשים חיבין.

וכל מצות עשה שהזמן גרמה – אנשים חיבין ונשים פטורות.
וכל מצות עשה שלא הזמן גרמה – אחד אנשים ואחד נשים חיבין.
וכל מצות לא תעשה, בין שהזמן גרמה, בין שלא הזמן גרמה – אחד אנשים ואחד נשים
חיבין, חוץ מבל תשחית, ובל תקיף ובל תטמא למתים.

A.1. All father-to-son commandments – men are obligated, women are exempt.

A.2. All son-to-father commandments – men and women are equally obligated.

B.1. All timebound, positive commandments – men are obligated, women are exempt.

B.2. All non-timebound, positive commandments – men and women are equally obligated.

B.3 and 4. All negative commandments, irrespective of whether they are timebound or non-timebound – men and women are equally obligated, except "do not mar [the corners of your beard]" "do not round [the corners of your head]," and "do not become impurified through contact with the dead." (m. Kid. 1:7)

---

[14] This reading follows the Palestinian MS tradition.

The two sets of rules (A and B) are complementary in obvious ways. Both divide commandments into related sets of categories, and both evaluate men's and women's obligations with respect to each of the stated categories. Nonetheless, there is one significant way in which the juxtaposition of these two rules is problematic – they contradict each other! The rule that women are exempt from father-to-son commandments (A.1) encompasses the stipulation that they are exempt from Torah study.[15] This ritual, however, is *not* timebound, and therefore this stipulation directly contradicts the second line of the rule about timebound commandments (B.2), which states that women are *obligated* to perform all non-timebound, positive commandments.

As statements regarding women's ritual obligation, the stipulations within the two matrices of categories (A and B) have significant areas of incompatibility. On one hand, the rule stating women's exemption from timebound, positive commandments (B) is set within a matrix of four categories that encompass the entirety of all commandments. In part B of the mishnah, timebound, positive commandments appear to be the *only* set of commandments from which women are exempt. But in part A, women are exempt from a second class of commandments: father-to-son commandments. Nothing in part A suggests that father-to-son commandments are a subset of timebound, positive commandments. In fact, the categories in part A appear to be conceived by reflecting on an altogether different set of traits from those used to generate the categories in part B.

How are we to make sense of this blatant contradiction in the space of a single mishnah? I will argue that those who formulated the mishnah did not sense the contradiction in the same way that we do because they did not understand the rule exempting women from timebound, positive commandments to be a *comprehensive* statement of male–female difference under the law. As already noted, m. Kid. 1:7 locates the rule concerning women's exemption from timebound, positive commandments within a grid of four categories that cover the entirety of all commandments. Insofar as the grid provides a comprehensive overview of all commandments, the specification that women are exempt from only timebound, positive commandments takes on important meaning. The rule appears to provide a *complete* statement of how the law treats women differently from men. So the question is this: Is it possible to read m. Kid. 1:7's four-part structure in a way that *does not* assume it accounts for women's involvement in the entire field of commandments?

The rule is included in two lists of male–female difference, in addition to the one that includes m. Kid. 1:7. Notably, in the other lists, the rule is not located in a matrix of four categories. In the other lists, the rule is presented in the context of a binary structure of categories. As I will demonstrate below, when the rule

[15] See t. Kid. 1:11, which lists Torah study among the father-to-son commandments from which women are exempt. For a more complete discussion of the relationship between women's exemption from Torah study and the rule, see Chapter 7.

is located in the context of a two-part structure, there is no rhetorical claim to account for the entire field of all commandments. In these other sources, the stipulation that women are exempt from timebound, positive commandments appears to be a *limited* statement of how the law treats women differently from men. When the rule is framed as an account of women's ritual involvement in a *limited* field of commandments, the rule's stipulation that women are exempt from timebound, positive commandments does not conflict with the stipulation that they are also exempt from father-to-son commandments.

T. Sotah presents the rule as follows:

האיש עובר על מצות עשה שהזמן גרמה, מה שאין כן האשה.

והאיש עובר על בל תשחת ועל בל תקיף ועל בל תטמא במתים, מה שאין כן האשה.

1. A man can transgress timebound, positive commandments, which a woman cannot.

2. A man can transgress "do not mar [the corners of your beard]," "do not round [the corners of your head]," and do not become impurified through contact with the dead, which a woman cannot. (t. Sot. 2:8)

The Tosephta is clearly familiar with the stipulations of the rule, but it rehearses them in a less direct manner than does m. Kid. 1:7. In line 1, t. Sot. 2:8 states that men are capable of transgressing timebound, positive commandments. The reason they are held responsible when they fail to perform timebound, positive commandments is because they are *obligated* to perform them in the first place. Women, by way of contrast, cannot be held responsible for transgressing timebound, positive commandments because women were never obligated to perform them.

Notably, t. Sot. 2:8 presents the rule as part of a binary structure (lines 1 and 2). Line 1 treats positive commandments, and line 2 treats negative commandments. Within each category, there are certain exceptional commandments that women do not perform. In the category of positive commandments, women do not perform the "timebound" ones. In the category of negative commandments, they do not perform three specified commandments ("do not mar the corners of your beard, do not round the corners of your head, and do not become impurified through contact with the dead"). These three commandments also appear in the locus classicus (m. Kid. 1:7, A.3–4) as an exceptional set of negative commandments that women are not obligated to perform.[16] Though the binary structure of positive versus negative commandments does encompass the entirety of all commandments, the rule as it appears here does not dictate the extent of *women's involvement* for all commandments. Rather, the rule legislates women's exemption for *a small exceptional group of commandments in each of the two categories* (positive and negative). Unlike m. Kid. 1:7's four-part structure, the binary structure in the t. Sot. 2:8 is open-ended. T. Sot. 2:8

---

[16] See also t. Bik. 2:4.

specifies that women are exempt from a particular set of commandments (time-bound, positive ones and the three specified negative ones), but it leaves open the question of women's exemption from other commandments. Furthermore, it does not make a definitive statement about women's obligations.

T. Bikkurim likewise alludes to the rule when discussing male and female obligation concerning positive and negative commandments. Like t. Sotah, t. Bikkurim structures its allusion to the rule in a binary division of commandments into positive and negative commandments. T. Bikkurim also does not employ the four-part structure found in m. Kid. 1:7. The context in t. Bikkurim is a discussion of the androgyne, a hybrid person who has genitalia of both men and women. The discussion seeks to clarify when the halakhah regards the androgyne as a man, when as a women, when as both, and when as neither. Though the tosephtan discussion of the androgyne is not formally a list of male–female difference, it appears to draw on such a list in its assessment of the androgyne.

T. Bikkurim 2:3–7 lists the ways in which the androgyne resembles men and women in a number of different areas of law. In compiling the list, t. Bikkurim appears to draw on instances where the differences between men and women have already been established. The rule is alluded to while clarifying one of the ways in which the androgyne resembles a man.

דרכים ששוה בהן לאנשים: . . .

וחייב בכל מצות האמורות בתורה כאנשים . . .

ואין מטמא למתים כאנשים ועובר על בל תקיף ועל בל תשחית כאנשים.

[The androgyne] is similar to men [in the following] ways: . . .

1. He is obligated in all the commandments that are mentioned in the Torah, like men . . .

2. He may not be impurified by the dead, like men, and he trangresses "do not round [the corners of your head]" and "do not mar [the corners of your beard]," like men. (t. Bik. 2:4)

As in t. Sot. 2:8, t. Bik. 2:4 represents commandments as belonging to two basic categories: positive and negative (lines 1 and 2). The phrase "all of the commandments that are mentioned in the Torah" (כל המצות האמורות בתורה) is widely used to refer to positive commandments.[17] Assuming this phrase's idiomatic (rather than literal) sense, the first line notes that the androgyne, like men, is obligated to perform all positive commandments. This stipulation is especially meaningful when read against the understanding that woman are exempt from some positive commandments. Though this source does not state explicitly that

---

[17] See, e.g., t. Peah 3:8, where the context indicates that the term must refer to a positive commandment (something that is done, rather than something that is not done). See also t. Shab. 1:7; t. BB 8:14; Sem. 10:1 and 13:1, which list a number of the commandments traditionally assumed to be "positive commandments" as "all of the commandments stated in the Torah."

women are exempt from timebound, positive commandments, it does assume that there is a subset of positive commandments from which women are exempt. It is reasonable to assume that the implied set of positive commandments from which women are exempt is the timebound ones. This assumption is supported by the fact that line 2 lists the negative commandments from which women are exempt. The list of negative commandments from which women are exempt ("do not become impurified through contact with the dead," "do not mar the corners of your beard," and "do not round the corners of your head") is cited in conjunction with the rule exempting women from timebound, positive commandments in both t. Sot. 2:8 and m. Kid. 1:7. If t. Bik. 2:4 does indeed presume women's exemption from timebound, positive commandments, then timebound, positive commandments are once again represented as a small subset within the larger field of positive commandments. Here the rule stipulates women's exemption from only a small, specified group of positive commandments. Timebound, positive commandments are not represented here, as they are in the four-part structure of m. Kid. 1:7, as the *only* subset of commandments from which women are exempt.

Line 2 of t. Bik. 2:4 notes that the androgyne is obligated to perform the three exceptional negative commandments that women do not perform. As in t. Sot. 2:8, t. Bik. 2:4 assumes that women are exempt from a specific, limited group of positive commandments and a specific, limited group of negative commandments. As noted above, all three citations of the rule in the context of the lists of male–female difference (m. Kid. 1:7; t. Sot. 2:8; and t. Bik. 2:4) note that women are exempt from these three negative commandments ("do not become impurified through contact with the dead," "do not mar the corners of your beard," and "do not round the corners of your head"). As in t. Sot. 2:8, t. Bik. 2:4 does not try to account for women's involvement with all commandments. It leaves open the possibility that women are exempt from commandments other than the ones specified here. Likewise, it makes no definitive statement about women's obligations.

There are important differences between the binary division of categories into "positive" and "negative," which is attested in t. Sot. 2:8 and t. Bik. 2:4, and the four-part structure found in m. Kid. 1:7. In the binary structure (in t. Sot. 2:8 and t. Bik. 2:4), timebound commandments are a discrete group of positive commandments from which women are exempt. By way of contrast, in the four-part structure (in m. Kid. 1:7), timebound, positive commandments are the *only* subset of commandments from which women are exempt. In the binary structure, the matter of women's obligations and exemption is left open for all unmentioned commandments. The Tosephta, therefore, provides a relatively limited statement about women's obligations and exemptions. By way of contrast, the Mishnah makes a positive statement about women's involvement with the entire network of commandments. To put the point in slightly different terms, the Tosephta represents timebound commandments as an exceptional subset of positive commandments. The fact that this subset has been specified, however, does not preclude the possibility that other subsets – like father-to-son commandments – might also be specified as exceptional. By way of contrast, the Mishnah locates the category of timebound, positive commandments in a four-part structure where it is depicted as the *only* exceptional subset.

Recognizing that an alternate understanding of the rule circulated during the tannaitic period gives us a way to make sense of the contradiction in m. Kid. 1:7. I would argue that the open-ended understanding of the rule attested in t. Sot. 2:8 and t. Bik. 2:4 was available as a frame of reference for those who formulated m. Kid. 1:7. Even though the authors of m. Kid. 1:7 generated a four-part structure that makes the rule appear to account for women's involvement with *all* commandments ("women are exempt from *only* this subset of commandments"), the fact that they juxtaposed the rule to the "contradictory" rule about father-to-son commandments suggests that they nonetheless thought about the rule as a more open-ended statement ("women are exempt from this subset of commandments and may be exempt from other subsets, as well").

It may be that the authors of m. Kid. 1:7 knew from other contexts that the rule was a limited statement of male–female difference.[18] If this is the case, we still need to make sense of the fact that the Mishnah represents the rule as a comprehensive statement of male–female difference by locating it in a matrix of four categories. In my view, the Mishnah's four-part structure is best understood as an expansion of the Tosephta's two-part structure. It is a common technique in the Mishnah to manipulate variables in order to produce overarching symmetrical structures that serve as a container of sorts for information.[19] Such structures do not organize information hierarchically, but rather propose that there is a series of related bins into which information can be conveniently placed for storage.[20] The rhetorically symmetrical structures assist in the oral mastery of information, but they do not necessarily map into a single, conceptually coherent system.[21]

---

[18] Here I draw on the suggestion of John Miles Foley that audiences and composers in traditional societies are always listening to and composing material against the backdrop of a broader network of associations and motifs. See John Miles Foley, *Immanent Art: From Structure to Meaning in Traditional Oral Epic* (Bloomington: Indiana University Press, 1991), 39–60. See also the discussion of Foley in Alexander, *Transmitting Mishnah*, 48n24.

[19] B. Ned. 2b. cites a number of mishnayot that have been composed in this manner. I thank Shlomo Naeh for alerting me to the relevance of this source.

[20] Both Shlomo Naeh and Mary Carruthers discuss metaphors used to represent memory as a series of storage bins. See Shlomo Naeh, "The Art of Memory, Structures of Memory and Paradigms of Text in Rabbinic Literature" (Hebrew), in *Mehqerei Talmud: Talmudic Studies*, ed. Yaacov Sussman and David Rosenthal (Jerusalem: Magnes Press, 2005); and Mary Carruthers, *The Book of Memory: A Study of Memory in Medieval Culture* (Cambridge: Cambridge University Press, 1990), 33–45.

[21] Yitzhak Gilat writes about the inconsistency of early tannaitic sources and their failure to map into a single coherent system. See Gilat, *Development of Halakha*, esp. 19–31. See also Moscovitz, *Talmudic Reasoning*, 96–97, who discusses the lack of abstract thinking in tannaitic

As discussed in Chapter 1, both parts of m. Kid. 1:7 (A and B) seem to have been expanded from an early kernel into a broader rhetorical structure. The first part of the mishnah (A) begins with a statement about father-to-son commandments (A.1).[22] Reversing the position of these two subjects yielded the category of son-to-father commandments (A.2) and gave the sense that the topic of commandments involving fathers and sons had been treated thoroughly. In the second half of the mishnah (B), the early kernel appears to have been two related statements: One statement noted women's exemption from the time-bound commandments among the positive commandments (B.1), and the other noted women's exemption from three specified commandments among the negative commandments (B.3–4).[23] Insofar as the first line (B.1) notes that some commandments are timebound, the idea that some commandments are *non*-timebound is also suggested. The authors of the mishnah's four-part structure would have generated the second line of the mishnah (B.2) by articulating what is merely implicit in the first line: namely, that women are obligated to perform *non*-timebound, positive commandments. The authors of the mishnah's four-part structure would have then carried the marker of "timeboundedness" down in the statement about women's exemption from negative commandments, noting that they too can fall into the categories of timebound and non-timebound (B.3–4). As in Chapter 1, I argue that the four-part structure is a secondary development of the rule concerning timebound, positive commandments.

One way to make sense of the four-part structure of the Mishnah is to fail to see it as a comprehensive overview of the entirety of all commandments. In this way of thinking, the structure is *rhetorically, but not substantively,* comprehensive. Like the two-part structure that juxtaposes father-to-son commandments to son-to-father commandments (A.1–2), the four-part structure (B.1–4) deals with all the "bins" of information suggested by its language, but it does not offer a comprehensive account of women's involvement with *all* commandments. Accepting this hypothesis requires that we read the term "all" that introduces each line of m. Kid. 1:7 in a somewhat counterintuitive manner.[24] The commonsense understanding of the phrase "all timebound,

---

materials. See also the recent dissertation by Moshe Simon-Shoshan, who notes the degree of specificity in the Mishnah's narration of cases. He calls this feature of the Mishnah "narrativity." Moshe Simon-Shoshan, "Halachah Lema'aseh: Narrative and Legal Discourse in the Mishnah" (PhD diss., University of Pennsylvania, 2005).

[22] Though m. Kid. 1:7 and its tosephtan parallel, t. Kid. 1:11, mention both father-to-son commandments and son-to-father commandments, elsewhere we find only a reference to "father-to-son" commandments, suggesting that it is the older of the two categories. See Mek., Bo 18, ed. Horowitz and Rabin, 72–73.

[23] Again, though m. Kid. 1:7 and its tosephtan parallel (t. Kid. 1:10) mention timebound, positive commandments and *non*-timebound, positive commandments, all other tannaitic sources mention only timebound, positive commandments. The earliest reference appears not even to allude to negative commandments, as do the tosephtan sources (t. Sot. 2:8 and t. Bik. 2:4) discussed in this chapter. See Sif. Num., Shellah 115, ed. Horowitz, 124.

[24] I thank Ishay Rosen-Zvi for calling this observation to my attention.

positive commandments – women are exempt" reads the term "all" as referring to all commandments that possess the traits of being both "positive" and "timebound." Likewise in the phrase "all non-timebound, positive commandments – women are obligated," the term "all" is understood to designate all commandments that can be accurately described by the terms "positive" and "non-timebound." Against common sense, I am proposing that we read the term "all" as having a more limited point of reference. Rather than indicating the full range of commandments possessing the traits of being "positive" and "timebound" or "positive" and "non-timebound," I suggest that the term "all" would have referred to *only those commandments that were already known to belong to this category and already known to be subject to this rule.* Admittedly, in this way of reading the term "all," the rule becomes somewhat tautological. It rehearses and summarizes what is already known about a limited phenomenon rather than prescribing law for a broad range of unknown situations. I think, however, that this is the best way to make sense of the internal tensions within m. Kid. 1:7. Only when we find a way to read the four-part structure (B.1–4) without requiring that it function as a comprehensive statement of male–female difference does the problem of internal contradiction within m. Kid. 1:7 (i.e., between A and B) resolve itself.

In sum, the most obvious reading of m. Kid. 1:7 sees the rule exempting women from timebound, positive commandments as a comprehensive statement of the way in which the law regards women differently from men. In spite of the appeal of this reading, I have argued that during the tannaitic period, an alternative understanding of the rule prevailed – one that saw it as a *limited* statement regarding male–female difference.[25] In t. Sot. 2:8 and t. Bik. 2:4, the phrase "timebound, positive commandments" designates a specific subset of positive commandments from which women are exempt. The rule as recorded in t. Sot. 2:8 and t. Bik. 2:4 leaves open the possibility that women might also be exempt from other sets of commandments.

Interestingly enough, the Talmuds attest to the viability of *both* readings during the rabbinic period. The Yerushalmi relates to the rule as it is set within the binary division of categories. It ignores the category of *non*-timebound, positive commandments (B.2) that represents that main difference between the binary division of the Tosephta and the four-part structure of the Mishnah.[26] Obviously the Yerushalmi is familiar with the second of the mishnah's four categories (B.2), but the Yerushalmi does not bother to comment on women's obligation regarding non-timebound, positive commandments. For the Yerushalmi, only the two statements that I have argued represent the core of the mishnah's four-part structure (B.1 and B.3–4) warrant comment. This is not to suggest

---

[25] See also Menachem Fisch, *Rational Rabbis: Science and Talmudic Culture* (Bloomington: Indiana University Press, 1997), 171–88, discusses the gap between the Mishnah's rhetorical claims as law code and and the limits of its legal capacities.

[26] See y. Kid. 61c.

that the Yerushalmi had a different version of m. Kid. 1:7 than we do today. Rather, it is to propose that one can know of m. Kid. 1:7's four-part structure *and nonetheless* view the rule in the open-ended manner in which it is presented in the Tosephta.

The Bavli, on the other hand, recognizes and accepts the Mishnah's rhetorical claim to present a comprehensive statement of the way in which the law regards women differently from men and directly engages this claim. It notes exceptions to both the first *and* second lines of the rule (B.1 and B.2).[27] For the Bavli, dealing with the rule means relating to and commenting upon all four parts. The Bavli activates the meaning that is latent in m. Kid. 1:7's four-part structure, but that earlier transmitters seem to have ignored.

This finding is significant because the Bavli has provided a framing lens for all subsequent readers who have encountered the Mishnah. The medieval and contemporary readers who see the rule as a legal response to female "nature" do so because they assume that the rule represents a comprehensive statement of the ways in which the law treats men and women differently. As we have observed, however, the rule was not always seen to provide such a comprehensive overview. The earliest trend of interpretation, attested in both the Tosephta and the Yerushalmi, sees the rule as pointing to a limited phenomenon of male–female difference. Nonetheless, the rule was associated with the project of distinguishing men from women more generally.

Lists of Male–Female Difference

Though the rule exempting women from timebound, positive commandments primarily functions as a limited statement of male–female difference, it does play an important role in the broader cultural project of distinguishing men from women. That the tannaitic sages are engaged in such a project can be discerned from the fact that no fewer than four different lists enumerate the legal differences between men and women.[28]

A sample of the items brought in the lists provides a taste of the kinds of issues that clarified for the rabbis the difference between men and women. The lists observe the following ways in which the law treats women differently from men: Whereas male lepers rend their clothes and bare their heads, female lepers do not; whereas a man can submit his son to a Nazirite oath, a woman cannot; whereas a man convicted of a capital crime is stoned naked, a woman is not; whereas a male executee is hanged, a female is not; whereas a father can sell his daughter to be a slave or give her away in marriage, a mother may not. One

---

[27] See b. Kid. 33b–35a.

[28] The four lists: m. Sot. 3:8; t. Sot. 2:7–9; t. Bik. 2:3–7; and m. Kid. 1:7–8. In addition to these four lists, which are eclectic in nature, there are also lists that focus on male–female difference in a specific area of law: Sem. 11:2 (mourning practices) and m. Shab. 6:1–5 (the prohibition of carrying on the Sabbath).

thing that is evident from even a cursory review of the lists is how concrete and specific the cited differences are. The list is not compiled by contemplating the matter of male–female difference as a theoretical issue, but by surveying existing legal sources and extracting those rulings that treat men differently from women.

Ishay Rosen-Zvi has observed that the list in m. Sotah 3:8 contains a significant number of laws that deal with the issue of exposing the female body.[29] For example, a female leper does not bare her head, and a woman convicted of a capital offense is neither stoned naked nor hanged for all to see. Rosen-Zvi notes that the chapter in which the list appears begins by outlining the ordeal for the suspected adulteress, which subjects the woman's body to a significant amount of humiliating exposure. In this context, the list (which enumerates instances in which the female body is treated with dignity and respect) provides a rhetorical counterbalance to the ordeal (which exposes and humiliates the female body). Rosen-Zvi argues that the rhetorical claim of the chapter's structure is to contain and contextualize the ordeal of the suspected adulteress. Though the ordeal requires baring the woman's head and breast in a public forum, the chapter polemicizes that this action should be understood as a consequence of the woman's actions and *not* as a function of the posture of halakhah toward female bodies. Halakhah's dominant approach to female bodies can be discerned from the list in m. Sotah 3:8, where they are treated with great respect.

While this account of the motivation for including the list in chapter 3 of m. Sotah makes good sense, it falls short of explaining the phenomenon of the list in its entirety. Though the list does include instances where the law requires the female body to be treated with dignity, the list also enumerates differences that have nothing to do with the female body. For example, a man may impose a Nazirite oath on his son, but a woman may not; a son may take over responsibility for his deceased father's Nazirite oath, but a daughter may not; a man may sell his daughter as a maidservant, but a woman may not; a man may betroth his daughter, but a woman may not. Given the fact that many of the legal differences listed in m. Sotah 3:8 do not serve the polemical purpose suggested by Rosen-Zvi, it is likely that the list originated outside the setting of m. Sotah 3.

The idea that the rabbis were working on the project of enumerating legal differences between men and women outside of m. Sotah 3 is supported by the fact that several other lists exist that catalogue male–female difference.[30] Each of the lists has its own unique emphases informed by the particular redactional

[29] Ishay Rosen-Zvi, "The Sotah Ritual in Tannaitic Literature: Textual and Theoretical Studies," (Hebrew) (PhD diss., Tel Aviv University, 2004), 148–49.
[30] See t. Sot. 2:7–9; t. Bik. 2:3–7; and m. Kid. 1:7–8. For lists of male–female difference in a specific area of law, see Sem. 11:2 (male–female difference in mourning practices) and m. Shab. 6:1–5 (male–female difference regarding the prohibition to carry on the Sabbath).

contexts in which the lists find themselves. Nonetheless, they share the common feature of focusing on discrete legal differences dealing with the same legal topics. Like the list from m. Sotah 3:8 the other lists touch on marriage law, the Nazirite oath, the laws of the Hebrew slave, and leprosy.

T. Sotah 2:7–9 records an expanded version of the list found in m. Sotah 3:8. While touching on some of the same topics treated in m. Sotah 3:8 (marriage law, laws of the Hebrew slave, and leprosy), the tosephtan list also mentions differences from other areas of law. The tosephtan list notes that whereas men are subject to the law of the stubborn and rebellious son, women are not; and whereas men can violate timebound, positive commandments and three specified negative commandments, women cannot. The theme that lends coherence to the list in t. Sotah 2:7–9 is less evident than that which lends coherence to the list in m. Sotah 3:8. It is possible that the list in t. Sotah 2:7–9 was not compiled to fit into a redactional context. Instead, it might be an informal record of other lists that circulated during the tannaitic period and from which the mishnaic list was compiled.[31]

Two other versions of the list of differences between men and women can be found in tannaitic literature. The second chapter of t. Bikkurim draws on one version of the list. As noted earlier, the second chapter of t. Bikkurim examines the androgyne, who has both male and female genitalia. The list in t. Bik. 2:3–7 opens with a statement that makes clear the hybrid character of the androgyne: "There are ways in which he is similar to men; there are ways in which he is similar to women; there are ways in which he is similar to both men and women; and there are ways in which he is similar to neither men nor women" (t. Bik. 2:3). The majority of the chapter consists of lists that outline situations in which the law treats the androgyne as a member of each of these different categories. For example, s/he is like a man insofar as s/he becomes impure through white genital secretions, but s/he is also like a woman insofar as s/he becomes impure through red genital secretions. S/he is like a man insofar as s/he cannot be alone with two women, but s/he is like a woman insofar as s/he cannot be alone with one man. Charlotte Fonrobert has argued that though the hybrid creature fits neatly into neither category, s/he becomes the occasion to clarify the boundaries of the established categories.[32] Indeed, the chapter does convey a strong sense

---

[31] See Judith Hauptman, *Rereading the Mishnah: A New Approach to Ancient Jewish Texts* (Tübingen: Mohr Siebeck, 2005), who argues that in many instances, tosephtan parallels are the raw materials of the Mishnah we have today. See also Shamma Friedman, *Tosefta Atiqta. Pesah Rishon: Synoptic Parallels of Mishna and Tosefta Analyzed with a Methodological Introduction* (Hebrew) (Ramat-Gan: Bar Ilan University Press, 2002), which argues for the primacy of tosephtan parallels.

[32] See Charlotte Fonrobert, "The Semiotics of the Sexed Body in Early Halakhic Discourse," in *How Should Rabbinic Literature Be Read in the Modern World?* ed. Matthew Kraus (Piscataway: Gorgias Press, 2006), 79–108. See also Jacob Neusner, *Judaism: The Evidence of the Mishnah*, 256–70, and Alexander, *Transmitting Mishnah*, 155–67, on the Mishnah's general interest in ambiguous legal phenomena.

of where the pertinent legal differences between men and women lie. The legal differences treated in this source overlap to a certain extent with those treated by the lists in m. and t. Sotah. Among the shared topics are marriage law, the Hebrew slave, leprosy, the Nazirite oath, and a statement noting men's obligation to perform certain positive and negative commandments from which women are exempt. In addition, t. Bik. 2:3–7 treats many additional topics: the laws of impurity, inheritance, seclusion, civil law, rights of testimony, levirate marriage, and the priesthood. One distinctive feature of the list in t. Bik. 2:3–7 is the foregrounding of sexual issues. The two leading items of the list deal explicitly with the sexualized body: genital excretions and the laws prohibiting the seclusion of unrelated men and women, which are designed to prevent inappropriate sexual liaisons. This emphasis is likely occasioned by the redactional context in which the list is cited: a discussion of the sexual ambiguity of the androgyne. Even though the list touches on topics unique to its redactional context, it also rehearses the differences associated with the other lists like the laws of the marriage, the Hebrew slave, leprosy, and the Nazirite oath.

Finally, the second half of m. Kid. 1 also includes a list of male–female differences.[33] I have already discussed the fact that this list includes a reference to male–female difference in the area of timebound, positive commandments and father-to-son commandments (m. Kid. 1:7). In addition, m. Kid. 1:8 also notes that, unlike men, women do not participate in any of the rituals related to sacrifice, except that they wave sotah and Nazirite offerings when appropriate. This list (m. Kid. 1:7–8) has the least in common with the other lists. It does not include a reference to the laws of marriage, the Hebrew slave, leprosy, and the Nazirite oath as the other lists do. It does, however, touch on the issue of women's engagement with commandments, which appears in two of the other lists (t. Sot. 2:8 and t. Bik. 2:4). By noting that women do not participate in sacrificial rites, it also touches on a topic that is treated in t. Bik. 2:5, namely that women are excluded from the priesthood. Natan Margalit has argued that the list in m. Kid. 1:7–8 emphasizes women's second-class status with regard to men and establishes the social context within which marriage is contracted.[34]

---

[33] Early critical scholars of rabbinic literature assume that the the the two halves of m. Kid. were originally composed as two different compilations and only subsequently spliced together. See, e.g., Chanoch Albeck, *Introduction to the Mishnah* (Hebrew) (Jerusalem: Dvir, 1959), 89; and J. N. Epstein, *Introduction to the Text of the Mishnah*, 3rd ed. (Hebrew) (Tel Aviv: Dvir and Magnes Press, 2000), 51–53. That is to say, quite early in the history of modern scholarship, it was recognized that the list in the second half of the chapter was initially transmitted as a discrete source.

[34] See Margalit, "Priestly Men and Invisible Women: Male Appropriation of the Feminine and the Exemption of Women from Positive, Time-Bound Commandments." See also Hauptman, *Rereading the Rabbis*, 222–28, who makes a similar argument about the fact that in M. Kid. 1:7, the rule confirms women's second-class social status. See also the unpublished Hebrew paper by Noam Zohar on chapter 1 of Kiddushin.

The four lists, then, have significant areas of overlap, but also distinctive emphases depending on the redactional context in which they are transmitted. The list in m. Sot. 3:8 emphasizes the general tendency of Jewish law to respect female bodies and treat them with dignity. The list in t. Bik. 2:3–7 highlights the sexualized body as the source of male–female difference. The list in m. Kid. 1:7–8 emphasizes women's second-class social and religious standing as the basis for the marital relationship. In addition to these distinctive emphases, the lists also appear to have drawn on a staple of tradition that was known to attest to male–female tradition: laws regarding marriage, leprosy, Nazirite oaths, and the Hebrew slave. In spite of the fact that none of the lists touches on all the same topics, they share the common goal of trying to discern what is at stake in being female versus male. The lists do not provide a conceptual analysis of the nature of gender. Instead they gather together material from throughout the legal tradition and place it in a new context. In that new context, the laws succeed in performing a new cultural function: They help define what it means to be male and female.

The Rule within the Larger Project

It is not insignificant that the rule exempting women from timebound, positive commandments appears on three of the four lists. Like other items on the lists, the rule is a tradition that is attested and established elsewhere in tannaitic legal tradition.[35] When the tannaitic sages surveyed legal tradition to find instances where the law treats women differently from men, they found the rule to be a relevant datum. Unlike almost every other item on the lists, however, the rule is not located within a particular sphere of law. It is the most unspecific statement of difference on the lists. Nonetheless, the lists provided an important transmissional context for the rule. In Chapter 1 I argued that the rule had limited legislative utility. I suggested that the rule was initially formulated to describe tefillin and other commandments with a similar profile. Only R. Shimon used the rule to determine women's ritual involvement, and even he used it to exempt them from only tzitzit. In this chapter, I have made related arguments about the rule's limited functionality. I have suggested that the phrase designating the sphere of women's exemption as "all timebound, positive commandments" should be read tautologically as indicating all those commandments from which women are *already* known to be exempt, rather than all commandments that are accurately described by the adjectives "timebound" and "positive."

With its limited legislative utility, the rule exempting women from timebound, positive commandments could easily have dropped off the radar screen of rabbinic sensibilities. Indeed, the rule's relevance to slaves has been all

<hr/>

[35] Sif. Num., Shelakh 115, ed. Horowitz, 125, attributes the rule to R. Shimon. See also MRSY, Bo, ed. Epstein and Melamed, 41, which cites the rule.

but forgotten. I argue that the rule endures and continues to be transmitted *because of its place within the lists of male–female difference.* In this context, it is remembered as a significant tradition because it contributes to the larger cultural project of distinguishing women from men. Notably, no such lists concerning the difference between slaves and freemen or between adults and minors were compiled, although these differences in status are reflected in numerous legal rulings.

The fact that the lists provide an important transmissional context that ensures the rule's future is underscored by an obscure version of the rule that has been preserved. Sifre Numbers attributes the rule to R. Shimon and names *both* slaves and women as its subjects.[36] No other attested version of the rule does this, though many sources list slaves together with women when discussing their various obligations and exemptions.[37] Every other version of the rule attested in tannaitic sources focuses on women alone as the appropriate subjects of the rule.[38] In post-talmudic times, including the contemporary period, the fact that slaves were originally subject to the rule has been all but forgotten.[39] I would argue that the rule's strong association with women, over and against slaves, results from the fact that the rule's dominant cultural function was to contribute to larger project of distinguishing men from women. In a formal sense, slaves were likely recognized as subjects of the rule during the tannaitic period. By the amoraic period, however, consciousness of that fact seems to have disappeared, in part because of the rule's legislative incapacity and in part because the rule's inclusion in the lists of male–female difference. As the rule's inclusion in three of the four lists suggests, the rule's main utility was as one patch in a broader collage of knowledge about male–female difference.

Some Differences Are More Equal Than Others

As I have noted, the lists provided a transmissional context that lent the rule meaning. It also appears, however, that the rule did emerge as a primary lens through which to view the matter of male–female difference. In at least one instance, the rule that women are exempt from certain commandments was used to indicate an overarching difference between men and women. Though the lists do not give prominence of place to the rule within the collage of

---

[36] Sif. Num., Shelakh 115, ed. Horowitz, 125.

[37] See, e.g., m. Ber. 3:3 on blessings; m. Suk. 2:8 on sitting in the sukkah; m. Hag. 1:1 on pilgramages; t. RH 2:5 on shofar. See additional material collected and discussed in Catherine Hezser, *Jewish Slavery in Antiquity* (Oxford: Oxford University Press, 2005), 76–82.

[38] This is especially significant in the case of the MRSY Bo, ed. Esptein and Melamed, 41, since this source knew and drew on the Mek., which discusses women and slaves in the same context. See also m. Kid 1:7 and t. Sotah 2:8 for other explicit mentions of the rule with regard to women only.

[39] An exception to this rule is Adler, "The Jew Who Wasn't There," 348–49.

male–female differences, the Tosephta records a tradition in the name of R. Yehudah that does privilege the rule over other male–female differences.

In t. Berachot 6:18,[40] R. Yehudah recommends that a man make three blessings every day. He should bless the Creator that He did not make him a gentile, a woman, or an ignoramus.[41] R. Yehudah explains that one thanks God for not making him a woman "because women are not obligated in the commandments."[42] This source reveals how at least one sage conceptualized the difference between men and women. For him, the salient and culturally significant difference is the fact that women do not engage the commandments in the same way men do. Though R. Yehudah may have been aware of the lists as a resource for understanding male–female difference, he did not refract the issue through the broad range of subjects treated therein. Rather, he understood male–female difference to be primarily a function of the fact that women do not perform all (or perhaps any) of the commandments. Here the rule's transmissional context shapes the cultural meaning attributed to the rule. Furthermore in the context of R. Yehudah's statement, the rule bears a cultural meaning, informed by, but now affirmed independently of, the transmissional context of the lists. Eventually the rule sustained this meaning without having to draw it from its context in the lists.

Conclusion

For the most part, tannaitic records indicate that the rule exempting women from timebound, positive commandments was understood to be a limited statement of male–female difference. As such, it finds its place within the lists of other legal differences between men and women. Within the context of the lists, male–female difference was not conceptualized as an abstract or essential quality. Instead, male–female difference was conceived as a patchwork of discrete legal stipulations that applied to men, but not women. Since the rule exempting women from timebound, positive commandments had limited legislative utility, it drew its primary cultural meaning from the context of the lists. In this context the rule functioned as a single statement within a broader collection. Furthermore, it was a limited, rather than comprehensive, statement of male–female difference.

---

[40] According to the numbering system in MS Vienna, which Lieberman chose as the basis for his critical edition. In MS Erfurt the dictum appears as 7:8. Saul Lieberman, *The Tosefta according to Codex Vienna, with Variants from Codices Erfurt, London, Genizah MSS. and Editio Princeps (Venice 1521)*, vol. 1 (Jerusalem: Jewish Theological Seminary of America, 1992), 38.

[41] A version of these blessings is today recited every day, with minor emmendations: gentile, woman, and slave.

[42] Shevah Yalon draws an explicit connection between this source and women's exemption from timebound, positive commandments. See Yalon, "'Women Are Exempted from All Positive Ordinances That Are Bound Up with a Stated Time,'" 127–28.

On the other hand, there were also ways in which the rule emerged as an outstanding and prominent example of male–female difference. R. Yehudah read the rule as having more significance when characterizing male–female difference than other items on the lists. R. Yehudah took the rule to be culturally significant in a way that the other differences were not. His reading of the rule paved the way for medieval and contemporary readers who see in the rule an allusion to essential female nature. It is important to note, however, that for the duration of the tannaitic period, R. Yehudah's perspective seems to have been a minority view. The interpretive trajectory that saw the rule as a comprehensive statement of male–female difference coexisted alongside a more widely attested tendency to view the rule as a limited statement of male–female difference. In the second, more commonly held view, the rule was a single element in a larger patchwork, the sum total of which offered the rabbis an inchoate impression of where male–female difference lay. The idea that the rule offers significant insight into the nature of women still lay in the future.

PART II

TALMUDIC INTERPRETATION AND THE
POTENTIAL FOR GENDER

3

How Tefillin Became a Positive Commandment *Not* Occasioned by Time

In this chapter I would like to explore the complex relationship between tefillin and the legal category of timebound, positive commandments. As in so many other areas of law, rabbinic literature preserves diverse ways of understanding the issue. The earliest recorded approach (and the one most broadly attested) positions tefillin as the prototypical member of this legal category. In this point of view, women's exemption from timebound, positive commandments is modeled on their exemption from the single timebound, positive commandment of tefillin; here tefillin is regarded as the paradigmatic timebound, positive commandment.[1] A second approach to the question is both later (found only in the latest redactional layers of the Bavli) and rarer (alluded to in only three discrete locations).[2] This strand of tradition denies that the observance of tefillin is timebound at all. In contrast to the dominant point of view, the second approach does not regard tefillin as subject to the rule that dictates female exemption from timebound, positive commandments, much less as its source. This chapter takes as its starting point that the emergence of a new tradition in the late rabbinic period was a significant development. The main work of the chapter is to investigate and document the exegetical processes and legal concerns that led to the emergence of this new tradition.

Before proceeding to develop the substance of the argument in this chapter, I must first clarify the relevance of this inquiry for the larger project of the book. In Chapter 1, I argued that the rule of women's exemption from timebound,

---

[1] See, e.g., MRSY, ed. Epstein and Melamed, 41, with roots in Mek., ed. Horowitz, Bo 17, 68–69; b. Kid. 34a, 35a. See also t. Kid. 1:10, which lists tefillin as a timebound, positive commandment. This baraita is cited in the Yerushalmi and the Bavli (and includes tefillin in the lists there as well). See y. Ber. 6b, y; Kid. 61c, and b. Kid. 33b–34a.

[2] See b. Kid. 35a, b; Eruv. 96a, b; Shab. 62a. My attribution of this tradition to post-amoraic sages is corroborated by Jay Rovner, who presented a paper arguing just this point at the Annual Meeting for the Association of Jewish Studies in Washington, DC, December 2005.

positive commandments emerged in a dynamic relationship with exegetical traditions about tefillin. A series of exegetical exercises in the Mekhilta yielded a description of tefillin as a "timebound, positive commandment from which women (and slaves) are exempt."[3] On the basis of this evidence, I argued that the rule in its earliest manifestation offered a description of a known legal phenomenon, that is, tefillin. It was not formulated to *determine* which of the many ritual commandments outlined in the Torah women need and need not perform. I also argued that other rituals eventually came to be regarded as subject to the rule only insofar as women had *already* been exempted from them by other means. Insofar as the rule did not determine women's exemptions, it is inappropriate to mine its stipulations for evidence of early rabbinic attitudes about women. The rule reveals far less than scholars have generally assumed about what the tannaitic sages thought about how women should or did use their time.

My historical reconstruction of how the rule came to be formulated notwithstanding, the fact remains that the rule *was subsequently* taken to have been formulated as a normative statement of law. In Chapter 5, I will argue that by the time the latest redactional layer of the Bavli was composed, a view of the rule as prescriptive – that is, as one that *did determine* women's ritual exemptions – solidified. From the perspective of a legal historian, it is interesting to consider how this transformation came to pass. How did a set of descriptive terms, initially illuminating tefillin, but gradually broadened to include other rituals from which women are exempt, eventually come to be viewed as a prescriptive principle?

This development had a significant impact on how the rule came to define gender roles in Judaism. Once the rule was seen as a prescriptive principle, it became possible to inquire into the purported motivations of those who formulated the rule. What, it came to be asked, did its authors think about women and how they should be using their time that led them to make this rule? It is significant, however, that these questions came to be asked only at a relatively late stage in the history of the rule's transmission. Only after the rule had been transformed from a descriptive to a prescriptive principle did such lines of thought become possible.

This chapter offers part of the answer to the question of how the transformation from description to prescription occurred. One part of the process involved the divorcing of the category of timebound, positive commandments from the generative member of the category, tefillin. Once the theoretical possibility that tefillin are not timebound was raised, even if only in the name of

---

[3] Chapter 2 documents the lists of male–female difference within which the rule is preserved and transmitted. In this transmissional context, the fact that the rule was about slaves, along with women, became insignificant. In the context of these lists, only women were mentioned as subject to the rule. Subsequent tradition almost completely disregards the fact that slaves are technically subject to the rule. Only women are considered "socially significant" subjects of the rule.

a small majority of sages, the category of timebound, positive commandments came to exist independently of its generative member. Such a move definitively freed the rule from its historic roots as a descriptive principle. Without a reason to regard the rule as descriptive, the mishnaic dictum was free to be interpreted as a prescriptive principle. Eventually interpreters inquired into the gender ideology envisioned by it. But it is important to recognize that the prescriptive interpretation of the rule was not inevitable, and it certainly was not the earliest attested understanding of the rule. Rather, this understanding of the rule emerged gradually in the context of broader legal and interpretive influences. This chapter aims to highlight some of the ambient issues in rabbinic culture that affected this transformation. Though these ambient influences were not directly concerned with gender matters, the version of the rule that emerged on the other end was highly influential in the subsequent discussions of who women are and what they should be.

To put it in slightly different terms, the goal of this chapter is to understand whence and why a heretofore unattested view – namely, that tefillin are *not* timebound – emerged. Documenting the emergence of this view sheds light on how the legal category of timebound, positive commandments became disengaged from the concrete phenomenon of tefillin.

The View That Tefillin Are Not Timebound

In its classic discussion of timebound, positive commandments (b. Kid. 34a–35a), the Bavli attributes the view that "tefillin are not timebound" to two tannaim, R. Meir and R. Yehudah. The Bavli does not, however, cite the source in which these tannaim state this view. Given the unanimity of the extant early sources that tefillin *are* timebound, the attribution of this view to two tannaim is curious. The Bavli's failure to cite the source that documents their view serves to pique our curiosity only further. On what basis did these two prominent sages come to understand, contrary to every other documented tannaitic opinion,[4] that tefillin were not a timebound commandment?

I will argue that it is very unlikely that these two tannaitic sages ever actually articulated this point of view. Instead, I propose that this view was *attributed* to them by later interpreters trying to make sense of an inherited set of sources about tefillin. It appears that a desire for certain kinds of legal coherence pushed the post-amoraic sages responsible for the latest redactional layer of the Bavli

---

[4] See MRSY, ed. Epstein and Melamed, 41; and Mek., ed. Horowitz, Bo 17, 68–69; t. Kid. 1:10, which is cited as a baraita by the two Talmuds; see y. Ber. 6b, y; Kid. 61c; and b. Kid. 33–34a. The tannaitic midrashim that regard tefillin as timebound are also cited in the two Talmuds, but not attributed to tannaim. See y. Eruv. 26a, b; Kid. 34a and 35a. David Weiss Halivni concludes that there are no tannaitic sources that state that tefillin are worn on the Sabbath (which is slightly different from the issue of whether tefillin are timebound). See David Weiss Halivni, *Sources and Traditions: A Source Critical Commentary on Tractate Eruvin and Pesahim* (Hebrew) (Jerusalem: Jewish Theological Seminary of America, 1982), 248.

to attribute this view to tannaitic sages who had never expressed it directly. Other scholars have already documented a persistent interest among the later talmudic sages in systematizing, organizing, and harmonizing their inherited legal sources.[5] I submit that this generally documented tendency toward legal conceptualization accounts for the interpretive choices that result in the view that tefillin is not a timebound commandment.

The current example illustrates just how forceful the Bavli could be when try-ing to harmonize, organize, and systematize its sources, insofar as it reverses a long-established tradition that tefillin *are* timebound. It also points to the unan-ticipated effects that such organizational work could have. Insofar as labeling tefillin as a non-timebound commandment opened up new ways of understand-ing the rule of women's exemption from timebound, positive commandments, it impacted the future understandings of this rule for many generations to come. In later chapters, I will discuss how this development impacted future understandings of the rule. For now, however, I wish to limit the discussion to tracing the exegetical and organizational processes that produced the tradition that tefillin are *not* a timebound, positive commandment.

Tefillin and Shabbat

In its classic discussion of timebound, positive commandments (b. Kid. 34a–35a), the Bavli briefly alludes to the fact that R. Meir and R. Yehudah hold that tefillin are not timebound. The reference there is frustrating for being so cryptic. The same attribution, however, also appears in b. Eruv. 95b–96b with wider discussion of related issues.[6] It is there that we will be able to discern the exegetical forces and legal concerns that gave rise to the previously unattested view that tefillin are not timebound.

---

[5] See Abraham Goldberg, "The Babylonian Talmud," in *The Literature of the Sages*, part 1, ed. Shmuel Safrai (Philadelphia: Fortress Press, 1987), 330–31; Benjamin De Vries, *Toldot Hahalakhah Hatalmudit* (Hebrew) (Tel Aviv: A Tsiyoni, 1966), 142–56; Ephraim E. Urbach, *The Halakhah: Its Sources and Development* (Tel Aviv: Modan Publishing House, 1996), 177–205; Jeffrey Rubenstein, "On Some Abstract Concepts"; and Moscovitz, *Talmudic Reasoning*. The focus among all of these scholars is noting how later rabbinic sources have an increased tendency toward abstract conceptualization. De Vries suggests that talmudic law is like other ancient legal systems in the fact that it evolves from a focus on particular concrete issues toward abstract conceptualization (142). Moscovitz notes that the goal of rabbinic conceptualization is to account for and explain *existing* cases, not to decide law in new cases (355). Robert Goldenberg, "The Talmud," in *Back to the Sources: Reading the Classic Jewish Texts*, ed. Barry Holtz (New York: Simon and Schuster, 1984), 150, 153; and Goldberg, "The Babylonian Talmud," 329–30, note that the Bavli tries to render the views of particular sages internally consistent.

[6] See also b. Shab. 62a. The allusion there is cryptic too. It appears that the tradition was for-mulated in the context of b. Eruv. and only secondarily imported to b. Shab. 62a and b. Kid. 35a.

The Bavli's discussion in Eruvin seeks to understand the following tannaitic dispute.

המוצא[7] תפילין, מכניסן זוג זוג.
רבן גמליאל אומר: שנים, שנים.

One who finds tefillin [in an exposed place where some harm may come to them], may bring them in [by wearing them] one pair at a time.

Rabban Gamaliel says: two pairs at a time. (m. Eruv. 10:1)

Both R. Gamaliel and his anonymous interlocutor agree that when tefillin are found in an exposed place on the Sabbath, they may be moved to a more secure site despite the prohibition against carrying on the Sabbath. The allowance is made, presumably, because the sanctity of tefillin allows for a limited violation of the Sabbath in order to protect them. The two parties differ, however, on how to move the tefillin most efficiently while violating the Sabbath to the least extent possible. Both parties agree that wearing the tefillin is preferable to carrying them.[8] They disagree, however, on whether one may wear one or two pairs at a time.

Both Talmuds discuss the basis for this dispute. The preferred explanation for the difference of opinion is that the two parties differ on whether one is obligated to wear tefillin on the Sabbath. To paraphrase the Bavli, the mishnaic debate about one versus two pairs is understood to be rooted in two opposing views as to whether "Shabbat is a time for tefillin" (שבת זמן תפילין) (b. Eruv. 95b). In both Talmuds, the anonymous first opinion is said to be based on the view that tefillin *are* generally worn on the Sabath, while R. Gamaliel's opinion is said to be based on the view that they are not.[9] As will be recalled from Chapter 1, tefillin came to be regarded as timebound because they are to be worn some times (weekdays, daytime hours), but not other times (Sabbath, holidays, nighttime hours). When the Talmuds suggest that the anonymous first opinion holds that tefillin are generally worn on the Sabbath, he implies that time of the day, week, or year does not determine tefillin observance. That is, their observance is not "timebound." Talmudic discussion of the mishnaic debate about saving tefillin on the Sabbath, then, is intimately connected with the issue of whether observance of tefillin is occasioned by time.

The two Talmuds employ many of the same sources and arguments in their discussion of m. Eruv. 10:1. The Bavli's discussion, however, distinguishes itself

---

[7] Palestinian MSS tradition has מוציא ("one who takes out [tefillin]"). Mishnah here is represented as it is cited in the Bavli. For the purposes of the present discussion, the variant does not seem to make much of a difference.

[8] Though the purpose of said act of wearing is to move the tefillin from one location to another, since one may wear certain necessary articles of clothing, the violation would be less severe.

[9] Saul Lieberman, *The Tosefta Ki-Fshutah: A Comprehensive Commentary on the Tosefta*, part 3 (Hebrew) (Jerusalem: Jewish Theological Seminary of America, 1992), 463, summarizes the talmudic engagement with this mishnah in like manner.

from the Yerushalmi in two key aspects. First, though the Bavli reproduces many of the sources and arguments found in the Yerushalmi, it arranges them differently to expose their interconnectedness and the coherence of the legal system as a whole. Second, though the issue of tefillin's timebound character is in the background of the discussion in both Talmuds, only the latest redactional layer in the Bavli produces a tradition claiming that the observance of tefillin is *not* occasioned by time. I submit that these two distinctive features of the Bavli's discussion are intimately related. That is, the Bavli's broadly attested legal program of organizing its sources into a coherent legal system accounts for the emergence of a previously unattested tradition that tefillin are not timebound.

I precede my discussion of the Bavli's interpretation of the mishnaic dispute with a discussion of parallel elements in the Yerushalmi's interpretation. Detailed analysis of the Yerushalmi allows us to monitor what is genuinely new and distinctive in the Bavli's treatment of the mishnah. Comparison with the Yerushalmi allows us to see the kinds of sources the Bavli's post-amoraic editors had available to them, and even more importantly, it allows us to see how the Bavli's editors manipulated their sources. Jeffrey Rubenstein has used the method of comparing parallel materials in the Yerushalmi and the Bavli to great effect in order to discern the cultural values unique to the latest stratum of the Bavli.[10] While Rubenstein works with aggadic materials, I aim to use the same methods here with halakhic materials.[11] I do not intend to take a stand on the historical question of whether the Bavli had access to the Yerushalmi as we

---

[10] See Jeffrey L. Rubenstein, *Talmudic Stories: Narrative Art, Composition, and Culture*, throughout, but esp. 15–26. Rubenstein draws heavily on Shamma Friedman, "Literary Development and Historicity in the Aggadic Narrative: A Study Based upon B.M. 83b–86a," in *Community and Culture: Essays in Jewish Studies in Honor of the Ninetieth Anniversary of the founding of Gratz College*, ed. N. M. Waldman (Philadelphia: Gratz College, 1987), 67–80, to whom he attributes the basic insight that underlies this study as well: "For our purposes, Friedman's study suggests that the Stammaim reworked their narrative sources with a considerable degree of freedom" (cited by Rubenstein on p. 20). Rubenstein's and Friedman's work (and mine, based on their methodological model) analyzes the post-amoraic embellishments for the insight they provide into late, Babylonian rabbinic culture.

[11] Christine Hayes makes clear that Friedman's insights are also useful in the analysis of halakhic materials. She writes, "Once one identifies within a Babylonian narrative the raw materials, associated link, and the literary patterns paralleled in Palestinian sources, what remains most likely emanates from a later Babylonian source and to that degree may provide insight into the later Babylonian period. In other words, the differential between the Babylonian and Palestinian versions of aggadah – the interpolated details, the redactional choices – may tell us something about the Babylonian Jewish world.... I have adopted a modified version of this method in my study of parallel halakhic sugyot in which the Yerushalmi preserves the amoraic core that lies at the base of the Bavli's dialectical structure." See Christine Elizabeth Hayes, *Between the Babylonian and Palestinian Talmuds: Accounting for Halakhic Difference in Selected Sugyot from Tractate Avodah Zarah*, 23. This chapter similarly focuses on a sugya in which the Bavli's dialectal structure incorporates and expands upon an amoraic core, which is attested in the Yerushalmi.

have it today. Such a claim, whether framed positively or negatively, continues to be debated among scholars and is beyond the scope of this chapter.[12] What I do ask is how we might see the Bavli more clearly if we were to heuristically assume that the Bavli had access to tradition in the form in which it appears in the Yerushalmi. Examining the parallels between the Yerushalmi and the Bavli allows us to isolate with relative confidence the materials in the Bavli that can reasonably be attributed to an amoraic provenance. Isolating the amoraic substratum in the Bavli's sugya makes it easier to discern the unique interests and activities of the post-amoraic sages responsible for the final editing of the sugya. So while I do not argue that the Bavli had access to the Yerushalmi as we know it, I use parallels in the Yerushalmi to discern the unique viewpoint of the post-amoraic sages. The inquiry begins with the knowledge that the late post-amoraic stratum records a heretofore unattested view that tefillin *are* time-bound. The goal is to identify the cultural forces at work in the post-amoraic period that would have led the Bavli, and only the Bavli, to express (or more properly, to construct) this view.

I begin by discussing relevant aspects of the Yerushalmi's interpretation of the mishnaic dispute.

The Yerushalmi on m. Eruv. 10:1

The Yerushalmi offers two basic interpretations of the mishnaic dispute between R. Gamaliel and the sages on the question of how many pairs of tefillin can be worn on the Sabbath in order to save them. The first (and dominant) view of the sugya is that the dispute arises because the interlocutors disagree on the question of whether tefillin are generally worn on the Sabbath. According to the Yerushalmi, if one holds that tefillin *are* generally worn on the Sabbath, one will allow only one pair at a time when trying to save the tefillin. Since a man will be wearing one pair of tefillin anyway on the Sabbath, he can don any pair he might wish, especially if so doing will help save a specific pair. On the other hand, if one holds that tefillin are *not* generally worn on the Sabbath, one will require that *two* pairs of tefillin be worn. In this way, the special procedure for saving tefillin on the Sabbath (wearing two pairs) is distinguished from routine weekday, ritual wearing of tefillin (wearing only one pair).

[12] Most recently, see Alyssa Gray, "A Talmud in Exile: The Influence of PT Avodah Zarah on the Formation of BT Avodah Zarah," (PhD diss., Jewish Theological Seminary, 2001), who argues that the Bavli did have access to the redacted Yerushalmi. Her most immediate and influential predecessors argued, conversely, that the Bavli did *not* have access to the Yerushalmi. See Yaacov Sussmann, "Once More on y. Nezikin" (Hebrew), in *Mehqerei Talmud (Talmudic Studies)*, ed. Yaacov Sussman and David Rosenthal (Jerusalem: Magnes Press, 1990), esp. 98–99; and Shamma Friedman, *Talmud 'Arukh*, vol. 2 (Hebrew) (Jerusalem: Jewish Theological Seminary of America, 1997), esp. 13n41.

A second interpretation of the mishnaic debate between R. Gamaliel and the sages understands it as revolving around a different issue. The second interpretation suggests that the debate is rooted in the interlocutors' differing views on the question of how many pairs of tefillin a man *usually* wears when observing the commandment of tefillin. One who thinks that regular, ritual tefillin wearing is done two pairs at a time will also allow two pairs to be worn on the Sabbath for the sake of saving the tefillin. Conversely, one who thinks that regular, ritual wearing of tefillin is done one pair at a time will permit only one pair on the Sabbath for the sake of saving them. Both interpretations of the mishnaic debate are equally viable from a theoretical perspective. The Yerushalmi, however, focuses significantly greater energy on analysis of the first explanation, namely, that the debate arises because the two interlocutors disagree on the question of whether tefillin should be worn on the Sabbath. The fact that the Yerushalmi focuses extensively on the question of whether tefillin are worn on the Sabbath sets the stage for the Bavli's construction of an opinion that tefillin are *not* timebound. If tefillin are generally worn on the Sabbath, one may conclude that their observance is not occasioned by time.

The Yerushalmi approaches its discussion of the mishnaic debate in a somewhat indirect fashion. Rather than stating at the fore that the mishnaic dispute arises because of a disagreement about whether tefillin are worn on the Sabbath, the Yerushalmi rehearses the scriptural basis for the opinion that tefillin not be worn on the Sabbath. Having presented the scriptural sources, the Yerushalmi then suggests that not all scholars accept the midrashic conclusion that can be derived from these sources. According to this presentation, the mishnaic dispute arises because not all scholars agree that the conclusion that tefillin should not be worn on the Sabbath "is clear" (מחוורא) from scripture.

The discussion begins with an *indirect* allusion to the midrashic basis for the non-observance of tefillin on the Sabbath.

רבי אבהו רבי אלעזר: הנותן תפילין בלילה עובר בלא תעשה,

שנאמר: ושמרת את החוקה הזאת מימים ימימה.

ימים, ולא לילות.

R. Abbahu, R. Elazar: One who puts on tefillin at night transgresses a negative commandment,

as it written: "And you shall guard this law throughout your days" (Exod 13:10).

Days, and not nights. (y. Eruv. 26a)

R. Abbahu here expresses the point of view that one is not permitted to wear tefillin at night lest one be in violation of a negative commandment. R. Abbahu also brings a scriptural prooftext (Exod 13:10) for his stipulation that tefillin not be worn at night, which is accompanied by a brief midrashic exposition. Though the midrashic interpretation is cited here in the name of an amora, it echoes the content of a tannaitic interpretation of the same verse. The

Mekhilta of R. Ishmael offers two glosses to the phrase from Exodus "throughout your days," specifying that the phrase comes to limit tefillin observance to both "daytime and not nightime" and to the "Sabbath and holidays," and not weekdays.[13] Significantly, the tannaitic midrash treats an additional point beyond that covered in the R. Abbahu, R. Elazar's later amoraic midrash. In addition to excluding the possibility of wearing tefillin at night, the tannaitic midrash *also* excludes the possibility of wearing tefillin on the Sabbath and holidays. Though only the first portion of the tannaitic midrash (which precludes wearing tefillin at night) is cited here by R. Abbahu, I suspect that the source's relevance to the current discussion derives from the second *uncited* portion of the tannaitic midrash (which precludes wearing tefillin on the Sabbath and holidays).[14] By engaging a midrash that (implicitly) discusses the permissibility of wearing tefillin on the Sabbath and holidays, the gemara anticipates the forthcoming discussion.

After a brief digression,[15] the Yerushalmi cites a second midrashic tradition concerning the appropriate times to wear tefillin. This second tradition (also attested in tannaitic sources[16]) stipulates that tefillin should not be worn on the Sabbath and holidays.

אית דבעי נישמעינה מן הדא: והיו לך לאות – מי שצריכין אות, יצאו שבתות וימים טובים שהן גופן אות.
ולא כתיב מימים ימימה?
לית לך אלא כיי דאמר רבי יוחנן: כל מילה דלא מחוורא, מסמכין ליה מן אתרין סנין

There are some who wish to learn it [the appropriate times to wear tefillin] from this verse:

"And it shall be for you a sign (*ot*)" (Exod 13:9).

For those [days] that need a sign. This excludes Sabbath days and holidays, which are themselves considered to be a sign (*ot*).

---

[13] See Mek., Bo 17, ed. Horowitz, 68–69. See Chapter 1 for a full discussion of this text.

[14] It is a common feature of rabbinic citation techniques that though only the first portion of a source is cited, the latter uncited portion is in fact the relevant portion. The fact that the uncited portion of the midrash is nonetheless implied is buttressed by a later comment that finds a second biblical passage discussing whence comes the prohibition against wearing tefillin on Sabbath and holidays, to be redundant. The second biblical passage appears to be redundant only if the first passage *also* discusses the prohibition against wearing tefillin on the Sabbath and holidays. Saul Lieberman, *Hayerushalmi kiphshuto: A Commentary based on Manuskripts* [sic] *of the Yerushalmi*, vol. 1: *Shabbat, Eruvin and Pesachin* (Hebrew) (Jerusalem: Darom, 1934), 353–54, notes that the parallel version of this statement in y. Ber. explicitly states the second half of the midrash. Lieberman notes, however, that most medieval commentators on the Berakhot passage do not confirm that reading. He suggests that the inclusion of the second half of the midrash is relatively late and was included in order to reconcile R. Abbahu's statement with the continuation of the sugya.

[15] The Yerushalmi interrogates the midrashic conclusion that tefillin are not worn at night, which is the explicit concern of R. Abbahu's statement.

[16] See MRSY, ed. Epstein and Melamed, 41.

But it is not written "throughout your days" [from which the same teaching can be derived]? This [apparent redundancy] can be resolved according to that which R. Yohanan said: Every matter which is not clear [in scripture], they support it from many places [in scripture]. (y. Eruv. 26a)

The Yerushalmi now presents a second midrash, which deduces the fact that tefillin are not worn on the Sabbath and holidays from the phrase "and it shall be a sign for you." It appears, however that the second midrash makes the exact same point as the first midrash. As noted above, the first midrash does not explicitly state that tefillin are not worn on the Sabbath and holidays. The first midrash explicitly states only that tefillin are not worn after nightfall. The surrounding context makes clear, however, that exegesis attested elsewhere (that the phrase "throughout your days" also precludes the wearing of tefillin on the Sabbath and holidays) is assumed here too.

The Yerushalmi regards the presence of two prooftexts for a single legal stipulation as troublesome. Why have two when one is sufficient to make the point? In order to resolve the difficulty of the redundant midrashim, the Yerushalmi calls on a teaching by R. Yohanan. He explains that when a matter is not "clear" or "self-evident" (מחוור) from scripture, it is useful to have more than one scriptural allusion. On the one hand, R. Yohanan's teaching helps resolve the problem of the apparently redundant scriptural allusions and so seems to support the midrashic conclusion that tefillin should not be worn on the Sabbath and holidays. On the other hand, the teaching also allows as the midrashic conclusion that tefillin are not worn on the Sabbath and holidays is not self-evident or "clear."

Throughout the rest of the sugya, the debate as to whether the midrashic allusion "is clear" (מחוור) is taken to be the critical issue at stake in the mishnaic debate between R. Gamaliel and the sages. For R. Gamaliel, the midrashic point "is clear," and tefillin are, therefore, not worn on the Sabbath. For the sages, the midrashic conclusion is not warranted, or "not clear," and tefillin, therefore, *should* be worn on the Sabbath.

After another short digression,[17] the Yerushalmi returns to its discussion of the mishnaic dispute between R. Gamaliel and the sages and connects it to the foregoing discussion of the scriptural basis for not wearing tefillin on the Sabbath.

הוו בעיי מימר: על דעתון דרבנן, אין מחוור; על דעתיה דרבן גמליאל, מחוור.

אמר רבי ירמיה בשם רבי שמואל: שיערו לומר עד מקום שגבהו של ראש מחזיק. וכמה מחזיק? שתים. מעתה אפילו בחול.

אמר רבי חגיי: אין בעי מיתב יהבו.

אמר רבי זריקא אסברי רב המנונא: עד מקום שמוחו של תינוק רופף.

---

[17] This digression will be discussed in the next chapter. In this part of the Yerushalmi's sugya, the discussion focuses on the scriptural basis for women's exemption from tefillin.

1. There are some who wish to say: In the view of the sages, [the scriptural source for the stipulation not to wear tefillin on the Sabbath and holidays] is not clear; whereas in the view of R. Gamaliel, [the scriptural source for the stipulation] is clear.

2. R. Yirmiah said in the name of R. Shmuel: Having taken a measurement, they stated [tefillin may be worn] in that space where the breadth of the head can accommodate [them]. And how many can be accommodated [in that space]? Two [tefillin].

3. If this is so, then even on weekdays [one could wear two].

4. R. Haggai said: If he wants to place [two], they give dispensation.

5. R. Zrika said: Rav Hamnuna explained: [One may wear tefillin only] in the place where the brain of a baby pulsates. (y. Eruv. 26a)

The gemara here offers two different explanations of the debate.[18] Paragraph 1 explains that the salient point of difference between the two interlocutors is their acceptance of the midrashic conclusions stated above. While R. Gamaliel accepts the midrashic conclusion that tefillin should not be worn on the Sabbath, the sages do not. For the sages, who say that tefillin *are* worn on the Sabbath, one may save tefillin only by wearing them in the prescribed manner, that is, one pair at a time. For R. Gamaliel, however, who does *not* believe that tefillin should be worn on the Sabbath, one need not wear tefillin in the ritually prescribed manner (i.e., one pair at a time). Thus, for R. Gamaliel two pairs at a time are perfectly acceptable.[19]

Paragraph 2 offers an alternate explanation for the tannaitic debate.[20] This second explanation of the debate takes the sages' view that only one pair of

---

[18] In seeing these two paragraphs as offering two explanations of the debate, I follow the reading of QE and Saul Lieberman, *Hayerushalmi kiphshuto*, vol. 1, 356.

[19] A few lines down in the sugya, two different intepretations of R. Gamaliel's position are offered. R. Yose suggests that R. Gamaliel permits wearing *only* two pairs at a time. In so doing, the wearer indicates that he is not wearing tefillin for the sake of fulfilling the commandment (so interpreted according to QE). Here, R. Gamaliel's belief that tefillin are not worn on the Sabbath is fundamental to the manner in which he considers it permissible to wear tefillin to save them. By way of contrast, R. Yose b. R. Bun understands R. Gamaliel differently. According to him, R. Gamaliel agrees with the sages that one may wear one pair at a time, but he adds that one may also wear two pairs at a time. In the interpretation of R. Yose b. R. Bun, Gamaliel's disagreement with the sages is not as extensive as it is according to the interpretation of R. Yose. See comments of R. Yose and R. Yose b. R. Bun on y. Eruv. 26a.

[20] QE and Lieberman understand R. Yirmiah as proposing an alternate way of understanding the dispute. The Bavli, however, attributes a different significance to the tradition that even during the weekday two pairs may be worn. It understands R. Yirmiah's tradition to be the basis on which Rabban Gamaliel allows two pairs of tefillin to be worn for the sake of saving them *on the Sabbath*. According to the Bavli, R. Gamaliel believes that one may wear tefillin on the Sabbath *only in the manner in which one regularly wears them on weekdays*. Therefore, R. Yirmiah's position is significant in that it allows for the fact that some people think that two pairs of tefillin are regularly worn on weekdays. It is important to note, however, that the Bavli uses R. Yirmiah's tradition differently than it is represented here. Here R. Yirmiah's tradition proposes a different reason for why R. Gamaliel would have disagreed with the sages. See b. Eruv. 95b. There the tradition that one may wear two pairs of tefillin during the weekdays is attributed to R. Shmuel b. R. Isaac.

tefillin can be worn for the sake of saving them on the Sabbath to be natural or self-evident. The text focuses its attention on understanding why R. Gamaliel permits two pairs at a time to be worn, which it takes to be the counterintuitive position. R. Yirmiah explains that the law actually permits one to wear *two* pairs of tefillin on the weekdays. The Yerushalmi here suggests a rationale for R. Gamaliel's position that permits two pairs on the Sabbath. Since two pairs are usually worn on the weekdays (for regular ritual observance of tefillin), two pairs are also permitted on the Sabbath (to save the tefillin from harm). Apparently the sages do not accept the tradition that one can wear two pairs of tefillin on weekdays. In their view, since only one pair is permitted on weekdays, one cannot wear two pairs on the Sabbath (even if one's intent is to save them from harm). This second explanation of the dispute appears to be rejected, however, when the gemara cites R. Zrika's position that the space where one may place tefillin is very limited (to the area in which the brain of a baby pulsates).[21] Apparently, there is not broad consensus that regular ritual observance of tefillin allows for two pairs.

In the last move of the sugya, the gemara tries to reconcile a related baraita with the mishnaic debate. The baraita states that women, as well as men, may employ the procedure of wearing tefillin to bring them in from an exposed site. The Tosephta records the following version of the baraita.

המוציא תפילין מכניסן זוג זוג
רבן גמליאל אומר שנים שנים
אחד האיש אחד האשה,
אחד חדשות ואחד ישנות.
ר' יהודה אוסר בחדשות ומתיר בישנות.

1. He who brings in tefillin [on the Sabbath] wears them one pair at a time.

2. R. Gamaliel says: two pairs at a time.

3. It is the same for men and women.

4. It is the same for old and new [tefillin].

5. R. Yehudah prohibits [the procedure] with new [tefillin], but permits it with old ones. (t. Eruv. 11:14)

Lines 1 and 2 of the baraita cite the two opinions already familiar to us from the Mishnah.[22] The anonymous sages permit the procedure of wearing tefillin to

---

[21] It is also possible that R. Zrika's position is cited as the basis for the sages' view. In that case, the debate between R. Gamaliel and the sages would mirror the debate between R. Yirmiah and R. Zrika.

[22] Saul Lieberman, *The Tosefta Ki-Fshutah: A Comphrehensive Commentary on the Tosefta*, vol. 1, 462, notes that two different versions of the baraita are attested. In MS Leiden and MS Erfurt, the first two lines appear as I have cited them here and as found in the Mishnah. In the printed edition and Geniza fragments, line two is attributed to R. Yehudah. Since both Talmuds assume the version of the baraita cited here, I use it as the basis for my discussion.

save them on the Sabbath one pair at a time. R. Gamaliel permits the procedure two pairs at a time. Lines 3–5 offer new information not found in the mishnaic version of the debate, and it is here that the Yerushalmi's interest in the baraita is focused. Line 3 states that women, as well as men, may perform the procedure of wearing tefillin in order to save them on the Sabbath. Lines 4–5 record a second debate about using the procedure to save new, as well as old, tefillin.

As preserved in the Tosephta, the attribution of line 3 (which extends permission to women to perform the procedure) is unclear.[23] On the one hand, the phrase equating women with men may be a continuation of R. Gamaliel's dictum from line 2. If so, then R. Gamaliel permits not only men to carry tefillin two pairs at a time, but women too. On the other hand, line 3 may represent a new statement of the anonymous majority. In that case, lines 1, 3, and 4 should all be attributed to the anonymous majority opinion. Lines 2 and 5 indicate local points of disagreement with the majority opinion. While R. Gamaliel (line 2) disagrees on the number of pairs that can be worn, R. Yehudah (line 5) disagrees with the permission that the sages extend to new tefillin. According to the second interpretation, all parties agree that women are regarded just like men in this matter, since the words are recorded in the voice of the anonymous majority. Both interpretations are equally legitimate on the basis of the text as it is preserved in the Tosephta.

The final segment of the Yerushalmi's discussion uses logic to attribute the ambiguous line 3 of the baraita to R. Gamaliel.

תני: אחד האיש ואחד האשה

הוון בעיי מימר מאן דמר מחוור הוא ניחא,

מאן דמר אינו מחוור, לא יהא מחוור אצל האיש, ויהא מחוור אצל האשה?

אמר רבי לעזר: מאן תנא אשה? רבן גמליאל.

It was taught [in a baraita]: It is the same for a man as for a woman (= t. Eruv. 11:14)

They could say that this baraita makes sense for he who holds that [the scriptural stipulation not to wear tefillin on the Sabbath] is clear.

However, for he who holds that [the scriptural stipulation not to wear tefillin on the Sabbath] is unclear, why would it be *unclear* for a man [who is commanded to wear tefillin for the purpose of saving in the manner in which he wears them for the sake of observance], but *clear* for a woman [who is commanded to wear tefillin for the purpose of saving in a manner in which she does *not* wear them to fulfill ritual observance]?

R. Elazar said: Who taught that women [may also wear tefillin to save them on the Sabbath]?

[Only] R. Gamaliel. (y. Eruv. 26a)

---

[23] Saul Lieberman, *The Tosefta Ki-Fshutah: A Comphrehensive Commentary on the Tosefta*, vol. 1, 462, is inclined to attribute line 3 to the anonymous majority.

The Yerushalmi initially assumes that all parties regard women like men in the matter of wearing tefillin on the Sabbath in order to save them.[24] That is, the Yerushalmi initially pursues the second of the two possible interpretations of baraita. The Yerushalmi observes, however, that though the stipulation that women, along with men, wear tefillin to save them accords well with R. Gamaliel's position, it leads to an internal contradiction in the sages' position. It will be recalled that in the Yerushalmi's view, *R. Gamaliel holds that men are not required to wear tefillin on the Sabbath.* Accordingly, for him, the law *does* treat men as it treats women. Like men, women are not permitted to wear tefillin on the Sabbath (for women, however, the prohibition applies during the weekdays too). Sharing the attribute of not being required to wear tefillin on the Sabbath, both men and women may wear them on the Sabbath for the specific purpose of saving them from the elements.

The baraita that equates men with women does not, however, accord well with the view of the sages who hold that men *should* wear tefillin on the Sabbath. The Yerushalmi suggests that it would be nonsensical for the sages to conclude that women, like men, can wear tefillin for the purpose of saving them on the Sabbath. An analogy between women and men is simply not possible for them, because, according to them, men save tefillin by *conforming* to the regular practice of wearing tefillin on the Sabbath, while women would save tefillin by *diverging* from their usual status as non–tefillin wearers. Men, who *are* required to wear tefillin on the Sabbath, have nothing in common with women, who are *not* required to wear tefillin on the Sabbath (or ever, for that matter). Line 3 of the baraita, then, cannot be reconciled with the sages' point of view. The gemara resolves this problem by attributing the view that equates women with men to R. Gamaliel exclusively. Given the inherent ambiguity of the baraita, the use of logic to resolve the question of attribution is not altogether inappropriate.

Here the Yerushalmi concludes its discussion of the tannaitic dispute between R. Gamaliel and his anonymous interlocutor on the matter of bringing in tefillin on the Sabbath. Though the gemara offers an additional interpretation of the dispute along the way, the preferred understanding is that R. Gamaliel and the sages disagree on the question of whether tefillin should be worn on the Sabbath. Though the gemara mentions traditions that restrict wearing tefillin to daytime hours, these traditions do not receive any extended treatment in the course of the sugya. For the Yerushalmi, then, the tannaitic dispute is *not* an occasion for discussing the timebound character of tefillin generally, but only the question of whether tefillin are worn on the Sabbath. Since the anonymous sages hold that tefillin *are* worn on the Sabbath, they allow one to save tefillin by wearing them in the regularly prescribed manner (i.e., one pair at a time). By way of contrast, since R. Gamaliel holds that tefillin are *not* worn on the

---

[24] So says Saul Lieberman, *Hayerushalmi kiphshuto*, vol. 1, 357.

Sabbath, he allows irregular ways of wearing the tefillin when donning them for the sake of saving them (i.e., two pairs at a time).

It is important to note that the Yerushalmi attributes a theoretical consistency to R. Gamaliel's position. When seeking to save tefillin on the Sabbath, R. Gamaliel allows one to wear them *only* in the manner in which they are *not* worn to fulfill the ritual command. Women, who are not generally obligated to wear tefillin, may wear them for the sake of saving them on the Sabbath. Men also, who are not obligated to wear tefillin on the Sabbath, wear two pairs; they thus distinguish "Sabbath-saving" wearing from weekday wearing for the sake of ritual observance. For R. Gamaliel, if one wears tefillin to save them on the Sabbath, *one should do so in a manner that distinguishes it from regular weekday observance of the ritual.* (Men distinguish Sabbath wearing for the sake of saving by wearing two, rather than the usual, one pair. Women distinguish Sabbath wearing for the sake of saving by wearing tefillin at all, since they are usually exempt from wearing tefillin.) For the Yerushalmi, only the sages, who regard the Sabbath as a time for ritual observance of tefillin, say that when seeking to save them, tefillin must be worn just as they are for ritual observance. For the sages, men may only wear one pair at a time because that is how tefillin are usually worn. On the basis of a similar logic, the sages prohibit women from wearing tefillin to save them because women do not wear tefillin as a regular ritual observance.

Observing the internal logic that the Yerushalmi attributes to R. Gamaliel's and the sages' positions allows us to see the Bavli's interpretation in sharp relief. As we will see momentarily, the Bavli is fundamentally uncomfortable with the idea that R. Gamaliel allows tefillin to be worn on Sabbath in a manner in which they are not regularly worn for the purposes of ritual observance. This discomfort leads the Bavli to read many of the sources and positions we have found in the Yerushalmi differently than the Yerushalmi does. Though the Bavli has access to many of the same sources as the Yerushalmi, it organizes the sources and arguments in different ways and uses them to reach different conclusions. Most importantly, the Bavli attributes the ambiguous line of the baraita to the anonymous sages (rather than to R. Gamaliel, as in the Yerushalmi). Additionally, the Bavli uses the baraita as tannaitic evidence for the view that tefillin are not timebound.

Finally, it is worth noting that most of the Yerushalmi's exegetical attention is focused on R. Gamaliel, who holds that tefillin may be worn two at a time for the sake of saving them on the Sabbath. The sages' view is apparently self-evident to the Yerushalmi since tefillin are usually worn one pair at time. For the Yerushalmi, it is R. Gamaliel's opinion that seems odd and in need of explanation. When we turn to the Bavli, we will see that equal exegetical attention is paid to both the anonymous sages' view and R. Gamaliel's view. Whereas the Yerushalmi's driving question is why wear two pairs, the Bavli's driving question inquires into the *source* of the sages' view that tefillin are worn on the Sabbath. The Yerushalmi has an answer to that question that proves unacceptable for the Bavli. The Yerushalmi offers no concrete source for the sages' view that tefillin are worn on the Sabbath; it simply says that the sages *do not accept* the midrashic derivation of the prohibition against wearing tefillin on the Sabbath. For them, the midrashic conclusion that tefillin are not worn on the Sabbath is "not clear." The Yerushalmi is perfectly comfortable with a negative argument: The sages reject a proposed midrash. The Bavli, on the other hand, requires that the sages support their view with a positive argument in favor of their position. The Bavli repeatedly attempts to locate an authoritative textual source for the sages' position that tefillin *are* worn on the Sabbath. The Bavli uses whatever sources it can muster to ground the position, borrowing many of them from the Yerushalmi's sugya.[25] These sources are, however, read in new ways. It is in this context that the Bavli rereads the baraita equating women with men as evidence for the view that tefillin are not timebound.

The Bavli on m. Eruvin 10:1

The Bavli's discussion of m. Eruv. 10:1 includes many of the sources and arguments that appear in the Yerushalmi's discussion of the same. Most fundamentally, the two Talmuds share the conclusion that the mishnaic dispute between R. Gamaliel and his anonymous interlocutor arises because the two parties have different views on the question of whether tefillin should be worn on the Sabbath.[26] In addition, they cite a number of the same sources and arguments. They both cite the tannaitic midrashim (without attributing them to tannaitic sources) on Exod 13:9–10 restricting tefillin observance to daytime hours and weekdays. They both propose an argument in which R. Gamaliel's opinion can be explained with recourse to a position that two pairs of tefillin are worn on the weekdays. Likewise, both know of the tradition that head tefillin should worn only in the area of the head where a baby's brain pulsates. Both also cite a tannaitic source (not discussed above) that Michal bat Kushi[27] wore tefillin without rabbinic censorship. Finally, both Talmuds cite the baraita that both men and women are allowed to employ the procedure of wearing tefillin on the Sabbath in order to save them.

---

[25] For the sake of a streamlined discussion, this chapter does not treat all of the parallels between the Yerushalmi and the Bavli. Several other elements of the Yerushalmi's discussion are picked up by the Bavli and worthy of note. Most significantly, a baraita about Michal bat Kushi (known in the Yerushalmi as Michal bat Shaul) is cited in both the Bavli and Yerushalmi, although put to different uses in each Talmud. The Bavli tries to use the baraita as evidence for the view that tefillin are not worn on the Sabbath, but this attempt fails.

[26] See Saul Lieberman, *The Tosefta Ki-Fshutah: A Comprehensive Commentary on the Tosefta*, vol. 1, 463, and David Weiss Halivni, *Sources and Traditions: A Source Critical Commentary on Tractate Eruvin and Pesahim* (Hebrew), 247, who notes the same thing.

[27] The Yerushalmi knows her as Michal bat Shaul. See y. Eruv. 26a. The earliest attestation of the tradition is in the Mek, Bo 17, ed. Horowitz, 68 (the midrash on Exod 13:9–10).

In spite of the common material, the Bavli differs from the Yerushalmi in its conclusions on two fundamental issues. First, the Bavli understands R. Gamaliel's position that two pairs can be worn on the Sabbath for the purposes of saving to be rooted in his belief that two pairs are *also* worn on weekdays. It will be recalled that the Yerushalmi understood R. Gamaliel in exactly the opposite manner. According to the Yerushalmi, R. Gamaliel allows two pairs of tefillin on the Sabbath precisely because that is *not* how they are worn on weekdays. By way of contrast, the Bavli concludes that R. Gamaliel allows two pairs on the Sabbath only if that is how they are worn on weekdays. Second, whereas the Yerushalmi attributes to R. Gamaliel the curious statement in the tosephtan baraita that women, like men, may employ this procedure, the Bavli attributes it to R. Gamaliel's anonymous interlocutor. How did the Bavli reach such different conclusions when it apparently had many of the materials available to the Yerushalmi?[28] I will argue the main difference between the two Talmuds concerns the extent to which the Bavli seeks to organize its inherited sources into a coherent system.[29] The post-amoraic sages responsible for the latest redactional layer of the Bavli sought to expose (or impose) consistency within and among its sources in a manner in which the Yerushalmi did not.[30] The Bavli's interest in exposing the systemacity of a network of related but diverse traditions provides the impetus for its unprecedented, and even revolutionary, interpretations. Importantly, these forces result in the production of a new tradition that tefillin are not timebound.

The Bavli begins its discussion of the mishnaic debate by examining the view of R. Gamaliel's interlocutor. As noted above, the Yerushalmi focuses most of its exegetical attention on R. Gamaliel's position because his is the view that seems counterintuitive and in need of explanation. The Bavli's interest in the view of the anonymous interlocutor seems to be motivated by a desire to treat matters systematically. The Bavli begins by clarifying the relationship between the anonymous interlocutor in m. Eruv. 10:1 and another anonymous mishnaic

---

[28] Irrespective of whether the Bavli had access to the Yerushalmi as we know it, it is possible to use the Yerushalmi to reconstruct the kind of raw materials ("early *talmud*") the Bavli had available to it. Current scholarly consensus suggests that the Bavli did not have access to the Yerushalmi as we know it. See Sussmann, "Once More on y. Nezikin" (Hebrew), esp. 98–99, and Shamma Friedman, "Literary Development and Historicity in the Aggadic Narrative: A Study Based Upon B.M. 83b–86a." Most recently, Gray, "A Talmud in Exile: The Influence of PT Avodah Zarah on the Formation of BT Avodah Zarah," argues that the Bavli did have access to the Yerushalmi.

[29] We are able to perceive these distinctive qualities in the Bavli precisely because we have undertaken a thorough analysis of the Yerushalmi, thereby highlighting how the Bavli treated and manipulated its raw source materials.

[30] As noted by Moscovitz, *Talmudic Reasoning*, 355, and Goldenberg, "The Talmud," 150–53. Closely related is the tendency of the post-amoraic stratum to conceptualize legal notions in a more inclusive, abstract manner than do earlier rabbinic sources. On this see De Vries, *Toldot Hahalakhah Hatalmudit*, 142–55; Jeffrey Rubenstein, "On Some Abstract Concepts"; and Moscovitz more generally.

tradition treating similar matters. The Bavli's discussion tries to account for and explain an apparent inconsistency between the two traditions.

לימא תנן סתמא דלא כרבי מאיר,

דאי כרבי מאיר האמר לובש כל מה שיכול ללבוש ועוטף כל מה שיכול לעטוף,

דתנן: ולשם מוציא כל כלי תשמישו, ולובש כל מהשיכול ללבוש, ועוטף כל מה שיכול לעטוף.

וההיא סתמא. ממאי דרבי מאיר היא?

דקתני עלה: לובש ומוציא ופושט ולובש ומוציא ופושט, אפילו כל היום כולו, דברי ר"מ.

1. Let us assume that the anonymous portion of the mishnah is not in accordance with R. Meir, for did not R. Meir say the following [which contradicts the anonymous portion of our mishnah]: One may wear as many clothes as clothes as one can wear and one may wrap oneself in whatever one can wrap around oneself [in order to carry them to safety from a fire on the Sabbath].

2. As it was taught: One may bring out all utensils to [the nearest courtyard out of reach from the fire], and one may wear as many clothes as one can at a time, and one may wrap oneself in whatever one may wrap. (= m. Shab. 16:4)

3. But this is [also] an anonymous mishnah. On what basis does it represent the teaching of R. Meir?

4. For a baraita was taught in connection with it: He puts on clothes, takes them out, undresses, puts on clothes, takes them out and undresses [as many times as he needs to], even all day long. These are the words of R. Meir. (b. Eruv. 95b)

The working assumption of the Bavli in this section is that any mishnah that is cited anonymously represents the teaching of R. Meir.[31] With this as a starting point, it makes sense to conclude that R. Gamaliel's anonymous interlocutor is R. Meir. The gemara questions this conclusion, however, because this anonymous mishnah is not consistent with material that is attributed to R. Meir elsewhere.[32] M. Shab. 16:4 states anonymously (and the gemara naturally attributes the material to R. Meir; see lines 3 and 4) that one may wear as many layers of clothing as one can at a time in order to carry them to safety from a fire on the Sabbath. Whereas the anonymous opinion in m. Eruv. 10:1 limits tefillin wearing to one pair, the anonymous opinion in m. Shab. 16:4 allows a limitless number of clothes to be worn for essentially the same purpose. Given this contradiction, it seems that the usual attribution of anonymous mishnaic opinions to R. Meir is not warranted in our case (= m. Eruv. 10:1).

---

[31] Strack-Stemberger notes that R. Meir "undoubtedly stands behind many anonymous halakhot [in the Mishnah]." Strack and Stemberger, *Introduction to the Talmud and Midrash*, 147. This principle that "the anonymous voice in the Mishnah is that of R. Meir" is first articulated explicitly by the early talmudic commentators (the Rishonim).

[32] David Weiss Halivni, "Sources and Traditions: A Source Critical Commentary on Tractate Eruvin and Pesahim" (Hebrew), 245, notes that several medieval commentators are disturbed by the gemara's question that R. Meir might not be the author of this mishnah, because a baraita cited at the very end of the sugya makes clear that R. Meir is the author of this position.

Rava resolves the problem by showing that the two anonymous opinions are compatible. He exposes the common logic that underlies both statements.

אמר רבא: אפילו תימא רבי מאיר

התם, דרך מלבושו כחול שוויה רבנן

והכא, דרך מלבושו כחול שוויה רבנן.

התם, דבחול כמה דבעי לביש, לענין הצלה נמי שרו ליה רבנן.

הכא, דבחול נמי זוג אחד אין, תפי לא, לענין הצלה נמי, זוג אחד אין, תפי לא.

1. Rava said: You can conclude that [the anonymous opinion in m. Eruv. 10:1 represents] R. Meir [and resolve the contradiction between his two statements in the following manner:]

2. There [in m. Shab. 16:4], the sages modeled [the manner in which he may dress on the Sabbath in order to save items] on the manner in which he is accustomed to dressing on the weekdays.

3. Here [too], the sages modeled the manner [the manner in which he may dress on the Sabbath in order to save items] on the manner in which is accustomed to dressing on the weekdays.

4. There, since one may wear as many layers of clothing as one wishes on the weekdays, the sages likewise permitted [as many layers of clothing as one wishes] for the purposes of saving.

5. Here, since one may wear one pair [of tefillin] and not two on the weekdays, the sages permitted one pair and not two for the purposes of saving. (b. Eruv. 95b)

Rava notes the common rationale that underlies both mishnaic statements, thereby making it reasonable for them to be the product of the same sage. According to Rava, both mishnaic statements permit one to wear items on the Sabbath for the purposes of saving them by wearing them *in the manner in which they are regularly worn on weekdays*. Since one may wear as many layers of clothing as one wishes on weekdays, one is permitted to wear as many layers of clothing as one wishes to save them from a fire on the Sabbath. Likewise, since one wears only one pair of tefillin on weekdays, one may wear only one pair on the Sabbath to retrieve them from an exposed site. The anonymous opinions are found to be consistent, and the Bavli concludes that the anonymous opinion in m. Eruv. 10:1 (like that of m. Shab. 16:4) represents the view of R. Meir.

Even at this early point in the Bavli's discussion, it is possible to detect several tendencies that distinguish its interpretation of this mishnah from the Yerushalmi's. First, the Bavli is proactive in seeking out related sources from within the tannaitic corpus and in trying to harmonize them as part of a single, coherent system.[33] The Bavli seeks to demonstrate the mutual compatibility

---

33 Note Hayes's discussion of this tendency: Christine Elizabeth Hayes, *Between the Babylonian and Palestinian Talmuds: Accounting for Halakhic Difference in Selected Sugyot from Tractate Avodah Zarah*, 105–6. "The rabbis clearly hold that mishnaic traditions are fully explicated

between seemingly contradictory traditions. Second, the Bavli is interested in identifying the personages behind anonymous mishnaic teachings. The Bavli is heir to a tradition that anonymous teachings represent the views of R. Meir. By instantiating this tradition in two separate cases (m. Eruv. 10:1 and m. Shab. 16:4), the Bavli exposes the consistency of the Mishnah. The Bavli's interpretive work reveals the extent to which what appears to be a network of related but diverse traditions is in fact a coherent and systematic whole.

Finally, one additional aspect of the Bavli's discussion thus far is noteworthy. When Rava explains the common logic underlying both of "R. Meir's" teachings, he provides the sugya with a conceptual vocabulary that will prove to be influential throughout the rest of the sugya. Rava articulates the idea that the manner in which one wears items on the Sabbath to save them should mirror regular weekday wearing habits. It will be recalled that the Yerushalmi reasons that R. Gamaliel allows two pairs on the Sabbath precisely because that is *not* how they are worn during the weekdays. The Bavli, on the other hand, introduces the idea that *all* wearing of tefillin on the Sabbath for the purpose of saving must be patterned after regular weekday wearing.

The sugya continues by examining the position of R. Gamaliel. Initially, the Bavli seeks to clarify his views on the question of whether tefillin are worn on the Sabbath. It is likely that the Bavli is familiar with the Yerushalmi's framing of the dispute as a function of disagreement about whether tefillin are worn on the Sabbath. It appears the Bavli is trying to figure out whether the Yerushalmi's conclusion that "R. Gamaliel holds that tefillin are *not* worn on the Sabbath" is logically sound.[34]

מאי קסבר?

אי קסבר שבת זמן תפילין הוא, זוג אחד אין, וטפי לא.

ואי קסבר שבת לאו זמן תפילין הוא, ומשום הצלה דרך מלבוש שרו ליה רבנן אפילו טפי נמי.

לעולם קסבר שבת לאו זמן תפילין הוא וכי שרו רבנן הצלה לעניין דרך מלבוש במקום תפילין.

אי הכי, זוג אחד נמי אין, טפי לא.

אמר רב שמואל בר רב יצחק: מקום יש בראש להניח בו שתי תפילין.

1. What does [R. Gamaliel] hold?

2. If he holds that the Sabbath is a time for wearing tefillin, then he would permit one pair [of tefillin on the Sabbath for the purpose of saving], but not more.

only when placed alongside other mishnaic and rabbinic traditions that contradict them, qualify them expand them or otherwise affect them. As we shall see, the juxtaposition of traditions can lead to a new understanding of a mishnah, and ultimately to a halakhic shift" (106). In our discussion, the juxtaposition of traditions here is one part of a larger interpretive complex that leads to the construction of a new tradition that tefillin are not timebound.

34 Alyssa Gray discusses a phenomenon in parallel sugyot between the Yerushalmi and the Bavli in which the Bavli address a question that is provoked or left unresolved by the Yerushalmi's treatment of matters. See Gray, "A Talmud in Exile: The Influence of PT Avodah Zarah on the Formation of BT Avodah Zarah," 61–62, 84–85, 254–68.

3. But, if he holds that the Sabbath is not a time for wearing tefillin, then since the sages permitted one to save [tefillin on the Sabbath] by wearing them, even more [than two pairs] should be permitted.

4. The fact is that he holds that the Sabbath is not a time for wearing tefillin, [and he allows only two pairs, and not more] because the sages permitted wearing tefillin for the purpose of saving them only in the place where tefillin [are usually worn].

5. If this is so, then he should permit [only] one pair, and not more.

6. Rav Shmuel b. Rav Yitzhak said: There is enough room on the head to put two tefillin. (b. Eruv. 95b)

This sequence uses logic to try to figure out whether R. Gamaliel believes that tefillin should be worn on the Sabbath. On the one hand, logic dictates that one who holds that tefillin *are* worn on the Sabbath will allow only one pair when seeking to save them. Since tefillin are worn for the sake of ritual observance on the Sabbath, one must wear them in the manner in which they are worn for ritual observance, namely, one pair at a time. On the other hand, logic also dictates that one who holds that tefillin are *not* worn on the Sabbath will allow a limitless number of pairs to be worn. The problem is, however, that R. Gamaliel's position does not accord with either of these theoretical positions. Unlike the first position, he allows more than one pair, and unlike the second position, he limits his permission to two pairs only. In line 4, the gemara establishes that R. Gamaliel indeed believes that tefillin should not be worn on the Sabbath. He parts ways with the theoretical position that allows even more than two pairs (i.e., line 3) because he follows the sages' ruling that one may wear tefillin for the purposes of saving them only in the spot on the head where tefillin are usually worn.

Here we encounter an allusion to Rava's tradition that the sages permit wearing on the Sabbath for the sake of saving *only* if one mimics the regular weekday manner of wearing. The Bavli here assumes that tefillin are usually worn in a particular spot on the forehead and arm. This way of understanding R. Gamaliel's position, however, raises a question. If he permits wearing tefillin on the Sabbath for the purpose of saving them only when they are worn in the specially designated spots, then he should allow only one pair. Surely, there is enough room in the designated "tefillin" spot for only one pair. The gemara responds by citing a tradition from R. Shmuel b. R. Yitzhak that, in fact, the designated spot on the head has enough room for *two* pairs of tefillin.[35] R. Shmuel's statement provides a weekday precedent for wearing two pairs, thus providing a basis for R. Gamaliel's position allowing two pairs on the Sabbath.

---

[35] The gemara continues its discussion by seeking a source that indicates that there is also enough room on the arm for two pairs of tefillin. I will not cite this section of the argumentation, for the sake of brevity. Conceptually, it establishes the same point that is established here: namely, that there is a legal precedent for wearing two pairs of tefillin during the weekdays.

In this sequence we again see how the Bavli's interest in integrating diverse sources into a coherent whole shapes its interpretive work. Having used Rava's tradition stating that Sabbath wearing for the sake of saving should mirror weekday wearing to understand "R. Meir's" position, the Bavli now tries to square the same tradition with R. Gamaliel's view. The Bavli assumes that the tannaim work within a common framework of fundamental assumptions, even if they reach different conclusions about specific points of law. The common working assumption is the idea that when one wears tefillin on the Sabbath for the sake of saving, one should follow the pattern of regular weekday wearing of tefillin.

This assumption has interesting implications for the Bavli's understanding of R. Gamaliel's position. It will be recalled that the Yerushalmi understood R. Gamaliel's position to be grounded in his belief that tefillin worn on the Sabbath should be worn precisely as they are *not* worn on the weekdays. By imposing a certain kind of consistency (namely, that both "R. Meir" and R. Gamaliel developed their positions in the wake of the sages' permission to save items on the Sabbath by wearing them *only* in the manner of regular weekday wearing), the Bavli reaches the exact opposite conclusion about the rationale behind R. Gamaliel's position. The Bavli understands R. Gamaliel to hold (like "R. Meir") that Sabbath wearing must be modeled on weekday wearing. This assumption leads the Bavli to seek a weekday precedent for wearing two pairs, which it finds in the teaching of R. Shmuel b. Yitzhak (line 6). The Yerushalmi also knows of a tradition that two pairs can be worn on the weekday, but it uses this tradition in a different manner than the Bavli does. The Yerushalmi offers *two* different explanations for the mishnaic dispute between R. Gamaliel and the anonymous interlocutor. *Either* it could be understood to result from their different ideas about the observance of tefillin on the Sabbath *or* it could be understood to result from their different ideas about the permissibility of wearing two pairs of tefillin on the weekdays. For the Yerushalmi, these are two *different* ways of explaining the mishnaic dispute. By way of contrast, the Bavli integrates these two proposals into a *single* argument. R. Gamaliel's position is explained *both* by the fact that he holds that tefillin are not worn on the Sabbath *and* by the fact that he holds that one may wear two pairs of tefillin on the weekdays. For the Bavli, these two explanations work in consort. Here is yet another example of how the Bavli integrates the diverse materials it has inherited into a coherent and systematic whole.

Weaving together what for the Yerushalmi are *alternate* explanations has serious implications for how the Bavli understands the baraita allowing women, like men, to employ the procedure of wearing tefillin on the Sabbath in order to save them. It will be recalled that the Yerushalmi attributes this baraita to R. Gamaliel because it is consistent with his position that people are permitted to wear tefillin on the Sabbath for the purpose of saving them *only* if they wear them in a manner in which they are *not* usually worn. Women may wear tefillin on the Sabbath to save them because in doing so they *diverge* from their regular pattern of wearing tefillin (i.e., usually they do not wear tefillin). The Bavli's new way of understanding R. Gamaliel, however, makes it impossible for the Bavli to attribute the baraita equating women with men to R. Gamaliel. On the Bavli's read, R. Gamaliel models Sabbath wearing of tefillin on regular ritual wearing of tefillin. Since women do not wear tefillin on the weekdays, it makes no sense for them to wear tefillin on the Sabbath to save them. This series of interpretive shifts creates an opening for the Bavli to reattribute the line of the baraita equating men with women. As we saw when we examined the Tosephta's version of the baraita, there is genuine ambiguity as to who articulated that position.[36]

The final section of the sugya returns to "R. Meir's" position and seeks a source for his view that tefillin *are* worn on the Sabbath. I have found no genuine tannaitic sources that state that tefillin *should be worn on the Sabbath*.[37] The Yerushalmi resolved this problem by speculating that whereas R. Gamaliel *accepted* the conclusions of the tannaitic midrashim (there attributed to R. Abbahu, R. Elazar), the anonymous interlocutor *did not* accept them. *The Yerushalmi never provides an independent source indicating that tefillin should be worn on the Sabbath*. I would conjecture that Yerushalmi does not supply such a source because no such source ever existed. Tannaitic sources portray tefillin as the timebound commandment *par excellence*. By way of contrast, in keeping with the Bavli's generally documented desire to provide a comprehensive treatment of its sources, the Bavli feels it necessary to supply this position with authoritative textual support.[38]

---

[36] This ambiguity is present on the literary level insofar as the text equally supports two readings. It should be noted, however, that according to the conventions of tannaitic, halakhic literature, Lieberman assumes that the ambiguous line 3 of the baraita should be attributed to the anonymous sages who also speak in lines 1 and 4 of the sugya. Saul Lieberman, *The Tosefta Ki-Fshutah: A Comphrehensive Commentary on the Tosefta*, vol. 1, 462–63. Insofar as the Bavli attributes line 3 of the baraita to the same "speaker" as line 1, one could say that it offers the more intuitive reading of the baraita. The Bavli's methods of drawing its conclusions, however, are hardly intuitive.

[37] See also David Weiss Halivni, *Sources and Traditions: A Source Critical Commentary on Tractate Eruvin and Pesahim* (Hebrew), 248: "It appears that we have no tannaitic source that tefillin are worn on the Sabbath."

[38] David Weiss Halivni, *Sources and Traditions: A Source Critical Commentary on Tractate Eruvin and Pesahim* (Hebrew), 246–48, also discusses the Bavli's impulse to supply a source for this position and sees it as curious in light of the fact that no genuine tannaitic source exists to support this position. Furthermore, Halivni notes that the Bavli's conclusions (that the ambiguous line of the mishnah was stated by R. Meir and that it implies women's obligation to tefillin as a non-timebound commandment) contradict the stipulation of another anonymous mishnaic teaching (which, by the logic used in this sugya, should be attributed to R. Meir) that exempts women from wearing tefillin. Halivni resolves these problems by suggesting that the textual source supplied at the end of this sugya to support the view that "tefillin are worn on the Sabbath" was initially brought to support a statement by Rav Sifra, on a similiar subject, which can now be found in b. Shab. 62a. The following analysis deals with the same question that Halivni identifies, but offers a different kind of solution. The explanation offered here highlights

The Bavli considers a number of different sources, each of which it rejects for various reasons. In the end, the Bavli proposes that the baraita allowing women to perform the procedure of wearing tefillin to save them on the Sabbath is the origin of the view that tefillin *should* be worn on the Sabbath.

אלא האי תנא היא דתניא:
המוצא תפילין מכניסן זוג זוג, אחד האיש אחד האשה,אחד החדשות אחד הישנות, דברי ר"מ.
ר' יהודה אוסר בחדשות ומתיר בישנות.
ע"כ לא פליגי אלא בחדשות וישנות, אבל באשה לא פליגי.
שמע מינה מצות עשה שלא הזמן גרמה, וכל מצות שלא שומן גרמה – נשים חייבות.

1. Rather, it is this Tanna who teaches [that Shabbat is a time for tefillin observance], as it is taught in a baraita:

2. He who finds tefillin may bring them in one pair at a time, a man and a woman may equally [employ this procedure, and the procedure may be done with] both new and old [tefillin]. These are the words of R. Meir.

3. R. Yehudah prohibits [the procedure] with new [tefillin], but permits it with old [tefillin].

4. If this is [what they said], then their argument is limited to the subject of new and old [tefillin]. But they did not argue about women.

5. Learn from this that [they both think] that [tefillin] is a positive commandment *not* occasioned by time, and women are required to perform positive commandments *not* occasioned by time. (b. Eruv. 96b)

According to the Bavli's interpretation of the baraita, the ambiguous third line of the baraita is stated by the same anonymous voice that states the first line (whom the Bavli understands to be R. Meir). With that assumption in mind, the Bavli reads the baraita as follows: The Bavli focuses on the fact that there is only one dispute in the second half of baraita. The final line of the baraita (in which R. Yehudah expresses the view that the procedure may be used only with old tefillin) is understood to be the sole point of disagreement between R. Meir (from line 3 of the baraita) and R. Yehudah (in line 5 of the baraita). The Bavli, therefore, concludes that *both* accede to R. Meir's statement in line 3, namely they both allow women to wear tefillin in order to save them on the Sabbath. Furthermore, if these two sages (R. Meir and R. Yehudah) allow women to wear tefillin in order to save them on the Sabbath, then they must also allow women to wear them on weekdays. Recall: according to the Bavli, one may save items by wearing on the Sabbath *if and only if* one wears them in the manner in which they are regularly worn during the week. Accordingly,

the characteristic academic tendencies exhibited by the post-amoraic stratum of the Bavli and attributes the Bavli's odd exegetical conclusions to that activity. See also Alexander, *Transmitting Mishnah*, chapter 4, in which I try to explain the Bavli's counterintuitive conclusions by characteristic academic concerns rather than processes of breakdown or loss in the course of transmission (as per Halivni).

a source that allows women to wear tefillin on the Sabbath *must also assume* that women wear them on weekdays.

Finally, insofar as this interpretation of the baraita allows women to wear tefillin on the weekdays, it diverges from the familiar position that women are exempt from tefillin.[39] The Bavli is, of course, familiar with the rule from m. Kid. 1:7 that exempts women from timebound, positive commandments and turns to this rule in order to make sense of R. Meir's and R. Yehudah's unusual permissiveness with regard to women and tefillin. The Bavli concludes that the sages who allow women to wear tefillin do not consider it to be a timebound commandment. According to them, therefore, women are not exempt from tefillin. In this convoluted manner, the Bavli reaches its final conclusion that one who holds that women may wear tefillin on the Sabbath in order to save them *also thinks* that tefillin are not a timebound commandment.

In contrast to the dominant position that regards tefillin as a timebound commandment, R. Meir and R. Yehudah hold that tefillin should be worn at all times, regardless of the hour of the day or the time of the week or year. They also hold that tefillin should be worn on the Sabbath.[40] One repercussion of their view that the observance of tefillin is *not* occasioned by time is that they think that women *do* wear tefillin.

Admittedly, this argument makes *indirect* use of the baraita to substantiate the position that tefillin should be worn on the Sabbath. Nonetheless, it conforms to the general tendencies we have already noted with respect to the Bavli. First, the Bavli reaffirms Rava's tradition that Sabbath wearing for the sake of saving must be modeled on weekday wearing. Second, the Bavli remains interested in establishing the extent to which individual sages are consistent in their views on different issues. It will be recalled that the tosephtan version of the baraita does not attribute the words allowing women, as well as men, to wear tefillin on the Sabbath in order to save them. Since the Bavli finds them to be consistent with the position it has already established as that of R. Meir, it attributes them to him. The interesting new development is that the Bavli sees these words as evidence for the view that observance of tefillin is *not* occasioned by time. As I have argued throughout, this interpretation is prompted by the

---

[39] As noted above in n38, Halivni finds it very problematic that the Bavli ignores the fact that elsewhere in the Mishnah (m. Ber. 3:3) the anonymous sages (which according to the logic of this sugya should be attributed to R. Meir) state explicitly that women are exempt from tefillin. See his discussion in David Weiss Halivni, "Sources and Traditions: A Source Critical Commentary on Tractate Eruvin and Pesahim" (Hebrew), 248.

[40] For the sake of brevity, I have not included a discussion of the final section of the argument establishing that R. Meir and R. Yehudah hold that tefillin are positive commandments *not* occasioned by time. The final stage of the argument considers the possibility that these two sages *permit* women to wear tefillin, but do not require them to do so. This possibility is rejected by showing that it is inconsistent with R. Meir's and R. Yehudah's views elsewhere. Again, we see the Bavli's interest in showing the consistency within the views of individual sages on diverse matters. See Goldenberg, "The Talmud," 150, 153, who notes this interest on the part of the Bavli.

Bavli's interest in organizing its inherited sources and showing them to be part of a coherent and systematic legal whole.

When we review our analysis, we find the following. In the very beginning of its discussion, the Bavli refers to a tradition that permits one to wear items to save them on the Sabbath if and only if they are worn as they are during on weekdays. Establishing the fact that both R. Gamaliel and his anonymous interlocutor were familiar with and accepted this tradition requires the Bavli to understand R. Gamaliel's position in a different way than the Yerushalmi had. Whereas the Yerushalmi assumes that R. Gamaliel permits two pairs of tefillin on the Sabbath precisely because they are *not* worn this way on weekdays, the Bavli has to account for R. Gamaliel's allowance of two pairs in a different way. Drawing on the alternate explanation of the debate from the Yerushalmi, the Bavli concludes that R. Gamaliel relies on a tradition that two pairs of tefillin are permitted on *weekdays also*. Interpreting R. Gamaliel's position in this manner disrupts the correspondence between his view on the number of tefillin that can be worn when saving them on the Sabbath and the baraita's view that women can employ the procedure as well. The Bavli is then free to reattribute the ambiguous line of the baraita as it sees fit.

The Bavli's concern to provide a comprehensive analysis of its sources moves it to consider a question that had remained outside of the purview of the Yerushalmi. Though both Talmuds agree that the dispute arises because of a fundamental disagreement over "whether the Sabbath is a time for tefillin," only the Bavli seeks a textual source for the view that tefillin are worn on the Sabbath. Since the baraita allowing women to employ the procedure is no longer viewed as compatible with R. Gamaliel's view, it is attributed to R. Meir and seen to be evidence for the position that women wear tefillin not only on the Sabbath, but also at all times. This series of interpretive accommodations produces the attribution to R. Meir and R. Yehudah that tefillin are a positive commandment *not* occasioned by time.

Conclusion

It is important to note that ideological concerns about gender are not responsible for the creation of a position allowing women to wear tefillin.[41] As I have

---

[41] Though my conclusions appear to agree with the argument put forward in Hauptman's *Rereading the Rabbis*, it is important to clarify where I differ. Hauptman observes that over the course of time, the rabbis exhibit an increased legal benevolence toward women, offering them more and more legal advantages. At first blush, the conclusion that the post-amoraic stratum constructed a position that stated that women were obligated to wear tefillin appears to conform to this pattern. I do not believe, however, that this view was ever anything but academic. Its relevance was only to be found among rabbis who debated the interpretation of sources. In her review of the history of rabbinic atttitudes toward women wearing tefillin, Aliza Berger does not even mention this source, suggesting that it had no practical implications. See Aliza Berger, "Wrapped Attention: May Women Wear Tefillin," in *Jewish Legal Writings by Women*, ed.

argued throughout this chapter, the major force compelling the Bavli's articulation of this position is its interest in organizing its sources into a coherent and integrated legal system. It is these concerns, and not gender ideological ones, that move the Bavli to reconceive the rationale behind R. Gamaliel's position. Redefining the rationale for R. Gamaliel's position leads the Bavli to attribute the baraita allowing women to wear tefillin to save them on the Sabbath to the anonymous interlocutor, whom the Bavli identifies as R. Meir. Additionally, the Bavli's dedication to providing a comprehensive analysis of its sources leads it to seek out a textual precedent for the view that tefillin are worn on the Sabbath. These concerns in concert bring about a series of interrelated shifts in the Bavli's understanding of the mishnaic dispute between R. Gamaliel and the sages, or "R. Meir." In the context of understanding the dispute in new ways, the view that observance of tefillin is not occasioned by time comes to be attributed to R. Meir and R. Yehudah. Though I do not believe that these sages ever historically held this view, the Bavli's belief that they did has a significant impact on the way in which it treats the topic of timebound, positive commandments. By severing the relationship between timeboundedness and tefillin, the Bavli affirms that the category of timebound, positive commandments has an existence and relevance beyond its descriptive function with respect to tefillin. Freeing the category of timebound, positive commandments from their historic tie with tefillin opens up the possibility of seeing the rule as prescriptive principle, governed by a patriarchal social vision of gender relations.

Micah D. Halperin and Chana Safrai (Jerusalem: Urim Publications, 1998), 75–188. Additionally, I do not believe that the creation of this view was occasioned by concern with "real" women and their legal empowerment. Rather, as I have argued throughout this chapter, I believe that the creation of this permissive position with regard to women grew out of interpretive pressures forced by the Bavli's academic agenda.

4

Shifting Orthodoxies

In the last chapter I concluded that ideological concerns about gender were not responsible for the creation of a new position in the Bavli requiring women to wear tefillin. I argued instead that the Bavli's interest in shaping the diverse legal sources it inherited into a coherent system triggered a series of interpretive shifts that *indirectly* resulted in the attribution of the view that tefillin are *not* a timebound, positive commandment to R. Meir and R. Yehudah. In this chapter I would like to interrogate this conclusion and push it a little bit further. After all, the sages who produced the interpretation discussed in the previous chapter were surely familiar with another anonymous mishnah that exempts women from wearing tefillin. M. Ber. 3:3 stipulates that "women, slaves and minors are exempt from recitation of the Shema and observance of tefillin." If the Bavli was so interested in achieving systematic consistency among its inherited sources, why did it not take into account this teaching, which clearly states women's exemption from tefillin?[1] The fact that this mishnah is also transmitted anonymously only deepens the question. Following the Bavli's presumption that all anonymous teachings in the Mishnah reflect the teachings of R. Meir, this mishnah should be attributed to R. Meir just as the anonymous mishnahs discussed in the previous chapter were. If, as I argued in the previous chapter, the Bavli was so interested in weaving its inherited sources into a coherent whole, why did it not discuss the problems that m. Ber. 3:3, with its *exemption* of women from tefillin practice, raises for m. Eruv. 10:1 and t. Eruv.

---

[1] Halivni is very troubled by this very question. See David Weiss Halivni, *Sources and Traditions: A Source Critical Commentary on Tractate Eruvin and Pesahim* (Hebrew), 248. His analysis provides a text-critical solution to the problem, suggesting that a splicing process involving two originally discrete discussions produced the odd source that contradicts m. Ber. 3:3.

11:14, which it understands to reflect R. Meir's and R. Yehudah's position that women are *obligated* in tefillin practice?

I will argue that the Bavli's disregard for this question is best understood as the result of a shifting set of orthodoxies. Whereas the Yerushalmi's primary orthodoxy concerns women's exemption from tefillin, the Bavli's primary orthodoxy concerns women's exemption from timebound, positive commandments. Each Talmud makes the sources available to it conform to the position it regards as an orthodoxy. It appears that the idea that women are exempt from tefillin is not an orthodoxy for the Bavli. The Bavli feels that there are *other* matters on which it cannot be flexible. Apparently, it is more important for the Bavli to demonstrate fidelity to these other principles than to confirm m. Ber. 3:3's stance that women are exempt from tefillin.

What occasioned this shift in priorities for the Bavli? Some may wonder if historical conditions impacted the Bavli in this matter. Is it possible that women were wearing tefillin in Sassanian Babylonia and the editors of this sugya sought a legal precedent for this activity? For women who seek a traditional precedent for the wearing of tefillin today, this is a tantalizing possibility.[2] Given the available evidence, however, I do not feel that such a conclusion is warranted. I am inclined to think that Bavli's permissiveness with regard to the traditional exemption of women from tefillin is a product of a shift in the perception of *where the law is flexible and where it is inflexible*.

For the Yerushalmi, the stipulation that women are exempt from tefillin is an orthodoxy; all interpretations of antecedent sources must affirm this principle. The Yerushalmi's interpretation of R. Gamaliel and his anonymous interlocutor takes their acceptance of women's exemption from tefillin for granted. The Bavli, on the other hand, understands women's exemption from the *category of timebound, positive commandments* to be an orthodoxy. That is, the Bavli is more concerned with showing how all legal positions are consistent with the *rule* of women's exemption from the category. For the Bavli, the question of which commandments are considered to be timebound is *secondary*. Apparently, there is some flexibility about which commandments get included in the category, as evidenced by the Bavli's willingness to ignore m. Ber. 3:3 and invent a position that obligates women to observe the ritual of tefillin. What is

---

[2] See, e.g., Aliza Berger, "Wrapped Attention: May Women Wear Tefillin." She examines the talmudic and post-talmudic sources that discuss women wearing tefillin and interrogates the contemporary halakhic conclusion that women may not wear tefillin. I admit to having been surprised that Berger did not cite R. Yehudah and R. Meir's position (discussed in the previous chapter) that tefillin are not timebound and therefore are an obligatory practice for women. Her disregard of this potential precedent for a position she wishes to bolster suggests to me how completely marginalized R. Meir's and R. Yehudah's position became in the post-talmudic history of interpretation. It is interesting that the post-talmudic decisors responsible for making pragmatic decisions about women's ritual engagement of tefillin seem to have completely ignored the position.

most important for the Bavli is that the rule itself be shown to be consistently applied.

This way of accounting for the Bavli's flexibility on the issue of women's exemption from tefillin actually strengthens the thesis promoted in the previous chapter. There I argued that the Bavli's legal interpretation distinguishes itself from the Yerushalmi's in the degree to which it seeks to expose the coherence of its diverse sources within a systematic whole. In this chapter, we see an additional manifestation of this tendency. Whereas the Yerushalmi affirms the authority of discrete traditions (i.e., the specific stipulation that women are exempt from tefillin), the Bavli affirms the overarching principles that provide an organizational structure for discrete traditions.[3] Apparently, the Bavli is more invested in the strong organizational scheme provided by the rule than the individual stipulations explained by it.

The Yerushalmi's Orthodoxy: Women's Exemption from Tefillin

The Yerushalmi's fundamental commitment to the position that women are exempt from tefillin is in evidence on two different occasions during its discussion of m. Eruv. 10:1. The first occasion arrives fairly early in the sugya. It will be recalled that the first section of the sugya brings a series of traditions debating the timebound character of tefillin. Though some sources stipulate that tefillin be worn only during daytime hours and weekdays, others suggest that tefillin may be worn at night. After the initial presentation of sources on the timebound character of tefillin, the Yerushalmi offers the following:

נשים מניין?

ולמדתם אתם את בניכם, ולא בנותיכם.

החייב בתורה חייב בתפילין; נשים שאין חייבות בתורה אין חייבות בתפילין.

התיבון: הרי מיכל בת שאול היתה לובשת תפילין, אשת יונה היתה עולה לרגל, ולא מיחו בידם חכמים.

רבי חזקיה בשם רבי אבהו: אשתו של יונה היא שבי, מיכל בת שאול מיחו בה חכמים.

1. From where do we learn women's [exemption from tefillin]?

2. *And you shall teach them [words of Torah] to your sons,* (Deut 11:19) and not daughters.

One who is obligated [to study] Torah, is obligated to wear tefillin.

Women, who are not obligated [to study] Torah, are not obligated to wear tefillin.

3. They replied: But behold there was the case of Michal b. Shaul who used to wear tefillin, and the wife of Yonah used to participate in the pilgrimages [which the Torah stated was an obligation for men only]. And the sages did not object.

---

[3] See Goldberg, "The Babylonian Talmud," 329–31; De Vries, *Toldot Hahalakhah Hatalmudit,* 142–56; Ephraim E. Urbach, *The Halakhah: Its Sources and Development,* 177–205; Moscovitz, *Talmudic Reasoning*; and Jeffrey Rubenstein, "On Some Abstract Concepts."

4. R. Hizkiya in the name of R. Abbahu [explained]: It was the wife of Yonah [to whom the statement that they did not object] refers; the sages did object to Michal b. Shaul. (y. Eruv. 26a)

The Yerushalmi's question seeking a prooftext for women's exemption from tefillin appears to be a non sequitor. The material immediately preceding this citation reviews several sources on the timebound character of tefillin, some of which affirm this status and others of which cast doubt upon it. The question about the source for women's exemption from tefillin may arise because this discussion casts doubt on the related question of women's obligation regarding tefillin. The Yerushalmi seeks to affirm that irrespective of the outcome of the debate about tefillin's timebound character, women are nonetheless exempt from this commandment. In adopting this position, the Yerushalmi follows the tannaitic sources in exempting women from tefillin on the basis of their analogous character with Torah study.[4] Insofar as women are exempt from Torah study, they are exempt from tefillin too. Line 3 challenges the conclusion that women are exempt from tefillin by citing a tradition that tells of Michal b. Shaul, who apparently *did* wear tefillin, and furthermore the sages did not censure her behavior. R. Hizkiya offers a sharp rebuttal. He suggests that the concluding phrase, which states that "sages did not object," applies to the second anecdote only, about the wife of Yonah. Apparently, the sages *did* object to Michal b. Shaul.

In this section, then, the Yerushalmi affirms the traditional source for women's exemption from tefillin with an analogy to Torah study.[5] Just as women are exempt from Torah study, so too they are exempt from tefillin. Though the debate over tefillin's timebound character might cast doubt on its status vis-à-vis women's participation, the prooftext confirms their exemption. The prooftext also establishes the rationale for women's exemption from tefillin. As with the tannaitic sources discussed in Chapter 1, women are not exempt from tefillin because they (tefillin) are a timebound, positive commandment. Women are exempt from tefillin because tefillin practice is an analogue of Torah study. The Yerushalmi also responds to the confusion that could arise as a result of the existence of a tradition that Michal b. Shaul used to wear tefillin. Though some might read the tradition as implying that the sages permitted this behavior, the Yerushalmi affirms that they did not sanction it. The Yerushalmi consistently projects its assumption that according to Jewish law, women do not wear tefillin.[6]

---

[4] The basic rationale for women's exemption from tefillin is provided in y. Ber. 4c and 6a. See also Saul Lieberman, *Hayerushalmi Kifshuto*, vol. 1, 355, who notes the same association.

[5] Women's exemption from tefillin on the basis of an analogy with Torah study is also established in the following sources: Mek., ed. Horowitz., 68; MRSY, ed. Epstein and Melamed, 41; y. Ber. 4c and 6a; and b. Kid. 34b.

[6] See Saul Lieberman, *Hayerushalmi Kifshuto*, vol. 1, 355, who discusses the difficulties raised by the difference between the Yerushalmi's interpretation of this baraita and the Bavli's.

The Yerushalmi's commitment to the position that women are exempt from
tefillin can be seen again in its discussion of the baraita that allows women to
wear tefillin on the Sabbath for the purpose of retrieving them from an exposed
site. It will be recalled that the Yerushalmi initially assumes that the baraita
represents the view of both R. Gamaliel and his anonymous interlocutor. In-
depth analysis, however, reveals that the baraita is not compatible with the
view of the anonymous interlocutor (the sages). As we will see, this analysis is
grounded in the assumption that women do not perform the ritual of tefillin.

The relevant text reads as follows:

הוו בעי מימר: על דעתון דרבנן, אין מחוור; על דעתיה דר' אחא, מחוור . . .

תני: אחד האיש ואחד האשה

הוון בעיי מימר מאן דמר מחוור הוא ניחא,

מאן דמר אינו מחוור, לא יהא מחוור אצל האיש, ויהא מחוור אצל האשה?

אמר רבי לעזר: מאן תנא אשה? רבן גמליאל.

1. There are some who wish to say: In the view of the sages, [the scriptural source for
the stipulation not to wear tefillin on the Sabbath and holidays] is not clear, whereas in
the view of R. Gamaliel,[7] [the scriptural source for the stipulation] is clear...

2.a. It was taught [in a baraita]: It is the same for a man as for a woman (= t. Eruv.
11:14)

2.b. They could say that this baraita makes sense for he who holds that [the scriptural
stipulation not to wear tefillin on the Sabbath] is clear.

2.c. However, for he who holds that [the scriptural stipulation not to wear tefillin on
the Sabbath] is unclear, why would it be *unclear* for a man [who is commanded to wear
tefillin for the purpose of saving in the manner in which he wears them for the sake of
observance], but *clear* for a woman [who is commanded to wear tefillin for the purpose
of saving in a manner in which she does *not* wear them to fulfill ritual observance]?

3. R. Elazar said: Who taught that women [may also wear tefillin to save them on the
Sabbath]?

[Only] R. Gamaliel. (y. Eruv. 26a)

The Yerushalmi begins by repeating an earlier set of conclusions about the
mishnaic debate between R. Gamaliel and the sages. As I discussed extensively
in the last chapter, the Yerushalmi understands the debate (about the number
of tefillin that may be worn on the Sabbath for the purpose of saving them)
to hinge on whether the interlocutors think that tefillin should be worn on
the Sabbath. Those who say that tefillin *are* worn on the Sabbath allow only
one pair, since that is how tefillin are regularly worn for the sake of ritual
observance. Those who hold that tefillin are *not* worn on the Sabbath require
two pairs, since the tefillin are not worn for the sake of ritual observance

---

[7] Lit. Rav Aha. All interpreters agree, however, that this is a scribal error and should read
R. Gamaliel. See Saul Lieberman, *Hayerushalmi Kifshuto*, vol. 1, 357, Pnei Moshe, QE and
Neusner's translation.

and must be distinguished from regular, weekday, wearing. The Yerushalmi assumes that R. Gamaliel (who holds that two pairs of tefillin may be worn) *accepts* the midrashic conclusions that tefillin are not worn on the Sabbath, while the sages (who hold that only one pair may be worn) *do not accept* them.

In this section the Yerushalmi tries to figure out how each interlocutor's position squares with the baraita that allows women to wear tefillin in order to save them on the Sabbath. As the Yerushalmi struggles with this question, *it takes for granted the fact that women are exempt from tefillin*. Assuming women's exemption from tefillin, the baraita accords well with R. Gamaliel's position. Just as he holds that men seeking to save tefillin on the Sabbath wear tefillin in a way they do *not* during the weekdays (i.e., two pairs at a time), he also allows women to wear tefillin in a way *they* do not during the weekdays. Only if he assumes that women do not wear tefillin on the weekdays, does this position make sense.

The Yerushalmi's analysis of the sages' position also assumes that women are exempt from tefillin. Regarding the sages, the Yerushalmi concludes that their position is *inconsistent* with the baraita stating that women may wear tefillin in order to save them on the Sabbath. Were the sages to allow women to wear tefillin to save them on the Sabbath, that would imply that they treat men *differently* from women. Whereas they *require men* to wear tefillin as they are worn for ritual observance (i.e., one pair at a time), they *allow women* to wear tefillin in a manner in which they are *not* worn for ritual observance. Again, the argumentation rests on the assumption that women do not wear tefillin for the purposes of ritual observance. As I noted in the previous chapter, the Yerushalmi neutralizes the inconsistency between the baraita and the sages' view by attributing the baraita to R. Gamaliel. What concerns us here, however, is not the flow of the argumentation and the manner in which questions are resolved. What I wish to highlight in this context is the extent to which the argumentation rests on the assumption that women are exempt from tefillin. If one does not grant this assumption, the argumentation simply makes no sense.

To the extent, then, that the Yerushalmi is trying to achieve legal consistency, its fundamental concern is to affirm the fact that women are exempt from tefillin.

The Bavli's Surprising Flexibility on the Issue of Women's Exemption from Tefillin

In the last chapter, I discussed extensively the Bavli's citation of a previously unattested view that women are obligated to wear tefillin. I explained the emergence of this unprecedented view by showing how the Bavli tries to reconcile the mishnaic dispute between R. Gamaliel and the sages with a tradition from Rava that all Sabbath wearing must mirror weekday wearing. The assumption that Sabbath wearing must mirror weekday wearing led the Bavli to attribute to the sages (or "R. Meir"), instead of R. Gamaliel (as had the Yerushalmi),

the baraita that allows women, along with men, to save tefillin on the Sabbath by wearing them. It appears that one underlying "orthodoxy" driving the
Bavli's interpretation is the idea that Sabbath saving wearing must mirror regular, weekday wearing. In the context of this chapter, however, I would like to
expose another orthodoxy that seems to influence the Bavli's interpretation of
this baraita. I propose that when considering the issue of women's relationship
to tefillin in the context of this baraita, it is much more important for the Bavli
to affirm the general rule that *women are exempt from all timebound, positive
commandments* than it is for it to affirm that any single commandment (such
as tefillin) is a member of this category.

We see a hint of the Bavli's commitment to the idea of women's exemption
from timebound, positive commandments over and against a commitment to
the idea of women's exemption from tefillin in its discussion of Michal, who
wore tefillin.[8] The Bavli, like the Yerushalmi, is familiar with the baraita that
discusses Michal's wearing of tefillin. The Bavli, however, resolves the problem Michal's actions pose in a different manner than did the Yerushalmi. It
will be recalled from the previous chapter that the last section of the Bavli's
sugya (b. Eruv. 95a–96a) seeks a textual source to substantiate "R. Meir's"
view that tefillin are worn on the Sabbath. It is in this context that the Bavli
considers the baraita about Michal, who wore tefillin. Though the baraita is
ultimately rejected as a suitable source for "R. Meir's" position that tefillin
are worn on the Sabbath, the discussion reveals important information about
the Bavli's underlying assumptions.[9] Whereas the Bavli demonstrates surprising flexibility about the stipulation that women are exempt from tefillin, it
reveals a wholehearted commitment to the rule that women are exempt from
timebound, positive commandments.

אלא האי הוא דתניא:

מיכל בת כושי היתה מנחת תפילין ולא מיחו בה חכמים, ואשתו של יונה היתה עולה לרגל ולא מיחו בה חכמים.
מדלא מיחו בה חכמים, אלמא קסברי מצות עשה שלא הזמן גרמה היא.
ודילמא סבר כרבי יוסי, דאמר: נשים סומכות רשות.
דאי לא תימא הכי, אשתו של יונה היתה עולה לרגל ולא מיחו בה, מי איכא למ"ד רגל לאו מצות עשה שהזמן גרמה?

1. Rather, let us say this tanna [held the view that tefillin are worn on the Sabbath],
as it is taught: Michal the daughter of Kushi used to put on tefillin and the sages did

---

[8] See discussion by Tal Ilan, *Jewish Women in Graeco-Roman Palestine*, 182–83n10, on the
different ways in which Michal is identified in the parallel sources. Whereas Mek. and the Bavli
identify her as Michal b. Kushi, the Yerushalmi identifies her as Michal b. Shaul. B. Moed Katan
16b tries to harmonize the two different identifications.

[9] Borrowing a phrase from Jacques Derrida, Aryeh Cohen discusses the idea that the Bavli introduces certain terms and ideas "under erasure." Even though such terms or ideas are *legally*
insignificant, insofar as they are rejected within the linear flow of the argument, they remain *lit-
erarily* significant. See Aryeh Cohen, *Rereading Talmud: Gender, Law and the Poetics of Sugyot*
(Atlanta: Scholars Press, 1998), 166–67.

not object. And the wife of Yonah used to participate in the [thrice-yearly festival] pilgrimage [to Jerusalem] and the sages did not object.

2. Since the sages did not object [to Michal's putting on tefillin], perhaps they assumed it was a positive commandment *not* occasioned by time, [which women are obligated to perform]?

3. Perhaps it is better to conclude that [the author of this baraita] thought like R. Yose [who allowed women the option of performing commandments from which they were exempt], as he said: It is optional for women to place their hands on a sacrificial offering.

4. For if we did not say this, how can we explain the situation of the wife of Yonah who used to participate in the [thrice-yearly festival] pilgrimage [to Jerusalem] and the sages did not object? Surely there is no one who would say that it is not a timebound, positive commandment? [No, there is not]. (b. Eruv. 96a)

The Bavli tries to use the baraita about Michal b. Kushi as a source for the view that tefillin should be worn on the Sabbath. The fact that the sages did not object to her putting them on suggests to the Bavli that they allowed women to wear tefillin. And if the sages allowed women generally to wear tefillin, they must have thought that tefillin are not a timebound commandment. And if they thought that tefillin were not a timebound commandment, they must have thought that tefillin should be worn on the Sabbath.

The Bavli offers an interesting reading of the baraita about Michal and Yonah's wife, which differs in significant ways from the Yerushalmi's reading. First, the Bavli upholds the surface meaning of the baraita, which explicitly states that a particular woman wore tefillin on a particular occasion and did not meet with rabbinic disapproval.[10] This possibility was problematic for the Yerushalmi. In fact, the Yerushalmi's discomfort with the plain sense of the baraita led it to read the baraita in a somewhat strained way. In order to accommodate its discomfort, the Yerushalmi associated the phrase of rabbinic approval with Yonah's wife's deeds alone. In spite of the apparent plain-sense meaning of the baraita about Michal, the sages *did* disapprove of her wearing tefillin. The Bavli, on the other hand, is not fundamentally uncomfortable with the idea that one woman once wore tefillin. Nor is the Bavli uncomfortable with the idea that the sages let it happen. Quite to the contrary, the Bavli suggests that the sages allowed this particular woman to wear tefillin because they *generally* permitted women to wear tefillin. Maybe these sages thought that tefillin were a *non*-timebound, positive commandment? If that were the case, then, tefillin would be worn on the Sabbath, and this source would be a good textual source for "R. Meir's" view that they are worn on the Sabbath.

In the end, the Bavli concludes that the sages' permissiveness with Michal did not result from their thinking that tefillin practice is not timebound. As we found in the previous chapter, the Bavli imposes legal consistency on its sources.

---

[10] See Saul Lieberman, *Hayerushalmi Kifshuto*, vol. 1, 355, who notes the way in which the Bavli, contra the Yerushalmi, upholds the straightforward meaning of the baraita.

The fact that the sages permitted one woman (Michal b. Kushi) to wear tefillin because it is *not* timebound suggests to the Bavi that they permitted another woman (Yonah's wife) to attend the pilgrimage for the same reason, namely they thought that it too is *not* timebound. But such a conclusion is absurd. On what basis can one conclude that attendance at the thrice-yearly festival pilgrimages is not occasioned by time? After all, scripture stipulates that these pilgrimages shall take place at specific times of the year. The Bavli must then reconsider the idea that the sages were permissive with Yonah's wife because they thought that she was obligated to perform the pilgrimage. This conclusion further requires reassessing the idea that the sages permitted Michal b. Kushi to wear tefillin because they thought that women were generally obligated to wear tefillin. In paragraph 3 the Bavli proposes an alternate explanation of the sages' permissiveness toward Michal b. Kushi and Yonah's wife. They assumed that women had the *option* of participating, even though they were officially exempt.[11]

Several features of the Bavli's interpretation are noteworthy. First, the Bavli reverses the Yerushalmi's interpretation stating the sages' disapproval of Michal's deeds. Unlike the Yerushalmi, it is not problematic for the Bavli to contemplate the possibility of extending permission to women to wear tefillin, at least in exceptional instances. Second, the Bavli introduces the language of timeboundedness to explain the sages' permissive stance toward Michal. In other words, the orthodoxy at stake for the Bavli is not whether women are exempt from tefillin, but whether they are exempt from timebound, positive commandments. When the Bavli encounters an instance of rabbinic permissiveness toward women, its natural reflex is to assume that the ritual in question falls into the category of commandments that woman *do* perform, namely, the *non*-timebound ones.

Conclusion

Our textual analysis reveals a shifting set of orthodoxies among the sages who compiled the Yerushalmi and the Bavli. For the Yerushalmi, all legal positions are assumed to conform to the norm that women are exempt from tefillin. The Bavli, on the other hand, takes the rule that women are exempt from all timebound, positive commandments to be the reigning norm. Legal positions are assumed to conform with the rule, but the Bavli has no overriding commitment to the idea that any particular commandment be considered a member of the category of "timebound commandments." The Bavli's preference for

---

[11] The issue of women's *option* to perform commandments for which they are not strictly obligated has stimulated much discussion, especially among the post-talmudic commentators interested in the pragmatic implications for women's ritual observances. For a discussion of rabbinic sources, see Hauptman, *Rereading the Rabbis*, 233–34, and Biale, *Women and Jewish Law: An Exploration of Women's Issues in Halakhic Sources*, 41–43.

upholding women's exemption from a broad-based category rather than from individual commandments offers another illustration of how its interpretive work is framed by a strong impulse to organize and streamline its legal sources. An overarching rule provides a stronger organizational structure than a list of individual commandments from which women are exempt. As I understand the matter, this accounts for the Bavli's flexibility with respect to the outcome of women's obligation vis-à-vis tefillin. As we will see in the following chapter, the Bavli's primary concern is to affirm the authority of the overarching rule.

5

From Description to Prescription

In this chapter I wish to document the emergence of a new way of understanding the rule that exempts women from timebound, positive commandments. In Chapter 1, I argued that the tannaim who formulated the rule that exempts women from this class of commandments envisioned it functioning descriptively. The category of "timebound, positive commandments from which women are exempt" initially emerged as a description of tefillin. Only secondarily was the category and its attendant rule extended to include other commandments with a similar profile (e.g., sukkah, lulav, shofar). I stressed that women's exemption from these other commandments had been determined by other means. Except in the single instance of R. Shimon's ruling on tzitzit, the rule was not used to *determine* women's ritual involvement. The rule's utility lay in describing a group of commandments from which women had already been exempted for other reasons. This view of the rule changed, however, before the end of the rabbinic period. The post-amoraic stratum of the Bavli (c. 450–600 CE) assumes that the rule was formulated for *prescriptive* purposes. Unlike earlier interpreters who encountered the rule, the post-amoraic stratum assumed that the rule *did determine* women's ritual involvement. This development represents a significant shift in the received understanding of the rule. The goal of this chapter is to describe how and why this new understanding of the rule developed. I will argue that the rule was read as a prescriptive principle without an awareness of how it would affect the construction of gender thenceforth. The new perception of the rule set the stage for medieval conversations about gender and the rule. I find no evidence to suggest, however, that it arose with a consciousness of the rule's ability to ground the construction of gender thenceforth.

The function of rules is to provide a general rubric within which a number of individual cases can be subsumed, but descriptive and prescriptive rules each give priority to a different end of the equation between particular cases and general rules. Whereas descriptive rules move from particular cases to broad generalization, prescriptive rules start with general stipulations that are applied to particular cases. The process resulting in the formulation of a descriptive rule begins with individual cases. When several individual cases offer the same judgment in similar circumstances, a descriptive rule can be formulated to summarize what they have in common. The utility of a descriptive rule is that it allows one to refer to cases collectively rather than enumerate them individually. By way of contrast, prescriptive rules start with a desired outcome and dictate the outcome to all appropriate cases. As long as the rule is enforced, all cases that fall under its jurisdiction will conform to its norms.

The two Talmuds expend considerable energy reflecting on how particular cases of women's ritual exemption and obligation relate to the general rule exempting them from timebound, positive commandments. They take note of individual cases that both instantiate and contradict the rule. These discussions offer crucial insight into how each of the two Talmuds conceptualizes the relationship between the rule and individual cases. While the Yerushalmi gives conceptual priority to individual cases (assuming that they precede the rule), the Bavli takes the rule as its conceptual starting point (assuming that the cases follow the rule). These observations form the basis for my claim that *only in the post-amoraic stratum of the Bavli* was the rule understood to be prescriptive. In an effort to document the shift from a descriptive to a prescriptive understanding of the rule, the body of this chapter examines how the two Talmuds reconcile the relationship between the rule and various cases that both instantiate and contradict it. Before proceeding to this task, however, it is useful to recall the broader interpretive context within which these observations are important.

The interpretive shift toward regarding the rule exempting women from timebound, positive commandments as prescriptive had a significant impact on the rule's ability to function as a marker of gender difference. Medieval and contemporary interpreters who have encountered the rule through the interpretive lens of the Bavli have assumed that it was formulated prescriptively. They have further assumed that the tannaitic prescription was instituted to realize a particular social vision. Accordingly, much post-talmudic interpretation of the rule seeks to articulate the social vision that interpreters imagine to be embodied by the rule. The irony, of course, is that these interpreters speculate about a process that never occurred historically, because, in point of fact, the rule was formulated to serve a descriptive purpose. It is noteworthy that the Bavli *itself* offers no theory regarding the social values that underpin the rule. For all the energy the Bavli expends defending its understanding of the rule as prescriptive, it has no interest in reflecting on the legislative content of the rule. Its entire exegetical program is taken up with clarifying the relationship between the rule and the individual cases that fall under its jurisdiction. The Bavli, then, crafts an understanding of the rule that allows it to function as a mechanism for gender differentiation, but only later interpreters realize the full potential of the Bavli's interpretive shift. The main accomplishment of the Bavli is to understand the rule in a manner that is *suggestive* to future interpreters. It shapes the rule into an empty vessel that can, but does not yet, contain a vision of that which distinguishes men from women.

I argue that gender concerns do not figure as part of the Bavli's interpretive agenda when it makes the shift to regard the rule as a prescriptive. Following up on the work of the two previous chapters, I again argue that the Bavli's interpretive innovations are motivated by a desire to reveal coherence and systematicity among inherited legal traditions. The post-amoraic stratum pursues the goal of resolving contradictions within inherited legal tradition in a more aggressive fashion than either the Yerushalmi (c. 220–425) or the amoraic stratum of the Bavli (c. 220–450).[1] When the post-amoraic stratum of the Bavli (c. 450–600) reads the rule as one that accounts for the entirety of women's involvement in ritual, it streamlines much diverse material into a simple and elegant legal framework.[2]

Instantiations of the Rule

Both Talmuds have occasion to note instances where the judgment in particular cases corresponds to that suggested by the rule, but they do so in different ways. The Yerushalmi notes the agreement between the rule and individual cases only *after* it establishes the judgment of individual cases *by other means*. For the Yerushalmi, individual cases have a conceptual priority over the rule. Even though the rule agrees with the cases, the rule is not assumed to be the means

---

[1] Richard Kalmin notes that differences between the Yerushalmi can be the function of either chronological factors (the Bavli was redacted more than a century after the Yerushalmi), geographical factors, or both. The following analysis focuses on Bavli-Yerushalmi differences that are a function of chronological differences. The materials I examine from the Yerushalmi (redacted c. 425) have much in common with materials from the amoraic stratum of the Bavli (c. 220–450). On retrieving historical data from early strata of the Bavli, see Richard Kalmin, "The Formation and Character of the Babylonian Talmud," in *The Late Roman-Rabbinic Period*, vol. 4 of *Cambridge History of Judaism*, ed. Steven Katz (Cambridge: Cambridge University Press, 2006), 840–76; and Richard Kalmin, *Jewish Babylonia Between Persia and Roman Palestine* (New York: Oxford University Press, 2006). On the use of the chronology gap between the Yerushalmi and the Bavli as the basis for historical reconstruction, see also Christine Elizabeth Hayes, *Between the Babylonian and Palestinian Talmuds: Accounting for Halakhic Difference in Selected Sugyot from Tractate Avodah Zarah*, 20–23; and Alexander, *Transmitting Mishnah*, 81–83.

[2] I build here on the work of other scholars who have noted that the post-amoraic stratum of the Bavli displays a concerted interest in organizing inherited traditions into a conceptually coherent and organized framework. See De Vries, *Toldot Hahalakhah Hatalmudit*, 142–56; Gilat, *Development of Halakha*; Moscovitz, *Talmudic Reasoning*; Goldberg, "The Babylonian Talmud," 330–31; Jeffrey Rubenstein, "The Sukkah as Temporary or Permanent Dwelling"; and Jeffrey Rubenstein, "On Some Abstract Concepts." Most recently, Barry Wimpfheimer describes this impulse in the Bavli as a drive toward "codification." See Wimpfheimer, *Narrating the Law: A Poetics of Talmudic Legal Stories*, 10–11.

of adjudicating individual cases. The Bavli, on the other hand, gives conceptual priority to the rule. Taking the prescriptive role of the rule for granted, the Bavli wonders why particular cases needed to be stated at all. The Bavli considers particular cases to be superfluous in the face of a rule that can achieve the same results. In the Bavli, particular cases, rather than the rule, are represented as extraneous. Examining how each Talmud treats the phenomenon of individual cases that instantiate the rule reveals that only the post-amoraic stratum in the Bavli gives conceptual priority to the rule and regards it as prescriptive. In order to highlight the novelty of the Bavli's approach to cases that instantiate the rule, I begin by discussing the Yerushalmi.

A Case-Based Discussion in the Yerushalmi

The Yerushalmi has occasion to note the correspondence between the rule of women's exemption from timebound commandments and their exemption from a particular commandment in its treatment of m. Ber. 3:3. The mishnah under discussion reads as follows:

נשים ועבדים וקטנים פטורין מקריאת שמע ומן התפילין, וחייבין בתפילה ובמזוזה ובברכת המזון.

Women, slaves, and minors are exempt from reciting the Shema and wearing tefillin; they are obligated to recite the Prayer, affix a mezuzah [to their houses and gates], and recite grace after meals. (m. Ber. 3:3)

This mishnah provides a short catalogue of commandments that women, slaves, and minors need and need not perform. The list is by no means complete, but focuses on commandments involving liturgy and text. Though one would have to ignore the fact the mishnah's stipulations are directed as much toward slaves and minors as to women, each of these judgments can be made to relate to the rule exempting women from timebound, positive commandments. Since the Shema is recited in the evening and the morning, it qualifies as a timebound commandment. Similarly, tefillin, by virtue of being worn only during daylight hours and on weekdays, is also a commandment whose performance is occasioned by time. The mishnah's stipulations that women are exempt from these two commandments accords well with the rule. Women's obligation to affix a mezuzah to their houses and gates also accords well with the rule, since this commandment is *not* occasioned by time and women must perform it. Their obligation to recite the traditional petitionary prayer, the Amidah, seems to contradict the rule, since the Amidah must be recited at specific points in the day. Women's obligation to recite the grace after meals stands in an unclear relationship to the rule. Depending on whether one thinks that meals are occasioned by time (and a reasonable argument can be made either way),[3] one may take the obligation to recite grace after meals to be timebound or not. This

---

[3] The Bavli provides a plausible argument for the fact that meals are occasioned by time. See b. Ber. 20b. It is equally defensible to suggest that though most meals are eaten at regular times,

mishnah, then, gives much interpretive leeway to a reader who wishes to gauge the impact of the rule on the adjudication of individual cases. It presents cases that agree with, disagree with, and are ambiguous as regards the rule exempting women from timebound, positive commandments.

The Yerushalmi, however, does not assume that the rule exempting women from timebound, positive commandments played a role in determining any of these judgments. It begins its discussion of this mishnah by assuming that each of these judgments was *scripturally determined*. It seeks the scriptural source for each judgment. Notably, the Yerushalmi addresses the mishnah in its entirety, providing prooftexts for the exemptions of women, *slaves, and minors.*

נשים מניין?

ולמדתם אותם את בניכם. את בניכ' ולא בנותיכם.

עבדים מניין?

שנ' שמע ישראל ה' אלהינו ה' אחד. את שאין לו אדון אלא הב"ה. יצא העבד שיש לו אדון אחר.

קטנים מניין?

למען תהיה תורת ה' בפיך. בשעה שהוא תדיר בה.

וחייבין בתפילה כדי שיהא כל אחד ואחד מבקש רחמי' על עצמו.

ובמזוזה, דכתיב: וכתבתם על מזוזות ביתך ובשעריך.

ובברכת המזון דכתיב: ואכלת ושבעת וברכת.

1. From where [do we learn] women's [exemption from reciting Shema and wearing tefillin]?

And you shall teach them to your sons (Deut 11:19). Your sons and not your daughters.

2. From where [do we learn] slaves' [exemption]?

Hear O Israel, the Lord is our God, the Lord is one (Deut 6:4). [This is addressed to] one who has no master other than the Holy One Blessed Be He. It excludes the slave who has another master.

3. From where [do we learn] minors' [exemption]?

In order that the teachings (Torah) *of the Lord shall be in your mouth* (Exod 13:9). In the hour [i.e., the age] when it is constantly there [i.e., adulthood].

4. And they are obligated to recite the prayer so that every single individual may request mercy for himself.

5. And [they are obligated to affix] a mezuzah, as it is written: *and you shall write them on the doorposts of your houses and on your gates* (Deut 6:9).

6. And [they are obligated to recite] grace after meals, as it is written: *and you shall eat and be satisfied and you shall bless* (Deut 8:10). (y. Ber. 6b)

In this sequence the Yerushalmi provides a scriptural source for almost all of the mishnah's stipulations. It is interesting to note that irrespective of whether

---

not every meal will be eaten at a regular time. According to this line of reasoning, recitation of the grace after meals is not timebound.

the exemptions from reciting Shema and wearing tefillin devolve upon women, slaves, or minors, the Yerushalmi assumes that *both* exemptions (from Shema and tefillin) derive from a single source. Women are exempt from Shema and tefillin because both are considered forms of Torah study, and women are exempt from Torah study. Slaves are exempt from these two rituals because they require the practitioner to pledge an allegiance to God alone. On account of the slave's primary allegiance to his earthly masters, slaves are also exempt from these rituals. Finally, minors are exempt because these two rituals are performed to inculcate a constant commitment to God's Torah, which minors, by virtue of their immaturity, cannot achieve. The obligation of women, slaves, and minors to recite the petitionary prayer commonly known as the Amidah is the only stipulation that is not backed by a scriptural prooftext. The Yerushalmi deviates from its usual pattern here because no such prooftext exists, seeing as the obligation itself is *rabbinic*, rather than biblical, in origin. Incapable of providing a biblical prooftext, the Yerushalmi offers the next best thing: a logical explanation. Women, slaves, and minors are obligated to recite the petitionary prayer because they need the same opportunity as free, adult men to request God's mercy. They are obligated to affix mezuzahs and recite the grace after meals because in each case the biblical verse prescribing the ritual is addressed to the whole congregation of Israel. While these prooftexts may or may not provide an accurate historical explanation of why women, slaves, and minors were obligated to or exempt from these rituals,[4] the *official discourse of the Yerushalmi regards them as the basis* for the exemptions and obligations. Significantly, the Yerushalmi does not assume that the mishnaic stipulations flow from the rule exempting women from timebound commandments.

The Yerushalmi does take note, however, of the correspondence between the rule and women's exemption from tefillin. After citing the scriptural source for each of these stipulations, the Yerushalmi cites a baraita that buttresses the stipulation that women are exempt from tefillin.

תמן תנינן: כל מצות עשה שהזמן גרמא, אנשים חייבין ונשים פטורות; וכל מצות עשה
שלא הזמן גרמא, אחד אנשים ואחד נשים חייבין.
אי זהו מצות עשה שהזמן גרמא? כגון סוכה לולב שופר ותפילין.
ואי זו היא מצות עה שלא הזמן גרמא? כגון אבידה ושילוח הקן מעקה וציצית.
רבי שמעון פוטר את הנשים ממצות ציצית שהוא מצות עשה שהזמן גרמא, שהרי כסות לילה פטור מן הציצית.
א"ר לייא טעמן דרבנן שכן אם היה היה' מיוחד' לו ליום וללילה, שהיא חייבת בציצית.

It was taught there: All timebound, positive commandments – men are obligated and women are exempt. All non-timebound, positive commandments – men and women are equally obligated (= m. Kid. 1:7).

What is a timebound, positive commandment? For example, sukkah, lulav, shofar and tefillin.

---

4 Chapters 6 and 7 attempt to provide a historical explanation of women's exemption from Shema and tefillin.

And what is a non-timebound, positive commandment? For example, returning lost property, sending the mother away from the nest before taking her eggs, building a parapet and wearing fringes on the corners of one's garments.

R. Shimon exempts women from wearing fringes since it is a timebound, positive commandment (= t. Kid. 1:10), seeing as nightwear is exempt from fringes.

R. Lia explained the reason behind the sages' rulings [that women are obligated to wear fringes, assuming that they are a *non*-timebound, positive commandment]. Should it happen that one has a special garment that he wears in both the day and the night, it would need to have fringes [i.e., sometimes nightwear must have fringes, so the commandment of fringes is *not* occasioned by time]. (y. Ber. 6a)

Having begun its discussion by giving equal weight to the matter of women's, slaves', and minors' exemptions, the Yerushalmi now turns its attention to the specific matter of women's exemptions. In order to buttress the stipulation of m. Ber. 3:3 that exempts women from tefillin, the Yerushalmi cites m. Kid. 1:7, which states the rule of women's exemption from timebound, positive commandments. One might speculate that the rule is cited because of its general compatibility with the mishnah as a whole. As noted above, several of the stipulations (women's exemption from reciting Shema and wearing tefillin and their obligation to affix mezuzah) clearly conform to the rule. Other stipulations (women's obligation to recite the petitionary prayer and recite grace after meals), however, contradict the rule or have an unclear relationship to the rule. It seems unlikely, then, that the rule is invoked because it is understood to complement m. Ber. 3:3 as a whole. A more likely explanation for its appearance here takes into account the tosephtan baraita that follows on the heels of the rule. In order to clarify what a "timebound, positive commandment" is, t. Kid. 1:10 offers several illustrative examples. Tefillin appears on the baraita's list of exemplary timebound, positive commandments. Taken as a complete unit, the mishnaic rule and its tosephtan gloss provide additional support for m. Ber. 3:3's stipulation that women are exempt from tefillin specifically.

Several aspects of the Yerushalmi's interpretation are noteworthy. First, the rule stating women's exemptions from timebound, positive commandments is not regarded as the *source* for the exemptions and obligations recorded in m. Ber. 3:3. Rather, the Yerushalmi understands the stipulations to be biblically mandated. Second, the rule is not invoked because it *determines* the female exemptions listed in m. Ber. 3:3, but because it *agrees* with the mishnah's conclusions in a single case. For the Yerushalmi, individual cases are the starting point of the discussion. The rule is cited because it confirms the adjudication of a particular case. Third, even though the rule conforms to *three* of the mishnah's stipulations (women's exemption from Shema and tefillin and their obligation to affix a mezuzah), the Yerushalmi notes the congruence only with tefillin. Why does the Yerushalmi not comment on the rule's agreement with other stipulations of this mishnah (i.e., women's exemption from Shema and their obligation in mezuzah)? The simple answer is that the Yerushalmi had a source designating tefillin as a timebound, positive commandment (from which women are exempt), but no source establishing the status of Shema as timebound or mezuzah as non-timebound. Whereas the tannaitic sources available to the Yerushalmi confirm m. Ber. 3:3's conclusions regarding tefillin, they are silent on the question of the mishnah's stipulations regarding Shema and mezuzah.[5] The deeper answer to this question, however, must consider *why* the Yerushalmi had access to a source listing tefillin as a timebound, positive commandment from which women are exempt. As argued in Chapter 1, tefillin was the first ritual to be described as a timebound, positive commandment. Yerushalmi's discussion, then, is very much shaped by the early sources that assume and reflect a descriptive understanding of the rule. The fact that the Yerushalmi discusses tefillin, and only tefillin, as a member of this class of commandments suggests that it retains a residual memory of both the close affiliation between the rule and tefillin and the rule's descriptive function.

In sum, when the Yerushalmi invokes the rule in its discussion of particular cases that fall under the jurisdiction of the rule, it gives all signs of relating to the rule in its descriptive capacity. First, the Yerushalmi does not presume that the rule determines women's exemptions or obligations. The rule is invoked only insofar as it buttresses conclusions that have already been reached by other means. Second, the Yerushalmi retains a residual memory of tefillin as the quintessential timebound, positive commandment. Its reticence to invoke the rule with regard to other commandments suggests that it does not readily associate the rule with them.

Conceptual Priority for the Rule in the Bavli

Like the Yerushalmi, the Bavli also has occasion to note the correspondence between individual cases and the rule of women's exemption from timebound, positive commandments. Interestingly enough, for the Yerushalmi the correspondence between the rule and the particular case of women's exemption from tefillin affirms the legitimacy of both the rule and the particular case. The Bavli,

---

[5] Though the Yerushalmi does not have a source establishing the timebound status of Shema and mezuzah, it does have a source establishing the sukkah, lulav, and shofar as timebound, positive commandments from which women are exempt. One can reasonably ask why the Yerushalmi does not invoke the rule when discussing these other rituals. We might have expected to see the rule invoked in the following places: y. Suk. 53b, where women's exemption from the sukkah is discussed; y. Suk. 53c, where women's involvement with lulav is discussed; and y. RH58c and 59a, where the minor's obligation regarding shofar is discussed. Apparently, only the link between the rule and tefillin deserves mention. I suspect that the Yerushalmi connects the rule to tefillin because of the tannaitic precedent for doing so. Judith Hauptman argues that talmudic sugyot develop in the wake of "proto-sugyot" consisting of associated tannaitic sources. The fact that several tannaitic sources correlated tefillin with the rule may explain why the Yerushalmi correlates tefillin, but not other timebound rituals from which women are exempt, with the rule. See Judith Hauptman, *Development of the Talmudic Sugya: Relationship Between Tannaitic and Amoraic Sources* (Lanham: University Press of America, 1988).

on the other hand, is not so sanguine about the existence of individual cases that instantiate the rule. Since the Bavli affords conceptual priority to the rule over and against individual cases, it assumes that instantiating cases render the rule *superfluous*. In the Bavli's view, where there is an all-encompassing rule, one does not need to state the individual cases of women's exemption and obligation. A major exegetical concern of the Bavli is explaining why individual cases need to be stated explicitly when applying the rule leads to the same legal outcome.

The Bavli considers the relationship between the rule and cases that instantiate it in two different textual settings. The first context is a treatment of m. Ber. 3:3 discussed above, which enumerates a number of women's ritual exemptions and obligations. The second context is a discussion of m. Kid. 1:7, the locus classicus of the rule. I will consider each of these textual settings in turn.

As noted above, m. Ber. 3:3 catalogues a number of women's ritual exemptions and obligations. While a number of the stipulations stated there conform to the rule's stipulations, one does not, and one has an unclear relationship to the rule. In the following passage, the Bavli assumes that all the mishnah's stipulations (except women's obligation to recite the petitionary prayer) conform to the rule. The Bavli also assumes that each individual case can be learned from the general prescription of the rule. Consequently, the Bavli regards the mishnaic stipulations in each individual case to be redundant and unnecessary. The passage seeks to justify the mishnah's inclusion of each individual stipulation, given that the same conclusions could be achieved by applying the rule. The Bavli's solution to this problem is to highlight the extenuating circumstances in each case that might compel a "rule override." In other words, for each case stated in m. Ber. 3:3, there are reasons to believe that the rule would have been overridden. According to the Bavli, m. Ber. 3:3 goes to the trouble of enumerating these exemptions and obligations explicitly in order to forestall any faulty judgments that might have resulted had logic alone been used.

קריאת שמע. פשיטא! מצות עשה שהזמן גרמא הוא, וכל מצות עשה שהזמן גרמא, נשים פטורות.

מהו דתימא: הואיל ואית בה מלכות שמים. קמשמע לן.

וזמן התפילין. פשיטא!

מהו דתימא הואיל ואתקש למזוזה.

וחייבין בתפילה, דרחמי נינהו.

מהו דתימא הואיל וכתיב בה "ערב ובקר וצהרים," כמצות עשה שהזמן גרמא דמי. קמשמע לן.

ובמזוזה. פשיטא!

מהו דתימא: הואיל ואתקש לתלמוד תורה. קמשמע לן.

ובברכת המזון. פשיטא!

מהו דתימא: הואיל וכתיב בה "בתת ה' לכם בערב בשר לאכל ולחם בבקר לשבע"

כמצות עשה שהזמן גרמא דמי. קמשמע לן.

1. [**Women, slaves, and minors are exempt from**] reciting the Shema (= m. Ber. 3:3). But is it not obvious [that women are exempt]? It is a timebound, positive commandment and women are exempt from timebound, positive commandments.

[It was stated specifically] lest you say: Since it [reciting Shema] involves acknowledging divine sovereignty [women should be obligated]. The mishnah teaches us [that it is not so].

2. **And from tefillin** (= m. Ber. 3:3). But is it not obvious [that women are exempt, since they too are a timebound, positive commandment]?

[It was stated specifically] lest you say: Since it [tefillin] can be likened to mezuzah, [and women should be obligated for tefillin, just as they are obligated for mezuzah]. The mishnah teaches us [that it is not so].

3. **And they are obligated to recite the petitionary prayer** (= m. Ber. 3:3), [is this not self-evident since] it is a request for mercy.[6]

[It was stated specifically] lest you say: Since it is written with regard to it, *Evening, morning and afternoon* (Ps. 55:18), it is *like* a timebound, positive commandment [from which women are exempt]. The mishnah teaches us [that it is not so].

4. **And [to affix] a mezuzah** (= m. Ber. 3:3). Is it not obvious? [It is a non-timebound, positive commandment and women are obligated to perform non-timebound, positive commandments].

[It was stated specifically] lest you say: Since it can be likened to Torah study, [women should be exempt from mezuzah, just as they are exempt from Torah study]. The mishnah teaches us [that it is not so].

5. **And [to recite] the grace after meals** (= m. Ber. 3:3). Is it not obvious [for the same reason as above]?

[It was stated specifically] lest you say: Since it is written in regard to it, *when God gave you meat to eat in the evening and bread in the morning until you were satiated* (Exod 16:8), it is like a timebound, positive commandment [from which women are exempt]. The mishnah teaches us [that it is not so]. (b. Ber. 20b)

In this passage the Bavli examines the list of women's ritual exemptions and obligations from m. Ber. 3:3.[7] As the Bavli proceeds through the list considering each item in turn, it wonders why the mishnah states each one. From the Bavli's perspective, each stipulation is self-evident and does not need special mention. Two assumptions undergird the Bavli's analysis of the mishnah here. First, the Bavli assumes that it is the nature of mishnaic language to avoid superfluity and redundancy. From the Bavli's perspective, the Mishnah always

---

[6] Text reproduced here follows the printed edition. Manuscript versions of this paragraph have same structure as other paragraphs. See discussion of manuscript variants and the textual emendation following Rashi in David Kraemer, *Reading the Rabbis: The Talmud as Literature* (New York: Oxford University Press, 1996), 90–91, 154nn1–3.

[7] Unlike the Yerushalmi, the Bavli disregards the fact that the mishnah stipulates exemptions and obligations for *slaves and minors*, as well as for women. In its interpretation, the Bavli focuses on the mishnah's stipulations for women, and *not* on those addressed to slaves and minors. Kraemer makes a similar observation. See David Kraemer, *Reading the Rabbis: The Talmud as Literature*, 89.

expresses itself with the greatest possible verbal economy.[8] For the Bavli, it is problematic that the Mishnah takes the trouble to enumerate each of the particular exemptions and obligations when elsewhere it offers a rule from which all can be derived. The body of the Bavli's analysis seeks to justify the inclusion of each stipulation in the mishnah.[9] The Bavli resolves its problem by showing the plausibility of conclusions that are diametrically opposed to those indicated by the rule. For example, even though the Shema is a timebound commandment, and the rule dictates that women should be exempt from reciting it, one could plausibly, but erroneously, reason that women should be obligated to recite it since it involves acknowledging divine sovereignty. Similarly, even though affixing a mezuzah is a non-timebound commandment, and the rule dictates that women are obligated to affix it to their homes, one could plausibly, but erroneously, reason that women are exempt from it as they are exempt from Torah study.[10] According to the Bavli, the mishnah states these stipulations explicitly precisely because they *cannot* be learned by applying the rule. The mere fact of having a rule that establishes women's exemption from timebound, positive commandments – and their obligation with regard to non-timebound, positive commandments – *is not sufficient* to arrive at each of the mishnah's stipulations. By showing that each stipulation is not, after all is said and told, as self-evident as was initially presumed, the Bavli succeeds in justifying the place of each in the mishnah and affirms that mishnaic language is not carelessly redundant but, in fact, very deliberate.

The second assumption that undergirds the Bavli's analysis is its presumption that the rule functions prescriptively to *determine* women's ritual involvement.[11] The Bavli assumes that one can derive almost all of the stipulations in m. Ber. 3:3 (with the single exception of women's obligation to recite the petitionary prayer) from the rule. The instantiations of the rule are considered self-evident precisely because one can reach the same conclusions from the rule. Without the assumption that the rule is prescriptive, the Bavli's pattern of remarking on the self-evident character of each of the mishnah's

---

[8] For a discussion of the Bavli's hermeneutical posture toward the Mishnah and its assumption that the Mishnah expresses itself with verbal economy, see Christine Elizabeth Hayes, *Between the Babylonian and Palestinian Talmuds: Accounting for Halakhic Difference in Selected Sugyot from Tractate Avodah Zarah*, 92–94; Alexander, *Transmitting Mishnah*, 77–115; and Goldberg, "The Babylonian Talmud," 331–32.

[9] The Bavli atomizes the mishnaic text insofar as it regards each stipulation as discrete and worthy of comment. On the Bavli's tendency to atomize the mishnaic text, see Alexander, *Transmitting Mishnah*, 84–103.

[10] Hayes discusses the Bavli's tendency to construct plausible, but erroneous, alternatives to the mishnah's formulation as a means of establishing the value of the mishnaic text as given. See Christine Elizabeth Hayes, *Between the Babylonian and Palestinian Talmuds: Accounting for Halakhic Difference in Selected Sugyot from Tractate Avodah Zarah*, 116.

[11] David Kraemer observes, "In the end, the only thing everyone in the gemara may agree on is that the Mishnah is right – women *are* exempted from affirmative, time-bound commandments." David Kraemer, *Reading the Rabbis: The Talmud as Literature*, 107.

stipulations simply makes no sense. Though the Bavli does not say so directly, the assumptions underlying its argumentation indicate that it regards the rule as a prescriptive one that actively *determines* to, rather than passively describes, individual cases.

The Bavli performs a similar kind of analysis in its discussion of m. Kid. 1:7, the locus classicus for the rule. After a brief discussion of rule's source, the Bavli examines the relationship between the rule and biblical stipulations that conform to it. Here too, the Bavli assumes that law is expressed in the most economical fashion possible. The Bavli also assumes that a rule exists that determines women's engagement with timebound, positive commandments. The interesting twist here, however, is that the Bavli does not assume women's *exemption* from this class of commandments. In this sugya, the evidence of the instantiating cases leads to the surprising conclusion that women should be *obligated* to perform timebound, positive commandments. The first biblical instantiation of the rule that the Bavli discusses is women's exemption from the commandment to sit in the sukkah during the holiday of Sukkot.

והרי סוכה, דמצות עשה שהזמן גרמא, דכתיב בסוכות תשבו שבעת ימים.
טעמא דכתב רחמנא "האזרח," להוציא את הנשים.
הא לאו הכי, נשים חייבות.

1. But what about [the commandment to sit in the sukkah]. This is a timebound commandment, as it is written, "you shall dwell in sukkot for seven days" (Lev 23:42).

2. But the reason [for women's exemption] is the fact that scripture states: *the citizen* (Lev 23:42). [The extra word "the"] comes to exclude women (= Sifra, Emor, perek 17.9).

3. Where [women's exemption] is not [explicitly stated, we must conclude] women are *obligated* [to perform timebound, positive commandments]. (b. Kid. 34a)

As in the previous sugya, the Bavli's line of questioning is generated by an apparent redundancy between the rule and its instantiations. The perceived redundancy here is between the rule and the biblical commandment to dwell in booths for seven days during the fall holiday of Sukkot, which is assumed to be a timebound, positive commandment. From the Bavli's perspective, the primary reason that women are exempt from this particular timebound commandment is because scripture exempts them (see paragraph 2). When scripture states that "each citizen in Israel shall dwell in booths," the word "the" is extraneous. Drawing on a tannaitic midrash that comments on the same textual irritant, the Bavli concludes that the extra word "the" is included in the scriptural text to indicate that women are exempt from dwelling in the booths.[12] According to another of the Bavli's assumptions, scripture has taken the trouble to specify women's obligations with regard to this ritual *because it does not conform to whatever rule is operating*. Though the Bavli assumes that a prescriptive

---

[12] See Sifra, Emor, perek 17.9.

rule determines women's participation in timebound, positive commandments, it initially envisions that as one that *obligates* women to perform timebound, positive commandments (see line 3). Since scripture takes the trouble to indicate women's exemption from sukkah (albeit obliquely), the Bavli assumes that this ruling could not have been achieved by applying whatever prescriptive rule is in place. Seeing as the biblical commandment to sit in a sukkah is a timebound commandment, and seeing as scripture specifies women's exemption from it, we must assume that the rule in place *obliges* women to perform timebound commandments in other cases (paragraph 3)! This is a creative and skillful argument. It challenges the legal content of the familiar rule from m. Kid. 1:7. It also, however, buttresses the idea that *women's involvement with ritual generally is regulated and determined by an overarching rule.*

The sugya continues by reasserting the legal content of the familiar rule. Initially, the Bavli rejects the conclusions of the familiar rule because the biblical stipulation exempting women from sitting in the sukkah redundantly duplicates conclusions that could be reached by applying the rule. If the Bavli can demonstrate, however, that the case of sukkah is not sufficiently addressed by the rule, then it can explain why scripture exempts women from this commandment specifically *even though* a rule exists that exempts them from timebound, positive commandments generally. The Bavli cites two different arguments (by Abaye and Rava) that explain how the rule alone is not sufficient to enable us to conclude that women are exempt from sitting in the sukkah.

אמר אביי: איצטריך.

סלקא דעתך אמינא: הואיל דכתיב "בסוכות תשבו," תשבו כעין תדורו.

מה דירה איש ואשתו, אף סוכה איש ואשתו.

ורבא אמר: איצטריך.

סד"א: נילף חמשה עשר חמשה עשר מחג המצות.

מה להלן נשים חייבות אף כאן נשים חייבות.

צריכא.

1.a. Abaye explained: [The biblical stipulation stating women's exemption from sitting in the sukkah] is needed lest it occur to you to say: Since it is written [with regard to sukkah], "In sukkot you shall sit" (Lev 23:42), "sitting" must be understood to be a kind of dwelling.

1.b. Just as men and wife dwell together in their usual habitation, so too man and wife should dwell together in the sukkah.

2.a. Rava explained: [The biblical stipulation stating women's exemption from sitting in the sukkah] is needed lest it occur to you to say: Let us establish an analogy between the "*fifteenth of the month*" (Lev 23:39) [as written in regards to Sukkot] and the "*fifteenth of the month*" (Lev 23:6) [as written in regards] to Passover.

2.b. Just as there women are obligated [to eat matzah], so too let them here be obligated [to sit in the sukkah].

3. [Therefore you must conclude that the stipulation regarding women's exemption from sitting in the sukkah] is needed [and is not redundant with the rule exempting women from timebound, positive commandments]. (b. Kid. 34a–b)

Both Abaye and Rava construct arguments to show that the question of women's participation in sukkah is not sufficiently addressed by the rule exempting them from timebound, positive commandments. Each demonstrates that though the obligation to sit in the sukkah is certainly timebound, other concerns exist that potentially override the rule exempting women from time-bound, positive commandments.

Abaye and Rava both argue that one can easily be misled to assume that women should be obligated to sit in the sukkah. Abaye observes that the biblical word articulating the obligation to sit in the sukkah has resonances with the concept of dwelling. He explains that one might erroneously conclude from the fact that men and women sit together in their regular dwellings that they should sit together in the sukkah. Alternatively, Rava observes that scripture sets up an analogy between the holidays of Passover and Sukkot by stipulating that both begin on the *fifteenth* of the month. He explains that one might be tempted to draw the erroneous conclusion that just as women are obligated to eat matzah on Passover, they should be obligated to sit in the sukkah on Sukkot. Both Abaye and Rava demonstrate that one can reach reasonable, but problematic, conclusions concerning women's involvement with sukkah when relying on the rule alone. In their view, scripture took the trouble to indicate women's exemption from sitting in the sukkah in order to counteract the reasonable conclusion that women should perform this ritual. The fact that scripture makes special mention of women's exemption from sukkah is *not*, therefore, evidence that the operative rule was one that *obligated* women with regard to timebound, positive commandments. Rather, scripture specifically mentions women's exemption from sukkah (even though it is timebound) to compensate for the fact that the rule *alone* does not sufficiently explain how the case of sukkah should be resolved. In the end, the Bavli concludes that the rule exempting women from timebound, positive commandments was in place when the decision about women's involvement with sukkah was made. Scripture needed to be explicit about women's exemption from sukkah because of extenuating circumstances that could lead one to view sukkah as outside the purview of the rule. The existence of a biblical stipulation that conforms to the stipulations of the rule is ultimately rejected as evidence for the conclusion that the rule is superfluous.

The Bavli offers a similar argumentational sequence when discussing a second biblical instantiation of the rule.[13] Like the obligation to sit in the sukkah, pilgrimage rituals are a timebound, positive commandment from which women are exempt. Scripture explicitly states that "every male shall appear before the

Lord three times a year" (Exod 23:17). Scripture's direct attention to the matter of women's non-participation in the thrice-yearly pilgrimage suggests to
the Bavli that a general rule exists that *obligates* women to perform timebound, positive commandments. After all, if women were generally exempt
from timebound, positive commandments, scripture would not need to state
women's exemption from pilgrimage. This conclusion is refuted by showing
that scripture went to the trouble to note women's exemption from pilgrimage because compelling reasons exist there too to override the general rule
exempting women from timebound, positive commandments.

In sum, when discussing cases that instantiate the rule exempting women
from timebound, positive commandments, the Bavli has a standard set of concerns that are generated by its prevailing assumptions. The Bavli assumes that
all individual cases are determined by an overarching rule. The Bavli also
assumes that halakhic norms are expressed in the most economical fashion
possible. Any congruence between particular cases and the general rule is considered redundant because the rule provides a more efficient means of determining the particular cases than stating them individually.

It is ironic that the Bavli regards cases that instantiate the rule as *problematic*.
Such cases do not reinforce the rule's authority, but call it into question. The
Bavli solves the problem by arguing that the congruence between the cases and
the rule is only partial. Though the instantiating cases appear at first glance
to be textbook cases of timebound, positive commandments, they actually
fall just outside the purview of the rule. In each case, there exist compelling
reasons to override the rule that exempts women from timebound, positive
commandments. According to the Bavli, scripture specifies women's exemption
from these particular cases to compensate for the reasonable, but erroneous,
conclusions one might draw. Though each of the "instantiations" appears to
agree with the rule, the Bavli argues that one could not have reached the right
decision by applying the rule alone. Here then is a second irony. Fundamental
to the Bavli's argumentation is the assumption that the rule functions in a
prescriptive manner. As noted above, the idea that the cases and the rule are
redundant flows from this assumption. Nonetheless, the Bavli *knows of no
cases that are actually determined by the rule*. Though the Bavli knows of
many cases that apparently agree with the rule (Shema, tefillin, mezuzah, grace
after meals, sukkah, and "appearing before the Lord three times a year"),
in the final analysis not one actually falls within the jurisdiction of the rule.
All of these exemptions and obligations are stipulated individually. None is
determined by the rule.

In spite of the ironic fact that the Bavli knows of no case that is actually
determined by the rule, I would argue that the Bavli considers the rule to be
a prescriptive one.[14] Essential to each of its argumentational sequences is the

---

[14] I make this argument by highlighting what is new and distinctive in the Bavli's discussion of the
     rule. Kraemer argues that the force of the Bavli's sugya is to *undermine* our confidence in the

assumption that the rule functions prescriptively, even if we never see evidence of this activity in specific rulings. Only if the rule is assumed to function prescriptively does the problem of redundancy between the instantiating cases and the rule arise. Perhaps the most revealing moment is when the Bavli allows for the possibility that an alternate rule (one that *obligates* women to timebound, positive commandments) is in effect. Even as the Bavli rejects the content and conclusions of the familiar rule, it affirms that women's participation in ritual is regulated by an overarching rule. Here we are able to see the extent to which the Bavli gives conceptual priority to "rules" over and against cases. Irrespective of which rule it ultimately endorses, the Bavli has a clear sense that *a* rule determines the judgment in particular cases. The Bavli seems to have lost all memory of the rule as descriptive.

The Talmudic Treatment of Cases That Contradict the Rule

As noted in the introduction to this chapter, descriptive and prescriptive rules have different levels of tolerance for individual cases that contradict them. Descriptive rules aim to describe only a limited number of cases. It is expected that many cases that appear to be related to the rule will nonetheless fall outside of its jurisdiction. Prescriptive rules, on the other hand, dictate outcomes to *all* appropriate cases. Accepting the conclusions of Chapter 1, that the rule was formulated to function in a descriptive sense, helps explain why the rule has so many exceptions. Initially, the rule did not aim to account for the exceptional cases. Only once the rule was assumed to function prescriptively did the contradictory cases become problematic.

It is possible to trace the shifting conception of the rule from descriptive to prescriptive by gauging the talmudic tolerance for cases that contradict the rule. The greater the tolerance for contradictory cases, the more we must assume that the rule was understood to function descriptively; the less the tolerance for contradictory cases, the more we must assume that the rule was understood to function prescriptively. As we move from the earlier to the later strata of the Talmud,[15] a clear trend from greater to lesser degrees of tolerance is perceptible. Evidence from the early amoraim reflects a high degree of tolerance for cases that contradict the rule. By way of contrast, the post-amoraic stratum

---

rule's prescriptive value. He reaches this conclusion because the Bavli considers so many cases that contradict the rule. See David Kraemer, *Reading the Rabbis: The Talmud as Literature*, 86–108. As I understand the matter, the Bavli's very interest in these cases is a function of the Bavli's view that the rule is prescriptive. If the Bavli did not consider the rule to be prescriptive (as earlier sources did not), then the Bavli would not be concerned with the cases that instantiate and contradict the rule (as earlier sources were not).

[15] Kalmin argues that amoraic sources preserved in the redacted Bavli reflect not only the perspectives of late redactors. When read appropriately they can give us valuable information about the amoraic period, as well. See Kalmin, *Jewish Babylonia Between Persia and Roman Palestine*, and Kalmin, "The Formation and Character of the Babylonian Talmud."

of the Bavli organizes a good part of its discussion of the rule as a systematic accounting of many contradictory cases.[16] Notably, only the post-amoraic stratum of the Bavli feels the need to provide a systematic accounting of the contradictory cases. I argue that the Bavli's compelling interest in contradictory cases follows from its assumption (not held by the Yerushalmi or the amoraic stratum of the Bavli) that the rule is prescriptive. Only when the rule is assumed to be prescriptive do the many contradictory cases raise a problem.

Early Amoraic Tolerance for Contradictory Cases

R. Yohanan (second generation, Palestinian amora) had an intuitive understanding for the fact that some rabbinic rules function descriptively. He offers the following statement about the limited prescriptive utility of general rules.[17] His comment is cited in conjunction with two mishnaic rules (m. Kid. 1:7 and m. Eruv. 3:1) that have many exceptions. I cite the tradition as it appears in the discussion of the rule exempting women from timebound, positive commandments.

אמר רבי יוחנן: אין למדין מן הכללות, ואפילו במקום שנאמר בו חוץ.
דתניא: בכל מערבין ומשתתפין חוץ מן המים ומלח.
ותו ליכא? והאיכא כמהין ופטריות?
אלא אין למדין מן הכללות, ואפילו במקום שנאמר בו חוץ.

R. Yohanan said: We cannot learn from general rules, even when exceptions are stated.

As it is taught: "We may place all kinds [of food] in a common courtyard or alley in order to create [the legal fiction that all adjoining households are part of a single domain so that one may carry among them on the Sabbath,] except salt and water" (= m. Eruv. 3:1).

---

[16] Jay Rovner explains why the Bavli accounts for the particular contradictory cases that it does. According to Rovner, these cases are all the cases for which biblical or midrashic evidence exists. In Rovner's view, the Bavli's sugya was structured to account for precisely those cases where midrashic exegesis leads to conclusions that contradict the rule. Jay Rovner, "Rhetorical Strategy and Dialectical Necessity in the Babylonian Talmud: The Case of Kiddushin 34a–35a," *Hebrew Union College Annual* 65 (1994): 191, 193–203.

[17] R. Yohanan's statement appears in the Bavli as a response to a question raised by the existence of numerous exceptions to the rule. The cases that contradict the rule would seem to suggest that the rule is not operative. In the context of the redacted sugya, R. Yohanan explains that the rule functions, but only in a limited way, and that is why there are so many exceptions to the rule. Source-critical analysis suggests that R. Yohanan's statement was not initially formulated as a response to the question raised by the contradictory cases. Jay Rovner notes the late date of the "exceptions" list. The post-amoraic stratum of the Bavli constructs a question out of the "exceptions" list, and R. Yohanan's statement is positioned as answer. On the late date of the "exceptions" list, see Rovner, "Rhetorical Strategy and Dialectical Necessity in the Babylonian Talmud: The Case of Kiddushin 34a–35a," 200n47. His conclusion is buttressed by the use of Aramaic in framing the exceptions list.

Are there not more exceptions? Aren't there morrils and mushrooms?

Indeed, we cannot learn from general rules, even when exceptions are stated. [b. Kid 34a (= b. Eruv. 27a)]

R. Yohanan here offers a warning. General rules give the appearance of being able to address all situations that fall within their jurisdiction. R. Yohanan suggests, however, that it is a mistake to apply rules without discretionary consideration. Apparently, many cases *appear* to fall under the jurisdiction of a rule, but actually do not. Unless one knows from an authoritative source how a particular case should be adjudicated, one should not take the initiative to decide it according to a general rule. In other words, general rules *do not* have prescriptive utility. Even when exceptions to a rule are enumerated in conjunction with the rule, one should not assume that these are the only exceptions. It is always possible that additional exceptions exist.

R. Yohanan has a high level of tolerance for cases that contradict the rule. He fully expects to encounter exceptions to the rule. R. Yohanan intuitively understands tannaitic rules to be descriptive, rather than prescriptive. His statement suggests that rules are formulated only after individual cases have been determined. They provide a convenient summary of legal decisions that have already been rendered.[18] Rules should not, however, be the basis for new legal decisions.

Non-problematic Contradictions to the Rule

It appears that other early amoraic sages also viewed the rule as a descriptive summary of cases that had already been decided rather than as a prescriptive principle that should determine women's ritual involvement thenceforth. The Talmuds record several amoraic decisions on women's ritual involvement that contradict the stipulations of the rule. Though the rule exempts women from timebound, positive commandments, a number of amoraic decisions preserved in the Talmuds *obligate* women to perform timebound, positive commandments.[19] When one reads the amoraic statements without the

---

[18] R. Yohanan apparently makes an observation about tannaitic rules that corresponds to an observation made by contemporary scholars, as well. Modern scholars observe that when the expression "this is the general rule:" (זה הכלל) is used, it summarizes cases that have already been stated. Tannaitic rules generally have little utility as free-standing statements. See discussion in Moscovitz, *Talmudic Reasoning*, 50–62; Ephraim E Urbach, *The Halakhah: Its Sources and Development*, trans. Raphael Posner (Tel Aviv: Modan Publishing House, 1996), 177–78; and Alexander, *Transmitting Mishnah*, 138–40.

[19] Hauptman notes the preponderance of decisions made during the amoraic period to obligate women in the performance of timebound, positive commandments. Hauptman assumes that the mishnaic rule had functioned prescriptively to determine women's ritual involvement during the tannaitic period. She therefore takes the amoraic tendency to obligate women in the performance of timebound commandments to be a *departure* from previous policy. Whereas women were excluded from much ritual practice in the tannaitic period, amoraic sages "recognized the

framing comments of the Talmud's post-amoraic editors,[20] one finds no concern for the fact that these decisions contradict the stipulations of the rule. I suspect that these overt violations of the rule did not prompt discussion during the first half of the amoraic period because *at that time the rule was not viewed as having prescriptive force to determine women's ritual exemptions*. Cases that did not comply with the rule would not have been viewed as contradicting the rule, because the rule was not assumed to have prescriptive power.

Several contradictions to the rule are attributed to the first-generation Palestinian amora, R. Yehoshua b. Levi.

R. Yehoshua b. Levi said: Women are obligated in the recitation of the scroll of Esther [on the Purim], for they were also part of the same miracle. (b. Meg. 4a)

R. Yehoshua b. Levi said: Women are obligated [to light] the candles of Hanukah, for they were also part of the same miracle. (b. Shab.23a)

R. Yehoshua b. Levi said: Women are obligated [to drink] these four cups [of wine on Passover], for they were also part of the same miracle. (b. Pes. 108a–b)

These rulings by R. Yehoshua b. Levi obligate women to participate in rituals that commemorate the miraculous victories of the Jewish people against their enemies. The scroll of Esther is recited on the holiday of Purim, which marks the defeat of the wicked Haman by Queen Esther and her uncle Mordechai. Candles are lit on Hanukah to commemorate the defeat of the Hellenizing Assyrians by the Hasmoneans. Four cups of wine are drunk on Passover in celebration of the freedom that the Jews gained from the evil Pharaoh when God brought them out of Egypt with signs and wonders. Women, R. Yehoshua b. Levi explains, were implicated in risks posed by these dangerous times; women, therefore, have as much of a stake in ritually commemorating the miracles as men do.

The rulings of R. Yehoshua b. Levi do not elicit a comment from the post-amoraic stratum of the Bavli. When the rulings of R. Yehoshua b. Levi are presented in the Bavli, the post-amoraic editorial voice does not note that they contradict the rule that exempts women from timebound, positive commandments. If sages of the post-amoraic period did regard the rule as a prescriptive principle that determines women's ritual involvement, why did they not comment on R. Yehoshua's noncompliance with the stipulations of the rule? Why were they not troubled by it? Two answers suggest themselves. First, the post-amoraic

importance of making religious practice more central to the lives of women" (231). See Hauptman, *Rereading the Rabbis*, 228–31. By way of contrast, I argue that amoraic noncompliance with the rule does not represent a change in policy or attitudes toward women' ritual lives. Rather, amoraic sages, like the tannaitic predecessors, assumed that the rule was descriptive of a few cases that had already been decided and should not impact rulings yet to be made in the area of women's ritual involvement.

20　My work here is grounded in conclusions reached by Kalmin, who writes, "Despite the extensive evidence to which later generations of anoymous commentators subjected tannaitic and amoraic sources, the basic integrity of these sources is often recoverable" (873). See Kalmin, "The Formation and Character of the Babylonian Talmud," 843–47, 862–73.

stratum does not work all amoraic materials into a post-amoraic superstructure. For some reason that is not entirely clear, the post-amoraic stratum seems to have ignored the potential for development offered by these statements. Second, it is possible that the post-amoraic stratum felt that R. Yehoshua b. Levi adequately explained why these cases fell outside the jurisdiction of the rule exempting women from timebound, positive commandments. R. Yehoshua b. Levi does, after all, cite *a* principle as the basis for his inclusive rulings: "for they [women] were also part of the same miracle." Though the rituals associated with the scroll of Esther, the Hanukah candles, and the four Passover cups are timebound, positive commandments, they mark a miracle that affected the lives of women as much as the lives of men. Women are, therefore, obligated to observe these rituals, in spite of women's usual exemption from timebound commandments.

Rav Ada bar Ahava (second generation, Babylonian amora) provides additional evidence for the fact that early amoraim did not regard the rule as a prescriptive principle. Ada b. Ahava decides in favor of obligating women to recite the sanctifying blessing over wine on the Sabbath (*kiddush hayom*).

אמר רב אדא בר אהבה: נשים חייבות בקדוש היום דבר תורה

Rav Ada bar Ahava said: Women are obligated to recite sanctifying blessing over the wine [on the Sabbath]. This matter is determined in the Torah. (b. Ber. 20b)

The Bavli also records a statement by Rava (fourth generation, Babylonian amora) that elaborates on Ada b. Ahava's ruling. Rava explains the exegetical grounds for Ada b. Ahava's position.

אמר רבא: אמר קרא זכור ושמור – כל שישנו בשמירה ישנו בזכירה,
והני נשי, הואיל ואיתנהו בשמירה – איתנהו בזכירה

Rava said: Scripture states: *Remember [the Sabbath day and keep it holy]* (Exod 20:8) and *Observe [the Sabbath day and keep it holy]* (Deut 5:12). Everyone who is obligated to observe [i.e., refrain from prohibited activities on the Sabbath] is likewise obligated to *remember* it [i.e., recite the sanctifying blessing over wine].

Women, because they are obligated to *observe* – they are likewise obligated to *remember*. (b. Ber. 20b)

These amoraic statements are unapologetic in their decision to obligate women to recite the blessing that sanctifies the Sabbath, though such a ritual can easily be construed as a "timebound, positive commandment." When these amoraic statements are read without the framing comments provided by the later editors of the Bavli, they display no sign of discomfort with the contradiction that arises between their obligation of women and the rule that exempts women from timebound, positive commandments. Such a concern is raised only by the post-amoraic editor of the sugya when the text in its final redacted form asks, "Why [are women] obligated? [Recitation of the sanctifying blessing on the

Sabbath] is a timebound, positive commandment, and aren't women exempt from all timebound, positive commandments?" (b. Ber. 20b).

We should not, however, be surprised to find the post-amoraic stratum expressing discomfort with a case that contradicts the rule. I have been arguing that the post-amoraic stratum *does* regard the rule as a prescriptive principle that determines women's ritual exemptions. When the post-amoraic reframes these early amoraic statements, it casts Rava's midrash as an *answer* to the question of why the rule is overridden and why women are obligated to recite the sanctifying blessing. Rava's midrash no longer merely articulates that which is explicit in Rav Ada b. Ahavah's ruling. Rava's midrash now provides the rationale for Ada b. Ahava's disregard of the general rule that exempts women from timebound, positive commandments. Reciting the sanctifying blessing on the Sabbath is a positive obligation (*remember*) that scripture has linked with its negative counterpart (*observe*, i.e., refrain from prohibited activities). These special conditions dictate that the general rule not be applied.

Finally, both Talmuds attribute to R. Elazar (third-generation Palestinian amora) the ruling that women are obligated to eat matzah on Passover. The Yerushalmi reports R. Elazar's ruling as a response to a question:

What is [women's ritual status] regarding matzah? R. Elazar said: Obligation. (y. Pes. 35d = y. Kid. 61c)

The Bavli attributes the same legal position to R. Elazar, but frames it differently.

As R. Elazar said: Women are obligated in the eating of matzah; this matter is determined in the Torah. (b. Pes. 43b)

The editorial superstructures in both the Yerushalmi and the Bavli are troubled by the fact that R. Elazar obligates women to eat matzah on Passover when the rule exempts women from timebound, positive commandments. It should be noted, however, that R. Elazar's statement does not telegraph its own concern with respect to the issue. The contradiction arises only for the later editors because they, unlike the earlier amoraim, assume that the rule functions prescriptively.

In sum, during the first four generations of amoraic activity (220–350), sages in both Palestine and Babylonia felt comfortable obligating women to perform timebound, positive commandments (sanctifying blessing over wine on the Sabbath, Hanukah candles, Purim scroll, four Passover cups, Passover matzah). They were aware, of course, of the rule that exempts women from timebound, positive commandments, but they apparently did not think that the rule rendered their noncompliant rulings inappropriate. In my view, this phenomenon is best explained by recognizing that the early amoraim did not imagine themselves to be acting in violation of the rule. I argue that the early amoraim whose rulings are collected here were like R. Yohanan in that they accepted the descriptive utility of the rule, but did not see it as the basis for making new rulings. While the rule adequately describes a number of legal rulings that had already been decided, the rule was not viewed as a prescriptive principle to be used to determine women's ritual involvement thenceforth.

From Description to Prescription

I argue that only the post-amoraic stratum of the Bavli operates under the assumption that the rule was in force during the tannaitic period as a prescriptive principle determining women's ritual involvement. This assumption is manifest in the Bavli's systematic treatment of rulings that contradict the rule. The Bavli's discussion of the rule is structured around what Jay Rovner calls the "exceptions list": a list of six exceptions to the rule that have a biblical or midrashic precedent.[21] By way of contrast, the Yerushalmi's editorial strata (c. 375–425) notes only one ruling that contradicts the rule. It will be useful to discuss the Yerushalmi's treatment of the contradictory rulings before discussing the Bavli's in order to gauge what is genuinely new in the post-amoraic stratum of the Bavli.

Evidence from the editorial strata of the Yerushalmi suggests that later Palestinian amoraim, unlike earlier amoraim discussed above, were attentive to the conflict created when a particular case contradicted the stipulations of the general rule. In their efforts to make sense of inherited legal traditions, they noticed and attempted to account for the contradiction between the rule and women's obligation to eat matzah. The redactors of the Yerushalmi probably did not view the rule as a prescriptive principle that determines women's ritual involvement broadly, but recognized that in one case the rule had been disregarded; they wanted to know why.

The Yerushalmi records an extended discussion of R. Elazar's ruling (quoted above), which obligates women to eat matzah on Passover. Two of R. Elazar's contemporaries (R. Zeira and R. Hila) disagree about the context in which Elazar made his decision. R. Zeira believes that R. Elazar represents one side in a dispute over women's obligation to eat matzah. R. Hila believes that R. Elazar states his position as one that was universally agreed upon by all. After citing the disputing voices of R. Zeira and R. Hila, the editorial voice of the Yerushalmi notes that a tannaitic source can be brought in support of both R. Zeira and R. Hila.[22] The Yerushalmi finds a tannaitic source that follows R.

---

[21] See discussion in Rovner, "Rhetorical Strategy and Dialectical Necessity in the Babylonian Talmud: The Case of Kiddushin 34a–35a," 191, 193–203.

[22] A standard procedure in talmudic argumentation demonstrates the viability of two mutually exclusive positions in a dispute. See discussion of this trait of talmudic argumentation in Elizabeth Shanks Alexander, "Why Study Talmud in the 21st Century: The View from a Large Public University OR Studying Talmud as a Critical Thinker," in *Why Study Talmud in the Twenty-first Century? The Relevance of the Ancient Jewish Text to Our World*, ed. Paul Socken (New York: Rowman and Littlefield, 2009), 17–18. See also Louis Jacobs, *The Talmudic Argument: A Study in Talmudic Reasoning and Methodology* (Cambridge: Cambridge University

Zeira in representing women's obligation to eat matzah as a disputed position; it also finds a tannaitic source that follows R. Hila in representing women's obligation to eat matzah as universally held by all. My discussion centers on the tannaitic source that supports R. Hila's position (namely, that R. Elazar's view that women are obligated to eat matzah was universally held by all).

מתניתא מסייעא לר' הילא נאמר לא תאכל עליו חמץ ונ' שבעת ימי' תאכל עליו מצו' לחם עוני

את שהוא בבל תאכל חמץ הרי הוא בקו' אכול מצה

ונשי' הרי הן בבל תאכל חמץ הרי הן בקום אכול מצה

והא תנינן כל מצות עשה שהזמן גרמא האנשים חייבין והנשים פטורות

א"ר מנא הוא מצות עשה שהיא באה מכח בלא תעשה

A tannaitic source supports R. Hila [who says that R. Elazar's position that women are obligated to eat matzah was universally held by all]:

It is written, *You shall not eat leaven with [the Passover sacrifice]* and it is written, *Seven days you shall eat matzah, the bread of distress* (Deut 16:3).

Whoever is obligated to refrain from [eating] leaven is obligated to actively eat matzah.

Behold women, since they are obligated to refrain from [eating] leaven, they are obligated to actively eat matzah.

But a tannaitic source [conflicts with this teaching. Does it not say:] *All timebound, positive commandments – men are obligated and women are exempt* (= m. Kid. 1:7)?

R. Mana says: [Eating matzah] is a positive commandment that is integrally connected with a negative commandment [refraining from leaven]. [y. Kid. 61c (= y. Pes. 35d)]

The editorial strata of the Yerushalmi begins by noting that a tannaitic midrash on Deut 16:3 supports R. Hila's representation of R. Elazar as a universally held position.[23] The tannaitic midrash notes that scripture speaks of the negative commandment to refrain from eating leaven and the positive commandment to eat matzah in the same verse. The juxtaposition of these negative and positive commandments teaches that anyone who is subject to the negative command to refrain from leaven is also subject to the positive command to eat matzah. The midrash concludes that women, being subject to the negative command of refraining from eating leaven, are also subject to the positive command to eat matzah. Since the midrash is not ascribed to any single sage, we must assume that its conclusions are universally held. As such, the tannaitic midrash supports R. Hila's position that R. Elazar's decision to obligate women to eat matzah was uncontested.

Press, 1984); and William Kolbrener, "'Chiseled from All Sides': Hermeneutics and Dispute in Rabbinic Tradition," *AJS Review* 28/2 (2004): 273–95.

[23] A version of this midrash appears in Sif. Dt. 130 (ed. Finkelstein, 187). The Sifre's version does not include the line that indicates that women in particular are obligated to eat matzah (line 4 above).

With tannaitic evidence to support R. Hila's position in place, the editorial stratum of the Yerushalmi raises another question. How can anyone reach the conclusion that women are obligated to eat matzah? Is not matzah a timebound, positive commandment? Are not women exempt from timebound, positive commandments? The editorial stratum of the Yerushalmi is disturbed by the contradiction between the two tannaitic sources. While one tannaitic source (the midrash on Deut 16:3) obligates women to perform a timebound, positive commandment (eating matzah), another (m. Kid. 1:7) exempts women from timebound, positive commandments. The Yerushalmi solves the problem by showing that the ritual of eating matzah is *unlike* other timebound, positive commandments. Given its distinctive qualities, it is not subject to the same rule as other timebound, positive commandments. Unlike other timebound, positive commandments, the ritual of eating matzah is a "positive commandment that is integrally connected to a negative commandment [refraining from eating leaven]." Apparently, positive commandments (like eating matzah) that are integrally connected to a corresponding negative commandment (refraining from eating leaven) are not subject to the rule that otherwise exempts women from timebound, positive commandments. In this manner, the contradiction between tannaitic midrash and the rule exempting women from timebound, positive commandments is resolved.

Insofar as the editorial stratum of the Yerushalmi is troubled by the existence of a ruling that contradicts the stipulation of the rule, it moves beyond the position of the early amoraim who did not expect decisions in specific cases to conform to the stipulations of the general rule. There are, however, important ways in which the Yerushalmi's discussion falls short of viewing the rule as broadly prescriptive. The Yerushalmi's discussion arises because it brings one tannaitic source (the midrash concluding that women are obligated to eat matzah) into dialogue with another (the rule exempting women from timebound, positive commandments). The Yerushalmi is not reflecting on *all* cases that might possibly conflict with the rule. Rather, the Yerushalmi reflects on the conflict between women's obligation to eat matzah and the rule in the context of a discussion of Passover rituals. The starting point for the Yerushalmi's discussion is a specific case (women's obligation to eat matzah), rather than a general rule (women's exemption from timebound, positive commandments).[24] It makes sense to conclude that the Yerushalmi's editors were initially thinking about women's obligation to eat matzah and as an afterthought recalled that such a decision conflicts with the rule that exempts women from timebound, positive commandments. It is less likely that the editors of the sugya were

---

[24] The dialectical conversation cited above is found in the Yerushalmi's discussion of Passover (y. Pes. 35d on m. Pes. 8:1) and in its discussion of timebound, positive commandments (y. Kid. 61c on m. Kid. 1:7). In both locations the primary topic of discussion is analysis of Passover rituals, not the rule exempting women from timebound, positive commandments.

reflecting on the rule and noted one – and only one – exception to the rule. The Yerushalmi's discussion does, however, seem to have prompted the Bavli to think more systematically about contradictions to the rule.[25]

The Bavli's Systematic Reflection on Contradictory Cases

The Bavli's discussion of the rule is structured around a discussion of the cases that both instantiate and contradict the rule. As noted above, cases that instantiate the rule are problematic for the Bavli because of the post-amoraic stratum's assumption that the rule functions prescriptively. The instantiating cases do not need to be stated explicitly because they can be deduced by applying the rule. The Bavli resolves this problem by showing that each case that instantiates the rule actually falls slightly outside the purview of the rule; apparently, the correct decision would not have been reached had the rule alone been available. The exceptional nature of the instantiating cases (sukkah, "appearing," and the paschal offering) requires that they be stated explicitly.

Cases that contradict the rule present a different sort of challenge for the post-amoraic stratum of the Bavli. The Bavli cites six cases that contradict the stipulations of the rule. Three cases contradict the first half of the rule (that women are *exempt* from timebound, positive commandments), and three cases contradict the second half of the rule (that women are *obligated* to perform non-timebound, positive commandments). After citing the mishnaic rule (m. Kid. 1:7) and the tosephtan baraita that enumerates examples of the rule (t. Kid. 1:10), the Bavli notes the following exceptions to the rule:

וכללא הוא?

הרי מצה, שמחה, הקהל, דמצות עשה שהזמן גרמא, ונשים חייבות!

ותו, והרי תלמוד תורה, פריה ורביה, ופדיון הבן, דלאו מצות עשה שהזמן גרמא הוא, ונשים פטורות!

Can this really be the rule?

Behold, matzah, "happiness," and "gathering" are timebound, positive commandments – and yet women are obligated to perform them.

And furthermore, Torah study, be "fruitful and multiply," and redemption of the first born are *non*-timebound, positive commandments – and yet women are exempt from them. (b. Kid. 34a)

In violation of the first part of the rule, women are obligated to perform the following "timebound" commandments. Women are obligated to (1) eat

[25] Alyssa Gray observes that sometimes a sugya in the Bavli is designed to address a question that is generated by the parallel sugya in the Yerushalmi. See Alyssa M. Gray, *A Talmud in Exile: The Influence of Yerushalmi Avodah Zarah on the Formation of Bavli Avodah Zarah*, Brown Judaic Studies 342 (Providence: Brown Judaic Studies, 2005), 149, 151, 153, 160–62, 172, 241. See also Elizabeth Shanks Alexander, "Art, Argument and Ambiguity in the Talmud: Conflicting Representations of the Evil Impulse," *Hebrew Union College Annual* 73 (2002): 108–10, 120–31.

matzah on Passover,[26] (2) offer a "happiness offering" on the festivals,[27] and (3) "gather" with the nation once every seven years to hear the Torah read publicly.[28] In violation of the second part of the rule, women are exempt from the following non-timebound commandments (even though the rule stipulates that should be obligated): (1) Torah study,[29] (2) be fruitful and multiply,[30] and (3) redemption of the firstborn son from the priests.[31]

The Bavli's treatment of the contradictory cases distinguishes itself from the Yerushalmi's in several regards. First, the Bavli's discussion is occasioned by reflecting on the rule, not the individual cases. We noted that Yerushalmi's discussion, by way of contrast, is occasioned by an interest in the laws of Passover. Only secondarily does the Yerushalmi reflect on the contradiction between women's obligation to eat matzah and the rule. Apparently, only the post-amoraic stratum of the Bavli thought of the rule as a piece of legislation that *by the mere fact of its existence* needed to be reconciled with contradictory rulings. Second, the Bavli treats many more contradictory cases than does the Yerushalmi. Jay Rovner explains that the Bavli's "exceptions list" is a complete list of exceptions that have biblical or midrashic roots.[32] The Yerushalmi, by way of contrast, treats only one contradictory case: matzah. Whereas the Bavli treats the question raised by the existence of contradictory cases in a systematic way, the Yerushalmi treats it only in an occasional way.

Finally, the Bavli notes exceptions to *both* halves of the rule. Women are observed to be obligated to perform several timebound commandments *and* exempt from several *non*-timebound commandments. The Yerushalmi, on the other hand, does not comment at all on the second half of the rule. Apparently, the Bavli conceptually frames the rule in a different way than does the Yerushalmi. The Bavli is troubled by contradictions to both halves of the rule because it takes seriously the mishnaic rhetoric that presents the rule as part of a four-part structure. As noted in Chapter 2, the four-part structure of m. Kid. 1: discusses women's ritual obligations as regards *four* categories of commandments: (1) timebound, positive commandments; (2) *non*-timebound, positive commandments; (3) timebound, negative commandments; and (4) *non*-timebound, negative commandments. In the context of the four-part structure, the rule appears to be a *complete list* of women's ritual obligations and exemptions. The Tosephta,[33] on the other hand, presents the rule in the context of a

---

[26] See Sif. Dt. 130 on Deut 16:3.

[27] See Sif. Dt. 138 on Deut 16:11.

[28] See Deut 31:12.

[29] See Sif. Dt. 46 on Deut 11:19 and t. Kid. 1:11.

[30] See m. Yev. 6:6.

[31] See Exod 13:1, 13.

[32] See Rovner, "Rhetorical Strategy and Dialectical Necessity in the Babylonian Talmud: The Case of Kiddushin 34a–35a," 191, 193–203.

[33] T. Sot. 2:8 and t. Bik. 2:8. See discussion of these sources in Chapter 2.

two-part structure. When framed within the two-part structure, the rule enumerates only a few exceptional positive commandments and a few exceptional negative commandments from which women are exempt. When the Bavli notes exceptions to the second half of the rule, it signals that it engages the rule within the conceptual rubric of the four-part structure. The four-part structure positions the rule as a complete account of all of women's ritual obligations. By contrast, the Yerushalmi completely ignores exceptions to the second half of the rule. In so doing, the Yerushalmi signals that it engages the rule within the conceptual rubric of the two-part structure. Since the two-part structure enumerates only a few commandments from which women are exempt, it leaves open the possibility that women will be exempt from commandments other than the timebound, positive ones stipulated by the rule. For the Yerushalmi, the rule does not claim to be a complete account of women's ritual obligations. In sum, I take the fact that the Bavli treats exceptions to the rule in a more thoroughgoing manner than the Yerushalmi to be a sign that the Bavli thinks about the rule differently than does the Yerushalmi. Where the Bavli regards the rule as a prescriptive principle that determines the broad scope of women's ritual involvement, the Yerushalmi regards the rule as a descriptive statement of limited scope. For the Yerushalmi, the sugya notes one area in which women are ritually exempt; the Yerushalmi, however, does not expect the rule to be universally and consistently applied.

In addition to treating more contradictory cases than the Yerushalmi, the Bavli also reconciles itself to the existence of the contradictory cases in a different way than the Yerushalmi does. It will be recalled that the Yerushalmi resolves the problem created by women's obligation to eat matzah by showing that this ritual falls outside of the purview of the rule. Since eating matzah is a positive commandment that is integrally connected with a negative commandment (refraining from eating leaven), eating matzah is a timebound, positive commandment for which women are obligated. The contradictory cases pose a different type of problem for the Bavli. In the context of the Bavli's argumentation, the contradictory cases suggest that the received tradition that women are exempt from timebound, positive commandments is false. In order to account for the fact that the mishnaic rule is routinely violated, the Bavli speculates that the rule that actually governs women's ritual involvement is the exact opposite of the mishnaic rule. Perhaps, the Bavli suggests, the "real" rule *obligates* women to perform timebound, positive commandments (unlike the mishnaic rule, which exempts women from them)? Perhaps the "real" rule *exempts* women from *non*-timebound, positive commandments (unlike the mishnaic rule, where women are obligated)?

The goals of the Bavli's argumentational sequence are to deny the existence of what I shall call the "obverse rule" and to affirm the validity of "the rule as we know it." The Bavli does this by showing that none of the contradictory cases has the capacity to serve as a prototype for the "obverse rule." Undoubtedly, the contradictory cases do not conform to the "rule as we know it," but the

Bavli attempts to demonstrate that they do not prevent the "rule as we know it" from functioning prescriptively. The Bavli seeks to prove that the contradictory cases do not ground an alternate rule that would render "the rule as we know it" null and void.

Consider the following example of the Bavli's discussion:

ואדילפינן מתפילין לפטורא, נילף משמחה לחיובא!

אמר אביי: אשה – בעלה משמחה.

אלמנה מאי איכא למימר?

בשרויה אצלו.

ונילף מהקהל! משום דהוה מצה והקהל שני כתובים הבאים כאחד, וכל שני כתובים הבאין כאחד אין מלמדים.

1. Rather than learning from [the prototype of] tefillin that women are exempt from all timebound, positive commandments, let us learn from [the prototype of] the "happiness" offering [which is timebound, and obligatory for women] that women should be *obligated* [to perform all timebound, positive commandments].

2. Abaye said: A woman – her husband is obligated to make the "happiness" offering for her. [This indicates that the obligation for the festival "happiness" offerings does not truly fall on a woman, but on her husband].

3. What about a widow [who has no husband, and yet is nonetheless obligated to offer the "happiness" offering]?

4. [The obligation falls on] the man with whom she resides.

5. Then let us learn from [the prototype of women's obligation to] "gather" [every seven years to hear the Torah read publicly that women should be obligated to perform *all* timebound, positive commandments].

6. [No, we cannot use "gathering" as a prototype] because matzah and "gathering" are two laws which teach the same thing, and one cannot learn general rules [that extend to other cases] from two laws that teach the same thing. (b. Kid. 34b)

The Bavli discusses cases that contradict the rule for the purpose of discounting them as prototypes for the "obverse rule." In the extract presented here, the Bavli shows that none of the three cases that contradict the first half of the rule (matzah, "happiness," and "gathering") can be used to ground the "obverse rule." The first paragraph (lines 1–4) eliminates "happiness" as a prototype for the obverse rule, and the second paragraph (lines 5–6) eliminates matzah and "gathering" as prototypes for the obverse rule. The first paragraph explains that the obligation for a woman to bring a "happiness" offering on the festivals actually falls upon the man in whose home she resides, be it her husband (line 2) or some other man (line 4). Women's obligation to bring a "happiness" offering on the festivals cannot serve as a prototype for the obverse rule because it is not a clear-cut case of women being obligated to perform a timebound, positive commandment. In the context of the Bavli's argumentation, the first paragraph demonstrates that the "happiness" offering cannot ground the obverse rule. The first paragraph also shows that a woman's obligation to bring a "happiness" offering does not violate the stipulations of the "rule as we know it": The obligation to bring the "happiness" offering actually falls on the male householder, and not on the woman residing in his domain.

The second paragraph eliminates matzah and "gathering" as prototypes for the obverse rule, but it does so in a way that maintains their status as cases that contradict the "rule as we know it." The Bavli begins the next phase of its argument by proposing that women's obligation to participate in the public "gathering" every seven years can serve as a prototype for the obverse rule. Having eliminated "happiness" as a prototype, the argumentation now seeks other prototypes for the obverse rule. Since the ritual of "gathering" every seven years to hear the Torah read publicly is a timebound, positive commandment for which women are *obligated*, it is a good candidate. But in line 6, the Bavli demonstrates that "gathering" too cannot ground the obverse rule. The Bavli does not eliminate "gathering" by showing that it falls outside the purview of the rule. Rather, the Bavli confirms that women's obligation to "gather" does indeed contradict the "rule as we know it." Nonetheless, women's obligation to "gather" cannot serve as a prototype for the obverse rule because of the existence of a competing principle. According to the Bavli, if two legal decisions (e.g., women's obligation to eat matzah and their obligation to "gather") can both potentially serve as prototypes for the same rule, neither may do so. In the words of Rovner, the two combine to form a "non-productive pair."[34] Apparently, in order to serve as a prototype for a rule, a legal decision must be unique. A prototype functions by being a unique paradigm for other cases. A "proper" prototype reaches a conclusion that has not been reached in other cases. Because women's obligations to eat matzah and to "gather" every seven years *both* point to the same conclusion (that women should be obligated to perform timebound, positive commandments), neither can serve as a prototype for the rule. Even though the Bavli never resolves the contradiction between women's obligation to eat matzah and gather every seven years, on one hand, and the rule exempting women from timebound, positive commandments, on the other, the Bavli does succeed in affirming the validity of the "rule as we know it."

Underlying the Bavli's argumentation sequence is the assumption that *a* rule – whether the obverse rule or the "rule as we know it" – governs women's ritual involvement. The explicit goal of the argumentation is to affirm the validity of the "rule as we know it." The Bavli concludes that the familiar mishnaic rule, rather than the obverse rule, determines women's ritual involvement. But it is important to note that the Bavli's argumentational sequence simply would not be possible without the assumption that the rule was formulated to determine women's ritual involvement. It is interesting that the Bavli does not try to

---

[34] See Rovner, "Rhetorical Strategy and Dialectical Necessity in the Babylonian Talmud: The Case of Kiddushin 34a–35a," 189. See also explication of this sugya in Jacobs, *The Talmudic Argument: A Study in Talmudic Reasoning and Methodology*, 133–43.

demonstrate that all cases that contradict the rule fall outside the purview of the rule. One might have expected the Bavli, with its presumption that the rule operates prescriptively, to take such an approach. Such an approach would dilute the force of individual rulings that contradict the rule. Instead, the Bavli maintains only a theoretical commitment to the idea that the rule functions prescriptively. The Bavli leaves open the possibility that some cases (like matzah and "gathering") genuinely contradict the rule. What the Bavli's argumentation does succeed in demonstrating is that the existence of contradictory cases does not undermine the prescriptive utility of the "rule as we know it."[35] Though discrete decisions were made to obligate women to perform the timebound, positive commandments of matzah and "gathering," the fact remains that a prescriptive rule remains in place that was formulated to determine women's ritual involvement. Even though the Bavli leaves in place the contradiction between some of the cases on the "exceptions list" and the rule exempting women from timebound, positive commandments, it does give the appearance of addressing the contradictory cases fully. Unlike the Yerushalmi, the Bavli wrestles with a full range of tannaitic rulings that contradict the rule that exempts women from timebound, positive commandments.

Conclusion

Early amoraim do not seem to have regarded the rule as a prescriptive principle that determined women's ritual involvement. We see evidence for this in the fact that early amoraim made many legal decisions about women's ritual involvement that violated the terms of the rule. By the end of the amoraic period when the editorial layer of the Yerushalmi did its work, the amoraim seem to have developed a discomfort with cases that contradict the stipulations of the rule. It is possible that the Yerushalmi's discomfort in this regard provoked the post-amoraic stratum of the Bavli to discuss the contradictory cases in a more thoroughgoing manner. Even more than the editorial stratum of the Yerushalmi, the post-amoraic stratum of the Bavli sought to understand inherited legal traditions as part of a coherent legal system. The impulse to structure inherited legal traditions as part of a harmonious whole became stronger as time went on. By the post-amoraic period, sages routinely brought conflicting traditions into dialogue with each other in order to reveal underlying consistencies within the legal system. As Leib Moscovitz has argued, during the

---

[35] In his literary reading of talmudic sugyot, Aryeh Cohen suggests that the talmudic presentation of material impacts the reader on levels other than that signaled by the rhetoric of argumentation. See Aryeh Cohen, *Rereading Talmud: Gender, Law and the Poetics of Sugyot.* He writes, "Even though [certain legal conclusions] are not accepted as *legal* reasoning, [they] still have rhetorical power" (167). Building on Cohen's suggestion, I would argue that even though the Bavli knows of no case that is actually determined by the rule, the force of the sugya with its presumption that the rule functions prescriptively is to construct the rule as a prescriptive principle.

post-amoraic period, sages also reflected on inherited legal traditions through a more conceptual lens.[36] In the context of these post-amoraic intellectual tendencies, viewing the rule as a prescriptive principle made sense.

In this chapter, I have tried to demonstrate that during the post-amoraic period a new view of the rule developed. During the post-amoraic period, sages began to think of the rule as one that had been formulated to determine, rather than describe, women's ritual involvement. It is important to note that the post-amoraic view of the rule as prescriptive did not lead them to employ the rule as a means of making new legal decisions. In fact, it is ironic that the Bavli knows of no case (not even the instantiating cases) that was actually decided by the rule. Nonetheless, when the post-amoraic stratum envisions legal decision making during the tannaitic period, it assumes that the rule functioned prescriptively.

The post-amoraic view of the rule as prescriptive lays the groundwork for medieval interpreters of the rule to reflect on the social motivations for the rule. Once the Bavli framed the rule as one that had been formulated to determine women's ritual involvement, it became possible to theorize about the social vision that guided the rule's authors. Undoubtedly, the post-amoraic reading of the rule as prescriptive had a lasting effect on the rule's ability to ground and support the construction of gender. It is important to stress, however, that there is no evidence to suggest that the post-amoraic sages read the rule prescriptively with an awareness of how it would support the construction of gender henceforth. Rather, it seems that a broadly conceived legal agenda led the post-amoraic sages to read the rule prescriptively. In general, post-amoraic sages emphasized the conceptual priority of general rules over individual cases. Within this context, reading the rule prescriptively made sense. While the rule now had the potential to ground the edifice of gender, it did not acquire this attribute as the result of post-amoraic interests in gender. The rule acquired this attribute in the context of the post-amoraic interest in organizing received sources into a conceptually coherent legal system.

[36] See Moscovitz, *Talmudic Reasoning*. See also Goldberg, "The Babylonian Talmud," 330–31.

PART III

GENDER IN WOMEN'S RITUAL EXEMPTIONS

6

Women's Exemption from Shema and Tefillin

M. Berakhot 3:3 provides a short catalogue of women's exemptions and obligations vis-à-vis various liturgical and textual practices.

Women, slaves and minors are exempt from the recitation of Shema and from tefillin, and obligated with regard to the Prayer, the mezuzah and grace after meals.

Here we learn that women are exempt from reciting the Shema and wearing tefillin, but obligated to pray the Amidah, recite the grace after meals, and post a mezuzah on their doorposts. Unfortunately, in classic fashion the Mishnah states these legal conclusions without providing a rationale for them.[1] Women's exemption from reciting the Shema, in particular, provokes curiosity since the Shema is a liturgical affirmation of the key doctrinal commitments underlying rabbinic Judaism (belief in one God and dedication to God through performance of the commandments). What is it about the recitation of Shema and wearing tefillin that makes it inappropriate to require women to perform these rituals? What distinguishes Shema and tefillin from the other liturgical and textual practices listed in m. Ber. 3:3?

This chapter seeks to answer this question by highlighting the fact that the rabbis regarded recitation of Shema and the wearing of tefillin as forms of Torah study. Since the rabbis claimed to know from elsewhere that women are exempt from Torah study, they concluded that women are also exempt from the rituals that are the functional equivalent of Torah study. The bulk of this chapter offers a reception history of the biblical verses that eventually constituted the Shema liturgy in an effort to reveal how the rabbis came to regard Shema and tefillin practices as forms of Torah study.

---

[1] According to David Weiss Halivni, the Mishnah is exceptional within the Jewish legal corpus in its tendency to state laws apodictically, i.e., without justification. See Halivni, *Midrash, Mishnah, and Gemara: The Jewish Predilection for Justified Law*, 38–65.

By the time the Mishnah was recorded in 200 CE, the rabbis took for granted the existence of a liturgical practice that consisted of reciting three biblical passages (Deut 6:4–9; Deut 11:13–21; Num 15:37–41) twice daily, framed on either end with a set of blessings. The fact that such a practice was standardized and considered of ancient origin by tannaitic times, however, does not negate the fact that certain interpretive moves had to be made in order for the Shema verses to be understood as a liturgical unit subject to daily recitation.

The rabbinic practices of reciting Shema and wearing tefillin derive from a particular reading of Deut 6:7–8 (see also Deut 11:18–20):

You shall repeat [these words which I command you this day] to your children and you shall speak of them when you sit in your house and when you go on your way, and when you lie down and when you rise up. And you shall bind them as a sign upon your hand and they shall be a frontlet between your eyes.

The rabbinic interpretation of these verses assumes that "the words" to be recited in the evening and morning ("when you lie down" and "rise up") and "the words" to be worn as frontlets and on the arm are the full text of the paragraph containing these verses, that is, Deut 6:4–9. In other words, the rabbis understand the term "these words" to be self-referential.[2] Reviewing the process by which this interpretation came about reveals how and why the rabbis came to regard the recitation and binding of "these words" as forms of Torah study.

During the latter half of the Second Temple period, the biblical verses that make up the rabbinic Shema were attracting attention because of their doctrinal centrality and the fact that they prescribe a concrete set of embodied rituals. Though a variety of sources attest to the importance of the Shema verses during the Second Temple period, the sources differ widely on their reasons for engaging the Shema verses. A survey of the Second Temple sources that allude to, discuss, or cite the Shema verses reveals the range of meanings that these verses carried in the period before the rabbis were active. Examining these sources highlights the distinctive meanings the Shema and its attendant rituals had for the rabbis, among them the idea that recitation of the Shema and wearing tefillin were forms of Torah study. Before turning to the Second

---

[2] Following an established trend in scholarship, Cohn characterizes this interpretation as "literalist" as opposed to "figurative." See Yehudah B. Cohn, *Tangled Up in Text: Tefillin and the Ancient World*, 87–88, 92, 100, and elsewhere. His characterization focuses on the interpretation of the scriptural words "recite" and "bind": Is one to recite and bind the words literally, or is this a mere figure of speech indicating one should "internalize" the words? Within the "literalist" interpretation, one can further distinguish between different ways of interpreting the term "these words," which are the subject of the ritual: Does the term "these words" refer to the instructional verses (i.e., is the text self-referential?), or does it refer to some other entity (like justice, law, or Torah generally)? The self-referential interpretation might be referred to as "doubly literalist" since it requires a literal reading of the terms "recite"/"bind" and a literalist reading of the term "these words."

Temple sources, however, it will be helpful to review the contents of the three biblical passages that eventually came to be the rabbinic Shema.

The Rabbinic Shema

The rabbinic Shema consists of three biblical passages (Deut 6:4–9; Deut 11:13–21; Num 15:37–41) framed by a set of two blessings preceding the biblical passages and one or two blessings following them.[3] The order and the content of the biblical passages are attested in several tannaitic sources.[4] Conventional scholarly wisdom sees the Shema liturgy as a ritual reenactment of Israel's covenantal dedication to God.[5] When performed liturgically, these verses were understood to speak not only to a historic set of relationships, but also to a relationship that endures in all its vitality in the present context.[6]

Rabbinic sources provide a title for each of the three paragraphs; the titles correspond to the first word or several words of each paragraph.[7] The first

---

[3] Kimelman discusses the theological framing provided by the framing blessings. He argues that the *emet veyaztiv* blessing is quite early and that it, alongside the biblical passages, formed the earliest core of the Shema liturgy. He further argues that in its earliest form, the ritual functioned as a reenactment of the covenant. The first and last blessings were added at a later stage and form an envelope structure around the covenantal reenactment material lending it a new set of meanings. In its new configuration, the Shema liturgy functions as a coronation of God as King/Master of the Universe. See Reuven Kimelman, "The Shema` Liturgy: From Covenant Ceremony to Coronation," in *Kenishta: Studies of the Synogogue World*, ed. Joseph Tabory (Ramat Gan: Bar-Ilan University Press, 2001), 9–105.

[4] See m. Ber. 2:2; Sif. Dt. 34–35; and Sif. Num. 115. M. Tam. 5:1 refers to a Shema liturgy that was recited by the priests as part of the morning sacrificial rites. In this source, three paragraphs of the rabbinic Shema are preceded by a recitation of the Ten Commandments. On the reliability of *m. Tam.* 5:1 as a description of Second Temple practice, see E. E. Urbach, "The Role of the Ten Commandments in Jewish Worship," in *The Ten Commandments in History and Tradition*, ed. Ben-Zion Segal and Gershon Levi (Jerusalem: Magnes Press, 1985), 161–89; Kimelman, "From Covenant to Coronation," 13n13, 68–80; and Joseph Tabory, "Prayers and Berakhot," in *Literature of the Sages*, part. 2, ed. Shmuel (z"l) Safrai et al. (Amsterdam: Royal Van Gorcum and Fortress Press, 2006), 290–94.

[5] See Levenson, *Sinai and Zion: An Entry into the Jewish Bible*, 81–86; Moshe Weinfeld, *Deuteronomy 1–11: A New Translation with Introduction and Commentary*, vol. 5 (New York: Doubleday, 1991), 349–54; Kimelman, "From Covenant to Coronation," esp. 77; Lawrence Schiffman, *Reclaiming the Dead Sea Scrolls* (Philadelphia: Jewish Publication Society, 1994), 293; and Tabory, "Prayers and Berakhot," 292. Levenson, for example, writes, "The recitation of the *Shma* is the rabbinic covenantal renewal ceremony." Levenson, *Sinai and Zion: An Entry into the Jewish Bible*, 86. Another popular view is that recitation of the Shema functions as an affirmation of faith. See Albert Baumgarten, "Invented Traditions of the Maccabean Era," in *Geschichte–Tradition–Reflexion*, vol. 1: *Judentum*, ed. Peter Schaefer (Tübingen: Mohr Siebeck, 1996), 202; and Alan Mintz, "Prayer and the Prayerbook," in *Back to the Sources: Reading the Classic Jewish Texts*, ed. Barry Holtz (New York: Simon and Schuster, 1985), 408–13.

[6] Levenson writes, "To recite the *Shma*... is ... to become a citizen of the kingdom of God ... in the historical present." See Levenson, *Sinai and Zion: An Entry into the Jewish Bible*, 85.

[7] This is the same method by which the rabbis name the books of the Pentateuch and chapters of the Mishnah.

word of the first paragraph is *shema`* (lit. "hear" or "listen"), and the whole liturgical cycle takes its name from this paragraph. The first paragraph of the Shema is drawn from Deut 6 and reads as follows (all biblical translations are taken from NJPS):

[DOCTRINAL PROLOGUE:] (4) Hear, O Israel! The Lord is our God, the Lord alone. (5) You shall love the Lord your God with all your heart and with all your soul and with all your might.

[TRANSITIONAL VERSE:] (6) Take to heart these instructions (*devarim*) with which I charge you this day.

[RITUAL INSTRUCTIONS:] (7) Impress them upon your children. Recite them when you stay at home and when you are away, when you lie down and when you get up. (8) Bind them as a sign on your hand and let them serve as a symbol on your forehead; (9) Inscribe them on the doorposts of your house and on your gates.

As understood by the rabbis, this passage contains two key elements. The first two verses of the paragraph (6:4–5) offer a doctrinal affirmation.[8] Israel is called upon to acknowledge the oneness of God.[9] Acknowledgment of God's unity leads to the next verse, which commands Israel to love God. Biblical scholars generally assume that the love requested here is a concrete sign of loyalty – that is, obedience to God's law.[10] The first two verses, then, proclaim the uniqueness of God and ask Israel to love and obey God as the appropriate expression of their recognition. The next verse (6:6) is transitional, and it sets the stage for all that follows. The transitional verse states that one should place upon one's heart these instructions (*devarim*, lit. "words"). In other words, one should internalize them. The biblical text is unclear as to what the "instructions" or "words" to be internalized are.[11] The rabbis assumed that the term "these words" referred to the very words of this passage (Deut 6:4–9), but as we will see later on, this interpretation is not reflected in most Second Temple sources. As Weinfeld notes, the term may refer to "the general paraenetic discourse of Deuteronomy."[12] It could also refer to the Decalogue, which is the chapter that immediately precedes this passage and which is named

---

[8] Weinfeld observes, "Verses 4 and 5 form … a unit." See Weinfeld, *Deuteronomy 1–11: A New Translation with Introduction and Commentary*, 351.

[9] Weinfeld discusses the range of ways the term "one" can be understood. See Weinfeld, *Deuteronomy 1–11: A New Translation with Introduction and Commentary*, 337–38, 349–50.

[10] See Weinfeld, *Deuteronomy 1–11: A New Translation with Introduction and Commentary*, 338, 351.

[11] For a range of interpretations of the term *devarim*, see Weinfeld, *Deuteronomy 1–11: A New Translation with Introduction and Commentary*, 340; and Yehudah B. Cohn, *Tangled Up in Text: Tefillin and the Ancient World*, 42.

[12] See Weinfeld, *Deuteronomy 1–11: A New Translation with Introduction and Commentary*, 340.

in the biblical text as "these words."[13] Alternatively, the term may refer to the first two verses of the paragraph (Deut 6:4–5).[14] In any event, the rhetorical function of the transitional verse is to introduce the second section of the paragraph (6:7–9), which alludes to a series of concrete acts by which the covenantal relationship with God is affirmed in one's daily life and transmitted to the next generation. One is to (1) teach these words to one's children, (2) recite them, (3) bind them on one's hand or arm[15] and on one's forehead, and (4) inscribe them on the doorposts and on one's gates.

The second paragraph of the Shema has a similar structure. It too begins with a doctrinally oriented prologue, has a transitional verse, and concludes with a list of concrete ritual instructions. This paragraph is called "if, then, you obey" (*vehayah 'im shamoa`*) according to the first few words of the passage. Like the first paragraph, the second paragraph is also drawn from Deuteronomy, this time chapter 11, and reads as follows:

[DOCTRINAL PROLOGUE:] (13) If, then, you obey (*shamo`a tishmi`u*) the commandments that I enjoin upon you this day, loving the Lord and serving him with all your heart and soul, (14) I will grant the rain for your land in season, the early rain and the late. You shall gather in your new grain and wine and oil – (15) I will also provide grass in the fields for your cattle – and thus you shall eat your fill. (16) Take care not to be lured away to serve other gods and bow to them. (17) For the Lord's anger will flare up against you, and He will shut up the skies so that there will be no rain and the ground will not yield its produce, and you will soon perish from the good land that the Lord is assigning to you.

[TRANSITIONAL VERSE:] (18) Therefore impress these My words (*devarai*) upon your very heart:

[RITUAL INSTRUCTIONS:] (18 cont'd) Bind them as a sign on your hand and let them serve as a symbol on your forehead, (19) teach them to your children – reciting them when you stay at home and when you are away, when you lie down and when you get up, (20) and inscribe them on the doorposts of your house and on your gates – (21) to the end that you and your children may endure, in the land that the Lord swore to your fathers to assign to them, as long as there is a heaven over the earth.

---

[13] This interpretation receives support from the fact that the term *devarim* is used to describe the Decalogue in Deut 5:22. See discussion in Weinfeld, *Deuteronomy 1–11: A New Translation with Introduction and Commentary*, 340; Yehudah B. Cohn, *Tangled Up in Text: Tefillin and the Ancient World*, 42; and David Nakman, "The Contents and Order of the Biblical Sections in the Tefillin from Qumran and Rabbinic Halakhah" (Hebrew), *Cathedra* 112 (2004): 23.

[14] See Othmar Keel, "Zeichen der Verbundenheit," in *Mélanges Dominique Barthélemy*, ed. Pierre Casetti, Othmar Keel, and Adrian Schenker (Fribourg: Editions Universitaires, 1981), 165. Cohn also argues that the term was understood at Qumran as referring to Deut 32 (Song of Moses), which in Deut 32:42 is called "these words" (*hadevarim ha'eleh*). See Yehudah B. Cohn, *Tangled Up in Text: Tefillin and the Ancient World*, 93.

[15] Cohn explains what is at stake in understanding the term *yad* as hand versus arm. See Yehudah B. Cohn, *Tangled Up in Text: Tefillin and the Ancient World*, 109.

The doctrinal prologue to the second paragraph (Deut 11:13–17) shares a number of linguistic features with that of the first paragraph. Like the first paragraph, the second paragraph calls upon Israel to "hear" or "obey" (both are English translations for the Hebrew root *sh.m.`.*). The object of the call is different, however. In the second paragraph, Israel is called to heed the commandments, rather than to affirm the unity of God. On the basis of this difference, the rabbis read the first paragraph as being about "the acceptance of the yoke of the kingship of heaven," and they read the second paragraph as being about "the acceptance of the yoke of the commandments."[16] As in the first paragraph (Deut 6:5), Israel is commanded to love God and serve him with all the heart and soul (Deut 11:13). Deut 11:14–17 introduces a new theme. Here we see the trope of reward and punishment commonly associated with Deuteronomy: If Israel hearkens to God's word, they will receive abundant blessings; if not, the heavens will close up so that no rains fall and the earth yields no produce.

The first half of Deut 11:18 is transitional, moving from the doctrinal framework to the concrete domain of action. The transitional verse shares many features with the transitional verse in the first paragraph. Both speak of placing "words" (*devarim*, earlier translated as "instructions") upon the heart. As above, the term "words" (*devarim*) has an unclear referent. The term could refer to deuteronomic instruction generally,[17] to the chapter immediately preceding (Deut 10),[18] to the verses immediately preceding (Deut 11:13–17),[19] or, as the rabbis understood it, to the full text of this paragraph (Deut 11:13–21). Like the first paragraph of the Shema, the second paragraph concludes with a list of the ritual instructions by which one is to affirm one's covenantal devotion to God. The only difference in the concluding sections of the first and second paragraphs is the order in which the rituals are listed. In the second paragraph, one is instructed to (1) bind these words on one's hand or arm and place them on one's forehead, (2) teach these words to one's children, (3) recite them, and (4) inscribe them on the doorposts and on one's gates. The instruction to bind the words on one's hand and place the words on one's forehead has been moved, from third place (where it appears in Deut 6) to first place (where it appears here). Finally, the paragraph ends with the blessing that Israel will endure on the land into perpetuity when they follow these instructions.

The third paragraph of the rabbinic Shema is taken from the book of Numbers. Unlike the first two paragraphs, the order in which it appears as part of the liturgical text does not conform to the order in which the paragraph

[16] See m. Ber. 2:2; Sif. Dt. 34 and 35; and Sif. Num. 115 for this language.

[17] See Weinfeld, *Deuteronomy 1–11: A New Translation with Introduction and Commentary*, 340; and Yehudah B. Cohn, *Tangled Up in Text: Tefillin and the Ancient World*, 43.

[18] Nakman explains that Deut 10 conveys the content of Moses' speech and therefore can appropriately be understood as "these words." See Nakman, "The Contents and Order of the Biblical Sections in the Tefillin from Qumran and Rabbinic Halakhah" (Hebrew), 23.

[19] See Keel, "Zeichen der Verbundenheit," 165–66.

appears in the canonical biblical text. Some scholars think that the third paragraph was added to the liturgy after the first two paragraphs had already been
used together as a liturgical unit.[20] The third paragraph, from Num 15, reads
as follows:

[RITUAL INSTRUCTIONS:] (37) The Lord said to Moses as follows: (38) Speak to the
Israelite people and instruct them to make for themselves fringes on the corners of their
garments throughout the ages; let them attach a cord of blue to the fringe at the corner.
(39) That shall be your fringe; look at it and recall all the commandments of the Lord
and observe them, so that you do not follow your heart and eyes in your lustful urge.

[REITERATION OF HISTORICAL BASIS FOR COVENANT:] (40) Thus shall you be reminded
to observe all My commandments and to be holy to your God. (41) I the Lord am your
God, who brought you out of the land of Egypt to be your God: I, the Lord, your God.

The central feature of the third paragraph is the command to perform a ritual act: One is to attach fringes to the corners of one's garment. The ritual
function of the fringes is to serve as a reminder: One will look at the fringes
and recall God's commandments. Looking at the fringes keeps Israel from
lusting after other gods and reminds them of their connection to God. The
paragraph ends with a recollection of God's great historical act on behalf of
Israel (the Exodus from Egypt); it is this act that serves as the foundation for
the covenantal relationship between Israel and God that endures throughout
the ages. Many scholars assume that this paragraph was included in the Shema
because the Exodus supplies the grounds for Israel's covenantal fealty to God,
the relationship that is at the heart of the Shema's proclamation.[21]

Iterations of the Shema Verses in the Second Temple Period

There is no doubt that the verses in what later came to be the rabbinic Shema
liturgy attracted attention among Jews of the Second Temple period. What is
less clear is that these verses were understood as a coherent and fixed liturgical
unit in the manner in which the later rabbis took them to be. Based on the
patterns of citation, paraphrase, and allusion, it appears that Second Temple

---

[20] See Tabory, "Prayers and Berakhot," 291–92; Ismar Elbogen, *Jewish Liturgy: A Comprehensive
History*, trans. Raymond P. Scheindlin (Philadelphia: Jewish Publication Society; New York:
Jewish Theological Seminary of America, 1993), 23; and Naomi G. Cohen, *Philo Judaeus:
His Universe of Discourse* (Frankfurt Am Main: Peter Lang, 1995), 108, 167–76. My work
takes these researchers' conclusions as a starting point and assumes that the third paragraph
was added to the Shema as a secondary development. In light of this assessment, I seek to
understand the impetus for reciting only the first two paragraphs of the Shema.

[21] See Levenson, *Sinai and Zion: An Entry into the Jewish Bible*, 83–84. See also Elbogen, *Jewish
Liturgy: A Comprehensive History*, 23; and Nahum Sarna, *Exodus* (Philadelphia: The Jewish
Publication Society, 1991), 271. M. Ber. 1:5 refers to this paragraph as "the going forth from
Egypt," thereby highlighting its function as affirmation of the covenant. Kimelman offers an
interesting review of answers to the question of how the third paragraph is connected with the
first two paragraphs. See Kimelman, "From Covenant to Coronation," 16–25.

Jews were drawn to reflect on two different subsets within these verses for two distinct reasons. In one trend, we find Second Temple Jews citing, alluding to, or paraphrasing the first two verses of the first paragraph (Deut 6:4–5) because these verses call on Israel to reaffirm their covenantal commitment to God as they did at Sinai when they accepted all of God's commandments. In an altogether different trend, we find Second Temple Jews citing, alluding to, or paraphrasing the verses that prescribe concrete ritual practices (i.e., the second part of first and second paragraphs [Deut 6:7–9 and Deut 11:18–21] and the verses in the third paragraph about placing fringes on the corner of one's garments [Num 15:38–39]). It is interesting to note that Second Temple sources generally engage the Shema verses with either one or the other of these interests in mind, but not usually with both at the same time.

I argue that the different patterns of citation attest to two distinct sets of interest in the Shema verses. While both of these ways of engaging the Shema verses contribute to the eventual recitation of these verses as a liturgical unit, they suggest that two distinct cultural trends converged and reinforced each other in the creation of the Shema verses as liturgy. On one hand, the sources that cite, allude to, or paraphrase the doctrinal prologue of the first paragraph (Deut 6:4–5) suggest that the Shema liturgy developed because ritual repetition of these verses was a way to reaffirm the covenantal pact made at Sinai in which Israel affirmed God's uniqueness and dedicated themselves to performance of God's commandments. Ritual repetition of these verses affirmed that the covenantal relationship was not an artifact of history, but a vital relationship in the ongoing present.[22] On the other hand, the sources that cite, allude to, or paraphrase the verses of ritual instruction suggest that these three paragraphs became linked in the ancient imagination because each refers to concrete ritual practices (tefillin, mezuzah, and tzitzit) that mark one's Jewish commitments on one's body. Eventually the understanding emerged that the rituals should be fulfilled by means of the very text that was assumed to prescribe them. This understanding of the rituals opened up the possibility for a new interpretation of the instruction to "repeat [these words] to your children, speaking of them when...." Though earlier interpreters took this verse to require meditation on God generally, the rabbis understood this verse to require that the Shema verses themselves be recited as liturgy. Whereas others had understood the Shema rituals to be a means of internalizing basic Jewish commitments, the rabbis took them to be a means of internalizing biblical text.

The impulse to recite the Shema verses as liturgy, then, seems to have arisen as the result of two distinct understandings of what could be ritually accomplished thereby. On the one hand, recitation of the Shema verses was a ritual means of reenacting the covenantal commitments of Sinai. We learn of this

[22] This is a classic example of the process that Yerushalmi describes whereby memory is cultivated through liturgy and ritual. See Yosef Hayim Yerushalmi, *Zakhor: Jewish History and Jewish Memory* (Seattle: University of Washington Press, 1982), 1–26.

ritual sensibility from the sources that engage the doctrinal prologue of the first paragraph. On the other hand, recitation of the Shema verses served as a ritual mechanism by which the practitioner could incorporate biblical text into the self, just as one incorporated biblical text onto the body when one wore tefillin. We learn of this ritual sensibility from the sources that discuss the Shema rituals. Undoubtedly, for the rabbis, these two meanings of the Shema ritual were integrally connected and mutually compatible. Contemporary scholarship, however, has tended to emphasize that aspect of the Shema ritual that functions as covenantal reenactment while neglecting that aspect of Shema ritual that seeks to incorporate the biblical text into the self.[23] This chapter seeks to recover the full range of ritual meanings associated with the rabbinic Shema. When we recognize that recitation of the Shema also functioned as a ritual means of incorporating biblical text into the self, we are alerted to the fact that this ritual has much in common with Torah study, which for the rabbis was the premiere ritual by which one engaged the divine within scripture.[24] I argue that the rabbinic exemption of women from Shema (and tefillin) makes most sense when understood in the context of the second ritual sensibility underlying Shema practice, a sensibility that scholars have tended to neglect. This book's attention to rabbinic conceptions of gender stands to illuminate broader trends within rabbinic Judaism generally, trends that have been hitherto ignored.

Recognizing the Unity of God and the Command to Love God

The doctrinal prologue to the first paragraph of the Shema (Deut 6:4–5) calls on Israel to recognize the unity of God and commands Israel to love God. When Second Temple sources invoke these verses, they connect them with Sinaitic revelation and the Decalogue. In what follows, I will argue that this pattern of citing, alluding to, or paraphrasing the Shema verses follows from the status of these verses as a pseudo-commandment and the fact that repeating them

---

[23] Exemplars of this scholarly trend are Kimelman, "From Covenant to Coronation"; Schiffman, *Reclaiming the Dead Sea Scrolls*, 293; Levenson, *Sinai and Zion: An Entry into the Jewish Bible*, 80–86; Moshe Weinfeld, *The Decalogue and the Recitation of "Shema": The Development of the Confessions* (Hebrew) (Tel Aviv: Hakibbutz Hameuchad, 2001), 144–62; Elbogen, *Jewish Liturgy: A Comprehensive History*, 22–23; and Alan Segal, "Covenant in Rabbinic Writings," *Studies in Religion* 14/53–62 (1985): 60–62. An important exception to this trend is Marc Hirschman, who in his recent book argues that there were some rabbis who saw both the first and second paragraphs of the Shema as forms of Torah study. See Marc Hirshman, *The Stabilization of Rabbinic Culture, 100 C.E.–350 C.E.: Texts on Education and Their Late Antique Context* (Oxford: Oxford University Press, 2009), 32–39. See also Moshe Benovitz, "*Shinun*: Recitation of the Shema in the Teaching of R. Shimon Bar Yohai" (Hebrew), *Sidra* 20 (2005): 25–56.

[24] Hirshman, for example, writes: "For at least some of the Jewish sages, the words of Torah were essentially divine. God's words were part and parcel of God's essence.... The goal of the sage is to attach one's self and to cleave to these divine words, the Torah." See Hirshman, *The Stabilization of Rabbinic Culture*, 30.

recalled the original sealing of the covenant at Sinai when the Ten Commandments were first articulated. Second Temple sources do not appear to respond
to the instructions to "speak of [these words] when you lie down and when
you rise up" – or at least, they do not invoke the instruction verses – when
citing, alluding to, or paraphrasing the doctrinal prologue.

One important context in which these verses were invoked was rituals that
reenact the covenantal dedication of Israel to YHWH at Sinai. During the
Second Temple period, the event of Sinaitic revelation was increasingly seen
not as a one-time event in the past, but as an event that was to be ritually
reperformed on a regular basis to affirm the ongoing character of the covenantal
relationship that it created.[25] Several scholars argue that Pss 81 and 50 were
written against the backdrop of a covenantal reenactment ceremony that took
place on either Shavuot (the holiday that commemorates the giving of the law
at Sinai)[26] or Rosh Hashanah (the holiday of the New Year).[27] A central feature
of the ceremony of covenantal reenactment was affirming the importance of
the Decalogue, which was understood to be the central content of the Sinaitic
revelation. The first two commandments, which announce God as the redeemer
of Israel and demand Israel's fealty to YHWH exclusively, were of special
importance within the ceremony of covenantal reenactment. Ps 81 invokes the
first two commandments in its recalling of the Sinaitic event: "You shall have
no foreign god, you shall not bow to an alien god. I am the Lord your God who
brought you out of the land of the Egypt" (Ps 82:10–11). In a more condensed
form, Ps 50 alludes to only the first commandment:[28] "I am God, your God"
(Ps 50:7). In addition to recalling the revelation at Sinai, these two psalms also
call Israel by name, asking her to "hear" (*shema`*) or obey God: "Hear, My
people and I will admonish you; O Israel, if you would but listen to Me!" (Ps
81:9) and "Hear, My people and I will speak, O Israel, and I will arraign you"
(Ps 50: 7). These verses from Pss 81 and 50 do not employ the same syntactical
structure that the first paragraph of the Shema does ("Hear, O Israel! The
Lord is our God, the Lord alone"), but they do reflect a common tradition in
that they use the verb "hear" (*shema`*) to call Israel to show loyalty to God

---

[25] See Sigmund Mowinckel, *The Psalms in Israel's Worship*, vol. 1 (New York: Abingdon Press,
      1962), 155–61; Levenson, *Sinai and Zion: An Entry into the Jewish Bible*, 80–86; and Weinfeld,
      Deuteronomy 1–11: A New Translation with Introduction and Commentary, 257–62. Also rel-
      evant to this discussion is Ezra's ceremony of covenant renewal discussed in Hindy Najman,
      "Torah of Moses: Pseudonymous Attribution in Second Temple Writings," in *The Interpre-
      tation of Scripture in Early Judaism and Christianity: Studies in Language and Tradition*, ed.
      Craig A. Evans (Sheffield: Sheffield Academic Press, 2000), 206.
[26] See Weinfeld, *Deuteronomy 1–11: A New Translation with Introduction and Commentary*,
      260–62, 267–75.
[27] See Mowinckel, *The Psalms in Israel's Worship*, vol. 1, 155–61; and Levenson, *Sinai and Zion:
      An Entry into the Jewish Bible*, 80.
[28] For a precise definition of biblical allusion and other strategies of invoking earlier scriptural
      texts, see Benjamin D. Sommer, *A Prophet Reads Scripture: Allusion in Isaiah 40–66* (Stanford:
      Stanford University Press, 1998), 6–31.

alone.[29] Though not quoting the Shema verses in tandem with the first two commandments, they attest to a tradition that associated the first two verses of the Shema with the first one or two commandments in the Decalogue.

The community at Qumran had an elaborate initiation process that members had to undergo in order to formalize their membership in the sectarian community. Like the ceremonies reenacting the covenant, formal entrance into the sectarian community was a ritual way to affirm the endurance of God's covenantal act at Sinai. The sectarians thought that they alone remained God's covenantal partners. Two different documents from Qumran (both c. 100 BCE) suggest that the sectarians used language from the second verse of the doctrinal prologue of the first paragraph (Deut 6:5: "You shall love the Lord your God with all your heart, with all your soul and with all your might.") to think about what it meant to enter the sect.[30] Weinfeld argues that the sectarians understood the first clause in this tripartite dedication ("love God with all your heart") to require commitment of one's mind to God. The second clause ("with all your soul") required dedication of one's power or strength, and the third clause ("with all your might") required dedication of one's wealth or possessions.[31] Echoing the tripartite structure of Deut 6:5, a passage in the *Rule of the Community* reads, "All those who freely devote themselves to His truth shall bring all their knowledge,[32] powers and possessions into the Community of God" (1QS 1:12). Those who enter the sectarian covenantal community are understood to be fulfilling the requirements of Deut 6:5. Weinfeld observes similar demands made on the entrant to the sect in the *Damascus Document* (13:11). There the new member is examined with respect to (1) "his works and intelligence" (to affirm that he dedicates himself with "all [his] heart"), (2) "his strength and power" (to affirm that he dedicates himself with "all [his] soul"),[33] and (3) "his wealth" (to affirm that he dedicates himself with "all [his] might").[34] In each of these documents (*Rule of the Community* and *Damascus Document*), entrance into the sectarian community involves a tripartite dedication similar to that demanded by the Shema verses. Qumran documents, then,

---

[29] For a discussion of the links between these psalms and the Decalogue, see Weinfeld, *Deuteronomy 1–11: A New Translation with Introduction and Commentary*, 337; and Kimelman, "From Covenant to Coronation," 13.

[30] See discussion in Weinfeld, *Deuteronomy 1–11: A New Translation with Introduction and Commentary*, 339–40.

[31] One of the requirements of entry into the sect's communal life involved renunciation of personal property to the sect. The rabbis similarly understand the clause requiring love of God "with all your might" as indicating a dedication of one's wealth. See discussion in Weinfeld, *Deuteronomy 1–11: A New Translation with Introduction and Commentary*, 339.

[32] Weinfeld documents an ancient Jewish interpretation of "heart" as "mind." See Weinfeld, *Deuteronomy 1–11: A New Translation with Introduction and Commentary*, 338.

[33] In its paraphrase of Deut 6:5, Mark 12:30 adds a fourth element to the biblical triplet demanding dedication of heart, soul, mind, and might.

[34] See Weinfeld, *Deuteronomy 1–11: A New Translation with Introduction and Commentary*, 340.

suggest that the second verse of the first paragraph of the Shema was linked to contemporary affirmations of the covenantal relationship. Whether linking Deut 6:4–5 to the first two commandments of the Decalogue or to entrance into the sectarian community, Second Temple Jews were thinking about these two Shema verses in the context of covenantal reenactment.

Like the passage in the *Rule of the Community*, Ben Sira (c. 180 BCE) draws on the language of Deut 6:5 to describe what it means to dedicate oneself to God. For Ben Sira, dedication to God does not find its fullest expression in joining the sectarian community, but rather in giving appropriate honor to God's agents in one's midst. Ben Sira 7 renders the biblical command to love God in three different ways as follows:

(27) <u>With all your heart</u> honor your father,

And the mother who bore you, do not forget.

(28) Remember that from them you came into being;

How can you repay them according to what they have done for you?

(29) <u>With all your soul</u> fear God,

And treat his priests as sacred.

(30) <u>With all your might</u>, love your maker,

Do not leave his ministers without support.[35]

According to Ben Sira, each of the three biblical phrases ("love God with all your [1] heart, [2] soul, and [3] might") compels dedication to a different one of God's representatives or agents on earth. The first phrase requires love for one's parents, the second respect for God's priests, and the third attention to God's servants.[36] For Ben Sira, loving God according to the threefold formula of Deut 6:5 means acting appropriately toward God's earthly representatives. It is interesting to note that Ben Sira connects Deut 6:5 with the Decalogue in that he refers to the obligation to honor one's father and mother. But he also connects Deut 6:5 with other obligations not mentioned in the Decalogue (treating priests as sacred, providing God's ministers with support). Though Ben Sira does not connect Deut 6:5 with the event of Sinaitic revelation, he does connect the verse with one of the commandments in the Decalogue. His testimony enriches our picture of the manifold ways in which Jews of the Second Temple period were linking Deut 6:4–5 with the Decalogue and thinking about these verses as a commandment.

---

[35] Translation of this phrase is drawn from Weinfeld, *Deuteronomy 1–11: A New Translation with Introduction and Commentary*, 339 (underlining added).

[36] Weinfeld understands this phrase as requiring financial support of God's ministers. See Weinfeld, *Deuteronomy 1–11: A New Translation with Introduction and Commentary*, 339.

The Synoptic Gospels (c. 65–90 CE) provide additional evidence that Second Temple Jews regarded Deut 6:4–5 as a commandment. Mark 12 relates the following encounter between Jesus and a scribe:

(28) One of the scribes came near and heard them disputing with one another, and seeing that he answered them well, he asked them, "Which commandment is the first of all?" (29) Jesus answered, "The first is: Hear o Israel, the Lord our God, the Lord is One; (30) and you shall love the Lord your God with all your heart, with all your soul, with all your mind, and with all your strength. (31) The second is this: You must love your neighbor as yourself. There is no other commandment greater than these."[37] (see also parallels in Matt 22:34–40 and Luke 10:25–28)

In Mark (and Matthew), Deut 6:4–5 is explicitly described as a commandment, indeed, the greatest of all commandments. It is especially interesting to note that Mark reads Deut 6:4–5 as a commandment without linking these verses to the Decalogue. Instead, the New Testament connects Deut 6:4–5 with Lev 19:18, the commandment to love one's neighbor as oneself.[38] Mark's connecting the command to love God with the command to love one's neighbor echoes Ben Sira, who likewise believes that the command to love God is best accomplished by loving God's human representatives on earth and alludes to commandments beyond those included in the Decalogue. Whereas Ben Sira suggests that God's presence is most immediately manifest in particular segments of the human community (parents, priests, and God's servants), Mark emphasizes that God is manifest in the entire human community (your neighbor). In both sources, love of God is linked to love of members of the human community.[39] The Synoptic Gospels, then, provide additional evidence that Jews in the Second Temple period read Deut 6:4–5 as a commandment.

In sum, the view that Deut 6:4–5 should be understood through the conceptual rubric of "commandment" was expressed in a variety of ways. Deut 6:4–5 was linked (1) with ceremonies of covenantal reenactment that featured the first two commandments, (2) with the commandment to honor one's parents, and (3) with the commandment to love one's neighbor as oneself. Though each of the sources discussed connects Deut 6:4–5 with commandments, each establishes this interpretative claim by different means. While Pss 81 and 51 and the Qumran documents link Deut 6:4–5 with Sinaitic revelation by invoking these verses in the context of covenantal reenactment, Ben Sira and the Synoptic Gospels associate Deut 6:4–5 with specific commandments, some of which

---

[37] Translation from NRSV. See also parallels in Matt 22:34–40 and Luke 10:25–28.

[38] See also Luke 10: 25–28, where a similar incident is related in abbreviated form. In Luke, Deut 6:4–5 is not described as a commandment. The question posed to Jesus is, "What is written in the Law?" The command to love God (Deut 6:5) and the command to love one's neighbor (Lev 19:18) are represented as the essence of the "law" (*nomos*).

[39] A passage by Paul, 1 Cor 8:6, is often taken to reflect early Christian interpretation of the command to love God. See discussion in Anthony C. Thiselton, *The First Epistle to the Corinthians: A Commentary on the Greek Text* (Grand Rapids: W. B. Eerdmans, 2000), 636–37.

are not even included in the Decalogue. While the Synoptic Gospels explicitly describe Deut 6:4–5 as a commandment, the other sources relate Deut 6:4–5 to the Decalogue by association, either by alluding to Sinaitic revelation as an event (as in Pss 50 and 81) or by citing specific commandments (like honor your mother and father, as in Ben Sira). What each of these sources has in common is the linking of Deut 6:4–5 with the Sinaitic revelation and the Decalogue as a symbol of Israel's covenantal commitment to God at Sinai. It is important to recognize that this trend of engaging the doctrinal prologue to the first paragraph of the Shema occurs without reference to the later verses in the first paragraph, which the rabbis understood as requiring recitation of the Shema verses as liturgy. The doctrinal prologue appears to have received attention on the basis of its status as pseudo-commandment that recalled Sinaitic revelation, and not because verses later in the paragraph called for its recitation.

Rabbinic Corroboration for Trend #1

The endurance of this conceptual framing of Deut 6:4–5 is attested in several tannaitic sources (c. 200–300 CE). When explaining the order of the Shema's three paragraphs, Sif. Num. 115 and m. Ber. 2:2 have occasion to reflect on the essential message of the first paragraph. Both sources assume that the first paragraph (with its doctrinal prologue) articulates an individual's "acceptance of the yoke of the kingship of heaven." In the view of these sources, reciting the first paragraph of the Shema signals one's acceptance of God's claim to covenantal loyalty. Like a number of the Second Temple sources discussed above, the tannaitic sources identify the significance of the first two verses of the first paragraph in their affirmation of Israel's commitment to God within the context of the covenant. Sif. Num. 115 additionally points out that the first paragraph expresses one's refutation of the worship of other gods (*vemi'et bah avodah zarah*, lit. "it excludes [the possibility of] alien worship"), thereby establishing a connection between the first two verses of the Shema and the second commandment. Here we hear echoes of Ps 81:9–11, which also attests to a traditional linkage between the first two verses of the Shema and the second commandment, not to worship other gods.[40]

M. Tamid offers another example of a tannaitic text that links the Shema with the Decalogue. The passage, m. Tamid 4:3–5:1, describes the daily order of morning sacrificial rites and includes a reference to the priestly practice of reciting the Shema.

(4:3) They [the priests] went along and put them [the various animal parts they were carrying] on the lower half and western side of the ramp, and they salted them. Then they went down to the Chamber of Hewn Stone to recite the Shema.

---

[40] Kimelman notes the similarities between Sif. Num. 115 and Ps 81:9–11. See Reuven Kimelman, "The Shema and the Amidah: Rabbinic Prayer," in *Prayer from Alexander to Constantine*, ed. Mark Kiley (London: Routledge, 1997), 110, 118n10.

(5:1) The officer said to them: Recite (*barkhu*) the blessing! They blessed [accordingly] and they recited the Ten Commandments, the "*shema`*" [the first paragraph], the "*vehayah 'im shamoa`*" [the second paragraph], and the "*veyomer*" [the third paragraph].

This mishnaic tradition describes a priestly liturgical practice of reciting, shortly after dawn, the three paragraphs of the rabbinic Shema preceded by the Decalogue. Historians debate the extent to which this tradition accurately reflects liturgical practices during the Second Temple period, whether among the priests or laity.[41] Did the priests and/or Israelite laity recite these four biblical passages in this order as part of a regular daily liturgy? Several factors mitigate against accepting the evidence of the Mishnah at face value. First, the Mishnah assigns a name to the liturgical unit that makes sense to a rabbinic audience, but would not have made sense to Second Temple practitioners of the described practice. The mishnah says, "they went down . . . to recite the Shema," but as Joseph Tabory notes, it is not logical for a liturgical practice that has the Decalogue as its first element to be named according to the first word of its second paragraph.[42] It is more likely that the Mishnah anachronistically describes what it imagines to have been Second Temple practice in light of the contemporary rabbinic ritual practice.[43] Second, scholars have noted that while other Second Temple sources describe a practice of diurnal prayer, none explicitly names the three paragraphs of the rabbinic Shema as the content of the prayer.[44] Third, even allowing that some form of the rabbinic Shema may have been recited during the Second Temple period, scholars question whether the third paragraph would have been recited as part of the liturgical cycle during Second Temple

---

[41] Joseph Tabory is skeptical about many aspects of this source. See Tabory, "Prayers and Berakhot," 290–92. Kimelman is inclined to accept the account as historically reliable and uses the source to demonstrate differences between the Shema ritual in its Second Temple and rabbinic manifestations. See Kimelman, "From Covenant to Coronation," 68–80, 84–91. Baumgarten compares this passage with a description of Temple practices in Ben Sira 50:1–21 (which make no reference to the Shema) and concludes that the Shema was not recited in the Temple as late as 170 BCE. He argues that the Shema was introduced into the Temple rites during the Maccabean era. See Albert Baumgarten, "Invented Traditions," 203.

[42] See Tabory, "Prayers and Berakhot," 290.

[43] A number of recent studies suggest that tannaitic descriptions of Temple ritual are often generated by the imagination in the rabbinic study house, rather than by accurate historical memory regarding Second Temple practice. See Berkowitz, *Execution and Invention: Death Penalty Discourse in Early Rabbinic and Christian Cultures*; Rosen-Zvi, *The Mishnaic Sotah Ritual: Temple, Gender and Midrash*; Naftali Cohn, "Rabbis as Jurists: On the Representations of Past and Present Legal Institutions in the Mishnah," *Journal of Jewish Studies* 60/2 (2009): 245–63. This body of research may be less relevant to the current case because m. Tamid is conventionally assumed to constitute a relatively old stratum of the Mishnah. In any event, for the purposes of the current argument, I need not resolve the question of the accuracy of this tradition.

[44] See Tabory, "Prayers and Berakhot," 290–92.

times, as claimed by m. Tamid 5:1.[45] There are several reasons, then, to be skeptical about the accuracy of the Mishnah's ascription of a liturgical practice very similar to its own to the Second Temple period. Whether or not we accept the picture of Second Temple liturgical practice depicted by m. Tamid, however, is immaterial for the argument here. These mishnayot, like a number of the Second Temple sources discussed above, attest to a tradition of linking the Shema verses with the Decalogue.

The Qumran Tefillin and the Nash Papyrus

A number of tefillin slips and casings were found at Qumran, and they provide some of our earliest evidence for the fact that Jews in antiquity understood verses from the Shema (Deut 6:8; 11:18: "And you shall bind [these words] as a sign upon your hand, and as frontlets between your eyes") as requiring the binding of encased textual inscriptions onto the body.[46] Though later rabbinic practice requires binding four discrete paragraphs[47] containing reference to tefillin practice, the tefillin slips found at Qumran contain much longer sections of biblical text and include at least one passage that makes no reference to tefillin at all (Deut 32).[48] We will have occasion to discuss the variety in passages included in the Qumran tefillin at greater length later. For the moment, I wish

---

[45] See Tabory, "Prayers and Berakhot," 292. For the view that the third paragraph of the Shema was added to the liturgical cycle after the first two paragraphs were already fixed as a liturgical unit, see Elbogen, *Jewish Liturgy: A Comprehensive History*, 23; Cohen, *Philo Judaeus: His Universe of Discourse*, 108, 167–76.

[46] The bulk of tefillin slips and casings were published by Milik and Yadin. See J. T. Milik, "Tefillin, Mezuzot et Targums," in *Discoveries in the Judaean Desert*, vol. 6 (Oxford: Oxford University Press, 1977), 33–85; Yigael Yadin, *Tefillin from Qumran (XQPhyl 1–4)* (The Israel Exploration Society and the Shrine of the Book, 1970). For a full listing of the official publications of the slips and casings, see Yehudah B. Cohn, *Tangled Up in Text: Tefillin and the Ancient World*, 56n2. For a full evaluation of the practice, see Cohn's work generally and also David Rothstein, "From Bible to Muraba'at: Studies in the Literary, Textual and Scribal Features of Phylacteries and Mezuzot in Ancient Israel and Early Judaism" (PhD diss., UCLA, 1992).

[47] The four paragraphs or "sections" (*parshiyot*) included in rabbinic tefillin are Exod 13:1–10 (13:9 alludes to tefillin practice); Exod 13:11–16 (13:16 alludes to tefillin practice); Deut 6:4–9 (6:8 alludes to tefillin practice); and Deut 11:13–21 (11:18 alludes to tefillin practice). The last two paragraphs correspond to the first two paragraphs of the rabbinic Shema. Rabbinic practice dictates that the four passages be written on a single parchment and placed in a single cell in the arm tefillin. The same passages are written on four separate parchments and placed in four separate cells in the head tefillin.

[48] Milik was the first to establish that 4QPhyl N (which contains Deut 32) was a tefillin slip. See Milik, "Tefillin, Mezuzot et Targums," 34–37. Contra Milik, Nakman argues that 4QPhyl N was not a tefillin slip. See Nakman, "The Contents and Order of the Biblical Sections in the Tefillin from Qumran and Rabbinic Halakhah" (Hebrew), 35–37. Cohn argues that 4QDeut^j, 4QDeut^{kl}, and 4QDeut^n were probably tefillin slips also based on the visibility of folds and the small size of the parchment and handwriting on these fragments. If these scrolls are indeed tefillin slips, then they attest to the fact that Deut 8:5–10 was also included in Qumran tefillin. See Yehudah B. Cohn, *Tangled Up in Text: Tefillin and the Ancient World*, 67, 76.

merely to observe that a number of the sets of tefillin slips that were assumed to originate in a single tefillin contain both the Decalogue and the Shema verses. To take just one example, 4QPhyl G, H and I are identified as coming from a single set of slips, and they include the entire chapter of Deut 5 (which contains the Decalogue) along with the Shema verses from Deut 6 and Deut 11.[49] The Qumran tefillin, then, provide additional evidence that Second Temple Jews linked the Shema verses with the Decalogue.

It is also interesting to observe that four of the Qumran tefillin that include the Decalogue stop short of citing the full paragraph of the Shema.[50] They either cite Deut 5 (which includes the Decalogue) and continue in Deut 6 up to verse 3, stopping just short of the first paragraph of the Shema, or continue in Deut 6 up to verse 5, thereby including the doctrinal prologue, but not the verses of ritual instruction. In both cases, it is notable that the tefillin link the Shema verses with the Decalogue without direct recourse to the instruction verses. This evidence corroborates the trend noted above that the link between the Decalogue and the Shema verses was established with the doctrinal prologue of the first paragraph of the Shema, rather than with the instruction verses. The evidence of the Qumran tefillin complicates the matter somewhat, however, since many of them do include the verses of ritual instruction.

The Nash Papyrus (c. 165–100 BCE)[51] was found in Egypt about fifty years before the Qumran tefillin were found. Like some of the Qumran tefillin slips, the Nash Papyrus contains the Decalogue and the doctrinal prologue from the first paragraph of the Shema. In addition, the Nash Papyrus adds a short introduction to the Shema verses (also found in the Septuagint) between the Decalogue and the Shema verses. Like the Qumran tefillin slips, the Nash Papyrus was folded a number of times. Initially scholars assumed that the Nash Papyrus was a text that had been used in a liturgical setting.[52] The discovery of the Qumran tefillin slips with similar folds found in tefillin casings led scholars

---

[49] 4QPhyl G includes Deut 5:1–21 (with omissions, additions, and transpositions) on one side and Exod 13:11–12 on the reverse. 4QPhyl H includes Deut 5:22–6:5 (with omissions and additions) on one side and Exod 13:14b–16 on the reverse. 4QPhyl I includes Deut 11:13–21 and Exod 12:(43)44–13:10 (with omissions) on one side and possibly Deut 6:6–7 on the reverse. See Yehudah B. Cohn, *Tangled Up in Text: Tefillin and the Ancient World*, 65–67, for tables listing the contents of the Qumran tefillin slips.

[50] See (1) 4QPhyl L, M, and N, which originated in one set of slips and which include Deut 5:(1–6), 7–24, (25–33), and Deut 5:33–6:5; (2) 4QPhyl G, H, and I, which originated in a single set of slips and which include Deut 5:1–21, 22–6:5; (3) 4QPhyl A, which includes Deut 5:1–6:3; and (4) 4QPhyl J and K, which originated in a single set of slips and which include Deut 5:1–6:3. Verses placed in parentheses were not found, but scholars have reasonably assumed that they were initially present. See also 4QDeut^j, which Cohn speculates was a tefillin slip also and which includes Deut 5:1–6:3. Information taken from charts in Yehudah B. Cohn, *Tangled Up in Text: Tefillin and the Ancient World*, 65–66.

[51] For this dating, see W. F. Albright, "A Biblical Fragment from the Maccabaean Age: The Nash Papyrus," *Journal of Biblical Literature* 56 (1937): esp. 149.

[52] See Moshe Greenberg, "Nash Papyrus," in *Encyclopaedia Judaica*, vol. 12 (Jerusalem, 1972), 833.

to reconsider how the Nash Papyrus was used. Scholars now believe that the Nash Papyrus was used in a manner similar to the tefillin slips found at Qumran: as a slip in tefillin.[53] What is particularly interesting for the purposes of this research project is that only the first two verses of the first paragraph of the Shema (Deut 6:4–5) are included in the Nash Papyrus. This feature of the Nash Papyrus provides one more piece of evidence that the first paragraph of the Shema attracted attention in the Second Temple period because of a link that was perceived between the Deut 6:4–5 and the Decalogue. As in the Second Temple sources cited above, the latter verses of the first paragraph of the Shema (i.e., the instruction verses) do not figure in this associative formation.[54] The Decalogue's link to the Shema verses arises when one focuses specifically on the doctrinal prologue to the first paragraph.

The Nash Papyrus and the Qumran tefillin, then, additionally attest to a perceived connection between the Decalogue and the doctrinal prologue of the first paragraph of the Shema.

A Cluster of Concrete Ritual Acts

A second set of Second Temple sources suggest that the Shema verses were simultaneously attracting attention for an altogether different reason. A number of sources cite, allude to, or paraphrase the Shema verses that prescribe concrete ritual acts. Notably, these sources do not invoke the doctrinal prologue. This fact suggests that the rituals were understood to function in a manner *other than* as an affirmation of the doctrinal prologue to the first paragraph. I argue that this second set of Second Temple sources reveals that the Shema verses were attracting attention because they were seen as the source for a group of concrete ritual acts that expressed commitment to *various* fundamental principles.

---

[53] See Baumgarten, "Invented Traditions," 206–7n38; Yehudah B. Cohn, *Tangled Up in Text: Tefillin and the Ancient World*, 67–68; Colette Sirat, *Les papyrus en caractères hébraïques trouvés en Egypte* (Paris: Editions du Centre national de la recherche scientifique, 1985), 29n30; and Ezra Fleischer, *Eretz-Israel Prayers and Prayer Rituals as Portrayed in the Geniza Documents* (Hebrew) (Jerusalem, 1988), 259n1.

[54] It is notable that four of the Qumran tefillin slips follow the pattern of the Nash Papyrus in this regard. They *do* include Deut 5 (which includes the Decalogue), but *do not* include the verses from Deut 6 that were later assumed to provide the ritual instructions for tefillin. Some of the tefillin slips stop short and cite no verses from the first paragraph of the Shema. Others stop short after citing the doctrinal prologue of the first paragraph of the Shema. See (1) 4QPhyl L, M, and N, which originated in one set of slips and include Deut 5:(1–6), 7–24, (25–33) and Deut 5:33–6:5; (2) 4QPhyl G, H, and I, which originated in a single set of slips and include Deut 5:1–21, 22–6:5; (3) 4QPhyl A, which includes Deut 5:1–6:3; and (4) 4QPhyl J and K, which originated in a single set of slips and include Deut 5:1–6:3. Verses placed in parentheses were not found, but scholars have reasonably assumed that they were initially present. See also 4QDeutʲ, which Cohn speculates was a tefillin slip also and includes Deut 5:1–6:3. Information taken from charts in Yehudah B. Cohn, *Tangled Up in Text: Tefillin and the Ancient World*, 65–66.

The rabbis eventually derived six distinct rituals from the Shema verses: (1) Tefillin of the arm fulfills the instruction to "bind them as a sign upon your hand" (Deut 6:8; 11:18), (2) tefillin of the head fulfills the instruction to "have them as a frontlet between your eyes" (Deut 6:8; 11:18), (3) mezuzah fulfills the instruction to "inscribe them on the doorposts of your house and on your gates" (Deut 6:9; 11:19), (4) diurnal prayer consisting of recitation of the Shema verses fulfills the instruction to "impress them upon your children, speaking of them... when you lie down and when you get up" (Deut 6:7; 11:19),[55] (5) Torah study fulfills the instruction to "impress them upon your children" (Deut 6:7; 11:19), and (6) tzitzit fulfills the instruction to "make fringes for themselves on the corners of their garments" (Num 15:38).

It is clear from Second Temple sources that these rituals were attracting attention and were connected with one another, though no Second Temple source attends to all of these rituals in a single discussion. What is less clear, however, is whether the conceptual clustering of these rituals resulted from an encounter with text of the Shema in liturgical form. It is also not clear that the rituals were understood to be a means of affirming the content of the doctrinal prologues. The available evidence suggests that *a variety of conceptual principles* governed how Second Temple Jews thought about the Shema rituals as a collectivity.

The Shema Rituals as Embodied Performance of Jewish Commitments

The *Letter of Aristeas* (c. 170 BCE) discusses the Shema rituals as part of an allegorical interpretation of the dietary laws. According to Aristeas, Jews are allowed to eat ruminants because they serve as a paradigm for recollection (*Let. Aris.*, 154). Ruminants naturally bring back up what has already been consumed, and Jews too are "exhorted through scripture to... 'remember the Lord who did great and wonderful deeds through you'"[56] (155). The dietary laws are one ritual means of recollection. The body, however, has multiple

---

[55] An interesting question can be asked here: From which verb in the phrase is the obligation to recite the Shema derived? Sif. Dt. 34 states, "*You shall teach them diligently* (veshinantam). These verses [and not other verses] are for diligent repetition (*shinun*)." This interpretation appears to root the obligation in the phrase "you shall teach them diligently" (*veshinantam*). The verb *sh.n.n.* here is not understood as an action directed toward one's children. Rather, it is an action one performs with one's *own* self-transformation as the *telos*. This interpretation of "you shall teach them diligently" (*veshinantam*), however, has the obvious difficulty of requiring that one ignore the verb's direct object. In its native literary context, the verb is directed toward children/sons (*banekha*). Maimonides resolves this exegetical difficulty by rooting the obligation to say Shema in a different phrase: "speaking of them" (*vedibarta bam*). See Moses Maimonides, *Sefer Ha-Mitsvot*, trans. Joseph Kapach (Jerusalem, 1930–31), 64–65. See discussion in Benovitz, "*Shinun*: Recitation of the Shema in the Teaching of R. Shimon Bar Yohai" (Hebrew), 25–28.

[56] According to Hadas, the scriptural reference here is to a combination of LXX Deut 7:17 and 10:21. The term "through you" refers to the human body. See Moses Hadas, ed. and trans., *Aristeas to Philocrates (Letter of Aristeas)* (New York: Ktav, 1973), 161.

points of sensory input (156), and therefore God "has ordained" a variety of rituals that can serve in "every time and place for a continual reminder of the supreme God and upholder [of all]" (157).

158a. Accordingly, in the matter of meats and drinks, He commands men to offer first fruits and to consume them there and then, straightaway.

158b. Furthermore, in our clothes He has given us a distinguishing mark as a reminder [= reference to tzitzit],

158c. And similarly on our gates and doors he has commanded us to set up the "words," so as to be a reminder of God [= reference to mezuzah].

159. He also strictly commands that the sign shall be worn on our hands, clearly indicating that it is our duty to fulfill every activity with justice, having in mind our own condition, and above all the fear of God [= reference to hand/arm tefillin].

160. He also commands that "on going to bed and rising" men should meditate on the devisings of God, observing not only in word but in understanding the movement and impression which they have when they go to sleep, and waking too, what a divine change there is between them – quite beyond understanding [= reference to diurnal prayer/meditation on God's devisings].[57]

Aristeas discusses the Shema rituals insofar as they are types of reminders, which he has been brought to consider through his discussion of the dietary laws. First, it is important to note that the Shema rituals are not conceived as a discrete unit unto themselves. The laws of firstfruits (158a) are part of the conceptual unit into which the Shema rituals are introduced. They too are regarded as a ritual means of recollection that engages the diverse senses "in every time and every place." Second, Aristeas's discussion is generated by a concern for the rituals as diverse types of reminders. He mentions tzitzit first among the Shema rituals (158b), even though they appear in the third paragraph of the Shema, presumably because the biblical text explicitly states that they function as a vehicle of recollection.[58] Aristeas next discusses the ritual of mezuzah (158c), even though it is the last of the rituals mentioned in the first and second paragraphs of the Shema. It too can easily be assimilated into the conceptual rubric of reminders. Finally, Aristeas discusses the other rituals that – in his view – less obviously serve as reminders (tefillin [159] and diurnal prayer/meditation [160]). We see Aristeas's hesitation about characterizing them as reminders in that he mentions other functions of these last rituals before noting that they serve as reminders of God.

---

57 Translation (with minor alteration) from R. J. H. Shutt, "Letter of Aristeas," in *The Old Testament Pseudepigrapha*, vol. 2, ed. James H. Charlesworth (Garden City: Doubleday, 1985), 7–34.

58 See Num 15:39 from the third paragraph of the Shema: "That shall be your fringe; look at it and *recall* all the commandments of the Lord and observe them, so that you do not follow your heart and eyes in your lustful urge" (emphasis added).

Aristeas does not mention tefillin worn on the head when he discusses the arm/hand tefillin in 159. Perhaps he knew only of the ritual of wearing tefillin on the arm/hand? Perhaps the head-tefillin ritual with which he was familiar could not be easily amalgamated in the rubric of reminders? Whatever the reason, it is an interesting fact that Aristeas does not discuss all the rituals that the rabbis eventually derived from the Shema verses.

The verses that the rabbis read as dictating the recitation of the Shema are read by Aristeas as requiring one to "meditate on the devisings of God." Though this meditation is presumably done twice daily ("upon going to bed and rising" [160]), there is no clear indication that the content of this meditation is a liturgical text consisting of the Shema verses. Rather, the subject of meditation is "the devisings of God" and the miraculous transition effected when one moves from sleep to wakefulness and vice versa.[59]

Aristeas also does not exhibit a uniform understanding of the term "these words" by which the rituals are fulfilled. According to the biblical instructions (Deut 6:7–9), one is to recite the same "words" that one attaches to the door-post and binds to one's arm/hand. In Aristeas, one mediates on "the devisings of God"[60] (*tas tou theou kataskeuas*) and the miracle of moving from sleep to wakefulness and vice versa. By way of contrast, the ritual of mezuzah is fulfilled by means of the ambiguous "these words" (*ta logia*), which also appears to be the case with tefillin. In the case of hand tefillin, the reminder works in an interesting way. Since the hand is an instrument for affecting justice (159), we must mark the hand with a sign to use it well. Tefillin are a sort of ritual mnemonic that prompts us to use the hands appropriately.[61] The only consistency behind the different rituals is that each aims to instill consciousness of God in the practitioner.

Aristeas clearly sees connections among the Shema rituals and thinks of them as a unit to be discussed in a single context, even though not all function obviously as reminders. What is less clear is whether the connection is generated for him by a familiarity with the Shema verses as a liturgical text. My sense is that the trope of embodied ritual as a means of remembering God plays a stronger role in shaping Aristeas's discussion of the rituals than does a daily encounter

---

[59] Aristeas's manner of understanding the ritual reflects a particular interpretation of the verse that states, "you shall teach them to your children, speaking of them ... when you lie down and when you rise up." Aristeas assumes that the *time* at which the ritual is to be performed ("when you lie down and when you rise up") indicates something about the *content and purpose* of the ritual (it involves meditation on the transition from sleep to waking and vice versa). A similar interpretive move is reflected in the first blessing that the rabbis add to the Shema liturgical cycle. In the morning one praises God for bringing light into the world, and in the evening one praises God for bringing darkness. Here too one reflects on the miracles that are wrought *at the time* of sleeping and waking. See Kimelman, "From Covenant to Coronation," 29–40, where he discusses the morning and evening blessings that precede the Shema in the rabbinic liturgy.

[60] Reflecting translation in Hadas, *Aristeas to Philocrates (Letter of Aristeas)*, 163.

[61] Philo also attests an interpretation in which the hand/arm tefillin call the wearer to use the hands for the purpose of executing justice (*Spec. Laws.* 4:138).

with a liturgical text consisting of the Shema verses. First, when discussing embodied ritual, Aristeas certainly focuses on the Shema-derived rituals, but not to the exclusion of other rituals. He refers to the laws of firstfruits (158a) alongside the Shema-derived rituals in his allegorical treatment of the dietary laws. Second, he treats the rituals in an order that ignores their layout in the (eventual) liturgical text. Third, Aristeas's interpretation of Deut 6:7–9 does not imply a consistent reading of "these words," which one would expect to result from the intimate familiarity engendered by ongoing repetition of the Shema verses as a discrete textual unit. Finally, to the extent that Aristeas does know of a ritual way to enact the instructions "to recite [these words] . . . when you lie down and when you rise up," he assumes that this phrase requires meditation on "God's devisings" and the miracle of the transition from sleep to wakefulness. Aristeas certainly recognizes that the rituals have roots in scripture.[62] Aristeas's encounter with the biblical verses, however, is not filtered through an experience of them as a liturgical unit, as well. Central to my argument is the recognition that the decision to excerpt a passage of biblical text to be performed as liturgy both rests upon and engenders new ways of interacting with the biblical text. Aristeas's discussion of the Shema rituals, while acknowledging their rootedness in scripture, does not respond to aspects of the text that are highlighted once the verses are regarded as a liturgical unit.

The Synoptic Gospels (c. 70–90) provide additional evidence that the Shema-derived rituals were conceptually clustered together and perceived as a means of marking one's body with one's Jewish commitments. Whereas for Aristeas one marks one's body to initiate an internal process (remembering), Matthew suggests that the Shema-derived rituals mark the body for onlookers. In remarking on how the Pharisees stand out from other Jews, Matthew calls attention to their tefillin and tzitzit: "They do all their deeds to be seen by others; for they make their phylacteries broad and their fringes long" (Matt 23:5). Here tefillin and tzitzit serve as reminders not for the person wearing them, but for the onlooker in the public arena. The Shema rituals mark one's Jewish commitments, in this case a specific brand of Jewish commitments (i.e., the Pharasaic kind), by reminding others of the degree of the wearer's piety.[63]

We find further corroboration for the idea that these rituals were linked to one another because of how they marked the body with one's Jewish commitments in early rabbinic texts. Sif. Dt. 36 (c. 250–300 CE) discusses the Shema rituals in its final comment on the last phrase of the first paragraph of the Shema.

---

[62] Hadas notes that the use of *hē graphē* in 155 to indicate biblical scripture may be the earliest attested usage with this sense. See Hadas, *Aristeas to Philocrates (Letter of Aristeas)*, 161.

[63] Justin Martyr, in his *Dialogue with Trypho*, also refers to tzitzit and tefillin as distinctive practices that visibly mark the wearer. See A. Lukyn Williams, trans., *Justin Martyr, the Dialogue with Trypho* (New York: Macmillan, 1930), ch. 46, paragraph 5.

1. Precious is Israel [to God], for Scripture (*Hakatuv*) surrounded them with command-ments: Tefillin on their heads, tefillin on their arms, mezuzah on their doors, tzitzit on their clothes. About them David said, "Seven times a day do I praise thee because of thy righteous ordinances" (Ps 119:164).

2. He went into the bathhouse, and saw himself naked, and said "Woe to me that I am naked of the commandments." Then he looked at his circumcision and began to sing praises for it, "For the leader, on the eighth [day], a Psalm of David" (Ps 21:1).

As in Aristeas and Matthew, the Shema-derived rituals are clustered together because they play a central role in marking the body of the (male) Jew. In the Sifre, an anthropomorphic "Scripture"[64] physically surrounds and encom-passes the body in rituals that have a spatial component. Tefillin are on the head and hands, mezuzah enfolds them when they sit in their homes, and tzitzit grace their garments. Perhaps because Sifre Deuteronomy is considering the rituals in their physical aspect, no mention is made of the intellectual and verbal Shema rituals (recitation of Shema and Torah study). Notably, here the rituals are discussed in the order in which they appear in the liturgical text (with the slight exception that the head and hand tefillin are mentioned in reverse order). This fact may indicate that the rabbis do encounter the rituals in the liturgical text of the Shema verses. Finally, it is interesting to observe that, as in the *Letter of Aristeas*, we find mention of an additional ritual beyond those derived from the Shema. Aristeas mentions the ritual concerning the firstfruits because it can be practiced in "all places and times." Sifre Deuteronomy mentions circumcision because it marks the body in the most private ways, even when the body is deprived of all other signs of socialization and protection. Collectively, these sources (*Letter of Aristeas*, Matthew, and Sifre Deuteronomy) suggest a second reason why the Shema verses were attracting attention during the Second Tem-ple period. Though the doctrinal prologue of the first paragraph drew notice because of its status as a pseudo-commandment, the verses of ritual instruction generated interest because they prescribe a cluster of ritual actions that were understood to express and perform Jewish commitments in and on the body.

Philo: "These Words" Equals "Justice"

In *On the Special Laws*, Philo (d. 50 CE) also engages the Shema verses of ritual instruction because they testify to a central corpus of ritual acts. Philo treats the Shema verses in his discussion of justice in accordance with his belief that the rituals steer the mind and body toward just behavior. Philo's discussion follows the biblical text closely, as he provides a paraphrastic rendering of

---

[64] Azzan Yadin observes that *Hakatuv* (as opposed to *Torah*) functions as an active agent in directing the reader toward interpretation. Though the use of *Hakatuv* here does not feature scripture directing interpretation, scripture does function as an active agent as in Yadin's description. See Yadin, *Scripture as Logos: Rabbi Ishmael and the Origins of Midrash*, 11–33.

each phrase in the second paragraph of the Shema.[65] In order to highlight the interpretive aspect of Philo's discussion, I present the biblical text alongside Philo's rendering of it. I cite selectively from Philo, as he comments on the verses at great length.

Spec. Laws 4.137–142	LXX, Deut 11:18–20[66]
(137) The law tells us that we must set **the rules of justice** in the heart	(18) And lay **these words** in your heart and in your soul,
and fasten **them** for a sign upon the hand	bind **them** as a sign upon your hand,
And have **them** shaking[67] before the eyes.	So that **they** shall be immovable[68] before your eyes,
The first of these is a parable indicating that **the rules of justice** . . . must be upon our lordliest part [i.e., the heart].	[Second treatment of "Lay **these words** in your heart and in your soul"]
(138) The second shows that we must . . . express our approval of **them** in unhesitating action, for the hand is a symbol of action, and on this the law bids us fasten and hang **the rules of justice** for a sign.	[Second treatment of "bind **them** as a sign upon your hand]
(139) And the third means that always and everywhere we must have the vision of **them** as it were close to the eyes.	[Second treatment of "So that **they** shall be immovable before your eyes."]

[65] Naomi Cohen likewise observes that Philo comments on the second, not the first, paragraph of the Shema. See Cohen, *Philo Judaeus: His Universe of Discourse*, 108.

[66] Text according to Rahlfs edition.

[67] Philo here indicates that he had before him a version of the LXX with "moving (*saleuton*) before the eyes," rather than the more commonly attested version "immovable (*asaleuton*) before the eyes." See discussion in Cohen, *Philo Judaeus: His Universe of Discourse*, 145–46; and Yehudah B. Cohn, *Tangled Up in Text: Tefillin and the Ancient World*, 84. Much scholarly discussion of Philo's interpretation of the LXX here revolves around the question of whether Philo was describing a concrete practice of wearing tefillin, albeit one that differs greatly from the rabbinic practice. This question will not detain us here.

[68] Most LXX manuscripts translate *totafot* in Exod 13:16; Deut 6:8; and 11:18 as "unmoving" or "immovable" (*asaleuton*). Some LXX manuscripts have "moving" (*saleuton*), which appears to be the version upon which Philo comments. See discussion of this issue in Weinfeld, *Deuteronomy 1–11: A New Translation with Introduction and Commentary*, 333–35, 341; Cohen, *Philo Judaeus: His Universe of Discourse*, 144–47; and Yehudah B. Cohn, *Tangled Up in Text: Tefillin and the Ancient World*, 79–80. Interestingly, Naomi Cohen sees a shared tradition between Aristeas and Philo in that Aristeas thinks that the ritual of tefillin focuses attention on the *movement* from sleep to waking and vice versa. See Cohen, *Philo Judaeus: His Universe of Discourse*, 146–47.

(141) Indeed he must be forward to teach **the rules of justice** to kinsfolk and friends and all the young people at home and in the street, both when they go to their beds and when they arise, so that in every place... they may be gladdened by visions of **the just**. For there is no sweeter delight than that the soul be charged through and through with **justice**...	(19) And you shall teach **them** to your children (*tekna*),[69] speaking them when you stay at home and when you are away, when you lie down and when you rise up.
(142) He bids them also write and set **them** forth in front of the doorposts of each house and the gates in their walls, so that those who leave or remain at home, citizens and strangers alike, may read the inscriptions engraved on the face of the gates and keep in perpetual memory **what they should say and do** [= justice], careful alike to do and to allow **no injustice**.[70]	(20) And you shall write **them** on the doorposts of your house and on your gates.

Unlike the sources discussed thus far, Philo's discussion of the Shema-derived rituals is generated by direct engagement with the biblical text. We see this in the fact that he treats the rituals in the exact order in which they appear in the biblical text. He even offers an explicit interpretation of the "transitional verse" that introduces the term "these words" (Deut 11:18a), even though it prescribes no concrete ritual. In 137, Philo paraphrastically renders the "transitional verse" as "The law tells us we must set the *rules of justice* in the heart." Here he introduces the interpretation that he will pursue consistently throughout the passage: the "words" or "things" that are subject to various rituals are the rules of justice (*ta dikaia*).[71] Philo explains that "the law bids us fasten the rules of

---

[69] While the LXX translates the *banim* of Deut 11:19 as *tekna* (= gender-neutral "children"), it translates the same term in Deut 6:7 as *huios* (= male son). The rabbis are emphatic in their understanding of the term in both paragraphs of the Shema as indicating "sons, and not daughters." Sif. Dt. 46 offers a gender-specific interpretation of the term *banakhem* as "sons, and not daughters." M. Ber. 3:3, which states that women do not recite the Shema, offers an implicit interpretation of *banekha* in Deut 6:7 as indicating "sons and not daughters." The fact that LXX does not translate the term consistently suggests that it was not familiar with a liturgical text of the Shema consisting of both of these paragraphs. If it had been, I speculate it would have offered the same interpretation of the Hebrew term *ben* in both places. I will have occasion to discuss the gendered character of the interpretation of this term at great length in the next chapter.

[70] Translation taken from F. H. Colson, trans., *Philo* (London: William Heinemann, 1939).

[71] Naomi Cohen offers an extended discussion of semantic range of the term "justice" (*dikaiosyne*) and its meaning in Philo's Jewish-Greek specifically. See Cohen, *Philo Judaeus: His Universe*

justice" to the hand (138) by way of accounting for what it means to "bind these words upon your arm." In reference to the head tefillin in which "these words" are placed between the eyes, Philo states, "always and everywhere we must have a vision of them [the principles of justice] as it were close to the eyes" (139). At 141, the initiate is to instruct others in the "rules of justice," that they may be "gladdened by visions of the just. For there is no sweeter delight than that the soul be charged through and through with justice." And in 142, Philo implicitly suggests that the mezuzah too aims to inculcate habits of just behavior by keeping in "perpetual memory what they should say and do." Unlike Aristeas, Philo offers a uniform reading of "the words" employed in the various rituals in the instruction verses.[72]

It will be recalled that Aristeas notes a connection between tefillin of the arm and the arm as an agent of justice. It is not surprising that Philo, coming from the same Alexandrian milieu, should know of the same tradition. What is noteworthy, however, is that Philo takes a trope (justice) that was associated with just one of the many Shema-related rituals (arm/hand tefillin) and assumes that it offers the key to understanding all the rituals. As a reader of the biblical text, Philo feels the need to render the passage in a coherent manner, and he reads each and every appearance of "these words" as a reference to justice.

As can be seen from the order in which Philo treats the different rituals, Philo's discussion focuses on the second, rather than the first, paragraph of the Shema.[73] This fact is of interest because it demonstrates that the doctrinal prologue to the first paragraph was not responsible for the attention that the verses of ritual instruction received from Philo. The verses of ritual instruction generated interest because of the rituals in and of themselves, and not because they were appended to the doctrinal prologue of the first paragraph. Evidence already reviewed from the *Letter of Aristeas*, Matthew, and Sifre Deuteronomy suggests that the rituals were attracting attention because they were an embodied means of performing Jewish commitments. For Philo, the rituals embody one's commitments to justice.

Finally, it is important to observe that Philo does not seem to know of a Shema-derived requirement to pray twice daily. Philo reads the latter part of the phrase "teach them to your children, reciting them when you stay at home and when you are away, when you lie down and when you get up" as an idiomatic expression that means at all times and in all places. By way of contrast, the rabbis understand the adverbial clause "when you lie down and when you get

---

   of *Discourse*, 106–28. She argues that the term refers to observance of Torah commandments, both ritual and ethical. The term refers to commandments between man and man, and it is often paired with *eusebeia*, which indicates commandments between man and God (128).

72 See discussion above where I note Aristeas's inconsistent reading of "these words."

73 It will be recalled that the rituals are discussed in a different order in the first paragraph than in the second paragraph. See discussion on p. 142. See also Cohen, *Philo Judaeus: His Universe of Discourse*, 108, who likewise states that Philo paraphrases the second, not the first, paragraph of the Shema here.

up" as indicating specific times when or specific positions in which recitation should be performed. Though the rabbis later understand the verb "speak" to mean "recite as liturgy," Philo takes the term to mean "recite in the context of study." Thus the initiate must instruct his friends, family, and young men "so that in every place . . . they may be gladdened by visions of the just." As we found in the *Letter of Aristeas*, Philo does not appear to be familiar with an interpretation of these verses that requires diurnal recitation of the Shema verses themselves.

Diurnal Prayer and the Shema Verses in Josephus and the Rule of the Community

In his *Jewish Antiquities* (c. 95 CE), Josephus has occasion to mention the rituals of the Shema when he discusses the government established by Moses. Amid various political and cultic arrangements, Josephus discusses several mechanisms that Moses put in place to fashion the people into responsible citizens who will uphold the laws. Every seven years on the holiday of Sukkot, all men, women, and children are to gather to hear the high priest read the laws, "for it is a good thing that those laws should be engraven in their souls, and preserved in their memories, so that it may not be possible to blot them out; for by this means they will not be guilty of sin, when they cannot plead ignorance of what the laws have enjoined of them" (*Ant.* 4.210).[74] In the same paragraph, Josephus suggests that the children have been given a separate instruction to learn the laws: "Let the children also learn the laws, as the first thing they are taught, which will be the best thing they can be taught, and will be the cause of their future felicity" (*Ant.* 4.211). This last stipulation may represent an interpretation of the Shema verses that require instruction of the children ("impress [these words] upon your children" [Deut 6:7]; "teach [these words] to your children" [Deut 11:19]). If Josephus is indeed paraphrasing the Shema verses here, he offers yet another interpretation of "these words." Children are to be taught "the laws," just as the entire nation hears the law once every seven years. On this reading, "these words" are understood to be the law.

Since a public review of the law once every seven years is not sufficient to inculcate citizens with the necessary degree of internal responsibility, Moses also stipulates a daily ritual to reinforce fealty to the law:

Let everyone commemorate before God the benefits which he bestowed upon them at their deliverance out of the land of Egypt, and this twice every day, both when the day begins and when the hour of sleep comes, gratitude being in its own nature a just thing, and serving not only by way of a return for the past, but also by way of invitation of future favors. (Ant. 4.212)

---

74 Translation of this and the following citations of Josephus from *Josephus, Complete Works*, trans. William Whiston, foreword by William Sanford LaSor (Grand Rapids: Kregel Publications, 1978), 117.

The broader context suggests that this daily ritual, like the ritual reading of the law every seven years and instruction of children, works to make citizens cognizant of the obligations that the law places upon them. An additional reason for the ritual of diurnal prayer is stated explicitly. It is appropriate to be grateful for favors already given, especially since appreciation can inspire additional benefaction.

The question that has vexed scholars is this: What is the verbal content of the diurnal prayer with which Josephus is familiar? Did such prayer involve the recitation of the Shema verses as liturgy? Several elements of Josephus's discussion support the conclusion that Josephus refers here to the recitation of the Shema verses. After discussing the obligation to acknowledge God's generosity twice daily, he suggests that the rituals of mezuzah and tefillin likewise instill mindfulness of the many blessings God has bestowed:

(213) They are also to inscribe the principal blessings they have received from God upon their doors, and show the same remembrance of them upon their arms; as also they are to bear on their forehead and their arm those wonders which declare the power of God, and his good will toward them, that God's readiness to bless them may appear everywhere conspicuous about them.

Scholars conclude from the fact that Josephus's discussion of diurnal prayer is set within a broader discussion of Shema-derived rituals that the diurnal prayer is also Shema derived and therefore consists of recitation of the Shema verses.[75] Additionally, Josephus specifies that the prayer is to be said "when the day begins and when the hour of sleep comes on," which echoes the Shema's stipulation to "recite [these words] ... when you lie down and when you rise up," albeit it in reverse order.

In spite of this evidence, Shlomo Naeh and Aharon Shemesh argue that Josephus's diurnal prayer did not consist of recitation of the Shema verses.[76] They observe that Josephus requires the supplicant to recount "the benefits which [God] bestowed them at their deliverance out of the land of Egypt." Though it is possible that this phrase alludes to God's kindness generally in taking Israel out of Egypt (a subject that the Shema verses could plausibly be stretched to include), Naeh and Shemesh argue that the term "benefits" should be understood quite specifically as a reference to the miraculous provisions

75 See Ezra Fleischer, "On the Beginnings of Obligatory Jewish Prayer," *Tarbiz* 59 (1990): 417–18; Emil Schurer et al., *The History of the Jewish People in the Age of Jesus Christ* (Edinburgh: T. and T. Clark, 1979), 455n153; Elbogen, *Jewish Liturgy: A Comprehensive History*, 19; Cohen, *Philo Judaeus: His Universe of Discourse*, 170–71; and Albert Baumgarten, "Invented Traditions," 206. Kimelman is more cautious, leaving the relationship between this passage in Josephus and the Shema unresolved. See Kimelman, "From Covenant to Coronation," 13. Tabory follows Naeh and Shemesh (see discussion below) and expresses skepticism that Josephus refers here to the Shema. See Tabory, "Prayers and Berakhot," 289–90.
76 See Shlomo Naeh and Aharon Shemesh, "The Manna Story and the Time of Morning Prayer," *Tarbiz* 64 (1995): 335–40.

that God provided Israel in their trials during their desert wanderings: the pillar of cloud, morning manna, evening quail, and the magically appearing well.[77] In their view, Josephus's diurnal prayer acknowledges specific generous provisions by God: the manna and quail. They note that the Bible states that God provided manna in order to give the people an opportunity to reflect on God's providential role in their lives.[78] In Naeh and Shemesh's reconstructed prayer, the people acknowledge the "benefits" conferred by God at the very times when they historically appeared (manna in the morning, quail in the evening). This derivation could account for the fact that Josephus mentions the morning prayer before the evening prayer: The obligation to recall God's beneficence is rooted in an interpretation of the manna verses. Since manna was received in the morning,[79] the prayer would have initially been said in the morning. Only secondarily (according to Naeh and Shemesh) was a prayer added in the evening to commemorate the quail.[80]

Naeh and Shemesh offer a compelling interpretation, as they account for several distinctive features of Josephus's description of diurnal prayer. If they are correct that Josephus refers to a prayer that acknowledges the miracles of God's desert provisions,[81] then this passage provides additional evidence that the Shema-derived rituals were clustered associatively with rituals that derive from other biblical passages. In a single context, Josephus discusses not only the Shema-derived rituals of mezuzah, arm/hand tefillin, and head tefillin and the instruction of children, but also the unrelated rituals of the public reading of the law every seven years and diurnal prayer. As we found in the *Letter of Aristeas*, the discussion is structured by an overarching concept (desire to instill conscientiousness toward the law and gratitude to God) and not by attention to the Shema verses as a liturgical text.

Even if Naeh and Shemesh's conclusions are rejected, several other factors mitigate against concluding that Josephus's diurnal prayer consisted of a recitation of the Shema verses themselves. First, Josephus does not offer a consistent reading of the terms "these words" by which the various rituals are performed. He explains that children should be instructed in "the law," one should recite "the benefits conferred by God," and one should inscribe "the principal blessings they have received upon their doors, and show the same remembrance of

---

[77] For further ancient reflections on these miracles, see *t. Sotah* 11:8 and *Liber antiquitatum biblicarum* 28:8, cited in Naeh and Shemesh, "The Manna Story and the Time of Morning Prayer," 336n9.

[78] See Deut 8:3, discussed in Naeh and Shemesh, "The Manna Story and the Time of Morning Prayer," 337.

[79] See Exod 11:12, 14.

[80] Naeh and Shemesh cite Wisdom of Solomon as the earliest source that requires prayer at the time of the morning manna. Josephus appears to be the first to require prayer in the evening also, which Naeh and Shemesh speculate arises as a response to the evening miracle of quail. See Naeh and Shemesh, "The Manna Story and the Time of Morning Prayer," 336–37, 339.

[81] Tabory regards their argument favorably. See Tabory, "Prayers and Berakhot," 289–90.

them upon their arms; as also they are to bear on their forehead those wonders which declare the power of God" (*Ant.* 4.213). The term "these words" is variously interpreted as "the law," "benefits conferred by God," "principal blessings," and "wonders which declare the power of God." It is counterintuitive to conclude that Josephus would read the term "these words" in each of these various ways when discussing mezuzah, tefillin, and instruction of children, but read the term as referring to the Shema verses when discussing diurnal prayer.

Finally, it should be observed that Josephus mentions morning prayer before he mentions evening prayer (they should bless "both when the day begins and when the hour of sleep comes on"). The Shema verses notably require one to "recite [these words]... when you lie down and when you rise up," which when interpreted according to the house of Hillel[82] requires praying at the time of lying down (evening) and at the time of rising up (morning). If Josephus understands the Shema verses to dictate diurnal prayer, he does not feel the need to describe the prayer in the terms provided by the biblical text, nor does he feel the need to mention the prayers in the order provided by the biblical text. This observation is central because certain interpretive stances with regard to the Shema verses (which Josephus does not exhibit) need to be in place before the instructions to "recite [these words]" can be understood self-referentially as requiring recitation of the Shema verses themselves. If one encounters the biblical text and understands it to require recitation of the Shema verses, one must have a hyper-literalist interpretation of the text. Such an interpretive stance enables the term "these words" to be read as referring to the text of the Shema verses themselves, but it also requires reading other features of the text hyper-literally. I am inclined to believe that someone who read the Shema verses as requiring their recitation as liturgy would also be attentive to the fact that evening prayer is mentioned before morning prayer and would reflect this attention in his or her explication of the ritual, as the house of Hillel does. We find no indications that Josephus interacted with the Shema verses in this hyper-literal manner.

The *Rule of the Community* from the Dead Sea Scrolls also contains an allusion to prayer that many scholars have taken to be a reference to the recitation of the Shema verses. Toward the end of the scroll, the text prescribes a daily, weekly, and yearly regimen of prayer. In that context we find the following instructions:

10. As the day and night enters (*'im mavo' yom velaylah*) I will enter into the covenant of God (*'avo'ah bebrit 'el*), and as evening and morning depart (*ve'im motze' `erev uvoker*) I will recite his statutes (*'emor hukav*)...

13. ... When I go out and come in (*bere'shit tze't uvo'*),

14. sit and rise (*lashevet vequm*), and when laid on my couch (*ve'im mishkav vetzu`i*), I will cry for joy to him (*'aranenah lo*).[83]

Here we find a reference to prayer that reenacts the covenant and is recited in both evening and morning[84] (1QS col. 10, line 10). Notably, the words used by the *Rule of the Community* to describe the ritual are not identical to the terms used in the Shema verses. Where the *Rule of the Community* speaks of "day and night entering" (*'im mavo' yom velaylah*) and "evening and morning departing" (*ve'im motze' `erev uvoker*), the Shema verses suggest recitation is to be done "when you lie down and when you rise up."[85] Where the *Rule of the Community* understands the ritual to consist of "reciting/saying His statutes" (*'emor hukav*), the Shema verses ask one to "speak of [these words]" (*vedibarta bam*). Nonetheless, the idea that one reenacts the covenant twice daily through a ritual recitation does have striking similarities to the significance attributed to the Shema liturgy by the rabbis.[86] Even more striking is the fact that one should "cry for joy" in a range of different positions and places: "when I go out and come in, sit and stand, and when laid on my couch" (lines 13 and 14). The plurality of circumstances that elicit prayer recalls the language of Deut 6:7: "Speak of them when you are sitting in your home, and when you are walking on your way, when you lie down and when you rise up." The *Rule of the Community*, however, switches the order of the situations that elicit prayer/recitation. Where the biblical verses speak of (1) sitting, (2) walking, (3) lying, and (4) rising, the *Rule of the Community* offers them in the following order: (1) going out (= walking?), (2) coming in (= ?), (3) sitting, (4) rising, and (5) lying (on your couch). If the *Rule of the Community*'s description of

---

[83] Text cited according to Elisha Qimron and James H. Charlesworth, "Rule of the Community (1QS)," in *The Dead Sea Scrolls – Hebrew, Aramaic, and Greek with English Translations – Rule of the Community and Related Documents*, vol. 1, ed. James H. Charlesworth et al. (Tübingen: Mohr Siebeck; Louisville: Westminster John Knox Press, 1994), 45.

[84] Talmon argues that the daily affirmations were recited six times, rather than twice, daily. See S. Talmon, "The 'Manual of Benedictions' of the Sect of the Judaean Desert," *Revue de Qumran* 2/8 (1960): 481–83. For a refutation of this view, see Schiffman, *Reclaiming the Dead Sea Scrolls*, 292; Esther Glickler Chazon, "When Did They Pray: Times for Prayer in the Dead Sea Scrolls and Associated Literature," in *For a Later Generation: The Transformation of Tradition in Israel, Early Judaism, and Early Christianity*, ed. Randal A. Argall, Beverly A. Bow, and Rodney A. Werline (Harrisburg: Trinity Press International, 2000), 44; and Albert Baumgarten, "Invented Traditions," 205.

[85] Esther Chazon suggests that the sectarian regimen of prayer in the morning and evening derives from their interest in heavenly cycles and is connected to their widely observed commitments to a solar calendar. See Chazon, "When Did They Pray?" 43–47.

[86] Baumgarten argues that this is a reference to the Shema. According to Baumgarten, the Shema liturgy was instituted at the Temple as part of the larger Hasmonean program to bolster their authority. In this view, the sectarians continued the new tradition of reciting the Shema, but adapted the liturgy so that it served as a repudiation of the version recited at the Temple in Jerusalem. See Albert Baumgarten, "Invented Traditions," 202–5.

prayer is informed by the language of the Shema verses, it is only loosely so.[87]
Once again, I would argue that the *Rule of the Community* does not reflect the
hyper-literal conception of the Shema verses necessary to read the term "these
words" self- referentially.

In conclusion, though both Josephus and the *Rule of the Community* know
of prayer practices that are associated with the Shema verses, neither source
offers conclusive proof that the hyper-literal conception of the verses that is
necessary if one is to read the instruction to "recite [these words]" as a reference
to the Shema verses is in evidence during the Second Temple period. If anything,
in their allusive strategies toward the Shema verses, Josephus and the *Rule of
the Community* reflect a mode of engaging the biblical text that is not focused
on fine textual details. When and where, then, do we find the hyper-literal way
of engaging the Shema verses that makes possible the recitation of the Shema
verses as liturgy?

From Qumran Tefillin to the Bar Kochba Tefillin

The tefillin slips found at Qumran date to the second and first centuries BCE
and constitute another piece of evidence as to how the term "these words" were
interpreted in the Second Temple period. As suggested earlier, the tefillin slips
contain a variety of different biblical passages in addition to those contained
in standard rabbinic tefillin.[88] Yehudah Cohn's research suggests that biblical
passages were included in Qumran tefillin for three distinct reasons, though
some passages could be included on the basis of more than one.

Cohn argues that the practice of tefillin emerged as an attempt to "Judaize"
pagan amulet practice.[89] Where pagans placed significant texts from their tradition into amulets intended to provide protection, Jews turned to their central
text (the Bible) to substantiate a similar practice. Cohn suggests that the promise
of long life in Deut 11:21 combined with the instruction in adjacent verses to
"bind [these words] on your arms/hand and place them as frontlet between
your eyes" led to the initial inclusion of the second paragraph of the Shema

---

[87] Qimron and Charlesworth remain noncommital regarding the question of whether this language
alludes to the Shema and Deut 6:4–7. See Qimron and Charlesworth, "Rule of the Community
(1QS)," 45. Chazon also adopts a cautious approach. See Esther Glickler Chazon, "Prayers
from Qumran and Their Historical Implications," *Dead Sea Discoveries* 1 (1994): 276. By way
of contrast, Talmon and Schiffman confidently assume that this passage refers to the Shema. See
Talmon, "The 'Manual of Benedictions' of the Sect of the Judaean Desert," 489; and Schiffman,
Reclaiming the Dead Sea Scrolls, 293.

[88] For a full list of the biblical passages contained in the Qumran tefillin slips, see Yehudah
B. Cohn, *Tangled Up in Text: Tefillin and the Ancient World*, 65–66. See also Nakman,
"The Contents and Order of the Biblical Sections in the Tefillin from Qumran and Rabbinic
Halakhah" (Hebrew), 41–42.

[89] See Yehudah B. Cohn, *Tangled Up in Text: Tefillin and the Ancient World*, 55–102, esp. 89–91.

(Deut 11:13–21) in tefillin.[90] Cohn assumes that the verses instructing one to "bind these words" were read figuratively in early Second Temple times, before tefillin practice is attested.[91] From the focus on Deut 11:13–21 emerged three bases for including biblical passages in the amulets. First, it was helpful if the passage offered a promise of long life and divine protection. On this basis, Cohn suggests that Deut 32 was sometimes the biblical passage of choice.[92] Cohn speculates that 4QDeut[n] and 4QDeut[j], which contain Deut 8:5–10, were also tefillin slips. Deut 8:5–10 promises bountiful life on the land as a reward for loyal performance of God's commandments. If these scrolls are indeed tefillin slips, then they provide evidence of another passage that was placed in tefillin because it offered divine blessing.[93] Second, since the instruction verses were understood to require placing "these words" in the amulet, it was also helpful if the passage was characterized in the biblical text as "words" or as "these words."[94] On this basis, Deut 32 (Song of Moses) and Deut 5 (the Decalogue) were included, since they are described by Moses as "words" or "these words." Finally, since the instruction verses from the second paragraph of the Shema (Deut 11:18) were initially included by virtue of their proximity to the promise for long life, there developed a sense that the instruction verses should also be included in tefillin. Most of the Qumran tefillin contain the instruction verses from the first and second paragraphs of the Shema (Deut 6 and 11), in addition to a substantial number of verses preceding the instruction verses (Deut 5 and 10). The Qumran tefillin also contain passages from Exodus 13 that require one to make a "sign on your hand and a reminder on your forehead." (Cohn argues that these verses were understood metaphorically during the early part of the Second Temple period.)[95]

---

[90] Though rabbinic tefillin and most Qumran tefillin slips (with the notable exception of 4QPhyl N) contain the four biblical verses that are understood to be instructions for tefillin practice, Cohn speculates that the practice first arose in connection with interpretation of Deut 11:21 alone. He argues that the association of tefillin with verses from Exodus was a secondary development. See Yehudah B. Cohn, *Tangled Up in Text: Tefillin and the Ancient World*, 69, 95.

[91] See figurative use of similar language in Prov 1:8–9; 3:3; 3:22; 6:20–22; 7:3. See discussion in Yehudah B. Cohn, *Tangled Up in Text: Tefillin and the Ancient World*, 46–48.

[92] See 4QPhyl N, which includes Deut 32:(9–13), 14–20, (21–31), 32–33. See also 4QDeut[j], 4QDeut[kl], and 4QDeut[q], which contain verses from Deut 32 and which Cohn suggests are tefillin slips (76). Deut 32:47 refers to length of days on the land. Cohn discusses the rationale for including Deut 32 in tefillin at Yehudah B. Cohn, *Tangled Up in Text: Tefillin and the Ancient World*, 93–94. Contra Milik, who was the initial editor of the Qumran tefillin, Nakman argues that 4QPhyl N is not a tefillin slip. See Nakman, "The Contents and Order of the Biblical Sections in the Tefillin from Qumran and Rabbinic Halakhah" (Hebrew), 35–37; Milik, "Tefillin, Mezuzot et Targums," 34–37, 70.

[93] See discussion in Yehudah B. Cohn, *Tangled Up in Text: Tefillin and the Ancient World*, 96.

[94] The Decalogue is called "these words" at Deut 5:19 and Exod 20:1. The Song of Moses (Deut 32) is called "these words" at Deut 32:45.

[95] See Yehudah B. Cohn, *Tangled Up in Text: Tefillin and the Ancient World*, 39–41, 45–53.

In many instances when the instruction verses are included in the Qumran tefillin slips, they are "padded" with substantial portions of the preceding passages. For example, even though no mention of tefillin practice is made until Exod 13:11, XQPhyl 1 includes Exod 12:43–13:10 (XQPhyl 3 from the same set and found in the same housing contain the instruction verses, Exod 13:11–16). We find here a pattern that is repeated in many places: The passages that precede the instruction verses are cited at great length. This practice suggests one additional way of reading the term "these words": "the words" to be included in the tefillin are the text immediately preceding the instruction verses.[96]

In conclusion, biblical passages were included in the Qumran tefillin for a variety of reasons. Passages were included because (1) they were thought to invoke divine protection (Deut 11:21; Deut 32; Deut 8:5–10); (2) they were named in the biblical text as "words," which seemed an appropriate way to fulfill the instructions regarding "these words" (Deut 5; Deut 32); (3) they included the instructions for the ritual (Deut 6; Deut 11; Exod 13); and (4) they immediately preceded the instruction verses (Deut 5; Deut 10; Exod 12). In point of fact, the content of most tefillin slips can be accounted for by more than one of these principles. Cohn emphasizes that reading the instruction verses as ritual instructions constituted a new interpretation of tefillin practice that emphasized the biblical roots of a practice that had pagan analogues.[97]

A second cache of tefillin generally dated to the period of the Bar Kochba Revolt (c. 135 CE) has been found in three sets of caves[98] in the Judean desert. It is very striking that these tefillin include only those passages that the rabbis include in their tefillin (Ex 13:1–16; Deut 6:4–9; Deut 11:13–21). The Bar Kochba tefillin are more narrowly focused on the instruction verses and the verses immediately preceding them. Apparently between the first century BCE and second century CE, a shift occurred.[99] Whereas earlier tefillin were

---

[96] Nakman explains that this practice resulted from an interpretation of "these words" as a reference to the speech Moses had given prior to giving the instruction verses. See Nakman, "The Contents and Order of the Biblical Sections in the Tefillin from Qumran and Rabbinic Halakhah" (Hebrew), 23.

[97] See Yehudah B. Cohn, *Tangled Up in Text: Tefillin and the Ancient World*, 89–92, 129. See also Cohn's discussion of Greco-Roman magical practices that include ritual instructions as part of the ritual: Yehudah B. Cohn, *Tangled Up in Text: Tefillin and the Ancient World*, 95–96.

[98] Six tefillin and one tefillin casing were found at Nahal Hever, Wadi Murabbat, and Nahal Seival. See catalogue and publication of these documents in Emanuel Tov, "Categorized Lists of the 'Biblical Texts': Appendix – Phylacteries (Tefillin)," in *Discoveries in the Judaean Desert*, vol. 39 (Oxford: Oxford University Press, 2002), 182–83; J. T. Milik, "Textes Littéraires," in *Discoveries in the Judaean Desert*, vol. 2 (Oxford: Oxford University Press, 1961), 80–86; Y. Aharoni, "The Expedition to the Judaean Desert, 1969, Expedition b'," *Israel Exploration Journal* 11 (1961): 22–23; and M. Morgenstern and M. Segal, "XHev/SePhylactery," in *Discoveries in the Judaean Desert*, vol. 38 (Oxford: Oxford University Press, 2000), 183–91. See discussion of these tefillin in Yehudah B. Cohn, *Tangled Up in Text: Tefillin and the Ancient World*, 103–6.

[99] Milik dates the shift to c. 100 CE. See Milik, "Tefillin, Mezuzot et Targums," 39.

understood to function as the fulfillment of several different principles, by the Bar Kochba period, the practice was understood to be a means of fulfilling the instruction verses.[100] In the Bar Kochba tefillin, we finally find an interpretation of the term "these words" that makes possible the recitation of the Shema verses as liturgy. The "words" that are included in the Bar Kochba tefillin are what later come to be known as the first and second paragraphs of the Shema (Deut 6:4–9 and Deut 11:13–21; Exod 13:1–16 was also included).[101]

I argue that the rabbis engaged in an interpretive strategy very similar to the one exhibited by Philo. Earlier I suggested that Philo was familiar with the Alexandrian trope (attested in the *Letter of Aristeas*) of associating the hand with justice. Philo took a motif associated with a single one of the rituals discussed in the instruction verses (hand/arm tefillin) and applied it uniformly to all the rituals, thereby offering a consistent reading of "these words" throughout the passage. Where the *Letter of Aristeas* had said that only hand/arm tefillin promote the performance of justice, Philo understood *all* the Shema rituals to be a means of instilling principles of justice. Philo was unique among Second Temple sources in his desire to impose uniformity on the passage. Neither the *Letter of Aristeas* nor Josephus offers a consistent read of the term "these words" by which the rituals are fulfilled.[102] I have suggested that the general reticence to read the term consistently throughout the passage results from the fact that Josephus and Aristeas attend to the verses insofar as they describe embodied practice. They are not primarily engaging the verses as text. Philo, by way of contrast, does engage the verses as a text, as he makes clear from the fact that he follows the biblical text so closely. His exegetical orientation leads him to impose uniformity on the passage so that the term "these words" has a consistent meaning throughout.

I speculate that the rabbinic practice of reciting the Shema verses as liturgy flows from a similar exegetical move. The Bar Kochba tefillin attest to a reading of the term "these words" as the instruction verses themselves. It makes sense that Judean interpreters wanted, like Philo in Alexandria, to read the paragraph in a uniform manner. They read the instruction to "recite [these words]" as requiring the recitation of the very same verses included in tefillin, namely the Shema verses.[103]

---

[100] Cohn suggests that pragmatic concerns were responsible for limiting the text included in the tefillin. See Yehudah B. Cohn, *Tangled Up in Text: Tefillin and the Ancient World*, 126.

[101] Exod 13:1–10 and Exod 13:11–16 are also included in the Bar Kochba tefillin, but they do not become part of the Shema liturgy because the biblical text there includes no instruction to recite these passages.

[102] See discussion of *Letter of Aristeas* and of Josephus on pp. 157, 165–66.

[103] In this argument I employ the "developmental model" of continuity between the Qumran tefillin, on one hand, and the Bar Kochba and rabbinic tefillin, on the other hand. That is, I posit a basic continuity between the two cultural phenomena and account for differences by suggesting a "development" in the culture. On the difference between the "developmental model" and the "reflective model" in considering the relationship between Qumran and rabbinic halakhah, see Aharon Shemesh, *Halakhah in the Making: The Development of Jewish*

The Textualization of Ritual and the Ritualization of Text

This review of Second Temple sources that cite, allude to, or paraphrase the Shema verses helps us see what is truly unique in the rabbinic interpretation. Contextualizing the rabbinic interpretation in this way also helps us understand what the rabbis thought they were accomplishing through the recitation of the Shema verses as liturgy.[104]

Several important shifts in the interpretation of the Shema verses are attested in rabbinic sources. The first and most important development in the tannaitic period is that the term "these words" is understood in a new way. The "words" by which one performs the rituals are not God's ordinances generally (as in the *Letter of Aristeas*). They are not the Decalogue or other texts assumed to have protective powers (as in the Qumran tefillin). They are not the principles of justice (as in Philo). For the rabbis, "the words" subject to ritualization are the very biblical texts that are presumed to prescribe the rituals. Thus we read in Sif. Dt. 35, "*And you shall bind them* (Deut 6:8). These [and not other verses] are for binding." I call this development the textualization of ritual because a ritual that formerly could be fulfilled through a variety of principles and passages was now fulfilled by means of the very text that was taken to prescribe the ritual.[105]

The new way of practicing tefillin rested on – and helped reinforce – a conception of the biblical text as deserving attention.[106] In a world of increasingly

---

Law from Qumran to the Rabbis (Berkeley: University of California Press, 2009), 3–7. Also following the developmental model in evaluating the relationship between Qumran and rabbinic tefillin are Yehudah B. Cohn, *Tangled Up in Text: Tefillin and the Ancient World*, 74–75; Nakman, "The Contents and Order of the Biblical Sections in the Tefillin from Qumran and Rabbinic Halakhah" (Hebrew); and Rothstein, "From Bible to Muraba'at: Studies in the Literary, Textual and Scribal Features of Phylacteries and Mezuzot in Ancient Israel and Early Judaism".

[104] It is important to note that my hypothesis regarding the process by which the Shema verses came to be recited as liturgy does not account for how the third paragraph (Num 15:37–41) came to be included in the liturgical cycle. In seeing the initial impetus for the Shema's recitation as coming from the first two paragraphs, I follow Elbogen, *Jewish Liturgy: A Comprehensive History*, 23; Tabory, "Prayers and Berakhot," 291–92; and Cohen, *Philo Judaeus: His Universe of Discourse*, 108, 167–76. My analysis does, however, suggest a reason for the eventual inclusion of the third paragraph: It, like the first two paragraphs, refers to a concrete ritual practice by which Jewish identity is marked and performed on the body.

[105] Cohn discusses a common ancient practice in which the instructions for or the mythical origins of a ritual become part and parcel of the ritual. See Yehudah B. Cohn, *Tangled Up in Text: Tefillin and the Ancient World*, 95–96, esp. n152.

[106] In his many writings, Kugel documents the attentions that the biblical text received during the late Second Temple period. See esp. James L. Kugel, "Two Introductions to Midrash," in *Midrash and Literature*, ed. Geoffrey H. Hartman and Sandford Budick (New Haven: Yale University Press, 1986), 77–103; and James L. Kugel, *The Bible as It Was* (Cambridge, Mass.: Belknap Press of Harvard University Press, 1997). See also Adiel Schremer, "'[T]He[Y] Did Not Read in the Sealed Book': Qumran Halakhic Revolution and the Emergence of Torah Study in Second Temple Judaism," in *Historical Perspectives: From the Hasmoneans to Bar*

potent biblical scriptural texts, the practice of tefillin galvanized the power of biblical scripture by incorporating it onto the body. The textualization of ritual that we find with tefillin was one part of a broader cultural process taking place during the latter part of the Second Temple period. During this period, biblical scripture began to assume a new significance as a locus of divine presence. The biblical text was increasingly attracting attention, increasingly assumed to be worthy of intense scrutiny, and significant in all of its details. In this cultural context, recitation, performance, and interpretation of scripture became new pious practices.[107] These other related developments contributed to a new framing of tefillin. What had formerly been a protective amulet was now a ritual means of incorporating biblical text onto the body.[108]

We can detect early signs of the "textualization of ritual" in Philo. On the one hand, Philo discusses the rituals because they offer an embodied way to internalize a foundational principle of Judaism, justice. (We saw the same tendency exhibited by the *Letter of Aristeas*, Josephus, and Matthew 23.) Unlike these other writers, however, Philo ties the rituals back to the biblical text from which they were assumed to derive. We see this in the fact that he frames his discussion as a paraphrastic rendering of the relevant verses and in the fact that he offers a consistent reading of "these words."

Kokhba in Light of the Dead Sea Scrolls, ed. D. Goodblatt, A. Pinnick, and D. R. Schwartz (Leiden: Brill, 2001), 105–26. Most recently Aharon Shemesh has argued that a new form of "text-centricity" emerged in the Hasmonean period: Sadducean Qumranites understood Jewish practices to be rooted in the biblical text. See Shemesh, *Halakhah in the Making: The Development of Jewish Law from Qumran to the Rabbis*, esp. 72–106.

[107] Cohn describes a phenomenon involving "literacy, literalism and interpretation of scripture" as setting the scene for the emergence of tefillin practice. See Yehudah B. Cohn, *Tangled Up in Text: Tefillin and the Ancient World*, 87–88. See also Albert Baumgarten, "Literacy and the Polemic Concerning Biblical Hermeneutics in the Second Temple Era," in *Education and History: Cultural and Political Contexts* (Hebrew), ed. Rivka Feldhay and Immanuel Etkes (Jerusalem: Zalman Shazar Center for Jewish History, 1999), 40. Tabory documents the use of scripture in public readings that served liturgical purposes. See Tabory, "Prayers and Berakhot," 288–90. Kugel proposes the accumulation of a fluid body of oral scriptural interpretations during the late Second Temple period. See James L. Kugel, *In Potiphar's House: The Interpretive Life of Biblical Texts* (Cambridge, Mass.: Harvard University Press, 1990), 266–68. Schremer documents the rise of study sessions and a new focus on the teacher among the Qumranites. See Schremer, "'[T]He[Y] Did Not Read in the Sealed Book': Qumran Halakhic Revolution and the Emergence of Torah Study in Second Temple Judaism," 112. Judith Newman discusses the incorporation of scriptural texts into liturgy. See Judith H. Newman, *Praying by the Book: The Scripturalization of Prayer in Second Temple Judaism*, no. 14 (Atlanta: Scholars Press, 1999). Shaye Cohen discusses the phenomenon more generally. See Shaye J. D. Cohen, *From the Maccabees to the Mishnah* (Philadelphia: Westminster Press, 1987), 72–73.

[108] Kugel discusses Ezekiel's being urged to eat a scroll containing God's words (Ezek 2:7–3:3) as an early example of the process of absorbing scripture in an intensely physical way. See Kugel, "Two Introductions to Midrash," 81–82. The sotah ritual described in Num 5 provides a biblical precedent for treating text as an element in ritual. There, a parchment containing the words of a curse are dissolved in water, and the suspected adulteress is made to drink the resulting concoction. She too incorporates text ritually into the body.

I further argue that the interpretation of "these words" exhibited by the Bar Kochba tefillin supports the possibility of a new ritual practice. Once the first and second paragraphs of the Shema came to be thought of as the "words" by which rituals (tefillin and mezuzah) are performed, it became possible to understand in a new way what it means to "repeat [these words] to your children, and speak of them, when you are at home and when you are away, when you go lie down and when you rise up" (Deut 6:7–8). While Philo derives from this phrase the imperative to instruct disciples and friends in justice and the *Letter of Aristeas* sees in it the obligation to meditate on God's devisings and the miraculous transition from sleep to waking, the rabbis take it to require recitation of the Shema verses themselves as liturgy. Thus we read in Sif. Dt. 34, "*And you shall repeat them to your children* (Deut 6:7). These [and not other verses] shall you repeat." The fact that the rituals alluded to in the Shema verses had been textualized brought renewed attention to the verses as a source of ritual. Recitation of the Shema verses emerges for the rabbis as a new kind of ritual.[109] The Shema verses were recited as liturgy because Judean Jews (maybe only the rabbis, maybe others as well?) sensed that these verses were a text that demanded to be internalized through ritual. What better way to internalize the text of these verses in ritual than by reciting them?

I call this second stage in the process by which the Shema verses came to be recited as liturgy the "ritualization of text." A text that was not formerly subject to liturgical recitation became so by virtue of the text's association with other rituals. As I have shown, these rituals had recently come to be seen as a means of internalizing and embodying the text of the instruction verses.

One interesting consequence of understanding the term "these words" to refer to the full paragraphs of the Shema is that the doctrinal prologues were now linked to the rituals. The textual rituals (Shema, tefillin, and mezuzah) now became, in part, about affirming the covenantal relationship between Israel and God (as expressed in the doctrinal prologues). The textual rituals, however, had another meaning that was equally central to them in their rabbinic iteration. These rituals engaged the Shema verses as scriptural text to be embodied and internalized. The rabbinic position was one among several about what the rituals aim to accomplish. For Philo, the rituals point the practitioner toward justice; for the *Letter of Aristeas*, they remind one of God; for Josephus, they cultivate consciousness of God's beneficence. For the rabbis, the rituals were a means of internalizing the biblical text. In this regard, they were understood to be a form of Torah study.[110] Insofar as these rituals incorporated the text of the Bible into the body, they functioned like Torah study, which was the

---

[109] Cohn speculatively proposes such a link between tefillin and Shema recitation. See Yehudah B. Cohn, *Tangled Up in Text: Tefillin and the Ancient World*, 101.

[110] Moshe Benovitz attributes the view that recitation of the Shema is a form of Torah study to R. Shimon b. Yohai. See Benovitz, "*Shinun*: Recitation of the Shema in the Teaching of R. Shimon Bar Yohai" (Hebrew). Hirschman extends Benovitz's thesis to include recitation of the *second* paragarph of the Shema. He argues that this paragraph also was viewed as Torah study.

premiere ritual by which the rabbis internalized scriptural verses. Thus we read
in the Mekhilta, "*They shall be a memorial between your eyes in order that the
Torah of God shall be in your mouth* (Exod 13:9). From here they said: Anyone
who wears tefillin is like one who reads Torah, and whoever reads Torah is
exempt from wearing tefillin" (Mek. Bo 17, ed. Horowitz-Rabin, 68).[111] In
this midrashic tradition, the practice of tefillin is taken to be redundant with
respect to the practice of Torah study. The two practices are so much of a piece
that one who is already engaged in Torah study does not need to perform the
distinct ritual of wearing tefillin. Wearing tefillin, like studying Torah, is a way
of integrating Torah into the self.

Several tannaitic sources draw a similar connection between Torah study
and recitation of the Shema.[112] The most explicit linking of the two practices,
however, is found in an early amoraic statement recorded in Bavli. There the
sages consider the question of how one is to fulfill properly the requirement of
Josh 1:8 that the "book of Torah should not depart from your mouth." Does
one need to study Torah all hours of the day and night? R. Ammi proposes
that it is enough to study just one chapter in the morning and one chapter in
the evening. Just as people use the expression "A to Z" to refer to all that
comes in between, so one may study a bit in the morning and in the evening
and thereby infuse all that comes in between with the flavor of Torah. R.
Yohanan in the name of the tanna R. Shimon b. Yohai offers a slight variation
of this tradition, making it even easier to fulfill the requirement to study Torah
always: "Even if a man only recites Shema in the morning and the evening
he has fulfilled the commandment of '*the book of Torah shall not depart
from your mouth*'" (b. Men. 99b).[113] In its essence, the ritual of reciting the
Shema verses is the same thing as the ritual of studying Torah. Therefore,
one fulfills the obligation to study Torah when one recites the Shema. This
is because recitation of the Shema is essentially constituted by recitation of
scriptural verses that are explicitly marked as text to be internalized through
ritual.

Hirschman follows Benovitz in attributing this view to R. Shimon b. Yohai. See Hirshman,
The Stabilization of Rabbinic Culture, 32–39.

[111] See also *t. San.* 4:7: [When the king] goes out to war, [his personal Torah scroll] is with
him....R. Yehudah says: A Torah scroll on his right [hand/arm] and tefillin on his left." Text
according to Vienna MS and *editio princeps*.

[112] The most explicit is *m. Ber.* 2:1, which regards recitation of Shema as a subset of the larger
category of Torah study. As long as one intends it, one's Torah study of Deut 6:4–9 may
do double duty as liturgical recitation of Shema. See also t. Ber. 2:12–13, which appears to
consider the recitation of Shema and Torah study as parallel phenomena.

[113] Hirschman notes a parallel in the Yerushalmi and speculates that this statement in the Bavli has
authentic tannaitic roots and can genuinely be attributed to R. Shimon b. Yohai. See Hirshman,
The Stabilization of Rabbinic Culture, 39. On the issue of Shema as a form of Torah study, see
also *Midrash Tehillim*, 1:17 (ed. Buber, 15) and discussion in Yalon, "'Women Are Exempted
from All Positive Ordinances That Are Bound Up with a Stated Time,'" 30–31.

Exempting Women from the Shema and Tefillin

I argue that the rabbis exempt women from the Shema and tefillin because they know from elsewhere that women are exempt from Torah study. The fact that in their essence wearing tefillin and reciting the Shema are a form of Torah study means that women are exempt from these rituals also.

The rabbis make explicit that women are exempt from tefillin because of the ritual's link to Torah study. "Can it be that women are obligated like men regarding tefillin? Scripture states, *In order that the Torah of God be in your mouth.* I said [tefillin] only regarding those who are [also] obligated with respect to Torah study" (Mek. Bo, 17, ed. Horowitz-Rabin, 68).[114] Here women's exemption from tefillin is explicitly linked to their exemption from Torah study. Since tefillin are in their essence a form of Torah study, anyone who is exempt from Torah study is also exempt from tefillin. On this basis, women are exempt from wearing tefillin.

The rabbis do not articulate their reasons for exempting women from the obligation to recite the Shema. M. Ber. 3:3 simply states that women are exempt from reciting the Shema and wearing tefillin, but obligated to perform other rituals involving texts (they are obligated to recite the Amidah and the grace after meals, and to place mezuzot on their doorposts and gates).[115] No reason for the exemptions is given.[116] Based on what I have shown about the development of the ritual recitation of the Shema verses in the rabbinic period, I believe that the Shema and tefillin were comparable textual rituals.

---

[114] This rationale for women's exemption from tefillin is also attested in b. Kid. 30a. See discussion of this exegesis in Alexander, "From Whence the Phrase 'Timebound Positive Commandments'?" 335–39, 343.

[115] One important question concerns the motivation for the rabbis obligating women in mezuzah. Why are women exempt from Shema and tefillin, on one hand, but obligated with regard to mezuzah, on the other? My gut instinct is that there was a long-standing tradition from the Second Temple period that women were obligated with respect to mezuzah and that rabbinic sources reflect this received tradition. See Philo, *Spec. Laws* 4:142: "He bids them also write and set them forth in front of the doorposts of each house and the gates in their walls, so that those who leave or remain at home, citizens and strangers alike, may read the inscriptions engraved on the face of the gates and keep in perpetual memory what they should say and do, careful alike to do and to allow no injustice, and when they enter their houses and again when they go forth *men and women and children and servants alike* may act as is due and fitting both for others and for themselves" (emphasis added). Two points are noteworthy in Philo's discussion of the ritual of mezuzah. First, he interprets the ritual as a means of instilling justice. Second, Philo assumes that the practice of mezuzah has an implication for *all persons* and people who pass by it: men and women, young and old, free and slave, citizen and stranger. Philo thus provides evidence of a pre-rabbinic tradition that mezuzah was relevant for a broad range of the Jewish (and human) community. I speculate that when the rabbis obligate women, slaves, and minors in mezuzah, they draw on an inherited tradition similar to the one that stands behind Philo.

[116] See David Weiss Halivni on the Mishnah's reticence to provide reasons (justifications) for its prescriptions. See Halivni, *Midrash, Mishnah, and Gemara: The Jewish Predilection for Justified Law*, 38–65.

Both rituals (as rabbinically conceived) were practiced according to a particular understanding of the meaning of the term "these words" in the first and second paragraphs of the Shema. Both rituals engaged the Shema verses as exemplars of scripture to be embodied and internalized. Both rituals incorporated the biblical text onto and into the body in a manner similar to Torah study.[117] I would argue that the rabbis exempted women from reciting the Shema for the same reason that they exempted women from wearing tefillin: because in its essence it was a form of Torah study, and the rabbis knew from elsewhere that women were exempt from Torah study.[118] In the next chapter, I ask how the rabbis know that women are exempt from Torah study, and we will see that the matter was not as self-evident as they represent it in the discussion cited here. For the moment, however, I want to grant the rabbis their claim.

Herein we see the logic behind exempting women from the most central doctrinal affirmation that exists in Judaism. The latest redactional layer of the Bavli (450–600 CE) recognizes that it is counterintuitive to exempt women from reciting the Shema: "You might say that [women should be obligated] because the Shema affirms the kingship of heaven" (b. Ber. 20b). I would argue that though it is compelling to think that women should be obligated because of the doctrinal centrality of the Shema verses, the deepest significance of the ritual recitation of the Shema lay in the way that it ritualized text study. By turning textual recitation into a daily liturgical ritual, the rabbis made it possible for (male) Jews of all stripes to be engaged in the most central of rabbinic pious practices, Torah study. As a form of Torah study, however, the Shema was also a ritual from which the rabbis had no choice but to exempt women. Or at least, that was how they saw the matter.

---

[117] Their parallelism is also manifest in Sif. Dt. 258, ed. Finkelstein, 282, which prohibits reciting Shema and wearing tefillin in "dirty" places (launderer's vat, bathhouse, or tannery). One important difference between Shema and tefillin is that the Shema may be recited in any language (m. Sot. 3:1), but tefillin may only be written in Hebrew letters (m. Meg. 1:8).

[118] See Yalon, "'Women Are Exempted from All Positive Ordinances That Are Bound Up with a Stated Time,'" 30–31, and 41n1.

7

Torah Study as Ritual

This chapter focuses on the tannaitic evidence regarding women's study of Torah. Torah study was a central ritual of the nascent rabbinic movement. Through Torah study, rabbinic disciples crafted a covenantal community in relationship with God. Torah study was a ritual means of re-experiencing Sinaitic revelation. It also provided a social forum through which disciples established relationships horizontally with their peers and vertically with their masters. The social makeup of the informal rabbinic disciple circles was almost certainly exclusively male.[1] As rabbinically practiced, then, Torah study was a pious practice from which women were certainly excluded. The initiates of the disciple circles, however, aspired to shape Jewish, pious practice beyond their own elite circles. Insofar as the rabbis envisioned broad lay participation in their ritualistic study of Torah, did they imagine women being included in the practice? Some passages unequivocally exempt women from Torah study. Other passages imply, however, that women could engage in the intellectual activities that are at the heart of Torah study. This chapter attempts to account for the complexity of this evidence.

I will argue that when the rabbis understood Torah study as the attainment and exercise of particular intellectual skills, they did not exempt women from it. When, however, they understood Torah study to be a ritual act that encompasses more than the intellectual activities involved, the rabbis did exempt women. The matter turns on what we take Torah study to be. Central to my argument in this chapter is the recognition that while rabbinic Torah study engaged the practitioner in certain intellectual exercises, in and of themselves these intellectual exercises do not constitute a ritual act. When these exercises

[1] Jaffee writes, "It is a virtual certainty that Torah in the Mouth was taught exclusively by male masters to a body of disciples from which females were excluded" (28). See Martin S. Jaffee, "Gender and Otherness in Rabbinic Oral Culture," 28–30.

were linked to a broader cultural narrative, they functioned as Torah study (*talmud torah*) in a formal sense. Ritualistic Torah study involved rabbinic disciples not only in intellectual exercises. It also reaffirmed their covenantal relationship with God and forged them into a community.[2] Their perception that they were helping to sustain and perpetuate central cultural narratives transformed "mere" intellectual exercises into ritually significant "Torah study."[3]

A particular cultural aspiration was achieved through lay Torah study. Attention to the complex evidence regarding women's involvement with Torah study helps us see what was at stake for the rabbis when they imagined it as a lay practice taking place within the social context of the family. The tannaitic sources that touch on the issue of women studying Torah break into two groups broadly conceived: One set unequivocally exempts women from Torah study, and one set implies that women could engage in Torah study. I argue that the passages that unequivocally exempt women from Torah study do so because they envision Torah study as a means of replicating the father's cultural and social identity. In these sources, Torah study is a means through which the lay *pater familias* reproduces himself in the next generation. By virtue of the fact that daughters could never reproduce their father's social identity – they could never become the *pater familias* of the next generation – it was also assumed that they could not reproduce their father's cultural identity. It turns out that the sources that unequivocally exempt women from Torah study do so because they understand Torah study as a means of (male) cultural reproduction. Applying gender as a category of analysis gives us insight into some of the cultural meanings that inhere in the rabbinic ritual of Torah study.

Making Sense of Contradictory Evidence

In the previous chapter I argued that the rabbinic decision to exempt women from wearing tefillin and reciting the Shema was based on the rabbinic understanding of both of these rituals as forms of Torah study. In the Mekhilta, for example, the rabbis explicitly link women's exemption from tefillin to their exemption from Torah study.

---

[2] In an essay exploring sacramental acts of Torah study, Martin Jaffee explains that Torah study transforms rabbinic disciples on two different levels: "1) the ritual actors incorporate into their being an element of the redemptive Word in a ritual performance that 2) incorporates the actors into a larger community of the redeemed" (66). In other words, Torah study as a sacramental act both transforms the self and creates a sacred community. See Martin S. Jaffee, "Oral Transmission of Knowledge as Rabbinic Sacrament: An Overlooked Aspect of Discipleship in Oral Torah," in *Study and Knowledge in Jewish Thought*, ed. Howard Kreisel (Beer Sheva: Ben-Gurion University of the Negev Press, 2006), 65–79.

[3] Michael Satlow argues that Torah study was a spiritual discipline that enabled rabbinic disciples to transform the self. See Michael L. Satlow, "'And on the Earth You Shall Sleep': *Talmud Torah* and Rabbinic Asceticism," *The Journal of Religion* 83/2 (2003): 204–25.

Can it be that tefillin... applies to women as it does to men?... No. I have stated [the obligation of] tefillin only with regard to one who is obligated to study Torah (*hayav bitalmud torah*). (Mek. Bo 17, ed. Horowitz-Rabin, 67)

The Mekhilta draws an analogy between tefillin and Torah study, applying a known legal stipulation regarding Torah study to the unmapped legal territory of tefillin. The reasoning works as follows: Since it is known and established that women are exempt from Torah study, and since tefillin are scripturally designated as a form of Torah study, women must also be exempt from tefillin. In the previous chapter, I speculated that the rabbis exempted women from the Shema on the basis of the same reasoning process: Since the Shema was conceived by the rabbis as a form of Torah study and since women were exempt from Torah study, women were exempt from reciting the Shema. Following these arguments requires that we grant the rabbis their assumptions. It turns out, however, that there is good reason to doubt the rabbinic claim to possess an independent, established tradition that women are exempt from Torah study.

I have been able to find only two other tannaitic sources that unequivocally exempt women from Torah study.[4] By way of contrast, as many as seven sources[5] imply that women could or did engage in something that looks like Torah study. Clearly these sources do not know of an established tradition that women are exempt from Torah study. Furthermore, one of the sources that unequivocally exempts women from Torah study derives the exemption from a verse in the Shema; this tradition is not entirely independent of the rabbinic conversations about the Shema and tefillin. The Mekhilta's assumption that there exists an independent, established tradition that women are exempt from Torah study falters in light of strong evidence to the contrary.

Steven Fraade offers a way to make sense of the rabbinic rhetoric that claims more than may actually have been the case. In his work on Sifre Deuteronomy, Fraade suggests that "these texts, when viewed in the historical context of the time of their creation, might be seen not so much as *reports* of a transformation already completed [but] as part of the *very work* of that transformation."[6] Rather than reading the sources that claim to know of or that look like an established tradition that women are exempt from Torah study as "*reports* of a transformation already completed," we might read them as "part of the *very work* of" making such a tradition." The sources that imply that women could

---

[4] Sif. Dt. 46 and t. Kid. 1:11. See discussion below.
[5] M. Ned. 4:2–3; m. Sot. 3:4; t. Ber. 2:12; t. Ket. 4:7; t. Sot. 7:9; Mek. on Exod 19:3; and t. Kel. BM 1:6. I will treat some, but not all, of these sources in this chapter. Discussion of these and other sources can be found in Ilan, *Jewish Women in Greco-Roman Palestine*, 190–204; Boyarin, *Carnal Israel: Reading Sex in Talmudic Culture*, 167–96; and David Goodblatt, "The Beruriah Traditions," *Journal of Jewish Studies* 26/1–2 (Spring–Autumn 1975): 68–85. See also Judith Hauptman, "A New View of Women and Torah Study in the Talmudic Period," *Jewish Studies: An Internet Journal* (2010): 249–92.
[6] Fraade, *From Tradition to Commentary: Torah and Its Interpretation in the Midrash Sifre to Deuteronomy*, 74.

and probably did study Torah help us see the extent to which the tradition was by no means fully established or consistently applied.[7] By virtue of their distinctive way of thinking about women's engagement with Torah study, they help us see what was at stake for the sources that felt it necessary to exempt women from Torah study. Insofar as they approach the issue of women studying Torah from a different vantage point, they help us see the logic compelling the position that women *are* exempt from Torah study. I argue that the sources that unequivocally exempt women from Torah study did so because they envisioned Torah study as a ritual means of perpetuating the covenantal identity of the lay *pater familias.*

Framing Torah study as a lay ritual, however, was only one part of the complex process of crafting Torah study into a ritual act. Another part of the process involved clarifying how Torah study functions in a lay setting. In that context, Torah study was a ritual means for the father to replicate his social and cultural identity in the next generation. The rabbis emphasized the male character of such study because the father was male.[8] Not all ritual Torah study took place in a lay environment where father-to-son reproduction was at stake, and so not all discussion of ritual Torah study emphasized the gendered (male) character of Torah study. When the rabbis imagined Torah study as a ritual act by which they forged themselves into an enduring covenantal community, they had to work through a *number* of issues concerning the relationship between biological and cultural reproduction. For example, what does one do when one's son (biological offspring) is not an exemplary sage? Are disciples (one's cultural offspring) just as good as sons (one's biological offspring)? (The rabbinic answer is a resounding yes!)[9] Or: Does the physical body that biologically reproduces and withers away have a role in Torah study, or does one need to distance oneself from reminders of one's vulnerability as a biological creature when studying Torah? (The answer is: better to distance oneself.)[10]

---

[7] It is interesting to observe that the "tradition" that women are exempt from Torah study seems to have been established by the post-amoraic period. We see evidence of this development in the Bavli's efforts to make sense of tannaitic sources that imply that women *do* study Torah. See Boyarin's discussion of the Bavli's interpretation of two tannaitic sources that imply that women study Torah (m. Sot. 3:4 and t. Ber. 2:12). Boyarin, *Carnal Israel: Reading Sex in Talmudic Culture,* 174–81. Ilan also observes the Bavli's recasting of t. Ber. 2:12. See Tal Ilan, *Mine and Yours Are Hers: Retrieving Women's History from Rabbinic Literature* (New York: Brill, 1997), 60–61.

[8] There is an affinity between my argument and that of Nancy Jay, who argues that women are excluded from sacrifice because it is conceived as a means to establish intergenerational continuity between father and son. See Jay, *Throughout Your Generations Forever: Sacrifice, Religion, and Paternity.*

[9] Rabbinic concern with these questions is documented by several scholars. See Boyarin, *Carnal Israel: Reading Sex in Talmudic Culture,* 206–19; and Jeffrey L. Rubenstein, *The Culture of the Babylonian Talmud,* 80–101.

[10] Jonathan Schofer has made a compelling argument for the fact that rabbinic consciousness of physical vulnerability shaped rabbinic spiritual disciplines. See Jonathan Wyn Schofer, *Confronting Vulnerability: The Body and the Divine in Rabbinic Ethics* (Chicago: University of

The rabbis were grappling with questions that arise when figuring Torah study as a ritual means of cultural reproduction. Gendering Torah study as male was the resolution to only one of the many questions that arose. The issue of women's exemption from Torah study surfaced only when gender was an integral part of thinking through the issues of Torah study as cultural reproduction, as it was when Torah study was figured as a ritual means for the (male) father to perpetuate his identity in the next generation. When the rabbis explored other ways in which Torah study functions as a ritual means of cultural reproduction, they did not emphasize women's exemption from Torah study, even if they silently assumed that those who properly study Torah are men.

Tannaitic sources engage the issue of women studying Torah according to three different paradigms. One set of sources envisions women exercising their intellectual faculties and attaining intellectual skills through Torah study, but the study is not framed as a ritual act. The other two sets of sources are actively wrestling with what it means to figure Torah study as a ritual act. When the rabbis performed Torah study as a ritual act, they were involved in serious intellectual "play."[11] Through the intellectual activity of Torah study, they were imagining a world in which their most dearly held cultural aspirations were achieved. Specifically, ritual Torah study enabled the rabbis to envision their covenantal community enduring beyond the present moment with all of its prosaic limitations: Fathers replicated their identity in their sons, and sages replicated their identity in their disciples.[12] Torah study was an important mechanism of cultural reproduction, which could complement, but sometimes stood in tension with, biological reproduction. While gender was a central concern when thinking through some aspects of figuring Torah study as cultural reproduction, it was not a central concern when thinking through other aspects of the problem.

The sources that frame Torah study as a ritual act break into two groups. One set engages questions in which gender is a central issue. This set of sources unequivocally exempts women from Torah study. The other set of sources wrestles with what it means to figure Torah study as a ritual act without

Chicago Press, 2010), esp. 21–76. I am extending Schofer's argument by suggesting that rabbinic consciousness of vulnerability as biologically reproduced creatures made sages anxious about their prospects of succeeding in the project of cultural reproduction. This anxiety was manifest in the rules they created to remove reminders of physical vulnerability during Torah study.

[11] I draw here on a recent study of ritual that argues that ritual operates in the subjunctive (the ritual actors adopt an "*as-if*-it-were-the-case" posture), which allows ritual actors to inhabit playfully worlds that might be. See Seligman et al., *Ritual and Its Consequences: An Essay on the Limits of Sincerity* generally, but esp. 69–101 on ritual and play. I will discuss this book more fully in the conclusion to this chapter.

[12] Jaffee envisions sacramental Torah study operating in the same manner in Martin S. Jaffee, "Oral Transmission as Rabbinic Sacrament." See also Martin S. Jaffee, "Gender and Otherness in Rabbinic Oral Culture."

directly raising questions that have to do with gender. This set of sources takes for granted that only men perform Torah study, but it is not emphatic about women's exemption because its attention is directed toward other issues. Though this set of sources does feature women studying Torah, I argue that it does not envision real women performing Torah study as a ritual act.

By the post-amoraic period, women's exemption was a firmly established feature of rabbinic thinking about Torah study.[13] Cultural work that in the tannaitic period was merely "in progress" was more fully completed by the post-amoraic period. Fraade, as cited above, alerts us to the importance of not projecting later cultural understandings onto tannaitic sources, even when the tannaitic sources display nascent features of what later becomes a more fully developed cultural phenomenon. Other scholars have already pointed out how the post-amoraic stratum of the Bavli enforces an orthodoxy that "women are exempt from Torah study" in its interpretation of earlier sources.[14] The sources on which we focus in this chapter shed light on the early stages of a complex process, but they also attract the attention of the post-amoraic stratum of the Bavli. The Bavli is interested in these sources precisely because they suggest that women *could* study Torah, which from its perspective is an impossibility. The Bavli rereads these sources so that they conform to its assumption that women do not study Torah.

My primary interest in this chapter remains squarely in the tannaitic period, and since others have already documented the Bavli's pattern of whitewashing the tannaitic sources that imply that women can study Torah, I will refer to the Bavli only in passing. My primary purpose is to learn what we can about why the rabbis exempt women from Torah study by looking at both the sources that exempt women and the sources that seem unconcerned with the gender of those studying Torah. I argue that when we recognize that some sources depict Torah study as a ritual act and others do not, we stand to gain much insight into the reasons for women's exemption. Why gender emerges as an explicit concern *in only some* of the sources that figure Torah study as a ritual act also requires an explanation, which I shall try to give. This chapter helps us see vividly what was at stake for the rabbis who exempted women from the textual rituals (Shema and tefillin) that in and of themselves are a form of Torah study.

I begin by examining the sources that figure Torah study as a ritual act, looking first at the sources that emphasize women's exemption and second at the sources that do not. After that, I examine the sources that do not figure

---

[13] Boyarin makes a forceful argument about the strength of this view in Babylonia during the post-amoraic period. See Boyarin, *Carnal Israel: Reading Sex in Talmudic Culture*, 167–96.

[14] As observed in an earlier note, post-amoraic sages edited and interpreted tannaitic sources that imply that women can study Torah (m. Sot. 3:4 and t. Ber. 2:12) to undo that implication. See Boyarin, *Carnal Israel: Reading Sex in Talmudic Culture*, 174–81; and Ilan, *Mine and Yours Are Hers*, 60–61.

Torah study as a ritual act and readily depict women engaged in such activity.
I conclude by summarizing recent theoretical insights about ritual that inform
the distinction I draw between ritual and nonritual study of Torah.

Torah Study as Cultural Reproduction

Two sources are unequivocal about women's exemption from Torah study.
Both sources address Torah study as it takes place in the family. The father is
the assumed legal subject in both cases. The issue of Torah study arises because
fathers are obligated to educate their (male) offspring and initiate them into
the covenantal community.

Sifre Deuteronomy addresses the issue of women studying Torah when it
comments on a verse from the second paragraph of the Shema. Deut 11:19, the
verse in question, reads, "Teach [these words] to your children (*baneikhem*) –
reciting them when you stay at home and when you are away, when you
lie down and when you get up." The Sifre focuses its attention on the word
that I have here translated, following the NJPS translation, as "your children." As we will discover, this translation is in and of itself an interpretation.
The Hebrew word *baneikhem* literally means "your sons." Why then does
the NJPS translate the word in a gender-neutral fashion as "your children"?
A peculiar feature of the Hebrew language is that every noun is grammatically gendered male or female. Even nouns representing things that are not
biologically gendered, like stones, wind, and the sun, are grammatically gendered male or female. The fact that a noun is grammatically gendered male
or female does not necessarily mean that the object to which it refers is biologically gendered in a corresponding manner. Furthermore, when one wishes
to talk about a group that contains both males and females, masculine grammatical forms are used. On the basis of this principle, the NJPS reads the
grammatically masculine term *baneikhem* as referring to a group that potentially contains both males and females, that is, children. The NJPS translation
is grammatically plausible and compelling for a contemporary audience that
wishes to affirm that both sons and daughters are implicated in the covenantal community created through recitation of the Shema.[15] Nonetheless, this

---

[15] I should note that the NJPS is not unique in offering this translation. I single out the NJPS in my
narrative only because it is the standard translation to which scholars refer when writing on the
Hebrew Bible as a Jewish text. Every prayerbook translation I have consulted (whether from
right-wing Orthodox groups, left-wing Orthodox groups, Chabad, Sephardi Orthodox groups,
Conservative groups, Reform groups, or Reconstructionist groups, pre-WWII U.S. Modern
Orthodox prayerbook) translates *baneikhem* as "your children." I suspect that the gender-
neutral translation of *baneikhem* reflects a modern interest in implicating girls and women in
the Shema's affirmation of faith. It is interesting to note that the inclusive translation practice
exists even in communities that do not accept the arguments of feminism and are traditionally
conservative. By way of contrast, tannaitic rabbis were emphatic in their gendered reading of
baneikhem with the implication that only men and boys recite the Shema and study Torah

translation does not accurately reflect the ancient rabbinic understanding of the term.[16]

The midrashic interpretation of Deut 11:19 indicates that the rabbis read the *baneikhem* of the Shema as referring to "sons," and not "children."[17]

And you shall teach them to your children (baneikhem). Your sons, and not your daughters,[18] so taught R. Yose b. Akiva.

Hence the sages have said: Once an infant begins to talk, his father should converse with him in the holy tongue, and should teach him Torah, and if he doesn't teach him Torah, it is as if he buries him. (Sif. Dt., piska 46)

Several features of this midrashic interpretation are worthy of comment. First, the legal subject addressed in this teaching is fathers. The obligation is not so much for sons to gain advantage as it is for fathers to transmit something. Second, the midrash proposes two elements to the father's curriculum. The father must teach his son the holy tongue, presumably Hebrew, and Torah. Parallel sources also include the Shema in the list of required subjects.[19] I would argue that the primary curricular interest is in Torah study. Hebrew and recitation of the Shema are included because mastery of these skills facilitates one's development as a student of Torah.[20] The ability to decode and pronounce

(Sif. Dt. 46 and m. Ber. 3:3). Already the post-amoraic stratum of the Bavli expresses some discomfort with the idea that women are exempt from Judaism's foundational affirmation of faith. See b. Ber. 20b.

[16] Another ancient Jewish translation, the Septuagint (c. third century BCE), translates the term *baneikhem* one way in the text that later becomes the first paragraph of the Shema and a different way in the text that later becomes the second paragraph of the Shema. *Baneikha* in Deut 6:9 is translated in a gender-specific manner as "sons" (*'ios*). *Baneikhem* in Deut 11:19 is translated in a gender-neutral manner as "children" (*tekna*). This inconsistency suggests that the translators of the LXX were not yet in possession of a fixed liturgical text of the Shema that included both the first and second paragraphs of the Shema. If they had been, they might have worked harder to achieve a consistent translation of the two paragraphs. Philo's paraphrastic rendering of the second paragraph implies a reading of *baneikhem* as "sons," rather than "children." See Philo, *Spec. Laws* IV, 141.

[17] The presumption that *banim* are male also emerges in the midrash commenting on the same words in the first paragraph of the Shema. Sif. Dt. 34 glosses *baneikha* of Deut 6:9 as "your students," who from a rabbinic perspective would have been male. By equating "students" with "sons," the midrash suggests that one's cultural offspring (one's students) can displace one's biological offspring ("sons"). The same motif of cultural connections superceding biological/genetic connections can be seen in mishnaic discussions of whether a son owes primary allegiance to his father or to his teacher. See m. BM 2:11 and m. Ker. 6:9. As in Sif. Dt. 34, these mishnaic traditions give priority to the cultural status of the master with his disciple over and against the biological/genetic relationship between father and son.

[18] See citation of this midrash as a baraita in y. Kid. 61a; y. Ber. 4c, 6b; y. Eruv. 26a; and b. Kid. 29b. In the Talmuds, the interpretation is presented as the majority anonymous position and is not attributed to R. Yose b. Akiva.

[19] See t. Hag. 1:2 and Sifre Zuta perek 15.

[20] Steve Fraade also reminds me that study of Hebrew was a means of perpetuating cultural and national identity.

Hebrew letters is, of course, a necessary prerequisite for Torah study, and reciting the Shema is one of the simplest ways to achieve the goal of studying Torah. The father must teach his son Hebrew and recitation of the Shema because these skills help him achieve the primary goal: getting the son to study Torah.

An additional observation to make about this passage concerns the purpose served by Torah study. When the father teaches his son, he holds at bay the threat of extinction. If a father ignores his educational obligations, it is "as if he had buried [his son]." Parallel texts say it is "as if [the son] had never [even] been brought into this world."[21] These traditions propose Torah study as means for the father to ensure the continuity of his line. Though the son may be alive and well, if the father fails to transmit his cultural identity, the physical endurance of his son in the world is of no consequence. Biological reproduction is *necessary, but not sufficient* if the father's identity is to endure beyond him. If the son is truly to perpetuate his father's line, the son must be a student of Torah. Torah study is here represented as means of cultural reproduction that strengthens the biological or genetic connection between father and son.[22]

Of course, there is one other notable feature of this text. The father does not teach Torah to his daughters. The midrash emphatically states that the father's obligation extends to his "sons, and not daughters." The two most striking features of this text – (1) the fact that it represents Torah study as a means for the father to perpetuate his line and (2) the fact that it exempts women from Torah study – are integrally connected. Fathers do not teach daughters precisely because as girls their identity will always be socially determined by the men in whose families they reside. When daughters grow into women, they will become someone else's wife. Unlike sons, daughters will never be the *pater familias* of the next generation. Torah study as a means for the father to ensure the survival of his cultural identity simply does not involve daughters.

---

[21] See t. Hag. 1:2 and Sifre Zuta perek 15.

[22] Cultural reproduction here supplements, rather than displaces, biological reproduction. In an essay on gender and Torah study, Jaffee focuses on Torah study as a means of cultural reproduction *over and against* biological reproduction within rabbinic disciple circles. See Martin S. Jaffee, "Oral Transmission as Rabbinic Sacrament." A key prooftext for the view that Torah study as cultural reproduction can displace and even replace biological reproduction is Sif. Dt. 34, which interprets "the sons" who are the recipients of Torah study as "disciples." Where the biblical text suggests that transmission proceeds from father to son, the rabbinic text envisions the continuity as running from master to disciple. Benjamin Wright notes that it is not uncommon for Wisdom texts to use the trope of a father–son relationship to describe the relationship between sage and disciple. See Benjamin G. Wright, "From Generation to Generation: The Sage as Father in Early Jewish Literature," in *Biblical Traditions in Transmission: Essays in Honour of Michael A. Knibb*, ed. Charlotte Hempel and J. Lieu (Leiden: Brill, 2006), 309–32. Boyarin argues that the rabbinic ideal is to perpetuate Torah through sons who are also rabbis. See Boyarin, *Carnal Israel: Reading Sex in Talmudic Culture*, 203–25. Rubenstein also observes tension between biological and cultural reproduction in the post-amoraic stratum of the Bavli. See Jeffrey L. Rubenstein, *The Culture of the Babylonian Talmud*, 80–101.

The second source that unequivocally exempts women from Torah study is also addressed to fathers. The Mishnah states that parents have certain obligations toward their children, and these fall only upon men, and that children have certain obligations toward their parents, and these fall upon men and women alike (m. Kid. 1:7). The Tosephta fills in important details missing from the Mishnah's presentation of this tradition:

What are the obligations of the father concerning the son [from which women are exempt]?

[The father must] circumcise him, redeem him, <u>teach him Torah</u>, teach him a trade, and marry him off. (t. Kid. 1:11)[23]

In this source, Torah study is one among several rituals through which the father initiates his son into the covenantal community. The text starts by rehearsing the rituals relevant to the beginning of the son's life. When a boy is born, the father must circumcise him in order to affirm membership in the covenantal community.[24] Genesis explicitly states the covenantal function of the rite of circumcision: "Thus shall My covenant be marked in your flesh as an everlasting pact" (Gen 17:13).

When the boy is thirty days old, his father again ritually affirms that the boy is a part of the covenantal community by redeeming him. Exod 13 stipulates that when the first issue of a woman's womb is a boy, the child belongs to God. The father must redeem the child from the priest. Exodus explains the reason for the ritual redemption: When God took Israel out of Egypt, God slew every firstborn. In recognition of God's miraculous acts on its behalf, Israel must dedicate all firstborn animals and children to God, since God could have slain Israel's firstborn also. Special allowance is made for families to redeem their firstborn sons. Redemption serves as a ritual reminder that Israel is forever indebted to God for the Exodus from Egypt. Such a ritual reminder affirms the participant's sense of standing in a covenantal relationship with God because God's miraculous acts on Israel's behalf are the basis for Israel's loyalty to God.[25]

---

[23] I have intentionally presented the text without the addendum so often quoted – "Others say: Also to teach him to swim" – because I do not believe that the addendum is part of the original tradition. The Mekhilta cites a variant of the Tosephta's addendum: "R. Akiba says: Also to teach him to swim. Rabbi says: Also to teach him affairs of state." My interpretation receives support from the Yerushalmi, which claims that the five obligations that fathers have toward sons correspond to five obligations children have toward their parents. See y. Kid. 61a.

[24] On the paradox that women are exempt from circumcision and yet are still members of the covenantal community, see Shaye J. D. Cohen, *Why Aren't Jewish Women Circumcised? Gender and Covenant in Judaism* (Berkeley: University of California Press, 2005).

[25] See Levenson, *Sinai and Zion: An Entry into the Jewish Bible*, 15–86; Edward L. Greenstein, "Biblical Law," in *Back to the Sources: Reading the Classic Jewish Texts*, ed. Barry Holtz (New York: Simon and Schuster, 1984), 83–89.

When the boy grows yet older, the father teaches him Torah. This act is also a covenantal ritual, since through Torah study the boy stands again as if at Sinai receiving revelation from God. Finally, by teaching his son a trade and marrying him off, the father creates the familial infrastructure that enables the process to begin all over in the next generation. The son will now become a father himself and he will be the subject of these instructions.

Once again we find that teaching Torah is an obligation fathers have to their sons. It is not an obligation mothers have to their sons, nor is it an obligation fathers have to their daughters. Women are neither the transmitters nor the receivers in this representation of Torah study. As above, the exemption of women from Torah study in this context is integrally connected with the larger cultural goal that is served by Torah study in this source. Torah study is represented as part of the ritual infrastructure by which a father perpetuates his identity as a member of the covenantal community. If the father wants to replicate himself in the next generation, it is not enough for the father to give his son the material means of accomplishing this: Teaching the son a trade and marrying him off are not sufficient. Neither is it enough to initiate the baby into the covenantal community (through circumcision and ritual redemption). Only when the father teaches his son Torah does the father make the son into an independent agent in the covenantal community, one who will surely perform all the same rituals for his son when he becomes a father.

In sum, the sources that unequivocally exempt women from Torah study do so because they envision Torah study as a means for fathers to replicate their cultural and social identities in their sons.[26] Torah study does not replace biological connections as a means of ensuring the father's continuity into the future. Rather Torah study works alongside and as a complement to the biological connections between father and son.

Tensions between Biological and Cultural Reproduction

Sources that theoretically allow for the possibility that women may engage in Torah study have sometimes been heralded by feminists as a beacon of light in an otherwise disappointing corpus.[27] For those who wish to recover historical evidence of women engaging in this central act of rabbinic piety,

---

[26] The Talmuds attest to the fact that these two sources (Sif. Dt. 46 and t. Kid. 1:11) were seen to be part of a single tradition. Both Talmuds cite the midrashic interpretation attested in Sif. Dt. 46 in the context of discussing t. Kid. 1:11. See y. Kid. 61a and b. Kid. 29a–b.

[27] Boyarin, for example, makes explicit the fact that one goal of his scholarship on women and Torah study is to make possible the "feminist restructuring of sex and gender … in our own time" (ix, see also 168n2). Boyarin acknowledges that the dominant voices in rabbinic literature oppose women's Torah study, but spends considerable energy reconstructing the suppressed voices of an alternate point of view. Boyarin explains that exposing this side of rabbinic literature may help contemporary Jewish feminists (women and men) forge a "vital connection with the historical, ancestral culture of their people" (168n2). Tamar Ross characterizes Boyarin's

these sources indicate that it was not beyond the pale for the rabbis to envision a woman studying Torah. My reading, however, will not be so immediately redemptive.[28] I am skeptical that the theoretical possibility introduced by these sources reflects genuine openness to and interest in women studying Torah. Rather, these sources consider the possibility of women studying Torah because it allows the sages to think through complicated issues about male Torah study. The figure of a woman studying facilitates theoretical speculation. As far as I can tell, however, these sources exhibit no interest in women studying as independent legal subjects.

Both of the sources considered below come from the Tosephta, which, like the Mishnah that it supplements,[29] presents itself as a collection of case law. Understanding the conventions of tannaitic case law will help discern rabbinic

feminist strategy as "revisionist" because he attempts to find models for a contemporary feminism in ancient sources that certainly did not espouse it in the way that contemporary feminists do. Ross acknowledges that Boyarin does not superimpose his contemporary ideals on the whole of rabbinic culture, and so she characterizes him as a "multiple thread" revisionist. Unlike the "golden thread" revisionists who find a single golden thread of beneficence running through Jewish sources, "multiple thread" revisionists "maintain continuity with the past by highlighting shreds of evidence that militate against a motif that is decidedly not golden" (108–9). They forge a connection only with the view that they succeed in reconstructing. The feminist strategy of "multiple thread" revisionism centers on identifying and reconstructing a strand of the tradition that regarded women favorably. Ross identifies several other works with the strategy of "multiple thread" revisionism: Chana Safrai, "Women in the Bet Midrash: Challenge and Dispute (Hebrew)," in *Ayin Tova: Du-Siach Vepulmus Betarbut Yisrael – Sefer Hayovel le-Tova Ilan*, ed. Ilan Nahem (Hakibbutz Ha-Meuchad, 1999), 160–69; Shulamit Valler, "Women and Womanhood in the Talmud," in *Women and Womanhood in the Talmud*, ed. Betty Sigler Rozen (Atlanta: Scholars Press, 1999). I would also add to the list Hauptman, *Rereading the Rabbis*. I follow Ross in finding "multiple thread" revisionism to be an insufficient salve to the wound inflicted by rabbinic androcentrism and patriarchy. I am less inclined than others might be, then, to find comfort in the sources discussed in this section that figure women studying Torah.

[28] In the Epilogue I address the issue of how my reading nonetheless engages me in a redemptive project. The emphasis in this sentence is on the word "immediately." The redemptive value of the reading I offer here will not be immediately perceptible. To understand the contribution of my reading to the feminist project, the reader is invited to turn to the Epilogue.

[29] Scholars assessing the relationship between the Mishnah and Tosephta offer three different models for describing the relationship: (1) Neusner and Halivni assume that the Mishnah was edited before the Tosephta and that the Tosephta was created to supplement the Mishnah, (2) Hauptman and Friedman argue that in some cases the tosephtan version of tradition predates the mishnaic version, and (3) Jaffee and Alexander emphasize the extent to which mishnaic and tosephtan parallels reflect different performative versions of a common tradition. This debate has no manifest impact on this following analysis, where I reflect on tosephtan tradition with no mishnaic parallels. See Jacob Neusner, *The Tosefta: An Introduction* (Atlanta: Scholars Press, 1992); David Weiss Halivni, "The Reception Accorded to Rabbi Judah's Mishnah," in *Jewish and Christian Self-Definition*, vol. 2: *Aspects of Judasim in the Graeco-Roman Period*, ed. E. P. Sanders with A. I. Baumgarten and Alan Mendelson (London: SCM Press, 1981), 204–12; Judith Hauptman, *Rereading the Mishnah* (Tübingen: Mohr Siebeck, 2005); Friedman, *Tosefta Atiqta. Pesah Rishon: Synoptic Parallels of Mishna and Tosefta Analyzed with a Methodological Introduction* (Hebrew); Martin S. Jaffee, *Torah in the Mouth: Writing and Oral Tradition*

views on women and Torah study from case law more effectively. Each case consists of a scenario and legal resolution. I have elsewhere argued that the legal scenarios in the Mishnah and Tosephta are constructed as a kind of question: If conditions a, b, and c are present, which raise legal issues x, y, and z, how should one rule? Should one employ resolution q as suggested by legal issue x, resolution r as suggested by legal issue y, or resolution s as required by legal issue z? The legal resolution in the case rhetorically functions as an answer to the question: Considering legal issues x, y, and z, raised by conditions a, b, and c, one should adopt resolution q. Before assuming that features a, b, and c in the scenario reflect historical conditions, it is important to consider the role they play in unfolding a question about competing legal concerns.[30] When reading scenarios that envision women studying Torah, one must pay due attention to the legal issues highlighted by the scenario. Only then can the scholar assess which elements of the scenario have historical value and which have been included to explore complex legal issues.[31]

The scenario that imagines women studying Torah is part of a larger unit (t. Ber. 2:12–16) that examines how a variety of physical states (ritual impurity, nakedness, and proximity to excrement) impacts one's ability to recite the Shema or study Torah. The first set of scenarios focuses on individuals who are impure by virtue of a leak from their genitals. The person who suffers the most severe limitations is the *baal keri*, the one who has had a seminal emission.

1. The *baal keri* who [cannot fully immerse in a ritual bath because he] is ill, upon whom one has poured nine qabs of water – behold, he recites [the Shema],

2. But he cannot exempt others from their obligation [to recite Shema] until he immerses himself in forty seahs [of water].

3. R. Yehudah says: [He must immerse himself in] forty seahs in any event [whether to recite Shema for himself or to exempt others].

4. Men with an irregular discharge, women with an irregular discharge, menstruating women, and women after childbirth are permitted to recite Torah, Prophets and Writings, and to study mishnah, midrash and aggadot,

5. But those who have had a seminal discharge are forbidden [to engage] in all [of the aforementioned activities].

---

in *Palestinian Judaism, 200 BCE–400 CE*, 106–25, 135–40; and Alexander, *Transmitting Mishnah*, 35–76.

[30] See discussion in Alexander, *Transmitting Mishnah*, 117–73, esp. 150–67.

[31] Christine Hayes cautions the historian not to draw conclusions about historical reality too facilely from talmudic dialectic that is constructed primarily with hermeneutical considerations in mind. The same caution should be exercised when trying to extract historical information from tannaitic case law. Scholars should assess the rhetorical function of legal scenarios before considering the extent to which they reflect historical conditions. See Christine Elizabeth Hayes, *Between the Babylonian and Palestinian Talmuds: Accounting for Halakhic Difference in Selected Sugyot from Tractate Avodah Zarah*. See also Alexander, *Transmitting Mishnah*, 152n168.

6. R. Yose says: But one may study routine halakhot, as long as he does not unpack the Mishnah.[32] (t. Ber. 2:12)

This passage considers the question of how one's status as impure by virtue of genital leaks impacts one's ability to recite the Shema or study Torah.

Lev 12–15 outlines a number of situations in which an individual becomes ritually impure. As Jonathan Klawans has explained, ritual impurity has consequences only in the ritual domain: A person who is ritually impure may not enter the holy precincts of the Temple, touch the Temple's sacred vessels, or consume sacrificial offerings (whether grain or animal). Furthermore, ritual impurity can be remedied by ritual means. After the problematic condition (genital discharge, proximity to death, skin disease) resolves itself, the impure individual waits an appropriate amount of time, takes a ritual bath, and brings an offering. Klawans rightly stresses that sin and moral wrongdoing are not imputed to the ritually impure individual.[33] Ed Greenstein explains that the impurities might be thought of as various forms of "life leaks."[34] Suffering a "life leak" is inimical to residing in or interacting with the holiness of the Temple, its vessels, and its offerings. At the center of the biblical purity system stands the Temple where God's presence dwells. In an interesting turn, the Tosephta considers the question of how ritual impurity affects one's ability to engage Torah, whether through recitation of the Shema or formal Torah study. At the center of the Tosephta's deliberations stands not the Temple, but the Torah.

Theoretically speaking, being in a state of ritual impurity should not affect one's ability to recite the Shema or study Torah. As explained above, ritual impurity has consequences only with respect to the Temple precincts, its vessels, and its offerings. Nonetheless, the *baal keri* cannot study Torah (line 5) or say the Shema (lines 1–3) until he has immersed, whether by having a minimal nine kabs of water poured over him (line 1) or in the full forty seahs of water generally required (lines 2–3).[35] Line 4 observes that other impure individuals *may* study Torah. Since certain kinds of impurity mentioned in Lev 12–15 occur only in women (e.g., menstrual impurity), the list refers to

---

[32] I follow the meaning implied by Jaffee's translation of the phrase ובלבד שלא יציע את המשנה. See Martin S. Jaffee, *Torah in the Mouth: Writing and Oral Tradition in Palestinian Judaism, 200 BCE–400 CE*, 70.

[33] See Jonathan Klawans, *Impurity and Sin in Ancient Judaism* (New York: Oxford University Press, 2000), 21–42. See also Christine E. Hayes, *Gentile Impurities and Jewish Identities: Intermarriage and Conversion from the Bible to the Talmud* (Oxford: Oxford University Press, 2002), 4–7.

[34] See Greenstein, "Biblical Law," 90–95, esp. 95.

[35] All agree that ideally the *baal keri* should immerse himself in forty seahs of water before reciting the Shema, but the anonymous position (lines 1 and 2) rules that when the *baal keri* is ill, special allowances are made and nine kabs of water are poured over him, thereby enabling him to recite the Shema. By way of contrast, R. Yehudah permits the *baal keri* to recite Shema only when he has been immersed in forty seahs (line 3).

women as well as men. We read, "Men with an irregular discharge, *women* with an irregular discharge, menstruating *women*, and *women* after childbirth are permitted to recite Torah, Prophets and Writings, and to study mishnah, midrash and aggadot." I submit that this list has been conceived to highlight the uniqueness of the *baal keri*. Unlike other people who have genital leaks that lead to impurity, the *baal keri* may *not* recite the Shema or study Torah. Through this juxtaposition, the Tosephta calls our attention to the fact that the reason that the *baal keri* cannot study Torah or recite the Shema has nothing to do with his being impure. His inability to recite Shema and study Torah derives from altogether different considerations.

The list of people who *may* study gives us insight into the reasons behind the *baal keri*'s disqualification. It is interesting to note that the list of people who may study Torah does not include *all* types of impure individuals mentioned in Lev 12–15. The person who suffers a skin disease (the *metzora`*) is notably absent.[36] The individuals listed in line 4 are all impure by virtue of a *genital* discharge. By way of contrast, the *metzora`* is impure because of a skin condition. The *metzora`* does not appear on the list because his impurity is not connected to the genital area. The Tosephta is apparently drawing a distinction among different kinds of activity in the genital area that produce impurity. Only the *baal keri*'s discharge is an expression of sexual desire. This unique feature of his impurity is the basis for disqualifying him from reciting the Shema and studying Torah. Having made manifest his sexuality, the *baal keri* must now ritually distance himself from it before engaging in the central act of rabbinic piety. The *baal keri* rectifies his disqualification by immersing himself in a ritual bath or, according to some, by having nine kabs of water poured over him if he is ill. Daniel Boyarin has written about the passion that rabbis expressed through Torah study, stressing that this passion was distinct from and in tension with the sexual passion that was physically expressed with their wives. This passage reveals similar tendencies. Physical expressions of sexuality are viewed as inimical to the encounter with the sacred afforded by Torah study and recitation of the Shema.

Somewhat more speculatively, this passage may be considered part of a larger group of traditions (attested in t. Ber. 2:12–16) that establish a rabbinic "purity system" that operates much as does the biblical purity system. The Torah stands at the center of this newly envisioned "purity system," and various physical states disqualify one from engaging the Torah, whether through Torah study or recitation of the Shema. In the scenarios that follow, we learn that one who is naked, one who can see his own genitals or someone else's sexually mature genitals, and one who is in close proximity to excrement and urine cannot recite the Shema.[37] In this "purity system," one is disqualified from

---

[36] The *metzora`* does appear in the list provided by the Bavli's version of the baraita. See b. Ber. 22a.

[37] See t. Ber. 2:12–16.

encountering the sacred when one is vividly reminded of the sexed, desiring, and excreting body. As with the biblical purity system, only when the "impurity" is sufficiently fenced off does it become possible to reengage the sancta. It should be noted that the rabbis never use the term "impurity" to label the states and statuses that disqualify someone from studying Torah or reciting the Shema. Linguistically and conceptually, they distinguish between the biblical purity system and the physical states that prevent one from saying Shema and studying Torah.

Jonathan Schofer has recently argued that consciousness of the vulnerabilities of the human body shaped rabbinic pious practice.[38] This passage from the Tosephta appears to exhibit an interest in those physical vulnerabilities that bring to mind the (male) body's involvement with biological reproduction. The body that excretes – and the body that is sexed and desires – is the body that engages in biological reproduction. But it is also a body that withers away. By distancing themselves from the sexed, desiring, and excreting body when engaging in Torah study and reciting Shema, the rabbis were fencing off Torah study from the other, lesser form of reproduction, the one that involves the physical body.

If this hypothesis has merit, this source provides an interesting point of contrast to the sources discussed earlier on fathers and sons. There we saw that Torah study strengthened the reproductive capacities of the father's body. Fathers made their biological offspring "count" by inducting their sons into the guild of Torah study. By way of contrast, in t. Ber. 2:12–16, the body that reproduces biologically is viewed as antithetical to Torah study. The two different sets of sources are exploring different aspects to the problem of what it means to figure Torah study as a ritual means of cultural reproduction. As suggested earlier, rather than seeing these sources as "reports" of a transformation already completed, we might see them as "part of the very work" of bringing the transformation about. These sources take us right to the heart of the process of figuring out what it means to ritualize Torah study as a form of cultural reproduction. Different sources deal with different issues that arise when conceiving of Torah study in this manner. Whereas the father–son sources represent Torah study as a way to strengthen the physical body's capacity to reproduce, t. Ber. 2:12–16 highlights the tension between the biologically reproducing body and Torah study.

It is, of course, also noteworthy that t. Ber. 2:12 allows for the theoretical possibility of women (as menstruants, parturients, and dischargers) studying Torah. Does this tradition suggest that the rabbis knew of women who studied Torah as a form of cultural reproduction? Does it indicate that the rabbis thought women could or should study Torah ritually? In spite of the appeal of a positive answer to these questions, I see no evidence in t. Ber. 2:12 that the rabbis thought that women's Torah study was ritually meaningful. First

[38] See Schofer, *Confronting Vulnerability: The Body and the Divine in Rabbinic Ethics.*

of all, all of the individuals listed in line 4 of t. Ber. 2:12 are mentioned as foils to the *baal keri*. Knowing that they *may* study Torah helps us see what is significant about the *baal keri* that he may *not* study Torah or recite the Shema. Second, if the authors of this passage seriously thought that women could ritually study Torah, the passage might raise questions about the impurities that disqualify *women* from studying Torah. The fact that the passage only considers male impurities (i.e., seminal emission) as capable of disqualifying one from reciting the Shema and studying Torah suggests that the passage is not really contemplating women as legal subjects who study Torah.[39] Women are introduced as theoretical students of Torah for what this allows us to see about the "real" legal subject, the *baal keri*. Since the Tosephta is not thinking through a question that involves the gender of the person studying Torah, it does not feel the need to emphasize women's exemption. By way of contrast, in the sources about fathers teaching Torah to their sons, the father's gender is a central issue. Those sources highlight women's exemption from Torah study because the gender of fathers and sons is central to understanding Torah study as a ritual means of cultural reproduction. Both sets of sources are thinking through what it means to figure Torah study as cultural reproduction, but gender is a consideration in only one of the deliberations.

The Wife Who Teaches Her Husband Torah

One additional tosephtan source introduces women studying Torah as a part of a legal scenario. Once again, it is important to attend first to the legal principles that are explored through the figure of a woman studying Torah before evaluating how the source contributes to our understanding of rabbinic attitudes about women studying Torah.

T. Ket. 4:7 allows a husband to write certain conditions into the wife's *ketubah* that will relieve him of the obligations a husband usually has toward his wife. Under ordinary circumstances, a husband provides his wife with her basic food and clothing needs (see m. Ket. 5:8–9). The Mishnah makes clear exactly the level at which the husband must maintain his wife: for example, designating figures for how much wheat, barley, oil, pulse, and figs he must provide a week. The Tosephta, however, gives the husband a means to extract himself from the obligations. When he marries her, he may make it a condition of the marriage that he will not maintain her in the manner typical of Jewish husbands. In fact, the husband may even go so far as to stipulate that his wife must maintain him.

---

[39] I thank Blaire French for calling my attention to this aspect of the text's framing. Michael Satlow makes a similar point about the androcentricism in rabbinic legal discussions of ritual. He notes that the nakedness that disqualifies one from engaging with holy things is *male* (not female) nakedness. See Michael L. Satlow, "Jewish Constructions of Nakedness in Late Antiquity," *Journal of Biblical Literature* 116/3 (Autumn 1997): 429–54.

1. A man may marry a woman on the condition that he will not feed [her] or support [her],

2. And not only that, but he may stipulate with her that [the marriage be] on the condition that she feed him, she support him and <u>she teach him Torah</u>. (t. Ket. 4:7)

This tradition examines the status of a marriage where the husband withdraws his usual support. Since the rabbis took the husband's provision of support to be a scripturally mandated feature of marriage,[40] one might think that a marriage where the husband fails to meet the minimal requirements of the law is not legally binding. This tradition establishes the legality of such an arrangement, unconventional though it is. The second scenario shows just how far the scriptural requirements of marriage can be distorted while still maintaining the status of a legal marriage. A husband can stipulate not only that he will withdraw his support, but that his wife must support him! The Tosephta observes that as long as these conditions are made explicit when the marriage is contracted, the union is legally a marriage.

The Tosephta imagines the wife's support of her husband taking three forms. First, she must feed him, reversing the traditional obligation he has to feed her. Second, she must support him (*mifarnasto*), reversing the traditional obligation he has to provide her with the necessities of life. Finally, she must teach him Torah. This obligation has no parallel in the husband's usual responsibilities to his wife. The husband meets the basic needs of his wife by providing food and support. By way of contrast, the wife meets the basic needs of her husband by providing food, support, and Torah study. When the Tosephta imagines the wife as the supporting figure, she must provide in three, rather than two, basic areas, because husbands have a different set of needs than wives. Husbands, unlike wives, have a basic need to study Torah.

What does this source tell us about women studying Torah? The text states that he may stipulate as part of the marriage contract that she "teach him Torah." Are we to imagine the couple sitting down together with the wife as the instructor? Or does she merely finance his study? Both readings are possible.[41] On one hand, the text states straight out that she teaches him Torah. On the other hand, in the surrounding traditions, the Tosephta's interest is with financial support. In the first scenario, the Tosephta considers situations in which the husband withdraws *financial* forms of support. In addition to his financial responsibilities, a husband must also provide his wife with regular conjugal relations. Notably, the text does not imagine the husband stipulating that they make the marriage conditional upon him not supplying her with regular relations. The text imagines the husband withholding only financial

---

[40] Derived from Exod 21:10.

[41] Ilan acknowledges the plausibility of both readings, though she seems to prefer the reading in which the "woman provides actual instruction." The basis for this preference is not clear, except perhaps that it appeals to contemporary feminist sensibilities. See Ilan, *Jewish Women in Greco-Roman Palestine*, 193–94.

resources. We might by extension conclude that the second scenario (with the wife as supporter) posits the wife supplying only financial resources, that is, she must agree to support his studies by paying for them, not by serving as educator herself.[42] Furthermore, in the story that follows, the issue of finances receives critical attention: A dispute arises during years of famine when a wife wishes to withdraw financial support. In my view the surrounding literary context supports a nonliteral reading of the phrase "that she teach him Torah" as "she financially support his studies." Even if, however, we adopt the first reading – the wife as instructor – this source does not provide strong evidence that the rabbis readily imagined women studying Torah ritually. The figure of a woman teaching Torah is introduced to clarify the nature and extent of the husband's basic needs. Torah study is a basic need of husbands, not of wives.

In sum, we have examined two sources from the Tosephta that depict women studying Torah. In these sources women appear as tools for giving voice to legal concerns. As far as I can tell, the women who study Torah in these sources have not been conceived in dialogue with real women who study Torah or who the rabbis felt should study Torah. These sources are not excited one way or the other about positioning women as students and teachers of Torah. Their main interest is to highlight a legal issue; the figure of a women studying or teaching Torah simply helps them highlight it. T. Ber. 2:12 presents women with genital leaks studying Torah in order to highlight that the (male) *baal keri* cannot study Torah. T. Ket. 4:7 presents a woman teaching her husband Torah in order to demonstrate that the (male) husband needs to study Torah. Women are foils against whom we see more clearly the men who, according to the rabbis, were the proper practitioners of Torah study.

Torah Study as a "Benefit" to the Individual: Gaining Skills

Two sources imply that women could, should, or did study Torah. Interestingly, these sources also locate Torah study in a family context by examining a father's educational obligations to his daughters. Women are envisioned as students of Torah not when they are grown women, but when they are younger and in their paternal home.

Chapter 4 of m. Nedarim examines the situation in which an individual (e.g., Reuven) vows not to derive benefit from another named individual (e.g., Shimon). It turns out, however, that Shimon can assist Reuven in a variety of ways. As long as Shimon does not confer "benefit" on Reuven, he may help him. "Benefit" here functions as technical legal term. While some actions appear to

---

[42] The issue of finances is especially highlighted in the story that follows, where during years of famine the wife wishes to withdraw support. I draw validation for my reading, which sees the sage story and the law as part of a single discursive framework, from Simon-Shoshan, "Halakhic Mimesis: Rhetorical and Redactional Strategies in Tannaitic Literature," *Diné Israel* 24 (2006): 101–23.

redound to Shimon's benefit, they do not confer "benefit" in a technical legal sense. The Mishnah is particularly interested in those actions that *appear* to confer benefit, but do not do so in the strict technical sense. For example, if Shimon returns a lost object to Reuven, Reuven does not technically "benefit" from Shimon's action. After all, the object has always belonged to Reuven. When Shimon returns the lost object, he is merely following the law to return lost objects to their owners. Reuven does not "net" any benefit from Shimon's action.[43]

The Mishnah considers a number of scenarios where Reuven appears to benefit from Shimon's action, but as in the case of the lost object, he does not "benefit" in the technical legal sense of the term.[44] Among the scenarios envisioned, we find several that involve Shimon serving as educator.

If a man [e.g., Reuven] is forbidden by vow to have any benefit from his fellow [e.g., Shimon]... he [Shimon] may teach him [Reuven] mishnah, halakhot and aggadot, but he [Shimon] may not teach him [Reuven] scripture (*mikra'*), <u>though he [Shimon] may teach scripture (*mikra'*) to his [Reuven's] sons and daughters.</u> (m. Ned. 4:2–3 according to the Venice printed edition, c. 1520–25)[45]

Shimon may teach Reuven the advanced elements of the rabbinic curriculum (mishnah, halakhot, and aggadot), but he may not teach him the basic foundational text (scripture). What logic undergirds this distinction? Why does teaching scripture confer "benefit" in the technical sense, while teaching mishnah, halakhot, and aggadot does not? I would argue that this source assumes a distinction between two different kinds of study: (1) rudimentary study whose goal is the attainment of basic skills and (2) higher-level study that serves a ritual function.[46] When Shimon engages Reuven in higher-level study, they are together performing a ritual that constitutes them as a covenantal community

---

43 For the Talmuds, financial gain is a key component of "benefit" in its technical sense.

44 Here we see the Mishnah exploring the "gray area" of the law: Shimon's actions have something in common with actions that confer benefit, but nonetheless do not belong in that category. For a discussion of how tannaitic law (especially in the Mishnah) often examines the ambiguous cases that fall between two clear-cut rulings, see Jacob Neusner, *Judaism: The Evidence of the Mishnah*, 256–69; and Alexander, *Transmitting Mishnah*, 150–67.

45 I thank Professor Robert Brody and R. Noah Bickart for alerting me to the late date of this version of the text. I later discovered that Tal Ilan also discusses it in print. See Ilan, *Mine and Yours Are Hers*, 82–84. Earliest versions of the text do not have the words "and daughters" in the underlined text. The addition or absence of these words is important for my discussion, since only the later variant implies women's involvement with Torah study. The significance of the original and variant versions will be discussed shortly.

46 I would like to thank Martin Jaffee, who led me to this interpretation in a consultative phone conversation. This interpretation receives support from scholarly reconstructions of educational school systems in antiquity. Gerhardsson distinguishes between elementary education focused on scripture and advanced education focused on more dialectical skills in ancient Jewish school systems. His reconstruction of the rabbinic educational system draws on Marrou's reconstruction of a similarly multi-tiered educational system consisting of elementary schools and advanced rhetorical schools in expressive and aesthetic rhetorical delivery. Francis Young

in relationship with God.[47] Even though Shimon may be more experienced
and knowledgeable, the interaction is transformative for *both* of them. Both
are involved in forming the community that emerges from Torah study. Both
are connected to the event of Sinaitic revelation.[48] By way of contrast, when
Shimon teaches Reuven scripture, Reuven receives something tangible from
Shimon that he did not have before. He now knows how to decode the letters
and pronounce scripture. Underlying the distinction between teaching mishnah, halakhot, and aggadot, on one hand, and teaching scripture, on the other,
is the distinction between Torah study as a ritual act and Torah study as vehicle
for gaining intellectual skills. Only when Torah study is performed to obtain
intellectual skills does it confer benefit in the technical sense. What is especially
important for our purposes is that this source indicates that the rabbis understood that sometimes Torah study could be a mundane act. Sometimes, Torah
study is merely the means by which a person equips him/herself to function in
this world.

Our understanding of how mundane Torah study operates is deepened by
considerations introduced in the next scenario. The mishnah notably regards
an individual who has made a vow as distinct from his children. Though
Shimon cannot teach scripture to Reuven (since Reuven would presumably
benefit thereby), Shimon *can* teach scripture to Reuven's children. The mishnah
assumes that Reuven himself does not benefit when Reuven's children are
taught. *They* are the ones who gain the skills of Torah literacy. If anyone
benefits, it is they! Even though Reuven is ritually obligated to educate his
sons, he does not technically benefit from Shimon's generosity toward his
children. The individual who gains intellectual competence is unambiguously
the beneficiary of nonritual scriptural instruction.

We also see that when Torah study is figured as a vehicle by which an individual gains intellectual competencies, a late medieval/early modern (c. 1520)
version of the Mishnah does not exclude daughters from the educational enterprise. In the Venice printed edition, the Mishnah says that Shimon may teach
scripture to "[Reuven's] sons *and his daughters.*" As I argued earlier in this

draws on Marrou's work to describe a multi-tiered educational system in Christian communi-
ties during the second and third centuries. See Birger Gerhardsson, *Memory and Manuscript:
Oral Tradition and Written Transmission in Rabbinic Judaism and Early Christianity* (Grand
Rapids: W. B. Eerdmans, 1961; repr. 1998), 56–66, 85–92, 124–26; Henri Irénée Marrou, *His-
toire de l'education dans l'antiquité* (Paris: Éditions du Seuill, 1965), 215, 230ff.; and Frances
M. Young, *Biblical Exegesis and the Formation of Christian Culture* (Cambridge: Cambridge
University Press, 1997), 76–96.

[47] Martin Jaffee discusses the transformative effects of Torah study in "Oral Transmission as
Rabbinic Sacrament." See also Martin S. Jaffee, "A Rabbinic Ontology of the Written and Spo-
ken Word: On Discipleship, Transformative Knowledge and the Living Texts of Oral Torah,"
Journal of the American Academy of Religion 65/3 (Autumn 1997): 27–61.

[48] Steve Fraade emphasizes how rabbinic Torah study re-creates the event of Sinaitic revelation.
See Fraade, *From Tradition to Commentary: Torah and Its Interpretation in the Midrash Sifre
to Deuteronomy*, 25–68.

chapter, here too the manner in which Torah study is framed and the attitude toward women studying are integrally connected.

When framed as a ritual act, Torah study builds relationships, whether between master and disciple or between father and son. Torah study as ritual is the means by which a sacred community is built. The covenantal community transcends the limits of mere biology and creates connections between unrelated individuals in contemporaneous disciple circles and between lay householders and their (male) progeny as the householders of the future. When Torah study is figured as a way to forge links where the connections are otherwise tenuous, gender seems to matter. Torah study is then represented, either explicitly or implicitly, as a male activity. The community it helps to fashion is male. By way of contrast, when Torah study is divorced from the social web of relationships that it helps solidify, and when it is framed instead as the attainment of intellectual skills by an individual, the gender of the person studying Torah does not seem to matter. Apparently, basic skills of literacy were as much a benefit to daughters as to sons. The late medieval/early modern reader of the Mishnah who added the words "and his daughters" to a manuscript where it was missing felt no need to emphasize a male privilege to the benefits of education, even if in point of fact it was more typical for boys to have access to formal education than for girls. It is fascinating to discover that only when Torah study is framed as a ritual does its gendered character become relevant. Without the ritual framing, Torah study is merely the attainment and exercise of particular intellectual skills. There was apparently no compelling reason to exempt women from Torah study when understood in this manner.

This interpretation makes much of the fact that Shimon can teach Reuven's daughters alongside his sons. The evidence of m. Ned. 4:3 comes with an important caveat. Only the text as it is preserved in the first printed edition of the Talmud (c. 1520) states that Shimon "may teach scripture to [Reuven's] sons *and his daughters*." The italicized words are omitted in all earlier manuscripts, which can reasonably be assumed to more accurately represent early tannaitic tradition. Most likely, then, an earlier version of the mishnah (as attested by the Palestinian manuscripts) stated that "Shimon may teach Reuven's sons." Given the fact that the printer chose to read the teaching as applicable to daughters, as well as sons, the original text was most likely not emphatic about excluding daughters (like Sif. Dt. 46). The later printer probably read the passage and assumed that this kind of teaching was applicable to daughters as well as sons, and he added the words "and his daughters" in accordance with his understanding of the mishnah's intent.

It is interesting to ask why the printer felt justified adding the words "and his daughters." The behavior of this transmitter is quite different from that of many of his colleagues. Tal Ilan has documented a phenomenon that she calls "censorship" whereby scribes edit women out of texts that they think properly should not have women in them. For example, as I earlier noted, t. Ber. 2:12 features women as students of Torah ("*women* with an irregular discharge, menstruating *women*, and *women* after childbirth are permitted to recite Torah, etc."). Ilan observes that a later version of the baraita (preserved in the Bavli) differs on an important point. The baraita has been rewritten so that the text now features only men studying Torah. Ilan argues that a later scribe assumed that the baraita could not have meant to say that women may study Torah, so he rewrote the text to read that *"men who have had intercourse with a menstruant . . . may study Torah, etc."*[49] He left the word menstruant in place, but recontextualized it so that the person engaged in Torah study was a man. The same phenomenon occurs over and over again. In places where scribes could not fathom the presence of a woman (e.g., as obligated to wear tzitzit, as the transmitter of a legal tradition, as students of Torah), they rewrote texts to accord with their own vision of women's behavior or roles.[50]

Our case, however, stands out as a violation of the pattern so well documented by Tal Ilan. Rather than writing a women *out* of the text, our scribe has written women *into* the text! What allowed him to feel comfortable doing this? On what basis did he feel that m. Ned. 4:3 ought properly to depict Shimon teaching Reuven's sons *and daughters*? It is possible that the fact that the earlier version of the mishnah (without "daughters") conceives of Torah study in a nonritual manner made way for later interpreters to include daughters as students.[51] Though the original mishnah most likely did not include a reference to daughters studying Torah, it framed Torah study as a kind of intellectual activity that could just as well have included them. Those who study scripture in m. Ned. 4:3 do so for their own benefit. They do not engage in Torah study as a means of transcending the limits of the self. Torah study is instead represented as something that enriches the individual who practices it. It is the very fact that Torah study is not figured as the means by which fathers reproduce themselves that makes it possible for later interpreters to imagine daughters involved in it.

Torah Study as a "Benefit" for the Individual: Gaining Perspective

One additional source shares the attributes of (1) figuring Torah study as a benefit to the individual who studies and (2) imagining women involved in

---

[49] See b. Ber. 22a.

[50] Ilan, *Mine and Yours Are Hers*, 51–130. Boyarin also notes that the later Bavli has less tolerance for the theoretical possibility of women studying Torah than the earlier Yerushalmi. Boyarin, *Carnal Israel: Reading Sex in Talmudic Culture*, 170–81. Hauptman notes that the Mishnah (which she regards as later than many of the traditions preserved in the Tosephta) often promulgates law that is less friendly to women's needs and interests than earlier tosephtan versions. See Hauptman, *Rereading the Rabbis*. See also scattered observations in Hauptman, *Rereading the Mishnah*.

[51] Ilan discusses several sets of circumstances that could have led the printer to revise the text. See Ilan, *Mine and Yours Are Hers*, 82–84.

Torah study. M. Sotah 3:4 attributes a position to Ben Azzai whereby daughters must be taught Torah.

The text presents the issue of women studying Torah as an aside. The main topic of discussion is the ritual of the bitter waters, which is performed to assuage the jealousy of a husband who suspects that his wife has committed adultery. The ritual as outlined in the Bible is a form of trial by ordeal: The suspected wife is made to drink a potion consisting of dirt from the Temple floor and the diluted words of a curse. If she reacts violently to the waters, then she is deemed guilty of adultery; if she does not react to the waters, she is deemed innocent. After describing the full sequence of events by which the ritual is administered, the Mishnah narrates the events that follow her drinking of the waters.[52]

1. She hardly finishes drinking when her face becomes pale, her eyes bulge and her veins swell, and they say, "Take her away! Take her away that the Temple court not be made unclean [when she dies]!"

2. If she has any merit, this defers [her reaction to the waters].

3. There are merits which defer [her reaction] for one year; there are merits which defer [her reaction] for two years; and there are merits which defer [her reaction] for three years.

4. On this basis Ben Azzai says: <u>A man (*adam*) should teach his daughter Torah so that if she must drink [the bitter waters] she will know that merit defers [her reaction].</u>

5. R. Eliezer says: Any man who teaches his daughter Torah, it is as though he teaches her licentiousness.

According to Ishay Rosen-Zvi, the Mishnah (in contrast to the Bible) presumes the women's guilt as an adulteress. The reaction engendered by the bitter waters, then, is not so much an ordeal to *determine* guilt as it is a *punishment* for presumed guilt.[53] Granting Rosen-Zvi's interpretation, this mishnah imagines that the punishment occurs in one of two possible ways. On one hand, the waters may have the expected effect: Her face will pale, her eyes will bulge, and her veins will swell (line 1). On the other hand, nothing may happen. But even if nothing happens, according to Rosen-Zvi's interpretation, we are not to assume that she is innocent. Lines 2–3 explain that the suspected wife may have merit, which has the effect of deferring her reaction to the waters for as long as three years. The punishment still takes effect, but it is not immediately manifest.

---

[52] Ishay Rosen-Zvi points out that the Mishnah presumes the guilt of the suspected adulteress and regards the ritual as a punishment rather than an ordeal to determine guilt. Ishay Rosen-Zvi, "The Sotah Ritual in Tannaitic Literature: Textual and Theoretical Studies" (Hebrew), 161–63.

[53] Rosen-Zvi, "The Sotah Ritual in Tannaitic Literature: Textual and Theoretical Studies" (Hebrew), 161–63.

As an aside, the mishnah now introduces Ben Azzai's statement that "a man (*adam*) must teach his daughter Torah so that if she must drink she will know that merit defers [her reaction to the waters]." Several features of Ben Azzai's imperative to teach daughters are notable. First, as we have found so many times, Torah study is imagined by the Mishnah as an interaction between a father and his offspring. It is interesting to note, however, that the father's status as such is not stressed in Ben Azzai's teaching. Whereas earlier we found that the father's obligation to teach his sons is directly connected to his identity as a father, here the mishnah pointedly ignores the paternal status of the instructor. The mishnah notably says that "a *man* (*adam*) must teach his daughter Torah." The term *adam*, as the English term "man" did in the 1950s, can refer to a person of either gender. The mishnah may, therefore, have used the word *adam* ("man") to indicate the fact that mothers, as well as fathers, had the obligation to instruct their daughters. About this we can only speculate. Even if, however, the mishnah imagines only fathers teaching daughters, the mishnah does not represent Torah study here as an act that serves the interests of the father in his role as father. It is an act he performs as an *adam* ("man"), rather than as a father. What is important in this teaching is that daughters receive certain information.

Second, it is interesting to observe the purpose served by Torah study in this instance. The father is instructed to teach his daughter "so that if she has to drink she should know that merit defers [her reaction to the waters]."[54] The knowledge that Ben Azzai proposes extending to daughters does not obviate their guilt, which, as Rosen Zvi argues, the Mishnah presumes, but it does give daughters a new perspective on the ritual. On one hand, if the daughter later commits adultery and must drink the bitter waters, she may feel less anxious than she would if she did not know that merit defers her reaction to the waters. Understood in this way, Torah study is a vehicle for calming anxiety.[55] Ben Azzai may aspire to have fathers teach their daughters Torah out of a concern for the psychological welfare of daughters, guilty though they may be of adultery. Alternatively, knowing of her guilt and seeing that the waters have not affected her, she may come to question the validity of procedure altogether. Knowing that merit defers the punishment gives the suspected adulteress a framework for continuing to respect the legal system of which the

---

[54] Rosen-Zvi and Ebner argue that initially Ben Azzai's position did not include the explanatory phrase "so that if she has to drink, she should know that merit defers [the punishment]." They have difficulty with the Mishnah's stated reason for why women should study Torah, and indeed it is bizarre. I would argue that the very feature of the text that they find improbable – that a woman should study Torah for a limited and pragmatic purpose – is the feature that makes it possible for the Mishnah to preserve the position. See Rosen-Zvi, "The Sotah Ritual in Tannaitic Literature: Textual and Theoretical Studies" (Hebrew), 167–69; and David Yechiel Ebner, "The Composition and Structure of Mishnah 'Sotah'" (Yeshiva University, 1980), 240–57.

[55] Judith Hauptman argues that Ben Azzai's goal is to assuage women's anxiety. Hauptman, *Rereading the Rabbis*, 22–23.

ritual is a part. Understood in this way, Torah study strengthens the daughter's commitment to the legal system because she will not misinterpret the fact that her body has not reacted to the waters.[56] In either way of understanding Ben Azzai's goals, Torah study gives the daughter a new perspective. She, not the father, benefits from having been taught. Once again the purpose served by Torah study and the attitude toward women studying are integrally connected. This source makes room for women to engage in Torah study because Torah study is figured as a means of gaining knowledge or perspective. Torah study here is a mundane, rather than ritualistic, act. It serves the daughter as an individual. Unlike ritualistic Torah study, it does not connect her to broader cultural narratives and give her a means of transcending her limited, situated existence. It serves a pragmatic, utilitarian function.[57] For those who may be seeking a source to justify the contemporary practice of women studying Torah, I believe that m. Sotah 3:4 provides a weak basis. Knowing that the rabbis let women study Torah to reframe the way a suspected adulteress approached the ordeal of the bitter waters does little to inspire me.

Finally, attention should be paid to the corpora from which the father instructs his daughter. The mishnah states that "a man must teach his daughter *Torah*." The phrase ("to teach Torah," *lilamed torah*) that is used here is also used when discussing fathers' educational obligations to their sons (t. Kid. 1:11).[58] In that context, teaching Torah implies teaching all elements of the rabbinic curriculum: scripture, mishnah, midrash, halakhah, and aggadah. What about here? There is good reason to think that the "Torah" that Ben Azzai thinks daughters ought to learn overlaps significantly with the "Torah" that sons learn. The study described here logically must include elements of rabbinic tradition (mishnah, halakhah, or midrash) because it alerts daughters to the fact that merit defers the effects of the bitter waters.[59] This feature of the ritual is articulated only in the rabbinic expansion of the biblical rite.[60] The text as it stands, then, does offer the possibility that Ben Azzai thought that

---

[56] I thank Agí Věto for bringing this interpretation to my attention. I later found that Menahem Kahana offers the same interpretation of the mishnah. See Menahem Yitshak Kahana, *Sifre Zuta on Deuternomy: Excerpts from a New Tannaitic Midrash* (Jerusalem: Magnes Press, 2002) (Hebrew), 151n10.

[57] This feature of the mishnah as it stands is troubling to Rosen-Zvi and becomes the basis for his suggestion that when Ben Azzai first voiced his view, he was not reflecting on the drinking of the bitter waters. In other words, Rosen-Zvi finds it unlikely that Ben Azzai would have framed Torah study as a pragmatic, utilitarian act. Rosen-Zvi, "The Sotah Ritual in Tannaitic Literature: Textual and Theoretical Studies" (Hebrew), 167–69.

[58] The linguistic similarities between Ben Azzai's statement on daughters learning Torah and t. Kid. 1:11 on sons learning Torah is the basis for Ebner's suggestion that Ben Azzai's statement arose in the same context as t. Kid. 1:11. See Ebner, "The Composition and Structure of Mishnah 'Sotah,'" 245–47.

[59] Menahem Kahana makes the same point: *Sifre Zuta on Deuteronomy*, 151n10.

[60] Consider also m. Avot 1:1, where the term "Torah" refers to both the Written and Oral Torahs.

daughters should engage in something beyond rudimentary study of scripture. This text provides an interesting point of contrast with m. Ned. 4:3 discussed earlier, where daughters are depicted learning only the most basic element of the curriculum (scripture, *mikra'*).

Rosen-Zvi suggests that at an earlier stage in its textual history, Ben Azzai's statement argued in favor of women studying Torah more generally.[61] On the basis of technical linguistic considerations, Rosen-Zvi hypothesizes that originally Ben Azzai's statement was made independently of the discussion of the rite of the bitter waters. He concludes that the explanatory clause ("so that she will know that merit defers [the effect of the bitter waters]") was added only when the tradition was linked to the ritual of the bitter waters.[62] Rosen-Zvi's reconstruction has Ben Azzai originally saying that "a person (*adam*) must teach his daughter Torah." Such a position would come closer than anything we have seen thus far to envisioning women engaging in Torah study as ritual. Such a position would not connect daughters' study to pragmatic or utilitarian purposes; the study would be for its own sake. I have already observed that Ben Azzai notably addresses himself to a generic person (*adam*) rather than to fathers, per se. We may have here hints of an alternative way of envisioning the ritual act of studying Torah. Rather than seeing Torah study as a vehicle for (male) cultural reproduction, Ben Azzai may have understood ritualistic Torah study in a manner that includes women *both as transmitters* (as indicated by the gender-generic term *'adam*) and as recipients of learning. Unfortunately, the mishnah does not preserve the logic that undergirded Ben Azzai's (hypothesized) inclusion of women in ritual Torah study.[63]

By failing to convey the logic underlying what Rosen Zvi speculates was Ben Azzai's original position, the transmitters of the Mishnah express their lack of interest in such a position. They may or may not have been actively hostile toward such a position, but at the very least they felt no loss when

---

[61] See also Ebner, "The Composition and Structure of Mishnah 'Sotah,'" 243–47.

[62] Rosen-Zvi argues that the Mishnah's editor imported Ben Azzai's statement about women and Torah study to resolve a question raised by the phrase "merit defers the effects of the punishment." This phrase implies that women accrue merit sufficient to delay the punishment. The question is: How did women accrue merit? According to Rosen-Zvi, the editor thought that Ben Azzai's statement granting women the right to study Torah offered a handy solution to this problem: Women earned merit through Torah study. See Rosen-Zvi, "The Sotah Ritual in Tannaitic Literature: Textual and Theoretical Studies" (Hebrew), 167–69.

[63] We could speculate regarding the cultural narrative that would be sustained by a gender-inclusive social rendering of ritual Torah study, but it would only be a heuristic exercise. Perhaps Ben Azzai's view stressed the fact that both men and women should study Torah in a contemporary setting because he wanted to connect contemporary Torah study to the revelation at Sinai, which was witnessed by both men and women? This speculation gains support from the midrashic interpretation of Exod 19:3, which emphasizes the presence of women at Sinai (Mek., Yitro 2, ed. Horowitz-Rabin, 207). There is, however, no strong methodological basis for connecting the midrashic tradition about Sinai to Rosen-Zvi's reconstruction of Ben Azzai's original statement.

Ben Azzai's original statement about women studying Torah as a ritual act was refigured. The process of text transmission in evidence here follows the more typical pattern identified by Ilan. Whereas an earlier version of Ben Azzai's statement may have promoted the idea of women studying Torah as a ritual act, later transmitters altered the tradition to conform to their view of appropriate roles for women. The text as we have it now presents women studying Torah in a nonritual manner: They study so that they can function better in the world. Torah study either relieves women of the emotional anxiety they have when drinking the bitter waters or prevents them from misinterpreting their failure to react to the waters. The key point is that for the mishnah as we have it, Torah study is no longer framed as a ritual act by which the individual transcends his or her limited existence. Torah study is now framed as a mundane transaction by which the student gains information and a perspective she did not previously have.

In sum, these sources indicate that some tannaim imagined women learning both biblical scripture and rabbinic tradition. When Torah study was figured as a mundane act, even later transmitters of tannaitic tradition had no difficulty conceiving of women engaged in intellectual exchanges with Torah at the center.[64] The fact that these sources express no discomfort with women studying highlights what is distinctive about the sources that *are* uncomfortable with women studying Torah. Throughout this chapter we have seen that when tannaim took the trouble to specify that Torah study properly excludes women, they did so precisely because they figured Torah study as a ritual means of transcending the self. Through ritual Torah study, men connected with their ancestors at Sinai, fellow sages in the contemporary world, and their sons destined to become the community of the future.

Conclusion: Ritual versus Instrumental Torah Study

I have argued that attention to gender indicates that the tannaitic rabbis had (at least) two different ways of framing the intellectual activity of studying Torah. At times, they understood their study to be a ritual means of perpetuating their covenantal community. Ritual Torah study gave fathers a means to ensure that their biological offspring would live, as the father had, as partners in covenant with God. Torah study envisioned in this manner was the provenance of men and boys only. At other times and in other situations, however, the rabbis understood study to be a vehicle for strengthening the assets of an individual, by giving him or her skills, knowledge, and perspective. Torah study envisioned in this manner could be practiced by both males and females. By way of summary

---

[64] In a recent article, Judith Hauptman argues that women were involved in Torah study, as attested by various anecdotes in the Yerushalmi and Bavli. Many of the cases she discusses could be understood to be instances in which the Torah study is instrumental, as opposed to ritual. See Judith Hauptman, *Jewish Studies: An Internet Journal* (2010): 249–92.

and conclusion, let me highlight some theoretical insights about ritual from the domain of ritual studies that inform my distinction between ritual and instrumental (or nonritual) study of Torah.

In a recent book entitled *Ritual and Its Consequences*, four authors collectively argue that ritual is a way of framing action. The book discusses two different ways of framing actions, which they call ritual and sincere. The authors acknowledge that these are not the only ways people frame action, but the ritual and sincere ways of framing action provide a useful framework for the four authors to make an argument about contemporary scholarship on ritual.[65] My use of their work does not revolve around the ritual–sincere dichotomy that structures theirs. Instead, I use their work to provide theoretical and comparative insights into what I have been calling "ritual Torah study" (in which the father produces his covenantal identity in the next generation). My reading of the tannaitic sources suggests that ritual Torah study is more fruitfully juxtaposed with "instrumental" (or "nonritual") Torah study than with "sincere" Torah study. The theoretical and comparative framework of the book *Ritual and Its Consequences* provides us insight into "instrumental" Torah study, even though it does not map directly onto the authors' construct of the "sincere way of framing action." When the features characteristic of "ritual Torah study" are absent, I suggest that Torah study functions in an instrumental (or nonritual) manner.[66] Broadly speaking, whereas ritual Torah study has sacramental aspects,[67] instrumental Torah study has utilitarian or pragmatic ends.[68] It is important to stress that I am not arguing that the sincere way of framing

---

[65] They write, "We do not claim that these [the ritual and the sincere] are the only possible orientations toward action, but they are at least two terribly important ones that reveal a lot about our world." See Seligman et al., *Ritual and Its Consequences: An Essay on the Limits of Sincerity*, 6.

[66] I also draw here on the work of Catherine Bell, who points out the difficulties in juxtaposing ritual and instrumental action from an anthropological perspective. Since my goal is not to devise terms appropriate to the broad swath of human behavior, but to describe aspects of the ancient rabbinic worldview, I retain the term "instrumental" while recognizing its limits. Bell uses the term "ritualization to draw attention to the way in which certain actions strategically distinguish themselves in relation to other actions. In a very preliminary sense, ritualization is a way of acting that is designed and orchestrated to distinguish and privilege what is being done in comparison to other more quotidian activities. As such, ritualization is a matter of various culturally specific strategies for setting off some activities from others" (74). Bell's discussion focuses on what is accomplished through ritualization as a "positive" strategy. The mundane, quotidian, and nonritual is that which gets left behind. I argue that the rabbis ritualized intellectual activity (ritual Torah study) so that it accomplished things other than that which could be achieved by mundane, instrumental, or nonritual Torah study. See Catherine Bell, *Ritual Theory, Ritual Practice* (New York: Oxford University Press, 1992), 69–93.

[67] On the use of this terms to describe Torah study, see Martin S. Jaffee, "Oral Transmission as Rabbinic Sacrament."

[68] The utilitarian value of Torah study can be seen in many of the cases of women's Torah study discussed by Hauptman in "A New View of Women and Torah Study in the Talmudic Period."

action (as articulated by the authors of *Ritual and Its Consequences*) accounts for the phenomenon of instrumental Torah study.

The authors of *Ritual and Its Consequences* are interested in what we can learn about ritual by comparing the ritual way of framing action to the sincere way of framing action. When one feels that actions matter only if they are performed with intention and integrity, one constructs a world from the viewpoint of sincerity. From this viewpoint, ritual action often appears to be rote, mindless repetition, performed as a meaningless outer shell for ritual's true "inner" meanings, which are often theological in nature. The authors argue that the sincere approach pervades our society, and as a result we have failed to appreciate the insights engendered by a ritual way of framing action. Their attention to the ritual way of framing actions helps them reconstruct ritual's role in society in a more sympathetic – and, they suggest, more illuminating – manner. They propose that when one frames actions in a ritual mode, one temporarily creates the ideal world that one would like to inhabit, a world that exists in the realm of the "subjunctive."[69] Ritual involves "the creation of an order *as if* it were truly the case."[70] For example, when friends answer each others' inquiry by stating that they are good, they are constructing such a world in the subjunctive. The authors write, "The 'as if' quality of the ritual invocation, its subjunctive sense, is also what makes it real. What is, is what can be."[71] Interpreting ritual activity through a sincere lens, one fails to perceive the value of ritual activity: Through ritual, one temporarily brings about an alternate reality by acting *as if* it really were the case.[72] Ritual has value because it gives us a means to project ourselves into worlds other than that of lived experience with all its fractures and disruptions.

This account of ritual resonates deeply with the rhetorical framing of Torah study in Sif. Dt. 46, discussed earlier in this chapter. There we read that if the father fails to educate his son by teaching him Hebrew and Torah, "it is *as if* he had buried him." Here the text uses the subjunctive to describe a ritual failure. When the father fails to teach his son Torah, it is as if the son dies. The case of ritual failure implicitly teaches about the case of ritual success: When the father does teach his son Torah, it is *as if* he keeps the son (as an extension of himself)

[69] They build on the work of J. Z. Smith, who emphasizes how ritual gives expression to a reality that does not currently exist. Smith writes, "Ritual expresses a realistic assessment of the fact that the world cannot be compelled [to conform to the reality that the ritual creates.] The ritual is incongruent with the way things are or are likely to be.... [Ritual is valuable because it] displays a dimension of [reality that though not actual] can be thought about and remembered in the course of things." See Jonathan Z. Smith, *Imagining Religion: From Babylon to Jonestown* (Chicago: University of Chicago Press, 1982), 53–65, esp. 65.

[70] Emphasis in the original. Seligman et al., *Ritual and Its Consequences: An Essay on the Limits of Sincerity*, 20.

[71] Seligman et al., *Ritual and Its Consequences: An Essay on the Limits of Sincerity*, 22.

[72] See Seligman et al., *Ritual and Its Consequences: An Essay on the Limits of Sincerity*, esp. 35–36.

alive.[73] The Torah study in this source is ritual precisely because of the way the intellectual activities are framed. The intellectual activity of Torah study is understood as a way of maintaining the line of continuity between father and son. If the father fails to teach the son, of course the son will not die. But the midrash imagines a world in which Torah study has the capacity to keep the son alive so that he can maintain his father's identity in the next generation. It posits Torah study as a means of overcoming the difficulty of transmitting identity from father to son. The Torah study is understood in a ritual sense precisely because the intellectual activities of study allow practitioners to experience an ideal world, a world in which sons live out the covenantal destiny of their fathers.[74]

The authors of *Ritual and Its Consequences* additionally argue that framing activities ritually, by operating in the subjunctive, enables people both to acknowledge boundaries between discreet entities and mediate them.[75] They write, "Ritual both posits boundaries and allows the move between boundaries. By recognizing limits, ritual provides as well the vehicle for transcending them."[76] This dynamic can be seen in the sources on ritual Torah study that acknowledge palpable social differences between father and son, but also provide a means of negotiating the boundaries. The father described in Sif. Dt. 46 and t. Kid. 1:11 is differentiated from the son by the authority and powers that he possesses, which the son lacks. The father wields the knife of circumcision over the son, he reads Hebrew and understands Torah, he makes money through his practice of a trade, he has a wife. But the very same texts that highlight the social differences between father and son offer Torah study as a means of overcoming these differences. Torah study helps turn the son into a father of the future.

The insights of *Ritual and Its Consequences* also help us recognize the places where Torah study is not framed as ritual. M. Ned. 4:3 and m. Sotah 3:4 suggest that Torah study benefits the individual by offering the student skills, knowledge, and perspective. These texts do not operate in the subjunctive mode. They do not imagine an ideal world. They operate in the world *as it is*. In these texts Torah study provides the student with concrete capacities that

---

[73] I thank Greg Schmidt Goering for alerting me to the fact that the Sifre speaks in the subjunctive only of the case of ritual failure.

[74] Nancy Jay observes that sacrifice (a specific type of ritual) in unrelated traditions combines exclusion of women with strong concern for intergenerational continuity in the male line (i.e., between father and son). There are some striking similarities between the anthropological phenomenon described by Jay and the textual patterns observed here. In both cases women are excluded from rituals that emphasize intergenerational continuity between father and son. I do not find sufficient evidence, however, to translate a stronger version of Jay's hypothesis to the rabbinic materials. She argues that "sacrifice is a remedy for having been born of woman" (xxiii). See Jay, *Throughout Your Generations Forever: Sacrifice, Religion, and Paternity.*

[75] See also Catherine Bell on this point.

[76] Seligman et al., *Ritual and Its Consequences: An Essay on the Limits of Sincerity*, 12–13.

help him or her function in the here and now. Additionally, these texts focus on how Torah study affects the student as an individual. Recall that m. Ned. 4:3 stresses that it is the children who benefit when learning scripture, not the father. Likewise, m. Sotah 3:4 provides Torah study to daughters because of the perspective it offers them when they find themselves having to drink the bitter waters. These sources do not frame Torah study as a means of connecting bounded social entities. In these sources, Torah study strengthens the capacities of the individual *qua* individual. Unlike the sources that represent Torah study as a way of connecting fathers and sons, these sources do not portray Torah study as a means of linking discrete social entities.

The authors of *Ritual and Its Consequences* also emphasize that ritual is "endless work" that must be performed over and over again. They explain that "the reality [of the subjunctive world] lasts only as long as we adhere to the illusion,"[77] that is, as long as we participate in the ritual. Ritual assumes that there is a vast difference between the world enacted through ritual and participants' experience of lived reality.[78] "The endless work of ritual is necessary precisely because the ordered world of ritual is inevitably only temporary. The world always returns to its broken state, constantly requiring the repairs of ritual."[79] Attention to this feature of ritual helps us recognize places where the rabbis are *not* framing Torah study ritually. M. Ned. 4:3 represents scriptural study as a kind of transaction, almost financial in nature, through which the student "nets" a benefit. When Reuven teaches Shimon scripture (*mikra'*), Shimon gains skills he did not previously have. Torah study here is a task with a finite end. Shimon gains the skills of literacy and no longer needs Reuven's services. Torah study for the sake of acquiring skills, knowledge, or perspective is distinct from ritual Torah study. When Reuven teaches Shimon mishnah, halakhot, and aggadot, Reuven has more knowledge than Shimon, but both are transformed by the study. Torah study here is undertaken for its own sake (*lishmah*) with no tangible goal in mind. The study itself is transformative. Study is performance rather than "service rendered."

Finally, the authors of *Ritual and Its Consequences* make one additional point that clarifies why the tannaitic sources depict women engaged in Torah study in diverse, and even conflicting, ways. Because ritual operates in the realm of the subjunctive, the worlds it imagines are always limited.[80] "[Ritual] is ... imperfect to the situation at hand and in endless need of constant, if only minor adjustment to make the disconnect [between the real and imagined worlds] less painful."[81] The world of lived experience presents the practitioner with any

---

77 Seligman et al., *Ritual and Its Consequences: An Essay on the Limits of Sincerity*, 22.
78 Paraphrased from Seligman et al., *Ritual and Its Consequences: An Essay on the Limits of Sincerity*, 20.
79 Seligman et al., *Ritual and Its Consequences: An Essay on the Limits of Sincerity*, 30.
80 Seligman et al., *Ritual and Its Consequences: An Essay on the Limits of Sincerity*, 42.
81 Seligman et al., *Ritual and Its Consequences: An Essay on the Limits of Sincerity*, 42.

number of quandaries. Ritual can never fix all of the problems definitively. It does not offer a single all-encompassing solution. Rather, "ritual ... becomes the repertoire of ... patterns, a repertoire that is endlessly growing, constantly changing, and always in danger of becoming inadequate."[82] Here the authors liken ritual to a series of experiments, each of which attends to a different challenge posed by the world of lived experience. I find that this description of ritual as a series of subjunctive proposals helps explain why the sources that figure Torah study as ritual only sometimes emphasize women's exemption. If social reality was such that only men engaged in studying Torah ritually, one would expect the sources that figure Torah study as a ritual to refrain from portraying women studying Torah. But t. Ber. 2:12 does depict women (as menstruants, parturients, and dischargers) studying Torah. I believe that this source is inattentive to the gender of these female students of ritual Torah study because it is operating in the subjunctive. The experiment with which this source is concerned is positing a form of reproduction that endures beyond anything the sexed, desiring, and excreting body is capable of. It is the fact that this experiment is conducted in the subjunctive that makes it possible for this source to depict women with genital leaks studying Torah and to use these women to make the larger point that only genital leaks that result from sexual desire disqualify one from studying Torah.

In conclusion, we have every reason to believe that in the social world of the tannaim women did not participate in ritual Torah study. This fact, however, did not preclude the rabbis from imagining scenarios in which women did study, if doing so helped them think through an issue that needed thinking through. This complexity notwithstanding, the sources that figure Torah study as a ritual act offer us tremendous insight into why this religious practice was associated with men and men only. Ritual Torah study was posited as a means of temporarily inhabiting an ideal world in which the covenantal community of rabbinic sages endured throughout the generations. Since the social identity of those involved in the rabbinic disciple circles was male, they envisioned a future community that shared the quality of being male. I have argued that the tannaitic rabbis imagined their ideal future by constructing the lay *pater familias* as someone who replicates his social and cultural identity in his male offspring. In the next chapter, we will see that this conception of Torah study as a ritual means of (male) cultural reproduction underlies the exemption of women from timebound, positive commandments.

[82] Seligman et al., *Ritual and Its Consequences: An Essay on the Limits of Sincerity*, 32.

8

The Fringes Debate

A Conclusion of Sorts

After all is said and done, what, if anything, can we say conclusively about the rule that exempts women from timebound, positive commandments? Throughout this book I have made observations that both limit and expand our ability to understand the rule. In this chapter, I review the conclusions reached in the preceding chapters and try to gesture beyond them.

In Part I, I argued strenuously against the common understanding of the rule. Typically, both traditional and academic scholars assume that the rule was formulated to *determine* women's involvement with ritual. If the rule is a prescriptive principle, then it appears to offer insight into the tannaitic rabbis' vision of women's roles. One need only ask why the tannaitic rabbis exempted women from this particular class of commandments. Whatever it is that makes it inappropriate to require women to perform this class of commandments is what marks women as different from men. Most theories about the rule thus focus on how timebound, positive commandments differ from the other three classes of commandments.[1] Identifying the distinctive characteristics of timebound, positive commandments reveals why the rabbis exempted women from only this class of commandments. If, however, we attend to the academic interests of the literature in which the rule is preserved, this reading of the rule falters.

Various chapters in Parts I and II of this book support the conclusion that the rule was neither formulated as a prescriptive principle nor motivated by a particular social vision of who women are or should be. Chapters 1 and 2 set the rule in the context of tannaitic scholastic exercises. By showing what the tannaitic sages *were* doing when they formulated and transmitted the rule,

---

[1] See, e.g., Hoffman, *Covenant of Blood*, 162–70; Berman, "The Status of Women in Halakhic Judaism," 121–22; Wegner, *Chattel or Person*, 150–59; and Hauptman, *Rereading the Rabbis*, 224–28.

I created a basis for understanding the rule as a product of something *other than* prescriptive legislation. Chapter 1 showed how the category of timebound, positive commandments emerged from exegesis of the tefillin verses (Exod 13:9–10). I argued that the rule was formulated as a summary of three exegetical conclusions reached regarding the tefillin verses: (1) that women are exempt from tefillin, (2) that tefillin are not worn at night, and (3) that tefillin are not worn on the Sabbath or holidays. These three conclusions yield the summary statement that "tefillin are a timebound, positive commandment from which women are exempt." Though the category of timebound, positive commandments from which women are exempt eventually included additional rituals (sukkah, lulav,[2] shofar[3]) beyond the initial exemplar of the rule (tefillin), I argued that the other rituals were named as timebound, positive commandments only *after* women's exemption from them had already been determined by *other means*. I could find no evidence that the rule was used to determine women's exemptions in these cases.[4]

Chapter 2 explored how another scholastic exercise of the tannaitic sages (listmaking) granted a *cultural significance* to the rule that it did not originally have as the summary of exegetical conclusions. By including the rule in the lists of legal differences between man and woman, the tannaitic sages made the rule into a marker of male–female difference. It is important to note, however, that the rule came to be associated with the project of distinguishing men from women only *after* it had been formulated and circulated as an independent tradition. Notably, in one of the few places where the rule is preserved outside the context of the lists, it is cited as a rule that applies to slaves as well as women.[5] In that context, the rule does not serve to distinguish women from men, and so the rule is not specific to women.

In Chapter 5, I observed that only in the post-amoraic period do the rabbis treat the rule as if it actually determined women's levels of ritual obligation. I concluded that the idea that the rule was formulated to determine women's involvement with ritual was a construct of the post-amoraic period.[6] In

---

2 Sukkah and lulav are mentioned as timebound, positive commandments in t. Kid. 1:10; y. Kid. 61a; and b. Kid. 33b–34a.

3 Shofar is included in the list of timebound, positive commandments only in the Yerushalmi's version of the baraita (see y. Kid. 61a).

4 Various amoraic rulings on women's involvement with ritual also suggest that the rule was not used to determine the extent of women's ritual participation. See discussion of amoraic rulings in Hauptman, *Rereading the Rabbis*, 230–31.

5 See Sif. Num. 115, ed. Horowitz, 124, discussed below.

6 I need to make a critical distinction here. I do not mean to suggest that during the post-amoraic period the rule was *viewed as a prescriptive principle*. That would imply that the post-amoraic sages *used* the principle to determine women's participation, which I certainly do not wish to claim. As far as I can tell, except in a single case during the tannaitic period (tzitzit, discussed in the body of this chapter), the rule was never used to determine women's involvement with ritual. What I do mean to suggest is that when post-amoraic sages looked back on tannaitic decisions regarding women's ritual participation, they assumed that the rule had been on the books as a

Chapter 3 I argued that also during the post-amoraic period the rule was no longer reflexively associated with tefillin; it was freed from its descriptive function vis-à-vis tefillin. As the result of post-amoraic interest in organizing received tannaitic sources into a coherent and structured system, the view developed that tefillin was *not* a timebound, positive commandment. This development made room for the rule to become something besides descriptive vis-à-vis tefillin. It could now be viewed as a prescriptive principle.

In sum, seeing that (1) the traditions recording the rule were formulated as part of a scholastic program in which shaping women's roles played no role, and (2) the view that the rule was formulated to function prescriptively is a relatively late construct, we must conclude that the legal stipulations of the rule do not offer broad insight into tannaitic ideas about women's essence or roles. However, it is worth reflecting here on what might be called the "fallacy of origins." Knowing what something originally meant does not necessarily shed light on what it has become. Though Parts I and II demonstrate that the rule did not originate as a prescriptive statement that was undergirded by a rabbinic vision of who women are or who they should be, there can be no doubt that the rule eventually came to function in that manner. In both popular and scholarly accounts from the twentieth century, the rule is taken to be a premiere statement about Judaism's ideas about the roles women should play.[7] It is unfortunately beyond the scope of this book to show how we got from the prescriptive principle of the post-amoraic period to the intensive gender work performed by the rule in contemporary Jewish society.[8] Undoubtedly, the post-amoraic notion that the rule was formulated to function prescriptively has grounded all subsequent theories of the rule's gender ideology. The idea that the rule accommodates or encourages women's domestic roles or that it reflects their heightened spiritual capacities assumes that the rule requires women to do what is appropriate for them as women. But the full fleshing out of the rule's twists and turns during the medieval and modern periods will have to wait for another time.

It is, however, within the scope of this book to offer one final reflection on what the rule meant in the tannaitic period when it first circulated. Though I did not linger on this point in earlier chapters, we do find one instance in which the rule was used to determine women's participation in ritual. In a dispute with the sages, R. Shimon cites the rule as the basis for exempting women from

prescriptive principle with normative force during the tannaitic period and had been used during the tannaitic period to determine women's involvement with ritual. My research suggests that the post-amoraic view was a revisionist view of history.

7 For an example of this view in the popular religious literature, see Meiselman, "The Jewish Woman in Jewish Law," 43–57. For an example in the scholarly literature, see Shmuel Safrai, "The *Mitzva* Obligation of Women in Tannaitic Thought." For an example in contemporary feminist literature, see Adler, "The Jew Who Wasn't There."

8 See Elisheva Baumgarten's forthcoming book on women's piety in the medieval period, which includes a discussion of the rule.

tzitzit.[9] When we take this piece of information into account, we find that the rule passed through four discrete stages during the period covered in this book:

1. In the first stage, the rule was formulated as a descriptive summary of exegetical conclusions reached regarding tefillin.
2. In the second stage, R. Shimon (unique among the tannaitic sages) used the rule to exempt women from tzitzit.
3. In the third stage, the rule was retroactively applied as a descriptive principle to several other rituals (sukkah, lulav, and shofar) in which women's involvement had already been determined by other means.
4. In the fourth stage (attested in the post-amoraic stratum of the Bavli), the rule was viewed as having been formulated as a prescriptive principle.

This chapter focuses on the second stage, when R. Shimon used the rule to exempt women from tzitzit. Regarding R. Shimon specifically, we can ask the following: When *he* invoked the rule, what ideas about gender informed *his* use of the rule? As long as we recognize that the rule was used to institute a social vision *only in the single case of R. Shimon's ruling regarding tzitzit*,[10] we can inquire into the gender ideology represented by the rule. It is important to understand, however, that R. Shimon's use of the rule to decide law was exceptional.[11] For the most part, during the tannaitic period, the rule was viewed as a descriptive principle. Only in the post-amoraic period was the rule generally perceived to have been formulated to determine the full range of women's involvement with ritual.

The project of trying to understand the logic governing R. Shimon's use of the rule is an admittedly antiquarian pursuit. What the rule meant to R. Shimon has little to do with "the rule" as it has come to exist in the popular imagination of the twentieth and twenty-first centuries. But the human mind abhors a vacuum, and having observed that R. Shimon does use the rule prescriptively, it is worth inquiring into the ideas about gender that inform his use of it. The research presented in Part III on women's exemptions from Shema, tefillin, and Torah study places R. Shimon's use of the rule in a cultural context that extends

---

[9] See t. Kid. 1:10 and Sif. Num. 115.

[10] We see that R. Shimon's use of the rule to exempt women from tzitzit was not universally accepted because the Bavli notes that two amoraic sages (Rav Avram the Pious and Rav Yehudah) attached tzitzit to the aprons of the women in their household. See b. Suk. 11a and b. Men. 43a.

[11] Louis Ginzberg (and Shevah Yalon following him) also picks up on the close association between R. Shimon and the rule. Ginzberg argues that a key difference between the sages and R. Shimon is that whereas R. Shimon used the rule to determine women's involvement in a broad range of ritual, the sages decided women's involvement with ritual on a case-by-case basis through exegesis of the relevant scriptural verses. Ginzberg notes, however, that the disparate methods of determining women's involvement with ritual produced only one point of genuine legal contention (the case of tzitzit, to be discussed extensively below). See Ginzberg, *Commentary on the Palestinian Talmud*, 160–63; and Yalon, "'Women Are Exempted from All Positive Ordinances That Are Bound Up with a Stated Time,'" 119–20.

beyond his single decision. Knowing the gender ideology that informed the sages' exemption of women from the related rituals of Shema, tefillin, and Torah study will help us understand what it meant for R. Shimon to use the rule to exempt women from tzitzit.

The Rule Is Limited in Scope

Although the rhetoric of the rule sounds like an all-encompassing statement about *all* commandments, in Chapters 1 and 2 I argued that the rule is best understood as a statement of relatively limited scope. In Chapter 1, I analyzed the four-part structure of the rule in m. Kid 1:7.

1. All **timebound, positive** commandments – **men** are obligated, **women** are exempt.
2. All **non-timebound, positive** commandments, **men and women** are equally obligated.
3. and 4. All **negative** commandments, irrespective of whether they are **timebound** or **non-timebound** – men and women are **equally obligated**, except "do not mar [the corners of your beard]," "do not round [the corners of your head]," and "do not become impurified through contact with the dead." (m. Kid. 1:7)

The four-part structure can be diagrammed as follows:

1. Timebound, positive: Men obligated, women exempt	2. Non-timebound, positive: Men and women obligated
3. Timebound, negative: Men and women obligated	4. Non-timebound, negative: Men and women obligated

When mapped in this manner, it appears that the rule divides all existing commandments into one of four categories. These four categories appear to take into account every type of commandment that exists in the Torah. I have argued, however, that the rule is best understood as a statement of limited scope about a discrete phenomenon.

In Chapter 1, I suggested that initially the rule consisted of only statement #1, and indeed R. Shimon invokes only statement #1 in his ruling on tzitzit. The rule was not therefore formulated to anticipate women's involvement in all commandments. Rather, it was formulated to describe women's involvement with the few commandments within its purview. I also argued that the four-part structure was a secondary development, generated by manipulating the variables in statement #1 to flesh out the other three implicit categories. One way, then, that the rule was of limited scope was that initially it addressed women's engagement with only a limited number of commandments.

In Chapter 2, I presented another argument that highlights the initially limited scope of the rule. I proposed an alternative reading for the word "*all*" in the phrase "*all* timebound, positive commandments." When read as a prescriptive principle, the rule appears to apply to all the commandments that can legitimately be described by the terms "timebound" and "positive." Referring back to the table, this class appears to be conceptually one-fourth of all commandments. When we do not read the rule prescriptively, however, we find other ways to read the term "all." In Chapter 2, I proposed that we read statement #1 in the mishnaic rule as follows: "All the commandments which we know to be timebound and positive and from which women are exempt – women are exempt from these." No doubt, when understood in this manner, the mishnaic rule sounds tautological. The apodosis ("women are exempt") tells us something we already know from the protasis ("this rule concerns timebound, positive commandments from which women are exempt"). The tautology is less problematic, however, when we recognize that the Mishnah is not legislating here, but organizing information. M. Kid. 1:7–8 comprises a short list of the ways in which the law treats women differently from men.[12] We might think of the four different parts of the rule as baskets, each of which contains a few commandments. This way of thinking about the rule is very different from the way suggested by the above table. While the table makes it seem as if *all* commandments will be covered by one of the four parts of the rule, the basket metaphor leaves open the possibility that there will be many commandments not contained in the available baskets. In other words, there are a large number commandments that we should not expect to be accounted for in the four parts of the rule. In this way of reading the rule – and to the extent that the rule functioned prescriptively, as it did for R. Shimon – the rule differentiates among only a very few commandments. It does not carve out the entire range of commandments into discrete categories. It makes distinctions within a much smaller subset of commandments. We might think of the four parts of the rule as mapping out a *rhetorically* complete structure, though not an actually complete one.

In Chapters 1 and 2, I argued that the rule was of limited scope because it seemed to be the best way to make sense of the redactional settings within which the rule was variously attested. But the claims remained theoretical. In this chapter I would like to venture a guess as to the specific ritual domain within which the rule was meaningful.

The Rule Concerns Only Shema-Related Rituals

The Tosephta names several rituals (tefillin, lulav, and sukkah) as timebound, positive commandments.[13] The Yerushalmi further characterizes shofar as a

---

[12] The reader will recall that similar lists can be found in t. Sot.2:2–7; and t. Bik 2:3–7. See also Sem. 11:2.

[13] See t. Kid. 1:10.

timebound, positive commandment.[14] Above I suggested that the rule developed in four stages.

1. Descriptive summary of exegesis concerning tefillin
2. R. Shimon uses the rule to determine women's involvement with tzitzit
3. Other rituals from which women were already exempt (sukkah, lulav, shofar) encompassed within the rule
4. The rule was perceived as having been formulated prescriptive

According to this timeline of developments, not all of the commandments that the Tosephta and Yerushalmi name as timebound, positive commandments are subjects of the rule in the same sense. I have argued throughout this book that tefillin was the prototypical timebound, positive commandment (stage 1). The other rituals were brought into the sphere of the rule only after women's involvement with them was determined by other means (stage 3). These other rituals were named as exemplars of the rule because their profile (they are, after all, timebound, positive commandments from which women are exempt) fit that of the rule. When I focus on R. Shimon's use of the rule, I mean to draw our attention to the *second* stage of the rule's evolution; this is a stage before sukkah, lulav, and shofar were regarded as exemplars of the rule. So even though the Tosephta and Yerushalmi name sukkah, lulav, and shofar as exemplars of the rule, I discount this evidence in my discussion of R. Shimon's use of the rule.

In what follows, I argue that in the short period when the rule functioned prescriptively for R. Shimon, *the rule was relevant to Shema-derived rituals only*. In Chapter 6, I discussed six ritual practices that the rabbis derive from the Shema verses: (1) tefillin of the hand ("Bind them as a sign on your hand"), (2) tefillin of the head ("let them serve as a symbol on your forehead"), (3) mezuzah ("inscribe them on the doorposts of your house and on your gates"), (4) recitation of the Shema verses as liturgy (speak of them "when you lie down and when you rise up"), (5) Torah study and instruction of children ("Impress them upon your children"),[15] and (6) tzitzit ("make for themselves fringes"). I propose that when R. Shimon invoked the rule that women are exempt from timebound, positive commandments, he used it within the limited domain of Shema-derived rituals. For R. Shimon the rule was a way to distinguish among the Shema-derived rituals. Whereas some Shema-derived rituals can be described as timebound (tefillin, Shema), others cannot (mezuzah). The rule gave R. Shimon a means of determining women's involvement with tzitzit (itself a Shema-derived ritual) by comparing it with other Shema-derived rituals in which women's involvement was already resolved.

In support of this hypothesis, I offer three pieces of evidence. First, I note that tefillin (a Shema-derived ritual) has a special status as the paradigmatic

---

[14] See y. Kid. 61a.
[15] Benovitz argues that rituals 4 and 5 are not distinct rituals. See Benovitz, "*Shinun*: Recitation of the Shema in the Teaching of R. Shimon Bar Yohai" (Hebrew).

timebound, positive commandment. The privileged status of tefillin as a timebound, positive commandment is reflected in the Mekhilta de R. Shimon b.
Yohai.[16]

1. Another interpretation: *In order that the teaching* (torah) *of God be in your mouth*
(Exod 13:9). [This verse comes] to exclude women [from wearing tefillin].

2. Just as tefillin are distinctive insofar as they are a timebound, positive commandment
from which women are exempt, so too let women be exempt from all timebound,
positive commandments. (MRSY, ed. Epstein-Melamed, 41)

As noted in Chapter 1, the first paragraph summarizes exegesis found in a more
fully developed form in the earlier Mekhilta de R. Ishmael. Since scripture characterizes tefillin as the "*torah* of God" (Exod 13:9), the midrash concludes that
tefillin is a form of Torah study. And since women are exempt from studying
Torah, the midrash exempts women from wearing tefillin. The second paragraph draws an altogether different conclusion. The midrash determines that
women are exempt from all other timebound, positive commandments because
they are exempt from tefillin. Here we see tefillin functioning as the paradigmatic timebound, positive commandment.[17] Indeed, in Chapter 1, I argued that
exegesis of the tefillin verses (Exod 13:9–10) helped to *generate* the category of
timebound, positive commandments. Though the category of timebound, positive commandments came retroactively to include additional rituals (sukkah,
lulav, and shofar), tefillin had a distinctive status as the paradigmatic timebound, positive commandment.

A second reason for suggesting that the rule initially functioned within the
limited domain of Shema-derived rituals is that the midrashic exegesis that
generates the rule singles out two different Shema-derived rituals – tefillin and
mezuzah – for comparison. This midrash was discussed extensively in Chapter
1, but I re-cite it here to make a slightly different point.

1. *In order that the teaching* (torah) *of God shall be in your mouth* (Exod 13:9). Why
is this said, since it is also stated, *And it shall be for you a sign* (Exod 13:9)?

2. Could I learn that the meaning is to include women also? After all, logic suggests
that since **mezuzah is a positive commandment** and **tefillin is a positive commandment**,
if you learned with respect to mezuzah that it applies with respect to women as to men,
could it be that tefillin also functions with respect to women as with men?

3. The Torah states, *in order that the teaching* (torah) *of God shall be in your mouth*.
It [the commandment of tefillin] has not been stated except with regards to he who is
required to study Torah.

---

[16] See also b. Kid. 34a.
[17] Tefillin serves the same function in an expanded version of this logical sequence in b. Kid. 34a.

From here they said: Everyone is required [to perform the commandment of] tefillin, except women and slaves, [since they are exempt from studying Torah]....

5. *Throughout your days* (Exod 13:10). Why is this said, since it is also stated, *And it shall be for you a sign* (Exod 13:9)?

6. Could I learn that the meaning is to include nights? After all, logic suggests that since **mezuzah is a positive commandment** and **tefillin is a positive commandment**, if you learned with respect to mezuzah that it is performed in the nights as well as the days, could it be that tefillin is also performed in the nights as well as the days?

7. The Torah states, *throughout your days*. During the day you put on [tefillin], and not at night.

8. *Throughout your days* (Exod 13:10). Why is this said, since it is also stated, *And it shall be for you a sign* (Exod 13:9)?

9. Could I learn that the meaning is to include Sabbaths and holidays? After all, logic suggests that since **mezuzah is a positive commandment** and **tefillin is a positive commandment**, if you learned with respect to mezuzah that it is performed on the Sabbath and holidays, could it be that tefillin is also performed on the Sabbath and holidays?

10. The Torah states, *throughout your days*. This excludes the Sabbath and holidays. (Mek., Bo 17, ed. Horowitz-Rabin, 68–69)

The reader will recall that this midrash repeats a pattern three different times. Each of the three paragraphs opens with the suggestion that the laws of tefillin should resemble the laws of mezuzah since both are "positive commandments" (see lines 2, 6, and 9). In each paragraph the midrash points out that scripture distinguishes tefillin from mezuzah. In contrast to the rules regarding mezuzah, scripture indicates (1) that women (and slaves) are exempt from wearing tefillin (line 4), (2) that tefillin are not worn at night (line 7), and (3) that tefillin are not worn on the Sabbath and holidays (line 10). Summarizing these three exegetical conclusions yields the statement that tefillin are distinguished from mezuzah by virtue of the fact they are a "timebound" commandment (not worn at night, or on Sabbath and holidays) from which women are exempt. In this exegesis, the paradigmatic timebound, positive commandment (tefillin) is juxtaposed to and differentiated from another positive commandment (mezuzah). It just so happens that both commandments under consideration are Shema-derived rituals. Tefillin is compared to the mezuzah on the basis of the fact that both are positive commandments. Different rules apply to tefillin, however, in that it is a timebound, positive commandment from which women are exempt. Here the key difference between one Shema-derived ritual (tefillin) and another Shema-derived ritual (mezuzah) is the fact that one is timebound and the other is not.[18]

---

[18] The implication here, as will become increasingly clear in the ensuing argument, is that mezuzah was the prototypical non-timebound commandment. Unfortunately for my argument, no tannaitic source describes mezuzah as a non-timebound commandment, though the Bavli includes

Finally, it is noteworthy that the one time when tannaitic literature documents a sage using the rule to determine women's ritual involvement, the ritual in question is tzitzit, another Shema-derived ritual. Sifre Numbers preserves evidence of a debate between the sages and R. Shimon regarding women's obligation to wear ritual fringes on the corners of their garments.[19]

1. *And God spoke to Moses saying: Speak to the children of Israel and say to them that they should make for themselves fringes* (tzitzit) (Num. 15:37–38). [The law of fringes] also pertains to women.

2. R. Shimon exempts women from fringes because [of the principle of] timebound, positive commandments, from which women are exempt.

3. For this is the rule: R. Shimon said: All timebound, positive commandments apply to men and do not apply to women, [and apply to] those qualified [to give testimony] and not to those disqualified [from giving testimony]. (Sif. Num. 115, ed. Horowitz, 124)

In the first paragraph, the sages obligate women to wear tzitzit on the corners of their garments. The logic behind the sages' opinion is not stated, and it will be discussed more extensively later in this chapter. On the other side of the debate stands R. Shimon, who exempts women from tzitzit on the basis of the fact that tzitzit are a timebound, positive commandment (paragraph 2). The rule is then cited and attributed to R. Shimon (paragraph 3). Tzitzit is the only ritual for which concrete evidence exists that women's level of obligation was adjudicated by the rule. Notably, tzitzit is also a Shema-derived ritual.

Each of the commandments that interacts with the rule in a meaningful way (tefillin as prototype of the rule, mezuzah as point of contrast to the rule, tzitzit adjudicated by the rule) is a ritual that derives from the Shema verses. On the basis of these observations, I offer a somewhat speculative hypothesis: The rule that women are exempt from timebound, positive commandments was initially conceived as a way to distinguish some Shema-derived rituals from other Shema-derived rituals. As I argued above, the rule was not initially intended to designate a subset of rituals within the entire spectrum of *all* commandments. Given the centrality of Shema-derived rituals in early traditions about the rule,

mezuzah in its list of commandments that are non-timebound (b. Kid. 34a). This fact suggests that the compilers of the Bavli were sensitive to the evidence that leads me to posit that mezuzah was a, if not the, prototypical non-timebound commandment. It is important to recognize, however, that earlier versions of the list in the Tosephta and Yerushalmi do *not* include mezuzah. It is extremely unlikely, then, that a tannaitic version of the baraita included mezuzah. What the Bavli does suggest, however, is that later tradents of the baraita saw mezuzah as a glaring omission. The Bavli's version of the baraita, then, supports the plausibility of my argument in a general way without providing direct evidence for a tannaitic tradition that regarded mezuzah as a non-timebound commandment. On the creativity of the Bavli in its transmission of baraitas, see Louis Jacobs, "Are There Fictitious Baraitot in the Babylonian Talmud?" *Hebrew Union College Annual* 42 (1971): 185–96.

[19] The debate is attested also in t. Kid. 1:10; y. Kid. 61a; and b. Men. 43a.

I suggest we consider the possibility that the rule was formulated to designate a subset of rituals within the limited domain of Shema-derived rituals. While mezuzah is a positive commandment that is *not* occasioned by time (and which women are obligated to perform), tefillin is a positive commandment that *is* occasioned by time (and from which women are exempt). According to R. Shimon, tzitzit should be considered like tefillin, and women should be exempt from them too. Or conversely, R. Shimon regards tzitzit as *unlike* mezuzah. If we wish to understand what the rule meant to R. Shimon, we need to ask what it meant to compare a Shema-derived ritual (like tzitzit) to tefillin. But before answering that question, we need to make a few more observations about the status of women's involvement in the Shema-derived rituals during the early tannaitic period.

Women's Involvement with Shema-Derived Rituals

M. Ber. 3:3, which was discussed in Chapter 6, lists women's obligations regarding several textual and liturgical rituals.

Women, slaves and minors are exempt from the recitation of Shema and from tefillin, and obligated with regard to Prayer, mezuzah and Grace after Meals. (m. Ber. 3:3)

The list of rituals discussed in this mishnah can at first glance appear somewhat random. Each of these rituals involves text that is either recited (Shema, Amidah, and grace after meals) or incorporated into a ritual (tefillin and mezuzah). While some of the texts are of biblical provenance (Shema, tefillin, and mezuzah), others are of rabbinic provenance (Amidah and grace after meals). While some of the rituals derive from the Shema (Shema, tefillin, and mezuzah), others do not (Amidah and grace after meals). What logic dictated which text-based rituals would be included for discussion in this mishnah? One way to make sense of the somewhat haphazard list of rituals in this mishnah is to recognize that each of the rituals corresponds to a topic treated at length in tractate Berakhot, in which the mishnah appears. For example, chapters 1–3 of the tractate present laws regarding recitation of the Shema. Correspondingly, the mishnah surveys women's obligations regarding rituals that derive from the Shema (Shema, tefillin, mezuzah). Likewise, chapters 4–5 of the tractate present laws regarding recitation of the Amidah and women's obligation to recite the Amidah is discussed in this mishnah. Finally, chapters 6–8 of the tractate present laws regarding meal practice. Correspondingly, women's obligation to recite the grace after meals is discussed in this mishnah. This mishnah, then, serves as a synopsis of women's obligations regarding the various topics treated in the tractate. For our purposes, the mishnah offers a nice summary of rabbinic views concerning women's involvement in Shema-derived rituals in the tannaitic period.

There is, however, one striking omission from this mishnah. If it does (among other things) provide a summary of women's involvement with Shema-derived rituals, then why is women's involvement with tzitzit not discussed? One possibility is that even though tzitzit is a Shema-derived ritual, it does not center on a text, as the other rituals do. Topically, tzitzit might be said to fall just outside the purview of this mishnah. Another possibility is that there was no consensus during the rabbinic period regarding women's involvement with tzitzit. By way of contrast, there is tannaitic consensus regarding women's involvement in each of the listed rituals.[20] If there is any merit to this explanation, then this mishnah is doubly interesting to us because it provides a summary of women's involvement in Shema-derived rituals *about which there was rabbinic consensus*. When R. Shimon used the rule to say that tzitzit was like tefillin or unlike mezuzah, he was using the "known" to understand the "unknown." In other words, he determined the law in a case where there was no consensus regarding women's involvement (tzitzit) from the cases where there was consensus regarding women's involvement (tefillin, Shema, mezuzah).

As noted in Chapter 6, the scholarly consensus is that the third paragraph of the Shema (which prescribes the ritual of tzitzit) was added to the liturgical cycle after the first two paragraphs had already crystallized as a liturgical unit.[21] As a result of the late (only in relative terms) inclusion of third paragraph, ritual observances related to the third paragraph were still contested in the tannaitic period. We are already familiar with the fact that R. Shimon and the sages disagreed about whether women should wear tzitzit. In addition, tannaitic sages disagreed about whether the third paragraph should be recited at night, as the first two paragraphs are. On the one hand, some sages assumed that the third paragraph was included as part of the liturgical cycle because it, like the first two paragraphs, refers to the covenantal relationship between Israel and God. (In this view, the reference to Exodus at the end of the third paragraph [Num 15:40–41] constitutes an allusion to the covenant.) Those who understood the third paragraph in this manner felt that it should be recited in the evening because the covenant and the Exodus from Egypt are as relevant at night as they are during the day.[22] A second school of thought saw the third paragraph as linked to the first two paragraphs by the fact that all three paragraphs prescribe concrete rituals by which one embodies one's

[20] Women's obligation vis-à-vis tefillin and Shema is additionally attested in Mek. Bo 17, ed. Horowitz-Rabin, 68, and MRSY, ed. Epstein-Melamed, 13:9, 41. Women's exemption from mezuzah is additionally attested in Mek. Bo 17, ed. Horowitz-Rabin, 68. Philo (*Spec. Laws* IV, 142) discusses mezuzah in a manner that stresses women's involvement in the ritual. Philo, therefore, provides another attestation that women were considered obligated regarding mezuzah at the time when the early rabbis were active.

[21] See Elbogen, *Jewish Liturgy: A Comprehensive History*, 23; Tabory, "Prayers and Berakhot," 291–92; and Cohen, *Philo Judaeus: His Universe of Discourse*, 108, 167–76.

[22] M. Ber. 1:5 learns this point from an intensive reading of scripture: Deut 16:3 states that "so that you may remember the day of your departure from Egypt *all* the days of your life." According to a midrash attributed to Ben Zoma, if the text had said during "the days of your life," we might have thought the third paragraph should be recited only during the day. The fact that scripture includes the word "all" and says "*all* the days of your life" implies that one should recite the third paragraph at night also.

Jewish commitments. In seeking to resolve the question of whether one should recite the third paragraph at night, these sages focused attention on the verses that describe the ritual of wearing tzitzit (Num 15:38–39). Because the verse states that one should "*look* at the fringes and recall all the commandments of the Lord," the sages from this school of thought determined that the third paragraph should only be recited during the daytime when the tzitzit can be seen.[23]

Underlying these two views are two different understandings of what the Shema is and what binds the three paragraphs together. As discussed in Chapter 6, the rabbis inherited two distinct ways of thinking about the Shema. While some focused on the Shema as an affirmation of doctrinal commitments, others focused on the cluster of practices prescribed by the Shema. The debate about whether the third paragraph should be recited at night illustrates that the sages were trying to determine how to observe practices deriving from the third paragraph based on their understanding of the first two paragraphs. Those who emphasized that the Shema was a doctrinal affirmation felt that the third paragraph should be recited at night because its doctrinal content was as relevant at night as during the day. Those who felt that the Shema was unified by the rituals it prescribes felt that the third paragraph should not be recited at night because its ritual is not practiced at night.

I argue that a similar process was at work in the debate between R. Shimon and the sages about tzitzit. In order to determine how to observe a practice associated with the third paragraph (tzitzit), the rabbis turned to what they already knew about practices from the first two paragraphs (tefillin, Shema, and mezuzah). The parties to the dispute disagreed, however, on where to find the precedent to tzitzit in the first two paragraphs. Where R. Shimon turned to timebound, positive commandments (i.e., tefillin and Shema), I speculate that the sages turned to the one Shema-derived ritual that was not a "timebound, positive commandment," namely, mezuzah.[24]

The Debate about Tzitzit

The debate between R. Shimon and the sages on the question of women's obligations regarding tzitzit is preserved in its fullest form in Sifre Numbers. The midrash there comments on the verses from which the obligation to attach fringes to the corners of one's garments is derived. Having cited only part of the debate earlier in this chapter, I now present the full discussion.

1. *And God spoke to Moses saying: Speak to the sons / children* (bnei) *of Israel and say to them that they should make for themselves fringes* (tzitzit) (Num 15:37–38). Women too are included in the meaning [of the verse].

[23] See m. Ber. 2:2.
[24] B. Kid 34a names mezuzah as a non-timebound commandment, though neither the Tosephta or Yerushalmi does. See discussion in n18.

2. R. Shimon exempts women from tzitzit because [of the principle of] timebound, positive commandments, from which women are exempt.

3. For this is the rule: R. Shimon said: All timebound, positive commandments apply to men and do not apply to women, [and apply to] those qualified [to give testimony (i.e., freemen)] and not to those disqualified [from giving testimony (i.e., slaves)[25]].

4. R. Yehudah b. Baba says: The sages exempted a woman's veil in particular from fringes and they only required [fringes for a woman's] cloak because sometimes her husband wraps himself with it [i.e., sometimes he wears it]. (Sif. Num. 115, ed. Horowitz, 124)

The midrash begins with an anonymous position (presumably the majority position of the sages) that states that women, like men, are obligated to wear ritual fringes on the corners of their garments (paragraph 1). The sages' position is offered as an interpretation of the biblical verse under consideration (Num 15:37–38). The biblical word *bnei* literally means "sons of," but the expression *bnei yisrael* ("sons of Israel") need not refer to only the male members of the nation. From a grammatical perspective, it is quite plausible that the expression (as used here and elsewhere) refers to the entire nation of Israel, including its female members. Here, as in many places throughout the Torah, scripture may be using grammatically male language to indicate subjects that are both male and female. The sages claim that scripture here has a more inclusive meaning, implying that women, like men, must wear tzitzit on their garments.

The fact that the sages' position is formulated here as exegesis does not, however, mean that it arose out of exegetical concerns exclusively. While there are certainly grammatical reasons to interpret the term *bnei yisrael* as the sages have, the tannaim are notoriously inconsistent in their resolution of the question that terms like *bnei yisrael* pose to the exegete. In some cases, tannaitic exegetes assume that the biblical term includes women.[26] In other cases, they assume that the biblical term excludes women.[27] While the basis for opening or closing the interpretation is sometimes apparent, many times it

---

[25] For this interpretation, see Ginzberg, *Commentary on the Palestinian Talmud*, 163n47.

[26] See, e.g., the interpretation of Lev 19:3 (obligation to fear parents) in Sifra Kedoshim, parshata 1:2–3. See also the interpretation of Lev 16:29 (obligation to fast on Yom Kippur) in Sifra Acharei Mot, Perek 7:9, in which the term *ha-ezrah* (the citizen) is interpreted as including women. The same term in Lev 23:41 is later interpreted by the Sifra to be excluding women. In its commentary on Exod 21:18, Mek. Mishpatim 6, ed. Horowitz-Rabin, 269 states the general principle that all of the Torah laws regarding civil damages apply to men and women equally.

[27] See, e.g., the interpretation of Exod 19:3 in the Mek. Yitro 2, ed. Horowitz-Rabin, 207, in which the term *bnei yisrael* is understood to indicate men only. See also the interpretation of Lev 23:41 (obligation to sit in a sukkah) in Sifra Emor, perek 17:9, in which the term *ha-ezrah* (the citizen) is understood to be excluding women. Note that the same term (as used in Lev 16:9) is seen by in Sifra Acharei Mot, Perek 7:9, as including women. See previous note.

is not.[28] Given the general inconsistency that exegesis of such terms displays, it is difficult to determine why the sages reach the conclusion that they do here. Were they heir to a halakhically framed position that women are obligated to wear tzitzit? Or did they have an exegetically driven reason to interpret this term as including women? In other words, does the exegesis come to support conclusions that have already been reached, or are the conclusions themselves the product of exegesis? The midrash preserves no trace of the process that led to the conclusion.

Notably, the sages' position is preserved elsewhere as a halakhic statement, though this fact alone does not prove that they derived their position on the basis of a halakhic principle.[29] T. Kid. 1:10 illustrates the rule as brought in the locus classicus (m. Kid. 1:7) by providing examples of both timebound and non-timebound, positive commandments. For current purposes, the section that lists the non-timebound commandments is most relevant.

1. What are [some] non-timebound, positive commandments?

2. For example, [returning a] lost [object or animal], sending [the mother bird from] the nest [before taking her eggs], [building] a parapet [for your roof], and tzitzit.

3. R. Shimon exempts women from tzitzit because [they are] a timebound, positive commandment. (t. Kid. 1:10)

T. Kid. 1:10 includes tzizit in the sages' list of non-timebound, positive commandments (which women are, of course, obligated to perform). R. Shimon disagrees with the sages and regards tzizit as a timebound commandment (from which women are exempt). Here it appears that the sages base their

---

[28] For example, the exegetical basis is clear in the interpretation of Lev 19:3 (obligation to fear parents) in Sifra Kedoshim, parshata 1:2–3. The exegetical basis is unclear in the interpretation of Lev 16:9 and 23:41, where opposing conclusions are reached regarding the same term *ha-ezrah* (the citizen). See Sifra Emor, perek 17:9, and Sifra Acharei Mot, Perek 7:9, discussed in the two previous notes. For attempts to find order within chaos, see Michael Chernick, "'Ish' as Man and Adult in the Halakic Midrashim," *The Jewish Quarterly Review* 73/3 (January 1983): 254–80; Tal Ilan, "'Daughters of Israel, Weep for Rabbi Ishmael': The Schools Rabbi Akiva and Rabbi Ishmael on Women," *Nashim* 4 (2001): 15–34. For the view that no patterns are evident in the exegesis, see Shaye J. D. Cohen, *Why Aren't Jewish Women Circumcised? Gender and Covenant in Judaism*, 122–24. Cohen writes that the texts leave "the distinct impression that the exegete knows in advance exactly what [halakhic] conclusion needs to be reached, even if some modern scholars have tried hard to prove that legitimate and real exegetical activity is taking place" (122).

[29] Melamed, Epstein, and Porton discuss the fact that many traditions are preserved as both exegetical traditions and halakhically stated norms. Epstein and Melamed argue for the priority of the traditions as halakhic norms. See J. N. Epstein, *Introduction to Tannaitic Literature: Mishnah Tosephta and Halakhic Midrashim* (Hebrew), ed. E. Z. Melamed (Jerusalem: Magnus Press, 1957), 511–15; Ezra Zion Melamed, *The Relationship between the Halakhic Midrashim and the Mishnah and Tosephta* (Jerusalem, 1966). Porton cites several examples of midrashic–mishnaic parallels to note that the phenomenon exists, but without weighing in on the question of which version of tradition is earlier. See Gary G. Porton, *Understanding Rabbinic Midrash: Texts and Commentary*, vol. 5 (Hoboken: Ktav, 1985), 6–8.

ruling on their characterization of tzitzit as non-timebound. In this regard, the Tosephta presents the sages' view as if is based on a halakhic principle.

Jay Rovner has observed that the list of non-timebound commandments provided by t. Kid. 1:10 is arranged according to the order in which the commandments are discussed in Deut 22:1–12.[30] Deut 22:1–4 requires one to return the animal of one's neighbor when it has gone astray. Correspondingly, the first item in the list of non-timebound commandments is "[returning] lost items" (*'avedah*). Deut 22:6–7 requires one to send a mother bird away before taking eggs from her nest. Correspondingly, the second item on the list is "sending [the mother] from the nest" (*shiluah haken*). Deut 22:8 requires one to build a parapet for one's roof when building a new home. Correspondingly, the third item on the list is "the parapet." Finally, Deut 22:12 requires one to place tassels (*gedilim*) on the four corners of one's garment. Correspondingly, the final item on the tosephtan list is tzitzit.

Why did the Tosephta turn to this passage from Deuteronomy to construct its list of non-timebound commandments? It is interesting to consider the possibility that the sages turned to this passage because it includes a reference to tzitzit, though it notably uses a different term (*gedilim*) to describe the practice. The fact that the sages and R. Shimon were arguing about whether tzitzit are timebound may have provided the occasion for the sages to articulate the position that tzitzit are non-timebound. The idea that a category of non-timebound commandments exists may have, in fact, been first articulated in the context of the debate about tzitzit. When the time came to fill out the list of non-timebound commandments, the sages turned to a passage that included a reference to tzitzit (albeit using a different technical term for the practice). According to this reconstruction, at the heart of t. Kid. 1:10 lies the sages' invocation of a halakhic principle to exempt women from tzitzit. They exempted women from tzitzit because they considered tzitzit to be a non-timebound commandment. Though we cannot be certain, then, the evidence leans slightly more heavily toward the conclusion that the sages obligated women to tzitzit not because of exegetical considerations, but because they were guided by their commitment to the halakhic principle that tzitzit are not timebound.

In contrast to the sages, in both the midrash and the Tosephta, R. Shimon makes evident that his ruling is guided by a halakhic principle.[31] He rules that women are exempt from wearing tzitzit on account of the rule that women are

---

[30] See Rovner, "Rhetorical Strategy and Dialectical Necessity in the Babylonian Talmud: The Case of Kiddushin 34a–35a," 191–92.

[31] The midrash represents the sages as if they derived their position through exegesis, and it represents R. Shimon as if he derived his from a halakhic principle. From the disparity between how the midrash presents the respective positions of the sages and R. Shimon, Ginzberg concludes that the sages and R. Shimon approached the question of women's involvement in ritual with different methods. According to Ginzberg, R. Shimon determined all cases of women's ritual involvement using the principle, while the sages determined them on an ad hoc basis using scriptural exegesis. See Ginzberg, *Commentary on the Palestinian Talmud*, 160–64.

exempt from timebound, positive commandments. What ideas about gender were implicit in his use of the rule?

I have been arguing that when R. Shimon invoked the rule he was saying that the tzitzit have more in common with the timebound Shema-derived commandments than with the non-timebound ones. For R. Shimon, tzitzit are a ritual that inscribes covenantal identity on the animated body in much the same manner that tefillin do. There are differences between the two rituals, of course. Unlike tefillin and the Shema, tzitzit does not employ scripture directly in the ritual. By likening tzitzit to tefillin, R. Shimon was saying that tzitzit function *as if* the ritual involves scripture. As argued in Chapter 6, women are exempt from tefillin and Shema because they are regarded as forms of Torah study in that they incorporate scripture into and onto the self in a manner similar to Torah study. In Chapter 7 I argued that women are exempt from ritual Torah study because it is a means for the (male) *pater familias* to ensure the survival of his social and covenantal identity in the next generation. Because daughters cannot replicate their father's social identity, Torah study as ritual is simply not relevant for them. When R. Shimon said that women are exempt from tzitzit because "they are a timebound, positive commandment," I believe that he was saying that though tzitzit do not literally incorporate scripture into the self, they function like tefillin to buttress the covenantal identity of the (male) citizen of Israel. When a man wears tzitzit, it is *as if* he incorporates scripture into the self because he (like one who wears tefillin, recites Shema, and studies Torah) embodies enduring covenantal commitments.

It is impossible to know with any certainty why the sages disagreed with R. Shimon and felt that women should be required to wear tzitzit. As stated above, it is possible that exegetical concerns for which we have no evidence drove their interpretation. Another possibility is that the sages, like R. Shimon, turned to the Shema-derived rituals about which there was already clarity in order to resolve the unclear case of tzitzit. Just as R. Shimon had a compelling reason to regard tzitzit like tefillin and Shema (the timebound Shema-derived commandments), we can speculate that the sages felt that there were compelling reasons to regard tzitzit like mezuzah. There is a vague comparability between the two rituals. Like mezuzah, tzitzit is a ritual object that decorates a space that people occupy. Mezuzah decorates the home. Tzitzit decorates the garment. The sages might have reasoned that just as women are obligated to dwell in a space that has been decorated with a mezuzah, women are obligated to be clothed by a garment that has been decorated with tzitzit. In this view, tzitzit is not a ritual that crafts a human being of a particular type (e.g., a *pater familias* whose covenantal identity endures beyond himself). Rather, tzitzit is a ritual that crafts the space (whether garment or home) into which the ritual actor steps.[32]

---

[32] The following source stresses the comparability between mezuzah and tzitzit as two rituals affixed to objects (home and garment) that encompass the Jew. "Precious is Israel, for Scripture

One way to understand the debate about women's involvement with tzitzit is to imagine that it turned on the question of which Shema-derived ritual tzitzit was most like. When R. Shimon invoked the principle of women's exemption from timebound, positive commandments, I believe that he was suggesting that even though tzitzit do not involve the incorporation of scripture onto the body of the ritual actor, they are like tefillin, where there was already clarity about the extent of women's involvement. For the sages, mezuzah was a more compelling analogue to tzitzit than tefillin. About mezuzah also, there was clarity regarding the ritual's relevance for women. We stand to gain insight into the sages' understanding of women's ritual observance of tzitzit by reflecting on the consensus view that women are obligated in mezuzah.

Women's Obligation regarding Mezuzah

Philo provides an interesting precedent to the rabbinic obligation of women, slaves, and minors in mezuzah. In his discussion of Shema-derived rituals, Philo observes that mezuzah has a broad applicability, being relevant for both Jews and gentiles, men and women, freemen and servants,[33] and adults and children. Understanding Philo's reasons for viewing mezuzah as relevant to a broad range of types may help us understand why the rabbis similarly saw mezuzah as relevant to a broad range of types. Philo discusses the ritual observance of mezuzah in a passage quoted at length in Chapter 6. Here I present his discussion of mezuzah in full.

[Moses] also bids [the people of Israel] write and set [the principles of justice] forth in front of the doorposts of each house and the gates in their walls, so that those who leave or remain at home, **citizens and strangers alike**, may read the inscriptions engraved on the face of the gates and keep in perpetual memory what they should say and do, when they enter their house and again when they go forth, **men and women and children and**

---

encompassed them with commandments: tefillin on their heads and tefillin on their arms, mezuzah at their doors and tzitzit on their garments" (Sif. Dt. 36, ed. Finkelstein, 67–68). See also t. Ber. 6:25. This source envisions the Jew whose body is surrounded by both home and clothes as a male Jew, as it goes on to specify that even when the Jew is naked in the bathhouse, his body is marked by his circumcision. Thus even when naked of the outermost conventions of socialization (home and clothes), he stills remains encompassed by commandments. This source imagines that mezuzah and tzitzit are both ritual objects that decorate the spaces that male Israel inhabits. I am suggesting that the sages who obligated women in tzitzit observed a comparability between mezuzah and tzitzit consisting of the feature of encompassing that is featured in this source, but they stressed the fact that the spaces that these ritual objects decorate are inhabited by *all* Israel (male and female).

33 The Greek term that Philo uses is *therapeia*. According to Liddell and Scott, this term implies less harsh servitude than *doulos* (slave); see *A Lexicon Abridged from Liddell and Scott's Greek-English Lexicon* (Oxford: Clarendon Press, 1990), 315. The Hebrew term *'eved* can encompass both terms within its range. Philo may be seen here as discussing the relevance of mezuzah for what in Hebrew would be called an *'eved*.

servants alike may act as is due and fitting both for others and for themselves. (Philo, *Spec. Laws* IV, 142)[34]

In Chapter 6, I noted that Philo sees each of the Shema-derived rituals as a means of instilling principles of justice (*ta dikaia*) in the practitioner. Tefillin, for example, place the principles of justice on the arm and before the eyes. Likewise, when fulfilling the requirement to study Torah, the master teaches the principles of justice to young men, friends, and family. Finally, the mezuzah places the principles of justice on doorposts and gates where all who pass can see and internalize them. One interesting feature of Philo's discussion of mezuzah is that he assumes that the ritual has relevance for a broad range of types: Citizens and strangers, men and women, adults and children, freemen and servants all view and are affected by the mezuzah. What is it about mezuzah that warrants this broad applicability?

First, it is important to note that Philo does not emphasize the ritual activity of affixing a mezuzah to the threshold of one's home. For Philo, one has a ritually significant interaction with the mezuzah when one *observes* it *in situ*. Seeing the mezuzah, not affixing it, is what is ritually significant. A second thing to comment upon is that Philo envisions people encountering the mezuzah both when they enter the house *and when they go forth again*. Philo here offers an interpretation of the Shema's instruction to keep "these words" in mind both "when you are at home and *when you go on your way*." Philo's mezuzah offers individuals a concrete mechanism to take the "principles of justice" with them when they are abroad.

Even though the mezuzah is located on the threshold of the house, it operates as a Roman public monument might have. Arthur J. Dewey discusses Roman public monuments that display images and text that cannot literally "be read," but which nonetheless form and inspire the viewing public.[35] Dewey's discussion focuses on Trajan's Column, which depicts Trajan's two victorious military campaigns in the Dacian Wars (c. 101–106 CE) as a continuous frieze that starts at the base of the column and spirals around the shaft until it reaches the top:

It has often been pointed out, that given the location of the column [between two libraries and behind Basilica Ulpia, which bordered the new Forum Traiani], there was no true opportunity for the viewer to walk around the column and see every scene in order. Although one could have seen the column from the flanking libraries, it does not seem that, until the modern age, the column could be viewed in its entirety. But attempts to gain a "literal" reading of the column may well miss the intended rhetorical effect. Viewers would have been impressed with the unrolling campaigns.... The initial impression would invite the viewer to become caught up in the momentum of

---

[34] Text cited with slight emendations from Colson, *Philo*, 97.

[35] See Arthur J. Dewey, "The Gospel of Trajan," in *Jesus, the Voice, and the Text: Beyond the Oral and Written Gospel*, ed. Tom Thatcher (Waco: Baylor University Press, 2008), 182–92.

victory.... The erection of Trajan's Column [was] a propaganda piece intended to be noticed and "read" by the public.[36]

When the public viewed the column, they were awed by the accomplishments of the august Trajan. The events inscribed on its face became stories that ordinary citizens could retell and claim as their own.

Dewey's discussion of Trajan's Column helps us imagine how Philo envisioned the mezuzah affecting those who passed by. The column was a large, imposing structure in the city's centrally located Forum. Philo's mezuzah was undoubtedly an inscription on a different scale, and it was not centrally located like the column, but it likewise displayed an inscription with the explicit purpose of forming and inspiring the viewing public when they encountered it. Philo does not appear to be familiar with the mezuzah in the form in which the rabbis later practiced it: as a scroll affixed in a casing. In Philo, the words themselves are "engraved on the face of the gates," adding to their monumental stature.[37] Charlotte Fonrobert characterizes the rabbinic mezuzah as a discrete marker of Jewish space that would have been perceptible only to those who knew that it was there.[38] Philo's mezuzah is imagined quite differently. It is visibly accessible to all and likewise has relevance for all.[39] It works to instill the principles of justice that serve the good of *society at large*.[40] In Philo, the mezuzah has relevance for a broad range of types because all are implicated in the ideal society that resides in the public domain. The mezuzah galvanizes the diversity of individuals who cross the threshold into public space and forms

---

[36] Arthur J. Dewey, "The Gospel of Trajan," 187–88.

[37] An inscribed door lintel from Palmyra (third century CE) provides a suggestive example of what such an inscription might have looked like. See R. J. P. Jean-Baptiste Frey, *Corpus Inscriptionum Iudaicarum*, vol. 2: *Asie-Afrique* (Rome: Pontificio Istituto di Archeologia Cristiana, 1952), 68–69.

[38] See Charlotte Fonrobert, "Neighborhood as Ritual Space: The Case of the Rabbinic Eruv," *Archiv Für Religionsgeschichte* 10 (2008): 257.

[39] Ellen Birnbaum discusses the role that vision plays in the universalizing of Jewish ideals in Philo. Wisdom that is accessed visually is generally available to both Jews and gentiles. See Ellen Birnbaum, *The Place of Judaism in Philo's Thought: Israel, Jews, and Proselytes* (Atlanta: Scholars Press, 1996).

[40] In an electronic communication (November 4, 2010), Gregory Schmidt Goering writes that seeing mezuzot in Proverbs has much in common with Philo's description of mezuzah practice. As in Philo, vision and mezuzah are integral to the acquistion of a universal Wisdom. In Proverbs, Wisdom personified proclaims, "Happy is the person who listens to me, keeping watch at my doors day after day, observing (at) the *mezuzot* (doorposts) of my gates" (Prov. 8:34). Unlike in Philo, here one does not *look at* the mezuzah. Rather, the mezuzot (in their literal meaning as "doorposts") are *where* one finds Wisdom. As in Philo, the Wisdom acquired at the doorposts is acquired by vision; there one is instructed to "keep watch" and "observe." Also as in Philo, Wisdom that is accessed visually is accessible to Jews and non-Jews in the same measure. As Goering writes, "The mezuzot of Wisdom's doorway have a public nature that potentially all can see. The mezuzot are where one who desires wisdom will keep vigil."

them into Philo's vision of an ideal society. The mezuzah as a ritual object constructs the threshold between the home and the street as a public thoroughfare undergirded by universal Jewish ideals.

The broad constituency that the rabbis envisioned interacting with the mezuzah may have engaged in a similar process. For the rabbis, on the other hand, the mezuzah constructs a different kind of space. Equally located on the threshold, the rabbinic mezuzah emphasizes not the public side of the interface, but the domestic and exclusively Jewish side. We might speculate that the rabbis implicate women, slaves, and minors in the observance of mezuzah because they (women, slaves, and minors) reflect the fullness of the Jewish household. In Philo, the mezuzah makes the threshold a public thoroughfare when it is viewed by a broad range of individuals. By way of contrast, for the rabbis, the mezuzah makes the threshold a boundary that helps contain and define the Jewish domicile.[41] For both Philo and the rabbis, the mezuzah forms what stands just over the threshold into a *social space*. Located on the boundary between public thoroughfare and private domicile, the mezuzah utilizes those who use and traverse the space to transform it into a particular type of social space. In Philo, the broad public interacts with the mezuzah as they would with a public monument. This activity transforms the space just beyond the

---

[41] Rabbinic sources emphasize the location of the mezuzah on the boundary: "Israel is precious as scripture encompassed them with commandments: . . . mezuzah at their openings (*mezuzah b'pitkheihem*)." See Sif. Dt. 36, ed. Finkelstein, 67–68; and t. Ber. 6:25. Fonrobert discusses similarities in how the mezuzah and eruv function in the creation of Jewish space. Both rituals involve a marker at the boundary that spatially differentiates the "Jewish" space from public, civic space. Fonrobert emphasizes that an additional activity is required in order for the eruv to construct the courtyard/neighborhood as a Jewish space. The space within the eruv is unified when the residents place an (albeit unconsumed) shared meal in one of the homes within the courtyard. See Fonrobert, "Neighborhood as Ritual Space." One might speculate that the mezuzah likewise helps constitute domestic space as "Jewish" on the basis of a unifying activity that takes place within the confines of the home. I would argue that it is participation in the social, economic, and religious affairs of a Jewish household that grants social significance – as being Jewish – to a domicile that has been marked at the boundary by a mezuzah. After all, a mezuzah need only be placed on domiciles where Jews live. The halakhic rules regarding the placement of a mezuzah help us see the extent to which the idea that "Jews live in a space" comes only in the aftermath of adherence to socially conceived norms. For example, a sukkah is not considered a domicile and therefore does not require a mezuzah (t. Eruv. 5:5) even though (male) Jews are required to "reside" in it during Sukkot. T. Yoma 1:2 makes this principle explicit: "Only houses which are [used] for living require [a mezuah]. Houses which are not [used] for living do not require [a mezuah]." Various chambers in the Temple (*beit hamikash*) do not require a mezuzah on the basis of this principle. Only the councillor's chamber in which the High Priest dwelled for the seven days preceding Yom Kippur required a mezuzah. One sees here the role that agreed-upon norms play in the construct of a "domicile." Whereas temporary residence in the sukkah does *not* constitute a domicile, temporary residence in the councillor's chamber does. The one instance is different from the other only because of a socially determined sensibility. See also b. Men. 44a on the fact that one needs to be living in a rented home for thirty days in order for requirement for mezuzah to kick in. Again, "living" is defined by agreed-upon social conventions.

threshold into a public thoroughfare. For the rabbis, various members of the household interact with the mezuzah. The very fact of their living in the space is what requires the mezuzah to be affixed. For the rabbis, space requires a mezuzah when Jews *live in it*.[42] Women, slaves, and minors are obligated in the observance of mezuzah because by participating in the social, economic, and religious activities of the household, they help constitute the Jewish home.[43]

Returning to the Fringes Debates

Understanding the rabbinic basis for obligating women in mezuzah puts into sharper relief what was at stake for the sages who modeled women's involvement with tzitzit on their involvement with mezuzah. The sages crafted an analogy between tzitzit and mezuzah. Like R. Shimon's analogy between tzitzit and tefillin, the analogy between tzitzit and mezuzah has strengths and weaknesses. On one hand, tzitzit is similar to mezuzah in that the ritual performance is passive. Though one must be active when affixing the mezuzah to the doorpost or the tzitzit to the garment, the point of the ritual is to dwell in a home that is graced with a mezuzah or to wear a garment that is adorned with tzitzit.[44] The ritual actor enters into a domain (home or garment) and encounters the ritual object (mezuzah or tzitzit) where it is affixed in space. If one can be said to "perform" these rituals (mezuzah and tzitzit) at all, it is only to the

---

[42] See sources discussed in the previous note about which kinds of "living" require a mezuzah. "Living" in a space is not the mere fact of sleeping, eating, working, and socializing there. Only when one sleeps, eats, works, and socializes according to agreed-upon conventions do those activities constitute "living." The stipulation that any domicile in which women, slaves, and children reside requires a mezuzah implies that their presence in a household meets the minimum requirement of "Jewish living" – even if there is no free, adult male living in the house.

[43] Cynthia Baker also stresses the constructed character of rabbinic domestic space. Archaeological findings show that there were no clear boundaries between public and private space in Roman Palestine, even though the rabbis write as if there were. See Cynthia Baker, *Rebuilding the House of Israel: Architectures of Gender* (Stanford: Stanford University Press, 2002). Baker's arguments are relevant to this discussion because in the one instance in which a mezuzah niche was found *in situ* at an archaeological site, it is located on the inside of the house once the door is closed. The presence of an extensive courtyard where domestic tasks took place suggests that the boundary between public and private could theoretically be postulated to lie at the entrance to the courtyard. See Yizhar Hirschfeld, *The Palestinian Dwelling in the Roman-Byzantine Period*, no. 34 (Jerusalem: Franciscan Printing Press; Israel Exploration Society, 1995), 250–52. Even though this mezuzah was not located at the boundary between public and private space, rabbinic tradition imagined such a mezuzah as signaling the transition from civic to domestic space.

[44] The Bavli implicitly indicates this understanding about tzitzit when it cites the fact that Rav Avram the Pious and Rav Yehudah attached tzitzit to the aprons of the women of their households. The Bavli cites the actions of these two rabbis to illustrate the position that women are obligated in tzitzit. If the main ritual observance consisted of attaching the tzitzit, then this anecdotal evidence would prove exactly the opposite because a *man*, not a woman, attaches the tzitzit to the aprons. See b. Suk. 11a; and b. Men. 43a.

extent that one enters a space where the appropriate objects have already been affixed. On the basis of these parallels, it makes sense to determine women's involvement with tzitzit on the basis of their involvement with mezuzah. On the other hand, we also see important differences between the two rituals. Women are obligated in mezuzah because they are essential participants in the social fabric of the household. The space adorned by a mezuzah is fundamentally a social space. A garment, on the other hand, is worn by only one individual at a time. There is no shared sociality in the space demarcated by the confines of a garment (though, of course, the conventions of what and how people wear clothes are highly socially determined). In light of this consideration, the analogy between tzitzit and mezuzah falters somewhat.

Attention to this problem may have been what motivated R. Yehudah b. Baba to refigure the sages' position. After the debate between R. Shimon and the sages is presented in the midrash, R. Yehudah b. Baba qualifies the sages' blanket obligation of women in tzitzit.

4. R. Yehudah b. Baba says: The sages exempted a woman's veil in particular from fringes and they only required [fringes for a woman's] cloak because sometimes her husband wraps himself with it [i.e., sometimes he wears it]. (Sif. Num. 115, ed. Horowitz, 124)

According to R. Yehudah b. Baba, the sages did not mean to obligate women to wear tzitzit when wearing exclusively feminine clothing (e.g., the veil). Only when wearing clothing that can be inhabited by both men and women (e.g., a gender-neutral outer cloak) are women obligated to wear tzitzit. R. Yehudah b. Baba's interpretation of the sages highlights the sociality of the space within the confines of the garment. Women become obligated in tzitzit only when the space adorned by them (i.e., the garment) can be occupied by more than one "resident." For Yehudah b. Baba, only when a garment is worn by both men and women does its sociality emerge. Only then is the analogy to mezuzah – and the obligation of women – relevant. The effect of R. Yehudah b. Baba's interpretation is to limit the cases in which women are required to wear tzitzit. Undoubtedly, he was motivated by an androcentric and/or patriarchal sensibility. The participation of men in the life of the clothes is what triggers the requirement for tzitzit. Nonetheless, it is interesting to consider the fact that his interpretation highlights the comparability between tzitzit and mezuzah.

Conclusion

My goal in this chapter was to shed light on the ideas about gender that informed R. Shimon's invocation of the rule to exempt women from tzitzit. I have argued that R. Shimon's use of the rule was informed by his intuition that tzitzit are comparable to tefillin. Though tzitzit do not physically incorporate scripture onto the self as tefillin do, R. Shimon's use of the rule suggests an analogy. R. Shimon stresses that like tefillin, tzitzit are a Shema-derived ritual by which one marks one's Jewish commitments on one's body. Like tefillin, Shema, and Torah study, tzitzit are seen as a means of perpetuating the social and covenantal identities of the (male) *pater familias*. Since a daughter can never reproduce her father's social identity, rituals that aim to reproduce his covenantal identity are deemed irrelevant for women. Since tzitzit are seen as ritually accomplishing the same thing as tefillin, Shema, and Torah study, R. Shimon determines that the observance of tzitzit is irrelevant for women. They are all Shema-derived rituals performed by an animated ritual actor moving through time.

In addition, I have also speculated about the sages' reasons for obligating women in tzitzit. We cannot know with certainty why the sages ruled as they did. Were their conclusions exegetically driven (as represented in the midrash), or were they guided by a commitment to a halakhic principle (as represented in the Tosephta)? Since the midrash leaves us few clues about the exegetical basis for their views, I have tried to reconstruct what it might have meant for them to claim that tzitzit are a non-timebound, positive commandment. I have suggested that the sages obligated women in tzitzit because of a perceived analogy between tzitzit and mezuzah. Just as one enters the domain of the household, and the mezuzah affixed to the threshold becomes ritually relevant – so too one "enters" the domain of the garment, and the tzitzit affixed to the corners become ritually relevant. Just as women are obligated to live in a house with a mezuzah, so too are they obligated to wear garments adorned with tzitzit. The sages may have seen tzitzit, like mezuzah, as a Shema-derived ritual whose observance is occasioned by its location in space. Though I cannot be certain that my readings reflect the "original" meaning of the legal rulings of R. Shimon and the sages, my hope is that they help readers see the texts discussed in new ways. If nothing else, my readings demonstrate one possible way to imagine the rule in light of the evidence presented in the body of this book.

Epilogue

In the Introduction, I noted that the subject of this book (gender and the rule exempting women from timebound, positive commandments) was conceived in light of the rule's prominent place in cultural debates over the appropriate roles for women in contemporary Judaism. In this final reflective essay, I would like to return to the cultural debates that first occasioned my interest in time-bound, positive commandments and consider how my research might impact discussions in that arena.

As noted in the Introduction, the rule received attention from Jewish feminists in the 1970s because it was seen to be emblematic of Judaism's patriarchal character. Popular understandings of the rule (in both traditional and feminist circles) had their roots in the medieval interpretations that first reflected on the reasons for women's exemption. Jewish feminist discussion of the rule focused on the two explanations that had strong currency in traditional circles. One explanation posited that women are exempt from timebound, positive commandments in order to accommodate the pressing demands that women already bear in the care of the home and young children.[1] The second explanation suggested that women are exempt on account of their heightened spiritual capacities, which do not require the discipline of timebound commandments to form a meaningful relationship with God.[2] Feminists dismissed the second explanation of the rule as apologetics to make women feel better about their more limited religious involvement.[3] The first explanation of the rule was subject to strong critique because it linked women's performance of piety to their

---

[1] This interpretation is discussed by Berman, "The Status of Women in Halakhic Judaism," esp. 121–22. See also Meiselman, "The Jewish Woman in Jewish Law," 43.

[2] See Hirsch, *The Pentateuch*, vol. 3: *(Leviticus Pt. II)*, 712; and Meiselman, "The Jewish Woman in Jewish Law," 43–44.

[3] See Adler, "The Jew Who Wasn't There," 348–50.

work as caretakers of children and domestic laborers.[4] Reflecting on the rule, feminists observed that its prescriptions limited the religious horizons of Jewish women in much the same manner that secular cultural norms limited the educational, professional, and economic self-realization of women. The rule (as did the social norms of the 1950s and early 1960s) defines women as mothers and homemakers, disregarding their human potential in other, notably more public, spheres.

In the body of this book, however, I have argued that the traditional explanations of the rule do not provide an accurate account of how the rule supported the construction of gender when it was first formulated and transmitted. Suggesting that the issue of time is a red herring, I directed our attention toward the rabbinic exemption of women from rituals derived from the Shema verses (tefillin, Shema, Torah study, and tzitzit). I argued that we learn more about the rule's role in structuring gender when we focus on women's exemption from a discrete *subset* of timebound, positive commandments than when we focus on women's exemptions from the category *as a whole*. Recalling that the category of timebound, positive commandments was initially formulated as part of a discussion on tefillin, in Chapter 6 I investigated the reasons for women's exemption from tefillin (and the related ritual of Shema). I concluded that the rabbis exempted women from both tefillin and Shema because they understood these rituals to be forms of Torah study. In Chapter 7, I explored the basis for women's exemption from Torah study, discovering that the kind of study from which they are exempt is the kind that is intimately connected with the Shema verses and its themes. Women are exempt from Torah study that serves as a means of cultural reproduction. For the rabbis, male ritual Torah study facilitates the creation of an (albeit temporarily) perfected world in which fathers reproduce their social and covenantal identity in their sons. Since daughters cannot reproduce their father's (male) social identity (daughters will never be the *pater familias* of the next generation), rituals like Torah study, Shema, and tefillin are simply not relevant for them. The rabbis do feature women studying Torah to gain skills, perspective, or knowledge. For women, however, Torah study is a not a ritual act; it is merely instrumental.

In Chapter 8, I argued that women's exemption from timebound, positive commandments is an extension of their exemption from Torah study. The original category of timebound, positive commandments would have included Shema and tefillin. As forms of Torah study, these rituals enable the ritual actor to incorporate words of Torah into and onto his body. By extending the category of timebound, commandments to include tzitzit, R. Shimon indicated that he felt that the same could be accomplished through another ritual associated with the Shema: tzitzit. As ritual actions that mimic, stand in for, and enact certain aspects of Torah study, timebound, positive commandments

---

[4] See Adler, "The Jew Who Wasn't There"; and Blu Greenberg, *On Women and Judaism: A View from Tradition* (Philadelphia: Jewish Publication Society of America, 1981), 82–92.

enable (male) Israel to create and perpetuate itself as a covenantal community in relationship with God.

In the aftermath of this study, one question remains outstanding: How might these findings impact the way that Jewish feminists think about timebound, positive commandments? I recognize, of course, that an author has little control over how her work is received. Nonetheless, during the time I have been researching and writing this book, I have had much opportunity to reflect on this question, and it is these thoughts I would like now to share.

First, it must be stated unequivocally that this book is not the bearer of "good news" to feminists interested in finding resources in classic Jewish sources for contemporary Jewish womanhood. Undergirding the rule is an assumption that women are not central actors in the creation and perpetuation of the covenantal community. This idea is surely anathema to any movement devoted to crafting a Judaism in which women are fully implicated religious actors. Though this book may posit new reasons for women's exemption from timebound, positive commandments, the rule's fundamental "unfriendliness" to feminist interests does not change.

If anything, my findings may intensify the difficulties that feminists experience with the rule. The rule as recorded in the Mishnah is ambiguous about the extent of women's exclusion from timebound, positive commandments. Throughout this book, I have been careful to speak of women's "exemption" from this and that: "exemption" from reciting the Shema, "exemption" from tefillin, and "exemption" from timebound, positive commandments. Much energy has been expended parsing this little word "exempt." Does it mean that women are not required, but nonetheless *may* perform these rituals? For some, the idea that women can voluntarily take on these commandments takes the sting out of not requiring women's performance a priori. This reading, however, raises other questions: How much merit accrues from the *voluntary* performance of ritual? Also, if women may perform these commandments, should they say a sanctifying blessing when doing so? Such a blessing would raise the holiness of the act and augment its ritual significance. But what is the meaning or value of saying "Blessed are you God who *commanded* us to perform this act" when one is not commanded? Or perhaps "exemption" is a euphemistic code for prohibition? Perhaps exemption is a gentle way to communicate that women should not perform these rituals at all? This is not the place to take up a linguistic analysis of how the term "exempt" functions in rabbinic discourse.[5] Nor will I discuss the very interesting history of how the

---

[5] Neusner observes that the terms "exempt" and "liable" in mishnaic literature function as fixed phrases plugged into appropriate slots in the apodosis. Analysis proceeding from Neusner's observations would consider the implications of this pattern of usage for the present case. See Jacob Neusner, *Oral Tradition in Judaism: The Case of the Mishnah* (New York: Garland Publishing, 1987), 71–73. Hauptman cites a talmudic passage that suggests that some amoraim thought that the term "exempt" did not preclude women from voluntary performance. See Hauptman, *Rereading the Rabbis*, 233–34.

medieval rabbis dealt with this question.[6] What I can explain in this context is why – in the aftermath of this study – I believe that the rabbinic exemption implies exclusion.

I have argued that the rabbis exempted women from Torah study because Torah study was a way for fathers to reproduce their social and cultural identity in their sons. Though the language is a language of exemption, the logic is a logic of exclusion. Women have no place as either transmitters or receivers in this system of discipleship because the identity being reproduced is socially male.[7] When Torah study aims to reproduce male identity, creative efforts at parsing the word "exempt" do not change the fact that women's engagement in Torah study is ritually insignificant. Women's Torah study, as conceived in these sources, simply has no role in enabling Israel to inhabit, however temporarily, a world in which the generations are connected to one another and the covenantal community endures.

Furthermore, the force of this exclusion is not mitigated by the fact that R. Shimon, a lone individual among the tannaitic sages, used the rule to determine women's ritual involvement. Some feminists might see in the majority sages who – *unlike* R. Shimon – did *not* use the rule to exempt women from tzitzit, a repudiation of the views I have associated with the rule. They might conclude that since R. Shimon represents a minority position, *only he* exempted women from rituals that were conceived as central to the perpetuation, maintenance, and endurance of the covenantal community. To understand the dispute in this manner, however, is to miss the force of my interpretation. I have argued that R. Shimon's distinction lies *not* in his belief that women are exempt from those Shema-derived rituals that perpetuate and maintain the covenantal community. In fact, *all* of the sages agree with him on this point; women's exemption from Shema and tefillin is uncontested. Rather, R. Shimon's distinction lies in his desire to apply the exemption to an *additional* Shema-derived commandment (tzitzit). Though R. Shimon is prominently associated with the rule,[8] and though his position is represented as a minority view, his position *reflects and*

---

[6] Elisheva Baumgarten places the halakhic deliberations of the medieval rabbis in historical context. See Elisheva Baumgarten, *Mothers and Children: Jewish Family Life in Medieval Europe*, 88–89, 214nn141–44. For a discussion of these positions from a feminist perspective, see Biale, *Women and Jewish Law: An Exploration of Women's Issues in Halakhic Sources*, 41–43. For a discussion of these positions from a traditionalist perspective, see Meiselman, "The Jewish Woman in Jewish Law," 47–49; and Michael Kaufman, *The Woman in Jewish Law and Tradition* (Northvale: J. Aronson, 1993), 210–11.

[7] The exclusion of women as both transmitters and receivers is emphasized in b. Kid. 29b. See discussion of this passage in Elizabeth Shanks Alexander, "The Impact of Feminism on Rabbinic Studies: The Impossible Paradox of Reading Women into Rabbinic Literature," in *Jews and Gender: The Challenge to Hierarchy*, ed. Jonathan Frankel (New York: Oxford University Press, 2000), 107–8.

[8] Ginzberg, and Yalon following him, stress R. Shimon's connection with the rule. See Ginzberg, *Commentary on the Palestinian Talmud*, 160–61; and Yalon, "'Women Are Exempted from All Positive Ordinances That Are Bound Up with a Stated Time,'" 117–32.

extends widely held views about women's participation in rituals that perpetuate and maintain the covenantal community.

In sum, to the extent that the rule structures gender in Judaism, it does
so in a manner that is inimical to the contemporary Jewish feminist project.
This book, then, reveals a conflict between the tradition and the contemporary
feminist ethos. The existence of such a conflict is hardly news. It is important
to recognize, however, that the Jewish feminist movement was conceived with
a basic commitment to working *within* the confines of this conflict. Since the
earliest beginnings of the movement, Jewish feminists have faced the question of whether they have something to gain by abandoning the androcentric
and patriarchal heritage of Jewish tradition. The most influential Jewish feminists have made their calculations, and each has concluded independently that
Judaism is too integral to their identity to be discarded casually. They have
noted that identities are complex and woven together from many strands.[9]
The loss entailed in rejecting Judaism is simply too profound to offset the
gain experienced when one frees oneself entirely from its objectionable vision
of gendered identities. As one's sense of fealty to the tradition increases, the
conflict is sharpened.[10]

Feminist Approaches to the Jewish Past

Jewish feminist approaches to the Jewish past have been shaped by two basic
assumptions and commitments. First, as noted above, Jewish feminists recognize that their contemporary reshaping of Judaism is enriched by a meaningful
engagement with the Jewish past, as accessed through textual and material
sources. They have no illusions, however, that the role imagined for women in
canonical Jewish sources does not comport with contemporary feminist visions
for women's religious life. Consequently, their work seeks to recover and discover resources in the Jewish past that androcentric and patriarchal tradents
of tradition have ignored and/or marginalized. Embedded in this approach is
the second assumption that undergirds feminist work with the Jewish past.
Feminists have generally assumed that artifacts from the Jewish past are most
usable to the contemporary feminist project when they *directly* support the
religious self-realization of women as women. For example, upon discovering
that some talmudic sources support the possibility of women's Torah study,
Daniel Boyarin writes, "For many women it seems important to have a vital
connection with the historical, ancestral culture of their people.... Providing a

---

[9] See discussions in Plaskow, *Standing Again at Sinai: Judaism from a Feminist Perspective*, ix–
xiii, 94–95; Adler, *Engendering Judaism: An Inclusive Theology and Ethics*, 48–51; and Ross,
Expanding the Palace of Torah: Orthodoxy and Feminism, 176–78.

[10] Ross argues that Orthodox Jewish women, who experience "the highest degree of tension
between their current secular reality and their more immediate universe of religious discourse,"
are "the ideal agents" for change. Ross, *Expanding the Palace of Torah: Orthodoxy and
Feminism*, 163–64.

place for feminist women (and male fellow travelers) to retain a positive sense
of identity seems to me consequential and empowering for such people."[11]
Artifacts from the Jewish past that evince concern for issues that trouble feminists today are understood to hold great potential for the feminist project.
Feminists can turn to these relics from the Jewish past and find affirmation for
how they wish to live and who they wish to become.

Working with these assumptions, Jewish feminists have found a number of
ways to establish a meaningful connection with the Jewish past. One strategy
involves turning to textual and material sources preserved *outside* the traditional canon of sacred texts, as they often reflect more "feminist-friendly"
configurations of gender than can be found in the traditional canon. Feminist
scholar Bernadette Brooten, for example, observes that there is no material
evidence for a women's gallery in ancient Palestinian synagogues, despite the
fact that archaeologists have assumed the existence of women's galleries in
the ancient synagogue on the basis of their familiarity with later synagogue
architecture.[12] Brooten's scholarly works invite feminists to destabilize the
authority of contemporary traditional synagogues that do place women on the
spatial margins of the synagogue.[13] In a slightly different vein, Chava Weissler
focuses on early modern women's prayer practices that took place beyond the
purview of the (male) religious elite. In modern eastern Europe, women developed a set of liturgical practices in the Yiddish vernacular known as *tkhines* to
express religious strivings in arenas of life unique to female experience.[14] Learning of these practices offers contemporary women access to antecedent Jewish
religious practices that are shaped by women's religious needs and interests.
Finally, feminist scholars of rabbinic literature Tal Ilan and Judith Hauptman
have observed that more marginalized works of rabbinic literature envision
women in more multidimensional ways than do the more authoritative and
centrally studied Mishnah and Bavli.[15] Though it is as yet unclear how Jewish feminists will make use of Ilan's and Hauptman's findings, they affirm the

---

[11] Boyarin, *Carnal Israel: Reading Sex in Talmudic Culture*, 168n2.

[12] Bernadette Brooten, *Women Leaders in the Ancient Synagogue: Inscriptional Issues and Background Evidence* (Chico: Scholars Press, 1982).

[13] Plaskow draws on another of Brooten's archaeological discoveries in her efforts to fashion a
contemporary feminist Judaism. See Plaskow, *Standing Again at Sinai: Judaism from a Feminist
Perspective*, 44–46. Shaye Cohen argues that since these materials were not preserved in the
corpus of authoritative sources that have normative force for contemporary Judaism, they
are interesting from a historical perspective, but not in the framing of contemporary Jewish
community. See Shaye J. D. Cohen, "Women in the Syngagogue of Antiquity," *Conservative
Judaism* 34 (December 1980): 28–29.

[14] Chava Weissler, *Voices of the Matriarchs: Listening to the Prayers of Early Modern Jewish
Women* (Boston: Beacon Press, 1998).

[15] See Ilan, *Mine and Yours Are Hers*, 51–84; and a series of articles by Hauptman, in which
she argues that the Mishnah preserves more restrictive laws with regard to women than the
Tosephta: Judith Hauptman, "Increasingly Stricter Rulings in *Mishnah Gittin*" (Hebrew), in
Proceedings of the Tenth World Congress of Jewish Studies, Division C, Jewish Thought and

perception that canonical sources are less friendly to the feminist cause than are noncanonical sources. Extracanonical and material/archaeological sources appear to be especially useful to Jewish feminists who wish to identify within the Jewish past resources for contemporary feminist Jewish living.[16]

Another feminist strategy for maintaining a connection with the Jewish past involves reading canonical sources in new ways so as to discover within them echoes of (even if not overt commitments to) contemporary feminists ideals. Dealing mostly with biblical texts, Judith Plaskow, for example, proposes that we read biblical texts creatively in light of what feminist historians like the above-mentioned Bernadette Brooten reveal about women's spiritual lives in the biblical period. Plaskow explains that the Torah as it has reached us records only *part* of the Jewish people's spiritual strivings – that of men. In order to offset the lopsided record of spiritual strivings that the canonical texts preserve, feminists must tell stories about the spiritual journeys of their female ancestors, even if they sometimes have to use their imagination to reconstruct them.[17]

Other feminist scholars find that it is not necessary to reimagine the past creatively in order to hear voices in the traditional canon that affirm contemporary feminist ideals. When read properly, canonical sources reveal themselves to be more complex than an initial read might suggest. Judith Hauptman, for example, shows that the rabbis introduced legal mechanisms that bettered women's lives. Though rabbinic society was undoubtedly patriarchal, the rabbis were involved in a project similar to that of contemporary feminists. Hauptman argues that the rabbis sought to affirm women's personhood and protect their legal rights.[18] Daniel Boyarin employs yet another strategy to re-mediate rabbinic texts. He observes that the views that discourage women's Torah study vied in antiquity with other views that saw value in women's Torah study. Though the view that is problematic, from a feminist point of view, emerged

---

Literature (Jerusalem, 1990), 23–30; Judith Hauptman, "Maternal Dissent: Women and Procreation in the *Mishnah*," *Tikkun* 6/6 (1991): 81–82, 94–95; Judith Hauptman, "Pesach: A Liberating Experience for Women," *Masoret* (Winter 1993): 8–9; Judith Hauptman, "Women's Voluntary Performance of Commandments from Which They Are Exempt" (Hebrew), in *Proceedings of the Eleventh World Congress of Jewish Studies, Division C, Jewish Thought and Literature* (Jerusalem, 1994), 161–68; and Judith Hauptman, "Women and Inheritance in Rabbinic Texts," in *Introducing Tosefta*, ed. Harry Fox and Tirzah Meacham (Hoboken: Ktav, 1999), 221–40.

[16] Plaskow discusses the value of extracanonical and archaeological sources for the feminist project. Plaskow, *Standing Again at Sinai: Judaism from a Feminist Perspective*, 36–52.

[17] See her discussion of feminist midrash that builds on feminist historiography: Plaskow, *Standing Again at Sinai: Judaism from a Feminist Perspective*, 36–56. Other examples of feminist midrash include Vanessa L. Ochs, *Sarah Laughed: Modern Lessons from the Wisdom and Stories of Biblical Women* (New York: McGraw-Hill, 2005); and Anita Diamant, *The Red Tent* (New York: St. Martin's Press, 2005). A Christian model for such reconstructive feminist interpretation can be found in Elisabeth Schüssler Fiorenza, *But She Said: Feminist Practices of Biblical Interpretation* (Boston: Beacon Press, 1992).

[18] See Hauptman, *Rereading the Rabbis*.

victorious in the end, Boyarin shows the cultural energy that was expended to suppress the protofeminist view. The difficulty posed by the patriarchal character of rabbinic culture is mitigated by showing that some ancient rabbis had sensibilities that are compatible with contemporary feminist ideals.[19]

Using admittedly different strategies – (1) focusing on noncanonical sources and (2) reading canonical sources in nontraditional ways – these feminists and scholars find a way to feel better about turning to the Jewish past as a resource for contemporary feminist living. As already noted, their strategies of maintaining connection with earlier generations of Jews and the sacred canon are predicated *on identifying within the tradition religious impulses that prefigure contemporary feminism.* Working with this assumption, however, precludes the possibility of feminist embrace of many Jewish sources. Miriam Peskowitz, for example, designed her study of ancient Jewish gender with a focus on archaeological sources with the hope that she would find resources for contemporary feminist living. She writes that she "began [her] project hoping to 'find women,' and the spindle [as an artifact of women's lives] seemed a good place to start."[20] But she did not find what she hoped she would: "The spindle was used to commemorate women and compliment women. [But] it also constrained them."[21] Peskowitz finds little reason to celebrate her findings, and she eventually recognizes her historic quest as flawed: "The nostalgic desire to find oneself in history – and to find friends among history's women – can be challenged."[22] She eventually recognizes that there is no past to which she wishes to return.[23]

If maintaining a connection with the Jewish past is predicated upon sharing an ideological profile regarding issues of feminist concern, *there will be much in the Jewish past with which contemporary feminists are unable to connect.* This book's findings, as stressed earlier in the Epilogue, do not reflect, prefigure, or echo contemporary feminist commitments. Nonetheless, I believe that feminists have not yet exhausted the possibilities for maintaining a connection with traditional sources *even when they (the sources) say things about gender that they (the feminists) find problematic.* In the second half of this essay, I would like to consider two strategies of maintaining a connection with the Jewish past that do not require feminists to disavow their contemporary commitments, even while they do not ask the past to be something other than

---

[19] Boyarin, *Carnal Israel: Reading Sex in Talmudic Culture,* 167–96.

[20] Peskowitz, *Spinning Fantasies,* 166–67.

[21] Peskowitz, *Spinning Fantasies,* 169.

[22] Peskowitz, *Spinning Fantasies,* 169.

[23] Judith Baskin expresses a similar sentiment when she writes that "the consequences of the general construction of women expressed in these texts have been long lasting and often pernicious in stifling female intellectual, spiritual, and social possibilities. The manifold changes in women's status in Judaism and in the larger world at the beginning of the twenty-first century offer strong grounds for hope that all such limitations on female aspirations will soon disappear." Judith R. Baskin, *Midrashic Women: Formations of the Feminine in Rabbinic Literature* (Hanover: University Press of New England for Brandeis University Press, 2002), 163.

what it was. These strategies of connecting past to present do not paper over the disparities between the Jewish patriarchal past and the current feminist project. Each pays unflinching attention to the tensions. Each also, however, proposes ways of conceiving the relationship between past, present, and future that diffuse or subvert the claim that patriarchal features of the Jewish past have on contemporary Jewish life.

The conclusions in this book place feminists squarely in front of what might be called the "feminist dilemma." The texts discussed in this book do not embrace the full human potential of women as religious actors. Feminists, like other Jews, would like to be able to turn to the rabbinic corpus as a wellspring of identity, yet they find it incapable of reflecting back to them a vision of the religious selves they would like to become. Compelling though the feminist approaches to the Jewish past discussed in this section may be, they do not provide feminists with the resources to *live with a tradition that cannot be remediated*. Reading the rule with integrity means accepting that the tradition contains much that is challenging, from a feminist perspective. Given the unequivocal difficulty that this book's conclusions pose to feminists who wish to remain engaged with the tradition, it seems important to reflect on how one might maintain a connection with a heritage that is forthrightly acknowledged as problematic. The two strategies discussed below require feminists to neither compromise their feminist commitments nor dissociate themselves from or disavow problematic teachings like the rule.

Marrying the Feminist Future to the Patriarchal Past

One reason that feminists submit the Jewish past and the sacred canon to creative reading strategies is because they wish to ground contemporary feminist life in an authority of comparable weight to that which stabilizes traditional patriarchal religion. Feminists have generally assumed that contemporary feminist ideals will be most successfully buttressed when God and Torah are reenvisioned in the image of feminism.[24] Several years ago I read a book that turns this assumption on its head. In *Expanding the Palace of Torah*, Tamar Ross argues that setting one's course toward a feminist future is *not contingent upon* finding traces of feminism in the sacred texts of the past. In a manner that strikes me as most counterintuitive – and yet brilliant because it is simple and yet no one thought of it before – Ross marries her commitment to a feminist future with her commitment to the patriarchal past. She does not feel the need to ground the feminist future in sacred texts that have an explicit commitment to the feminist enterprise. Quite the opposite, she gives the patriarchy of the Jewish past a "foundational" status.[25] She optimistically believes that feminism "can be absorbed by canonic texts bearing an initially patriarchal slant."[26]

[24] See Plaskow, *Standing Again at Sinai: Judaism from a Feminist Perspective*, 25–169.
[25] Ross, *Expanding the Palace of Torah: Orthodoxy and Feminism*, 207–10.
[26] Ross, *Expanding the Palace of Torah: Orthodoxy and Feminism*, 248.

The insight that makes it possible for Ross to grant the patriarchal past a foundational status, ironically, comes from feminism. As Ross understands the matter, feminism's key critique of traditional religion lies in its demonstration of the extent to which divine revelation is mediated by humans. One of feminism's most compelling insights is that gender relations generally, and patriarchal social organization specifically, are human constructs. To the extent that traditional religious texts project patriarchal social organization as normative or use male images and language to depict God, they attest to the indelible traces of their human (male) scribes. Feminism, then, highlights the extensive role of the human filter in the records of divine revelation that have reached us. Feminism observes that the records of divine revelation available to us have an undeniable human (and male) component. In other words, *there has never been and may never be* such a thing as unmediated access to the divine.

Ross parts ways from her fellow feminists in her reaction to this observation. For other feminists, this observation casts aspersions on the records of divine–human communication from the past. For many, the authority of patriarchal sacred texts is compromised by the fact that the texts record the divine–human encounter in an incomplete manner.[27] For Ross, however, the fact that we access past divine–human encounters through a human (male) filter does not diminish their authenticity or authority. She argues that *all* records of the divine–human encounter bear the traces of human mediation. Accepting that divine revelation is humanly mediated, however, cuts in *two* directions. On one hand, accepting this fact means that the patriarchally mediated revelation of the past is authentically divine. On the other hand, accepting that the divine will is expressed through human culture means that God can speak through feminism too![28] When women earnestly bristle against the constraints of the patriarchal tradition and when religious life changes to accommodate these concerns, such developments are no less divinely authorized than the patriarchal past. The feminist present is as authentically divine as the patriarchal past. For Ross, *commitment to a feminist present and future does not require disavowing the patriarchal past.*

A question that naturally arises is how one can tell if the social and cultural envelope in which divinity is packaged is authentically divine. Ross has

---

[27] Plaskow, who regards the Torah's record of Israel's God wrestling as incomplete because it ignores the experiences of half of the Jewish population, is a prime example of the kind of approach I describe here. Plaskow, *Standing Again at Sinai: Judaism from a Feminist Perspective*, 32–34. In her critique of this position, Ross writes, "Current feminist thinking tends to adopt an ethical absolutism that denounces patriarchy as wrong for all time." Ross, *Expanding the Palace of Torah: Orthodoxy and Feminism*, 216.

[28] Her section entitled "The Revelatory Status of Feminism" follows right on the heels of her section entitled "The Foundational Status of Patriarchy." The patriarchy of the past is authorized by the same complex interweaving of the divine into social conventions that in our day is manifest in feminism. See Ross, *Expanding the Palace of Torah: Orthodoxy and Feminism*, 207–12.

an admittedly conservative method of determining when social and cultural developments are divinely inspired. When social developments are incorporated into even the most conservative elements of Jewish society, Ross sees them as a manifestation of the divine will unfolding.[29] Ross demonstrates how this process works with the example of women's Torah study.[30]

Almost a century ago, Sarah Schenirer risked being ostracized for her vision to develop a religious educational system for girls that included serious Torah study. Today, the Beis Yaakov school system founded by Schenirer "works hand in hand with the once-reluctant religious establishment and serves as a powerhouse for the forces of religious conservatism."[31] The idea that Torah study serves an important role in girls' religious formation is now so commonplace that even groups that are unsympathetic to women's Torah study see no way to avoid teaching the girls in their community. The principal of an Ultra-Orthodox women's seminary is quoted as saying, "We are giving you an education so that your granddaughters will no longer have the need for one."[32] For this rabbi, the ideal social arrangement does not involve teaching girls Torah. He recognizes, however, that society has developed such that he has no choice but to participate in the trend of educating girls. I cite the case of this rabbi not because I endorse his viewpoint (I do not), but because the fact that even he supports teaching Torah to girls suggests that feminism has "trickled down" to even the most conservative elements of Jewish society.[33] Now that the idea of teaching girls Torah as part of their religious formation has been mainstreamed within the Orthodox world, Ross argues that we should understand it as a divinely authorized ideal.

[29] One hitch: It is only possible to know if a social and cultural development is divinely sanctioned after the fact. Ross recognizes the difficulty this feature of her theology poses when she writes, "If we admit that normative standards are sometimes established only over a considerable span of several generations (if ever), how are we then to understand that time period before a consensus has solidified?" The question raised here is how to regard feminism in its "emergent" stages, when consensus is not yet established. Ross, *Expanding the Palace of Torah: Orthodoxy and Feminism*, 219.

[30] See discussion of the revolution in women's Torah study in Ross, *Expanding the Palace of Torah: Orthodoxy and Feminism*, 72–87.

[31] Ross, *Expanding the Palace of Torah: Orthodoxy and Feminism*, 243.

[32] Cited in Ross, *Expanding the Palace of Torah: Orthodoxy and Feminism*, 176.

[33] In Ultra-Orthodox sectors of Jewish society, there continues to be ideological resistance to women's learning, even though as a practical matter, the practice of educating girls is widespread. Ross explains that rabbis justify the trend of educating women by distinguishing between Torah study as a ritual and Torah study as a practical support for one's religious life: "[They approve] women's study for practical purposes (leading either to greater appreciation of the law or to intensification of religious commitment) for women but endorse in-depth study 'for its own sake' only for men." Ross, *Expanding the Palace of Torah: Orthodoxy and Feminism*, 233. The distinction these members of the Orthodox community draw between study for practical purposes and study for "its own sake" is very similar to the one discussed in Chapter 7, where women are featured engaging in instrumental Torah study, but not ritual Torah study.

In more modern sectors of Orthodoxy, women's learning focuses on the Oral Torah, which has traditionally been restricted for study by men. She writes that "what is unique in the learning revolution instituted by Modern Orthodox women . . . [is] not simply the level of literacy they [seek], but also its subject matter and institutional setting."[34] Women now study technical halakhic texts in settings that create "a rarefied spiritual atmosphere akin to that of a men's yeshiva."[35] In the new institutions that have developed, women's "learning is not achievement oriented; the study is conducted without exams, grades, and other external measures of success. The goal is the learning itself, which is conducted 'for its own sake' (*lishmah*) rather than for practical benefit."[36] Elsewhere Ross explains that traditionalists try to limit the significance of women's study by introducing "new distinctions, approving women's study for practical purposes (leading either to greater appreciation of the law or to intensification of religious commitment) . . . but endorsing in-depth study 'for its own sake' only for men."[37]

Ross suggests that the idea that women can engage in study as long as it is instrumental is new. My argument in Chapter 7, however, suggests that the distinction between instrumental and ritual Torah study is in fact a very old device for making women's Torah study socially and religiously acceptable. The move by contemporary traditionalists to characterize women's study as practical or instrumental dissolves the tension that arises from the idea that women can partake of ritual Torah study. By suggesting that Torah study is *either* instrumental *or* undertaken "for its own sake," participants in the modern struggle over women's education have intuited what I found in the ancient sources: Ritual Torah study accomplishes something powerful and important that is not achieved by instrumental Torah study. By saying that Modern Orthodox women have begun to frame their study as nonpractical and noninstrumental, Ross is suggesting that women have begun to participate in the very kind of Torah study from which tannaitic sources exclude them. What's more, according to Ross, women's engagement with this kind of Torah study has received widespread rabbinic endorsement.[38]

At this point, Ross's work becomes particularly relevant to making sense of this research in a contemporary context. This book reveals that in antiquity ritual Torah study was central to the maintenance and perpetuation of the covenantal community. Since continuity was conceived as the reproduction of the *pater familias*'s identity, women's practice of ritual Torah study was inconsequential. My study further shows the extent to which the ritual

---

34 Ross, *Expanding the Palace of Torah: Orthodoxy and Feminism*, 72.
35 Ross, *Expanding the Palace of Torah: Orthodoxy and Feminism*, 72.
36 Ross, *Expanding the Palace of Torah: Orthodoxy and Feminism*, 72.
37 Ross, *Expanding the Palace of Torah: Orthodoxy and Feminism*, 233.
38 See the range of halakhic authorities discussed in Ross, *Expanding the Palace of Torah: Orthodoxy and Feminism*, 72–87.

of Torah study permeated a broader network of rituals. As forms of Torah study, timebound, positive commandments could accomplish all that Torah study accomplished. Ross argues that in the modern world ritual Torah study by women has received divine endorsement. To my mind, this development strains the entire edifice of women's exemption from timebound, positive commandments. If women's exemption from Torah study accounts for and lends significance to their exemption from timebound, positive commandments, and women are now studying Torah as a response to the divine will, this leads me to wonder how long their exemption from timebound, positive commandments will endure. When, how, or even if the structure of women's exemption from timebound, positive commandments will finally collapse under the weight of its own internal contradictions I do not know. What I do know is that this book reveals a fracture in the structure that supports women's exemption from the central rituals of rabbinic Judaism. For feminists seeking to make sense of this book's findings in a contemporary context, Ross's work points to the possibility that women's performance of timebound, positive commandments today should be understood to be divinely authorized. When my research is read in light of Ross's theological arguments, the fact that the ancient rabbis exempted women from timebound, positive commandments in the patriarchal past has no bearing on the possibilities for a *divinely authorized* feminist present and future in which women perform these commandments.

Reporting the Patriarchal Past, Performing the Feminist Future

Thus far in this essay, I have focused on the difficulties my conclusions regarding the social ideology underlying women's exemption from timebound commandments and Torah study pose to the feminist project. It would be a mistake, however, for feminists to evaluate this book's relevance *solely* on the basis of the undoubtedly important insight that underlying the rule is an assumption that women are not primary agents in the maintenance and perpetuation of the covenantal community. It is important to remember that the book's conclusions (presented in Part III) are possible *only in the aftermath* of the extensive text work performed in the first and second parts of the book. Parts I and II reconstruct the exegetical and argumentational processes that generate both the rule and our perception that the rule is a significant marker of rabbinic gender. Though modern readers are conditioned to read the rule as a significant marker of rabbinic gender, Part I argues that the rabbis were not self-consciously engaged in social engineering when they produced the rule. We risk misunderstanding the rule if we turn our attention overly quickly to gender. The processes that produced the rule as we know it were most explicitly concerned with (1) linking tradition to scripture, (2) organizing and consolidating tradition, and (3) mastering the tradition. These scholastic activities did not aim to legislate or institute a social vision. More than anything, these activities aimed to mold the sages as masters of rabbinic tradition.

Undoubtedly, the fact that tradition had been manipulated in these ways impacted the formation of gender at a later juncture – especially in the medieval and modern periods – *but not necessarily because the sages of the rabbinic period sought to realize a particular social outcome.* Rather, the religious marginalization of women was embedded in the social organization of the *beit midrash* (the study house), where these scholastic exercises were practiced. In the social context of the *beit midrash*, women's marginalization from ritual Torah study was naturalized.[39] This book seeks to make explicit that which the rabbinic sources take for granted. The *beit midrash* was a place where social identities were constructed; engaging in the intellectual exercises that took place there was also an important vehicle for the formation of religious selves.

Keeping these observations in mind, we can now consider a second way feminists might engage the research in this book. Even while this book *reports* to feminists (and interested others) that ritual Torah study in the *beit midrash* was accessible to males exclusively, *it makes the intellectual activities performed in the ancient* beit midrash *accessible to a wide audience.* A sympathetic reader of my manuscript observed that "Alexander manages to bring us into the Talmudic 'workshop' as she reconstructs the exegetical and argumentational process that generated the text – a reconstruction that is surprisingly stimulating and exciting." I hope that feminist readers too will find themselves caught up in and enjoy the intellectual drama of the *beit midrash* that I conjure in Parts I and II of the book.

Though this book's primary purpose is to articulate the social commitments that underlie the rule, this goal could be achieved only when other intellectual projects temporarily took priority. In order to discern the social interests of the ancient sages, contemporary readers must immerse themselves in the intellectual thrust and parry that is intrinsic to rabbinic scholasticism. My mentor, Steven Fraade, argues that it is impossible to understand what he calls the "social work of commentary" (that is, how the rabbinic texts shape members of the rabbinic movement into masters of Torah) "without attempting to pose ourselves in the place of such students."[40] He advocates that contemporary readers of ancient rabbinic texts "put [them]selves in the position of one who is progressively working through the text, ... even as [they] employ the distancing tools of ... critical analysis as controls."[41] In order to grasp what was

---

[39] See Peskowitz's discussion of the naturalization of gender through the repeated performance of daily labors, including Torah study for men in the *beit midrash.* Peskowitz, *Spinning Fantasies,* 49–76, esp. 74–76.

[40] Fraade, *From Tradition to Commentary: Torah and Its Interpretation in the Midrash Sifre to Deuteronomy,* 20.

[41] Fraade, *From Tradition to Commentary: Torah and Its Interpretation in the Midrash Sifre to Deuteronomy,* 20.

accomplished in the performance of rabbinic texts in antiquity, the contemporary reader must respond to the text's invitation to be brought to life. Herein lies an intriguing opportunity for feminist readers of this book.

Undoubtedly, the ancient rabbis whose intellectual and social formation is both recorded in and generated by these texts envisioned their texts being received in social settings similar to their own. They assumed that when the intellectual exercises preserved in their texts were re-vivified, it would be men, like themselves, responding to the text's invitation. But as a physical object, a page of Talmud is inert. A text cannot work on its own behalf to ensure that it will be received into the same social world in which it was produced. According to Fraade, the rabbis did not intend for the texts they produced to be read passively as the record of an oral exercise decisively performed and finished. Rather, rabbinic texts were recorded to serve as a prompt and script from which rabbis and disciples would perform new oral exercises, similar to those that lay behind the texts. When feminists in our day follow the rabbinic arguments and exegesis that I have re-animated in the pages of this book, they can be seen to be participating in the ritual Torah study that is prompted by the ancient texts. Feminist readers of the text reenact the work of organizing, analyzing, ordering, and mastering tradition that, in antiquity, was central to the social and religious formation of rabbinic sages. By implicating themselves in the scholastic afterlife of rabbinic texts, feminist readers paradoxically participate in a *beit midrash* from which they are excluded. It is intriguing to consider the fact that feminists can *report* something they find to be very discouraging (that women cannot participate in Torah study that has the effect of reproducing the covenantal community) even while they *perform* the exact opposite. When feminists reenact the exercises exposited in this book, they realize the texts' potential to reproduce the covenantal community. It is more than a touch ironic that the feminist selves formed through such activity do not share a vision regarding gender with the religious selves that the authors envisioned being created when the texts were to be performed.

In order to effectively achieve this book's scholarly goals, I had to linger in the rabbinic practice of ritual Torah study. Ironically, only when I moderated my interest in patterns of social organization could I discern the moments when social identity was in fact being formed. In the end, I found answers to my question about how the rule supports the construction of rabbinic gender, but not in the places I had expected to find them. I cannot help but wonder if feminists would find that they too can achieve their social goals when they linger in the rabbinic practice of Torah study, when they engage in ritual Torah study for its own sake without a predetermined sense of how their study might support the social structures they wish to fashion. When feminists re-animate the exercises that constituted ritual Torah study in the ancient *beit midrash*, they constitute themselves de facto as the next generation in the covenantal community forged by Torah study.

In Chapter 7, I used contemporary ritual theory to articulate what the ancient rabbis accomplished when they engaged in ritual Torah study. I suggested that the rabbis constructed ritual Torah study as a means of overcoming the threat of extinction. Ritual Torah study posits a subjunctive reality in which sons live out the social and covenantal identity of their fathers. Feminists might draw on this insight about ritual to claim that when they re-animate ancient rabbinic texts and perform ritual Torah study today, they imagine themselves in to a world where feminist repair is temporarily achieved. Though the *beit midrash* that feminists bring to life when they re-animate the ancient texts espouses ideals to which feminists cannot assent, their performance of ritual Torah study testifies to the shortsightedness of the rabbinic social vision as originally articulated. Adam Seligman and the other authors of *Ritual and Its Consequences* observe that ritual is "endless work" that must be performed over and over again. "The endless work of ritual is necessary precisely because the ordered world of ritual is inevitably only temporary. The world always returns to its broken state, constantly requiring the repairs of ritual."[42] Feminist performance of ritual Torah study imagined in this manner is no different from ritual writ large. Ritual's power lies in its ability to mediate between the world that is and the world one wishes to inhabit.

This book is primarily an offering to the scholarly community. Its claims are constructed in dialogue with the conventions of scholarly method. The social location of this book notwithstanding, in this essay, I have tried to sketch out ways in which this book might stimulate conversation beyond the walls of academia, for it is there that the seeds of my interest in the rule were first planted. In Part II of the book, I demonstrated how extensively the Bavli's reading of the rule shaped later understandings of the rule. Through its intensive reading practices, the Bavli turned the descriptive mishnaic rule into a prescriptive rule whose impact is felt in Jewish communities until today. Traditionalists and feminists alike live in the long shadow of the gender expectations enabled by the Bavli's reading. The post-amoraic sages of the Bavli whose concern it was to read mishnaic dicta as part of a coherent and systematic legal structure, however, could not have predicted or anticipated the edifice of gender that would be built on their work. In similar fashion, I do not presume to envision a future in which specific changes are achieved as the result of my study. I nonetheless hope that future conversations about the rule and the gender expectations it projects into the Jewish community will somehow be different on account of the earnest engagement I have given this subject. Were that to happen, my scholarship would function not only as a scholarly investigation of the Jewish past, but also as a medium for the transmission and transformation of a robust living tradition.

[42] Seligman et al., *Ritual and Its Consequences: An Essay on the Limits of Sincerity*, 30.

Bibliography

Abudraham, Abraham. *Sefer Abudraham*. Jerusalem, 1963.

Adler, Rachel. *Engendering Judaism: An Inclusive Theology and Ethics*. Philadelphia: Jewish Publication Society, 1998.

———. "The Jew Who Wasn't There: Halakha and the Jewish Woman." In *Contemporary Jewish Ethics*, edited by Menachem Marc Kellner, 348–54. New York: Sanhedrin Press, 1978.

Aharoni, Y. "The Expedition to the Judaean Desert, 1969, Expedition b'." *Israel Exploration Journal* 11 (1961): 22–23.

Aiken, Lisa. *To Be a Jewish Woman*. Northvale: J. Aronson, 1992.

Albeck, Chanoch. *Introduction to the Mishnah* (Hebrew). Jerusalem: Dvir, 1959.

Albright, W. F. "A Biblical Fragment from the Maccabaean Age: The Nash Papyrus." *Journal of Biblical Literature* 56 (1937): 145–76.

Alexander, Elizabeth Shanks. "Art, Argument and Ambiguity in the Talmud: Conflicting Representations of the Evil Impulse." *Hebrew Union College Annual* 73 (2002): 97–132.

———. "The Fixing of the Oral Mishnah and the Displacement of Meaning." *Oral Tradition* 14/1 (March 1999): 100–39.

———. "From Whence the Phrase 'Timebound Positive Commandments'?" *Jewish Quarterly Review* 97/3 (2007): 317–46.

———. "The Impact of Feminism on Rabbinic Studies: The Impossible Paradox of Reading Women into Rabbinic Literature." In *Jews and Gender: The Challenge to Hierarchy*, edited by Jonathan Frankel, 101–18. New York: Oxford University Press, 2000.

———. *Transmitting Mishnah: The Shaping Influence of Oral Tradition*. Cambridge: Cambridge University Press, 2006.

———. "Why Study Talmud in the 21st Century: The View Form a Large Public University OR Studying Talmud as a Critical Thinker." In *Why Study Talmud in the Twenty-first Century? The Relevance of the Ancient Jewish Text to Our World*, edited by Paul Socken, 11–24. New York: Rowman and Littlefield, 2009.

Anatoli, Jacob. *Sefer Malmad Hatalmidim*. Lyck: R. Siebert, 1866; repr. Israel, 1968.

Baker, Cynthia. *Rebuilding the House of Israel: Architectures of Gender.* Stanford: Stanford University Press, 2002.

Baskin, Judith R. *Midrashic Women: Formations of the Feminine in Rabbinic Literature.* Brandeis Series on Jewish Women. Hanover: University Press of New England for Brandeis University Press, 2002.

Baumgarten, Albert. "Invented Traditions of the Maccabean Era." In *Geschichte–Tradition–Reflexion*, vol. 1: *Judentum*, edited by Peter Schaefer, 197–210. Tübingen: Mohr Siebeck, 1996.

―――. "Literacy and the Polemic Concerning Biblical Hermeneutics in the Second Temple Era." In *Education and History: Cultural and Political Contexts* (Hebrew), edited by Rivka Feldhay and Immanuel Etkes, 33–45. Jerusalem: Zalman Shazar Center for Jewish History, 1999.

Baumgarten, Elisheva. *Mothers and Children: Jewish Family Life in Medieval Europe.* Jews, Christians, and Muslims from the Ancient to the Modern World. Princeton: Princeton University Press, 2004.

Bell, Catherine. *Ritual Theory, Ritual Practice.* New York: Oxford University Press, 1992.

Benovitz, Moshe. "*Shinun*: Recitation of the Shema in the Teaching of R. Shimon Bar Yohai" (Hebrew). *Sidra* 20 (2005): 25–56.

―――. "Time-Triggered Positive Commandments as Conversation Pieces." *HUCA* 78 (2007): 45–90.

Berger, Aliza. "Wrapped Attention: May Women Wear Tefillin." In *Jewish Legal Writings by Women*, edited by Micah D. Halperin and Chana Safrai, 75–188. Jerusalem: Urim Publications, 1998.

Berkowitz, Beth A. *Execution and Invention: Death Penalty Discourse in Early Rabbinic and Christian Cultures.* New York: Oxford University Press, 2006.

Berman, Saul. "The Status of Women in Halakhic Judaism." In *The Jewish Woman: New Perspectives*, edited by Elizabeth Koltun, 114–28. New York: Schocken Books, 1976.

Biale, Rachel. *Women and Jewish Law: An Exploration of Women's Issues in Halakhic Sources.* New York: Schocken Books, 1984.

Birnbaum, Ellen. *The Place of Judaism in Philo's Thought: Israel, Jews, and Proselytes.* Brown Judaic Studies 290. Atlanta: Scholars Press, 1996.

Bordieau, Pierre. "The Force of Law: Toward a Sociology of the Juridical Field." Translated by Richard Terdiman. *Hasting Law Journal* 38/5 (1987): 805–50.

Boyarin, Daniel. *Carnal Israel: Reading Sex in Talmudic Culture.* The New Historicism 25. Berkeley: University of California Press, 1993.

Brooten, Bernadette. *Women Leaders in the Ancient Synagogue: Inscriptional Issues and Background Evidence.* Chico: Scholars Press, 1982.

Butler, Judith. *Gender Trouble: Feminism and the Subversion of Identity.* New York: Routledge, 1990.

Cabezón, José Ignacio. *Buddhism and Language: A Study of Indo-Tibetan Scholasticism.* SUNY Series, Toward a Comparative Philosophy of Religions. Albany: State University of New York Press, 1994.

―――, editor. *Scholasticism: Cross-cultural and Comparative Perspectives.* SUNY Series, Toward a Comparative Philosophy of Religions. Albany: State University of New York Press, 1998.

Carruthers, Mary. *The Book of Memory: A Study of Memory in Medieval Culture.* Cambridge: Cambridge University Press, 1990.

Chazon, Esther Glickler. "Prayers from Qumran and Their Historical Implications." *Dead Sea Discoveries* 1 (1994): 265–84.

———. "When Did They Pray: Times for Prayer in the Dead Sea Scrolls and Associated Literature." In *For a Later Generation: The Transformation of Tradition in Israel, Early Judaism, and Early Christianity*, edited by Randal A. Argall, Beverly A. Bow, and Rodney A. Werline, 42–51. Harrisburg: Trinity Press International, 2000.

Chernick, Michael. "'Ish' as Man and Adult in the Halakic Midrashim." *The Jewish Quarterly Review* 73/3 (January 1983): 254–80.

Cohen, Aryeh. *Rereading Talmud: Gender, Law and the Poetics of Sugyot.* Atlanta: Scholars Press, 1998.

Cohen, Naomi G. *Philo Judaeus: His Universe of Discourse.* Frankfurt am Main: Peter Lang, 1995.

Cohen, Shaye J. D. *From the Maccabees to the Mishnah.* Library of Early Christianity. Philadelphia: Westminster Press, 1987.

———. *Why Aren't Jewish Women Circumcised? Gender and Covenant in Judaism.* Berkeley: University of California Press, 2005.

———. "Women in the Syngagogue of Antiquity." *Conservative Judaism* 34 (December 1980): 23–29.

Cohn, Naftali. "Rabbis as Jurists: On the Representations of Past and Present Legal Institutions in the Mishnah." *Journal of Jewish Studies* 60/2 (2009): 245–63.

Cohn, Yehudah B. *Tangled Up in Text: Tefillin and the Ancient World.* Providence: Brown Judaic Studies, 2008.

Colson, F. H., trans. *Philo.* Loeb Classical Library. London: William Heinemann, 1939.

de Beauvoir, Simone. *The Second Sex.* Translated by Constance Borde and Sheila Malovany-Chevallier, with an introduction by Judith Thurman. New York: Alfred A. Knopf, 2010.

De Vries, Benjamin. *Toldot Hahalakhah Hatalmudit* (Hebrew). Tel Aviv: A Tsiyoni, 1966.

Dewey, Arthur J. "The Gospel of Trajan." In *Jesus, the Voice, and the Text: Beyond the Oral and Written Gospel*, edited by Tom Thatcher, 181–96. Waco: Baylor University Press, 2008.

Diamant, Anita. *The Red Tent.* New York: St. Martin's Press, 2005.

Ebner, David Yechiel. "The Composition and Structure of Mishnah 'Sotah.'" PhD dissertation, Yeshiva University, 1980.

Elbogen, Ismar. *Jewish Liturgy: A Comprehensive History.* Translated by Raymond P. Scheindlin. Philadelphia: Jewish Publication Society; New York: Jewish Theological Seminary of America, 1993.

Epstein, J. N. *Introduction to Tannaitic Literature: Mishnah Tosephta and Halakhic Midrashim* (Hebrew). Edited by E. Z. Melamed. Jerusalem: Magnus Press, 1957.

———. *Introduction to the Text of the Mishnah* (Hebrew). 3rd edition. Jerusalem: Magnes Press, 2000.

Fiorenza, Elisabeth Schüssler. *But She Said: Feminist Practices of Biblical Interpretation.* Boston: Beacon Press, 1992.

Fisch, Menachem. *Rational Rabbis: Science and Talmudic Culture.* Bloomington: Indiana University Press, 1997.

Fish, Stanley. "The Law Wishes to Have a Formal Existence." In *The Fate of Law*, edited by Austin Sarat and Thomas Kearns, 159–208. Ann Arbor: University of Michigan Press, 1991.

Fishman, Talya. "A Kabbalistic Perspective on Gender-Specific Commandments: On the Interplay of Symbols and Society." *AJS Review* 17/2 (1992): 199–245.

Fleischer, Ezra. *Eretz-Israel Prayers and Prayer Rituals as Portrayed in the Geniza Documents* (Hebrew). Jerusalem: Magnes Press, 1988.

——. "On the Beginnings of Obligatory Jewish Prayer." *Tarbiz* 59 (5750): 397–441.

Foley, John Miles. *Immanent Art: From Structure to Meaning in Traditional Oral Epic.* Bloomington: Indiana University Press, 1991.

Fonrobert, Charlotte. "Neighborhood as Ritual Space: The Case of the Rabbinic Eruv." *Archiv Für Religionsgeschichte* 10 (2008): 239–58.

——. "The Semiotics of the Sexed Body in Early Halakhic Discourse." In *How Should Rabbinic Literature Be Read in the Modern World?* edited by Matthew Kraus, 79–108. Piscataway: Gorgias Press, 2006.

Fonrobert, Charlotte Elisheva, and Martin S. Jaffee, editors. *The Cambridge Companion to the Talmud and Rabbinic Literature.* Cambridge Companions to Religion. Cambridge: Cambridge University Press, 2007.

Fraade, Steven D. *From Tradition to Commentary: Torah and Its Interpretation in the Midrash Sifre to Deuteronomy.* SUNY Series in Judaica. Albany: State University of New York Press, 1991.

Frey, R. J. P. Jean-Baptiste. *Corpus Inscriptionum Iudaicarum*, vol. 2: *Asie-Afrique.* Rome: Pontificio Istituto di Archeologia Cristiana, 1952.

Friedman, Shamma. "Literary Development and Historicity in the Aggadic Narrative: A Study Based upon B.M. 83b–86a." In *Community and Culture: Essays in Jewish Studies in Honor of the Ninetieth Anniversary of the Founding of Gratz College*, edited by N. M. Waldman, 67–80. Philadelphia: Gratz College, 1987.

——. *Talmud `Arukh: BT Bava Metzi'a*, vol. 2 (Hebrew). New York: Jewish Theological Seminary, 1997.

——. *Tosefta Atiqta: Pesah Rishon: Synoptic Parallels of Mishna and Tosefta Analyzed with a Methodological Introduction* (Hebrew). Ramat-Gan: Bar Ilan University Press, 2002.

Gerhardsson, Birger. *Memory and Manuscript: Oral Tradition and Written Transmission in Rabbinic Judaism and Early Christianity.* Grand Rapids: W. B. Eerdmans, 1961; repr. 1998.

Gilat, Yitzhak. *Studies in the Development of Halakha* (Hebrew). Israel: Bar Ilan University Press, 1992.

Ginzberg, Louis. *A Commentary on the Palestinian Talmud*, vol. 2 (Hebrew). New York: Ktav, 1971.

Goldberg, Abraham. "The Babylonian Talmud." In *The Literature of the Sages*, part 1, edited by Shmuel Safrai, 323–36. Philadelphia: Fortress Press, 1987.

——. "The Mishna – A Study Book of Halakha." In *The Literature of the Sages*, part 1, edited by Shmuel Safrai, 211–51. Philadelphia: Fortress Press, 1987.

Goldenberg, Robert. "The Talmud." In *Back to the Sources: Reading the Classic Jewish Texts*, edited by Barry Holtz, 129–75. New York: Simon and Schuster, 1984.

Goodblatt, David. "The Beruriah Traditions." *Journal of Jewish Studies* 26/1–2 (Spring–Autumn 1975): 68–85.

Goren, Shlomo. "Women as Regards Timebound, Positive Commandments" (Hebrew). *Mahanayim* 98 (1965): 10–16.

Gray, Alyssa M. *A Talmud in Exile: The Influence of Yerushalmi Avodah Zarah on the Formation of Bavli Avodah Zarah.* Brown Judaic Studies 342. Providence: Brown Judaic Studies, 2005.

Greenberg, Blu. *On Women and Judaism: A View from Tradition.* Philadelphia: Jewish Publication Society of America, 1981.

Greenberg, Moshe. "Nash Papyrus." In *Encyclopaedia Judaica,* vol. 12, 833. New York: Macmillan, 1972.

Greenstein, Edward L. "Biblical Law." In *Back to the Sources: Reading the Classic Jewish Texts,* edited by Barry Holtz, 83–103. New York: Simon and Schuster, 1984.

Hadas, Moses, editor and trans. *Aristeas to Philocrates (Letter of Aristeas).* New York: Ktav, 1973.

Halberstam, Chaya T. *Law and Truth in Biblical and Rabbinic Literature.* Bloomington: Indiana University Press, 2009.

Halivni, David Weiss. *Midrash, Mishnah, and Gemara: The Jewish Predilection for Justified Law.* Cambridge, Mass.: Harvard University Press, 1986.

———. "The Reception Accorded to Rabbi Judah's Mishnah." In *Jewish and Christian Self-definition,* vol. 2: *Aspects of Judasim in the Graeco-Roman Period,* edited by E. P. Sanders with A. I. Baumgarten and Alan Mendelson, 204–12. London: SCM Press, 1981.

———. *Sources and Traditions: A Source Critical Commentary on Tractate Eruvin and Pesahim* (Hebrew). Jerusalem: Jewish Theological Seminary of America, 1982.

Handelman, Susan. "The 'Torah' of Criticism and the Criticism of Torah: Recuperating the Pedagogical Moment." In *Interpreting Judaism in a Post-modern Age,* edited by Steven Kepnes, 221–39. NewYork: New York University Press, 1996.

Hauptman, Judith. *Development of the Talmudic Sugya: Relationship between Tannaitic and Amoraic Sources.* Studies in Judaism. Lanham: University Press of America, 1988.

———. "Increasingly Stricter Rulings in *Mishnah Gittin*" (Hebrew). In *Proceedings of the Tenth World Congress of Jewish Studies, Division C, Jewish Thought and Literature,* 23–30. Jerusalem: World Union of Jewish Studies, 1990.

———. "Maternal Dissent: Women and Procreation in the *Mishnah.*" *Tikkun* 6/6 (1991): 81–82, 94–95.

———. "A New View of Women and Torah Study in the Talmudic Period." *Jewish Studies: An Internet Journal* (2010): 249–92.

———. "Pesach: A Liberating Experience for Women." *Masoret* (Winter 1993): 8–9.

———. *Rereading the Mishnah.* Tübingen: Mohr Siebeck, 2005.

———. *Rereading the Rabbis: A Woman's Voice.* Boulder: Westview Press, 1998.

———. "Women and Inheritance in Rabbinic Texts." In *Introducing Tosefta,* edited by Harry Fox and Tirzah Meacham, 221–40. Hoboken: Ktav, 1999.

———. "Women's Voluntary Performance of Commandments from Which They Are Exempt" (Hebrew). In *Proceedings of the Eleventh World Congress of Jewish Studies, Division C, Jewish Thought and Literature,* 161–68. Jerusalem: World Union of Jewish Studies, 1994.

Hayes, Christine E. *Between the Babylonian and Palestinian Talmuds: Accounting for Halakhic Difference in Selected Sugyot from Tractate Avodah Zarah.* New York: Oxford University Press, 1997.

_____. *Gentile Impurities and Jewish Identities: Intermarriage and Conversion from the Bible to the Talmud.* Oxford: Oxford University Press, 2002.

Hezser, Catherine. *Jewish Slavery in Antiquity.* Oxford: Oxford University Press, 2005.

Hirsch, Samson Raphael, trans. *The Pentateuch,* vol. 3: *(Leviticus Pt. II).* Rendered into English by Isaac Levy. Gateshead: Judaica Press, 1976.

Hirschfeld, Yizhar. *The Palestinian Dwelling in the Roman-Byzantine Period.* Collectio Minor 34. Jerusalem: Franciscan Printing Press; Israel Exploration Society, 1995.

Hirshman, Marc. *The Stabilization of Rabbinic Culture, 100 C.E.–350 C.E.: Texts on Education and Their Late Antique Context.* Oxford: Oxford University Press, 2009.

Hoffman, Lawrence. *Covenant of Blood: Circumcision and Gender in Rabbinic Judaism.* Chicago: University of Chicago Press, 1996.

Ilan, Tal. "'Daughters of Israel, Weep for Rabbi Ishmael': The Schools Rabbi Akiva and Rabbi Ishmael on Women." *Nashim* 4 (2001): 15–34.

_____. *Jewish Women in Greco-Roman Palestine.* Peabody: Hendrickson Publishers, 1996.

_____. *Mine and Yours Are Hers: Retrieving Women's History from Rabbinic Literature.* New York: Brill, 1997.

Jacobs, Louis. "Are There Fictitious Baraitot in the Babylonian Talmud?" *Hebrew Union College Annual* 42 (1971): 185–96.

_____. *The Talmudic Argument: A Study in Talmudic Reasoning and Methodology.* Cambridge: Cambridge University Press, 1984.

Jaffee, Martin S. "Gender and Otherness in Rabbinic Oral Culture: On Gentiles, Undisciplined Jews, and Their Women." In *Performing the Gospel: Orality, Memory and Mark,* edited by Richard Horsley, Jonathan Draper, and John Miles Foley, 21–43, 201–9. Minneapolis: Fortress Press, 2006.

_____. "Oral Transmission of Knowledge as Rabbinic Sacrament: An Overlooked Aspect of Discipleship in Oral Torah." In *Study and Knowledge in Jewish Thought,* edited by Howard Kreisel, 65–79. Beer Sheva: Ben-Gurion University of the Negev Press, 2006.

_____. "A Rabbinic Ontology of the Written and Spoken Word: On Discipleship, Transformative Knowledge and the Living Texts of Oral Torah." *Journal of the American Academy of Religion* 65/3 (Autumn 1997): 27–61.

_____. *Torah in the Mouth: Writing and Oral Tradition in Palestinian Judaism, 200 BCE–400 CE.* New York: Oxford University Press, 2001.

Jay, Nancy. *Throughout Your Generations Forever: Sacrifice, Religion, and Paternity.* With a foreword by Karen E. Fields. Chicago: University of Chicago Press, 1992.

Kahana, Menahem Yitshak. "The Halakhic Midrashim." In *Literature of the Sages, Part. 2,* edited by Shmuel (z"l) Safrai, Zeev Safrai, Joshua Schwartz, and Peter J. Tomson, 3–105. Amsterdam: Royal Van Gorcum and Fortress Press, 2006.

_____. *Sifre Zuta on Deuternomy: Excerpts from a New Tannaitic Midrash* (Hebrew). Jerusalem: Magnes Press, 2002.

Kalmin, Richard. "The Formation and Character of the Babylonian Talmud." In *The Late Roman-Rabbinic Period.* Vol. 4 of *Cambridge History of Judaism,* edited by Steven Katz, 840–76. Cambridge: Cambridge University Press, 2006.

_____. *Jewish Babylonia between Persia and Roman Palestine.* New York: Oxford University Press, 2006.

———. *The Redaction of the Babylonian Talmud: Amoraic or Saboraic?* Monographs of the Hebrew Union College 12. Cincinnati: Hebrew Union College Press, 1989.

Katz, Menachem. "The First Chapter of Tractate Qiddushsin of the Talmud Yerushalmi: Text, Commentary and Studies in the Editorial Process." PhD dissertation, Bar Ilan University, 2003.

Kaufman, Michael. *The Woman in Jewish Law and Tradition.* Northvale: J. Aronson, 1993.

Keel, Othmar. "Zeichen der Verbundenheit." In *Mélanges Dominique Barthélemy,* edited by Pierre Casetti, Othmar Keel, and Adrian Schenker, 159–240. Fribourg: Editions Universitaires, 1981.

Kimelman, Reuven."The Shema and the Amidah: Rabbinic Prayer." In *Prayer from Alexander to Constantine,* edited by Mark Kiley, 108–20. London: Routledge, 1997
———. "The Shema` Liturgy: From Covenant Ceremony to Coronation." In *Kenishta: Studies of the Syngogue World,* edited by Joseph Tabory, 9–105. Ramat Gan: Bar-Ilan University Press, 2001.

Klawans, Jonathan. *Impurity and Sin in Ancient Judaism.* New York: Oxford University Press, 2000.

Kolbrener, William. "'Chiseled from All Sides': Hermeneutics and Dispute in Rabbinic Tradition." *AJS Review* 28/2 (2004): 273–95.

Koltun, Elizabeth, editor. *The Jewish Woman: New Perspectives.* New York: Schocken Books, 1976.

Kraemer, David. *The Mind of the Talmud: An Intellectual History of the Bavli.* New York: Oxford University Press, 1990.

———. *Reading the Rabbis: The Talmud as Literature.* New York: Oxford University Press, 1996.

Kraemer, Ross Shepard. *Her Share of the Blessings: Women's Religions among Pagans, Jews, and Christians in the Greco-Roman World.* New York: Oxford University Press, 1992.

Kugel, James L. *The Bible as It Was.* Cambridge, Mass.: Belknap Press of Harvard University Press, 1997.

———. *In Potiphar's House: The Interpretive Life of Biblical Texts.* Cambridge, Mass.: Harvard University Press, 1990.

———. "Two Introductions to Midrash." In *Midrash and Literature,* edited by Geoffrey H. Hartman and Sandford Budick, 77–103. New Haven: Yale University Press, 1986.

Lakoff, George. *Women, Fire, and Dangerous Things: What Categories Reveal about the Mind.* Chicago: University of Chicago Press, 1987.

Levenson, Jon D. *Sinai and Zion: An Entry into the Jewish Bible.* San Francisco: Harper and Row, 1987.

Levine, Lee I. *The Rabbinic Class of Roman Palestine in Late Antiquity.* New York: Jewish Theological Seminary of America, 1989.

A Lexicon Abridged from Liddell and Scott's Greek–English Lexicon. Oxford: Clarendon Press, 1990.

Lieberman, Saul. *Hayerushalmi kiphshuto: A Commentary based on Manuskripts* [sic] *of the Yerushalmi,* vol. 1: *Shabbat, Eruvin and Pesachin* (Hebrew). Jerusalem: Darom, 1934.

———. *The Tosefta Ki-Fshutah: A Comprehensive Commentary on the Tosefta,* part 3 (Hebrew). Jerusalem: Jewish Theological Seminary of America, 1992.

———. *The Tosefta according to Codex Vienna, with Variants from Codices Erfurt, London, Genizah MSS. and Editio Princeps (Venice 1521)*, vol. 1 (Hebrew). Jerusalem: Jewish Theological Seminary of America, 1992.

Lorber, Judith. *Paradoxes of Gender.* New Haven: Yale University Press, 1994.

Maimonides, Moses. *Sefer Ha-Mitsvot.* Translated by Joseph Kapach. Jerusalem, 1930–31.

Margalit, Natan. "Priestly Men and Invisible Women: Male Appropriation of the Feminine and the Exemption of Women from Postive, Time-Bound Commandments." *AJS Review* 28/2 (November 2004): 297–316.

Marrou, Henri Irénée. *Histoire de l'education dans l'antiquité.* Paris: Éditions du Seuill, 1965.

Meiselman, Moshe. *The Jewish Woman in Jewish Law.* New York: Ktav, 1978.

Melamed, Ezra Zion. *The Relationship between the Halakhic Midrashim and the Mishnah and Tosephta.* Jerusalem: Self-published with the help of the Research Authority of Tel Aviv University, 1966.

Milik, J. T. "Tefillin, Mezuzot et Targums." In *Discoveries in the Judaean Desert*, vol. 6, 33–85. Oxford: Oxford University Press, 1977.

———. "Textes Littéraires." In *Discoveries in the Judaean Desert*, vol. 2, 80–86. Oxford: Oxford University Press, 1961.

Mintz, Alan. "Prayer and the Prayerbook." In *Back to the Sources: Reading the Classic Jewish Texts*, edited by Barry Holtz, 403–29. New York: Simon and Schuster, 1985.

Morgenstern, M., and M. Segal. "XHev/SePhylactery." In *Discoveries in the Judaean Desert*, vol. 38, 183–91. Oxford: Oxford University Press, 2000.

Moscovitz, Leib. *Talmudic Reasoning: From Casuistics to Conceptualization.* Tübingen: Mohr Siebeck, 2002.

Mowinckel, Sigmund. *The Psalms in Israel's Worship.* New York: Abingdon Press, 1962.

Naeh, Shlomo. "The Art of Memory, Structures of Memory and Paradigms of Text in Rabbinic Literature" (Hebrew). In *Mehqerei Talmud: Talmudic Studies*, edited by Yaacov Sussman and David Rosenthal. Jerusalem: Magnes Press, 2005.

———, and Aharon Shemesh. "The Manna Story and the Time of Morning Prayer." *Tarbiz* 64 (1995): 335–40.

Najman, Hindy. "Torah of Moses: Pseudonymous Attribution in Second Temple Writings." In *The Interpretation of Scripture in Early Judaism and Christianity: Studies in Language and Tradition*, edited by Craig A. Evans, 202–16. Sheffield: Sheffield Academic Press, 2000.

Nakman, David. "The Contents and Order of the Biblical Sections in the Tefillin from Qumran and Rabbinic Halakhah" (Hebrew). *Cathedra* 112 (2004): 19–44.

Neusner, Jacob. *Judaism: The Evidence of the Mishnah.* Atlanta: Scholars Press, 1988.

———, editor. *The Modern Study of the Mishnah.* Leiden: Brill, 1973.

———. *Oral Tradition in Judaism: The Case of the Mishnah.* New York: Garland Publishing, 1987.

———. *The Tosefta: An Introduction.* Atlanta: Scholars Press, 1992.

Newman, Judith H. *Praying by the Book: The Scripturalization of Prayer in Second Temple Judaism.* Early Judaism and Its Literature 14. Atlanta: Scholars Press, 1999.

Ochs, Vanessa L. *Sarah Laughed: Modern Lessons from the Wisdom and Stories of Biblical Women*. New York: McGraw-Hill, 2005.

Panikkar, Raimundo. "Common Patterns of Eastern and Western Scholasticism." *Diogenes* 21/83 (1973): 103–13.

Peskowitz, Miriam. *Spinning Fantasies: Rabbis, Gender and History*. Berkeley: University of California Press, 1997.

Plaskow, Judith. *Standing Again at Sinai: Judaism from a Feminist Perspective*. San Francisco: Harper and Row, 1990.

Porton, Gary G. *Understanding Rabbinic Midrash: Texts and Commentary*. The Library of Judaic Learning 5. Hoboken: Ktav, 1985.

Qimron, Elisha, and James H. Charlesworth. "Rule of the Community (1QS)." In *The Dead Sea Scrolls – Hebrew, Aramaic, and Greek with English Translations – Rule of the Community and Related Documents*, vol. 1, edited by James H. Charlesworth, F. M. Cross, J. Migrom, E. Qimron, L. H. Schiffman, L. T. Stuckenbruck, and R. E. Whitaker. Tübingen: Mohr Siebeck; Louisville: Westminster John Knox Press, 1994.

Rosen-Zvi, Ishay. *The Mishnaic Sotah Ritual: Temple, Gender and Midrash*. Translated by Orr Scharf. Leiden: Brill, 2012.

———. "The Sotah Ritual in Tannaitic Literature: Textual and Theoretical Studies" (Hebrew). PhD disseration, Tel Aviv University, 2004.

Ross, Tamar. *Expanding the Palace of Torah: Orthodoxy and Feminism*. Brandeis Series on Jewish Women. Hanover: Brandeis University Press, published by University Press of New England, 2004.

Rothstein, David. "From Bible to Muraba'at: Studies in the Literary, Textual and Scribal Features of Phylacteries and Mezuzot in Ancient Israel and Early Judaism." PhD dissertation, UCLA, 1992.

Rovner, Jay. "Rhetorical Strategy and Dialectical Necessity in the Babylonian Talmud: The Case of Kiddushin 34a–35a." *Hebrew Union College Annual* 65 (1994): 177–223.

Rubenstein, Jeffrey L. *The Culture of the Babylonian Talmud*. Baltimore: Johns Hopkins University Press, 2003.

———. "On Some Abstract Concepts in Rabbinic Literature." *Jewish Studies Quarterly* 4 (1997): 33–73.

———. "The Sukkah as Temporary or Permanent Dwelling: A Study in the Development of Talmudic Thought." *Hebrew Union College Annual* 64 (1993): 137–66.

———. *Talmudic Stories: Narrative Art, Composition, and Culture*. Baltimore: Johns Hopkins University Press, 1999.

Safrai, Chana. "Women in the Bet Midrash: Challenge and Dispute" (Hebrew). In *Ayin Tova: Du-Siach Vepulmus Betarbut Yisrael – Sefer Hayovel le-Tova Ilan*, edited by Ilan Nahem, 160–69. Hakibbutz ha-Meuchad, 1999.

Safrai, Shmuel. "The *Mitzva* Obligation of Women in Tannaitic Thought" (Hebrew). *Bar Ilan Annual* 26–27 (1995): 227–36.

Sarna, Nahum. *Exodus*. The JPS Torah Commentary. Philadelphia: The Jewish Publication Society, 1991.

Satlow, Michael L. "'And on the Earth You Shall Sleep': *Talmud Torah* and Rabbinic Asceticism." *The Journal of Religion* 83/2 (2003): 204–25.

————. "Jewish Constructions of Nakedness in Late Antiquity." *Journal of Biblical Literature* 116/3 (Autumn 1997): 429–54.

Schiffman, Lawrence. *Reclaiming the Dead Sea Scrolls*. Philadelphia: Jewish Publication Society, 1994.

Schofer, Jonathan Wyn. *Confronting Vulnerability: The Body and the Divine in Rabbinic Ethics*. Chicago: University of Chicago Press, 2010.

Schremer, Adiel. "'[T]He[Y] Did Not Read in the Sealed Book': Qumran Halakhic Revolution and the Emergence of Torah Study in Second Temple Judaism." In *Historical Perspectives: From the Hasmoneans to Bar Kokhba in Light of the Dead Sea Scrolls*, edited by D. Goodblatt, A. Pinnick, and D. R. Schwartz, 105–26. Leiden: Brill, 2001.

Schurer, Emil, Geza Vemes, F. Millar, and M. Black. *The History of the Jewish People in the Age of Jesus Christ*. Edinburgh: T. and T. Clark, 1979.

Schwartz, Seth. *Imperialism and Jewish Society, 200 B.C.E.–640 C.E.* Princeton: Princeton University Press, 2001.

Scott, Joan Wallach. *Gender and the Politics of History*. Gender and Culture. New York: Columbia University Press, 1988.

Segal, Alan. "Covenant in Rabbinic Writings." *Studies in Religion* 14 (1985): 53–62.

Seligman, Adam B., et al. *Ritual and Its Consequences: An Essay on the Limits of Sincerity*. Oxford: Oxford University Press, 2008.

Shemesh, Aharon. *Halakhah in the Making: The Development of Jewish Law from Qumran to the Rabbis*. Berkeley: University of California Press, 2009.

————. "Toward a History of the Terms Positive and Negative Commandments" (Hebrew). *Tarbiz* 72/1 (1993): 133–50.

Shutt, R. J. H. "Letter of Aristeas." In *The Old Testament Pseudepigrapha*, vol. 2, edited by James H. Charlesworth, 7–34. Garden City: Doubleday, 1985.

Simon-Shoshan, Moshe. "Halachah Lema'aseh: Narrative and Legal Discourse in the Mishnah." PhD dissertation, University of Pennsylvania, 2005.

————. "Halakhic Mimesis: Rhetorical and Redactional Strategies in Tannaitic Literature." *Diné Israel* 24 (2006): 101–23.

Smith, Jonathan Z. *Imagining Religion: From Babylon to Jonestown*. Chicago Studies in the History of Judaism. Chicago: University of Chicago Press, 1982.

Sommer, Benjamin D. *A Prophet Reads Scripture: Allusion in Isaiah 40–66*. Stanford: Stanford University Press, 1998.

Stern, Sacha. *Time and Process in Ancient Judaism*. Portland: Littman Library of Jewish Civilization, 2003.

Strack, H. L., and G. Stemberger. *Introduction to the Talmud and Midrash*. Translated by Markus Bockmuehl. Minneapolis: Fortress Press, 1992.

Sussmann, Yaacov. "Once More on y. Nezikin" (Hebrew). In *Mehqerei Talmud (Talmudic Studies)*, edited by Yaacov Sussmann and David Rosenthal, 55–133. Jerusalem: Magnes Press, 1990.

Swartz, Michael D. "Scholasticism as a Comparative Category and the Study of Judaism." In *Scholasticism: Cross Cultural and Comparative Perspectives*, edited by José Cabezón, 91–114. Albany: State University of New York Press, 1994.

Tabory, Joseph. "Prayers and Berakhot." In *Literature of the Sages*, part 2, edited by Shmuel (z"l) Safrai, Zeev Safrai, Joshua Schwartz, and Peter J Tomson, 281–326. Amsterdam: Royal Van Gorcum and Fortress Press, 2006.

Talmon, S. "The 'Manual of Benedictions' of the Sect of the Judaean Desert." *Revue de Qumran* 2/8 (1960): 475–500.

Teubner, Gunther, editor. *Autopoietic Law: A New Approach to Law and Society.* Series A–Law. Berlin: W. de Gruyter, 1988.

Thiselton, Anthony C. *The First Epistle to the Corinthians: A Commentary on the Greek Text.* The New International Greek Testament Commentary. Grand Rapids: W. B. Eerdmans, 2000.

Tov, Emanuel. "Categorized Lists of the 'Biblical Texts': Appendix – Phylacteries (Tefillin)." In *Discoveries in the Judaean Desert,* vol. 39, 182–83. Oxford: Oxford University Press, 2002.

Urbach, E. E. "The Role of the Ten Commandments in Jewish Worship." In *The Ten Commandments in History and Tradition,* edited by Ben-Zion Segal and Gershon Levi, 161–89. Jerusalem: Magnes Press, 1985.

Urbach, Ephraim E. *The Halakhah: Its Sources and Development.* Translated by Raphael Posner. Tel Aviv: Modan Publishing House, 1996.

Valler, Shulamit. *Women and Womanhood in the Talmud.* Translated by Betty Sigler Rozen. Atlanta: Scholars Press, 1999.

Wegner, Judith. *Chattel or Person: The Status of Women in the Mishnah.* New York: Oxford University Press, 1988.

Weinfeld, Moshe. *The Decalogue and the Recitation of "Shema": The Development of the Confessions* (Hebrew). Tel Aviv: Hakibbutz Hameuchad, 2001.

———. *Deuteronomy 1–11: A New Translation with Introduction and Commentary.* The Anchor Bible 5. New York: Doubleday, 1991.

Weissler, Chava. *Voices of the Matriarchs: Listening to the Prayers of Early Modern Jewish Women.* Boston: Beacon Press, 1998.

Whiston, William, trans. *The Complete Works of Josephus* with a foreward by William Sanford. Grand Rapids: Kregel Publications, 1978.

Williams, A. Lukyn, trans. *Justin Martyr, the Dialogue with Trypho.* New York: Macmillan, 1930.

Wimpfheimer, Barry Scott. *Narrating the Law: A Poetics of Talmudic Legal Stories.* Divinations, Rereading Late Ancient Religion. Philadelphia: University of Pennsylvania Press, 2011.

Wright, Benjamin G. "From Generation to Generation: The Sage as Father in Early Jewish Literature." In *Biblical Traditions in Transmission: Essays in Honour of Michael A. Knibb,* edited by Charlotte Hempel and J. Lieu, 309–32. Leiden: Brill, 2006.

Yadin, Azzan. "Resistance to Midrash? Midrash and *Halakhah* in the Halakhic Midrashim." In *Current Trends in the Study of Midrash,* edited by Carol Bakhos, 35–58. Leiden: Brill, 2006.

———. *Scripture as Logos: Rabbi Ishmael and the Origins of Midrash.* Divinations. Philadelphia: University of Pennsylvania Press, 2004.

Yadin, Yigael. *Tefillin from Qumran (XQPhyl 1–4).* Jerusalem: The Israel Exploration Society and the Shrine of the Book, 1970.

Yalon, Shevah. "'Women Are Exempted from All Positive Ordinances That Are Bound Up with a Stated Time': A Study in Tanaic and Amoraic Sources." PhD dissertation, Bar Ilan University, 1989.

Yerushalmi, Yosef Hayim. *Zakhor: Jewish History and Jewish Memory.* Seattle: University of Washington Press, 1982.

Young, Frances M. *Biblical Exegesis and the Formation of Christian Culture.* Cambridge: Cambridge University Press, 1997.

Zlotnick, Dov. *The Iron Pillar – Mishnah: Redaction, Form, and Intent.* Jerusalem: Ktav, 1988.

Zohar, Noam. "Women, Men and Religious Status: Deciphering a Chapter of Mishnah." In *Approaches to Ancient Judaism: New Series*, vol. 5, edited by Hebert Basser and Simcha Fishbane, 33–54. Atlanta: Scholars Press, 1993.

Subject Index

Abaye, 116–17, 131
Abbahu, R., 75, 89, 97
  on tefillin at night, 74–75
Abudraham, 2, 12, 13, 46
Ada b. Ahava, Rav, 123, 124
adam, 202, 204
Adler, Rachel, 2, 3, 47, 61, 213, 235,
  236, 239
adulteress, suspected, 57, 173, 201,
  202
adultery, 201, 202
aggadah, 72
  as element of rabbinic curriculum,
  203
Aha, Rav, 98
Aharoni, Y., 170
Aiken, Lisa, 3
Akiba, R., 32, 40, 187
Albeck, Chanoch, 59
Alexander, Elizabeth Shanks, 8, 10, 26,
  28, 29, 33, 53, 58, 90, 106, 114,
  121, 125, 128, 176, 189, 190,
  197, 238
Alexandrian exegesis. *See* Aristeas; Philo
Amidah, 8, 17, 107–9, 110, 112, 113–15,
  176, 221
Ammi, R., 175
amoraic period. *See also* Bavli, amoraic
  strata of; Yerushalmi
  definition of, 11

first four generations of, 124
amulets, 168, 169, 173
Anatoli, Jacob, 12, 13, 18, 46
androgyne, 51–52, 58
Aristeas, 160, 171, 174
  Shema rituals in, 155–58
Avram the Pious, Rav, 214, 232

baal keri, 190–92, 194
Baker, Cynthia, 232
banim. *See also bnei yisreal;* sons
  in Maimonides, 155
  in NJPS, 184–85
  rabbinic interpretation of, 96, 108,
  170–71, 174
  in Septuagint, 161
Bar Kochba tefillin, 170–71, 174
Baskin, Judith, 242
Baumgarten, Albert, 139, 151, 164, 167,
  173
Baumgarten, Elisheva, 12, 19, 154, 213,
  238
Bavli
  affirmation of overarching principles,
  96
  amoraic strata of, 121–25
  assumption of verbal economy,
  112–18
  conceptual priority of the rule in,
  111–19

Citation Index